A DUSTY BOOT SOLDIER REMEMBERS

Twenty-Four Years of Improbable but True Tales
of Service with Uncle Sam's Army

LARRY A. REDMOND
Colonel, U.S. Army Retired

Hellgate Press   Ashland, OR

A Dusty Boot Soldier Remembers
©2015 Larry A. Redmond

·Published by Hellgate Press
(An imprint of L&R Publishing, LLC)

Hellgate Press
PO Box 3531
Ashland, OR 97520
email: sales@hellgatepress.com

Editor: Harley B. Patrick
Interior design: Sasha Kincaid
Cover design: L. Redding

Library of Congress Cataloging-in-Publication Data

Redmond, Larry A.
A dusty boot soldier remembers : twenty-four years of improbable but true tales of service with Uncle Sam's Army / Larry A. Redmond, Colonel, U.S. Army Retired. — First edition.
    pages cm
Includes bibliographical references and index.
ISBN 978-1-55571-778-0 (alk. paper)
1. United States. Army—Airborne troops—Biography. 2. United States. Army. Special Forces—Officers—Biography. 3. United States. Army. Airborne Division, 101st—Biography 4. United States. Army. Airborne Infantry Regiment, 505th—Biography. 5. Vietnam War, 1961-1975—Aerial operations, American. 6. Vietnam War, 1961-1975—Personal narratives, American. I. Title. II. Title: Twenty-four years of improbable but true tales of service with Uncle Sam's Army.
  UD483
  [.R43 2015]
  355.0092—dc23
  [B]
                        2015022048

Printed and bound in the United States of America
First edition 10 9 8 7 6 5 4 3 2 1

DEDICATION

To all the "dusty boot" soldiers who trod the roads
and trails of this twenty-four year Odyssey with me. They
were Patriots and Heroes all, and I salute them.

---

*"I'd like to have two armies: one with lovely guns,
tanks, little soldiers, staffs, distinguished
and doddering Generals and dear little regimental
officers who would be deeply concerned
over their general's bowel movements,
or their Colonel's piles,
an army that would be shown for a modest fee
on every fairground in the country.*

*The other would be the real one, composed entirely
of young enthusiasts in camouflage uniforms,
who would not be put on display,
but from whom impossible efforts
would be demanded and to whom all
sorts of tricks would be taught.
That's the army in which I should like to fight."*

JEAN LARTEGUY
The Centurions

CONTENTS

VIII A DUSTY BOOT SOLDIER REMEMBERS

PREFACE

started writing this epistle for my children who asked that I do so in order that some of what I experienced while wearing the Army green is not lost. The experiences of their grandfather, Lieutenant Colonel Edward Devlin, in World War II and the Korean War, were never recorded. The children asked that I not let that happen to my service. I have tried to be totally candid laying out the good, and the bad, as my memory now recalls it. Although started at the request of my children, the more I remembered the many incidents I experienced, and put them on paper, the more I realized how much I had done and been involved with over the course of those twenty-four years. Some of what follows may be of interest to others even if they never served in the military. My tales may shock some and cause more than a few raised eyebrows. I assure you everything you will read did happen. Recognize that these stories are from my perspective and hence others involved may have a different view. Counsel was sought from those who shared these adventures with me when there was doubt in my mind as to exactly what happened. Some correction in my writing was necessary as points were made by comrades and my memory jogged to recall the facts. Amazing things happened starting in June 1962 until I took off the uniform in January 1987. It was truly a remarkable time for a poor American kid of Irish descent from the wrong side of the tracks in Columbus, Ohio in the service of what is, in my mind, the greatest country in the world. The United States may not be perfect but it is still the greatest. As I used to tell my troops, "Moses did not find the promised land, Christopher Columbus did. And we are privileged to live there." I hope this proves a memorable and enjoyable read whether you are family, friend or just an interested patriot.

1
THE BEGINNING:
PROVIDENCE COLLEGE, 1958

"Fly Town USA" we called it. The lower middle class section of Columbus, Ohio where I was born and spent my early years was a mixed neighborhood of Irish, Italian and Black families. The gangs were integrated and one needed to know which side of the street you could safely walk down. Most of the old neighborhood has long since been torn down and replaced by condos and freeways. I graduated from Aquinas College High School in 1958. I was fortunate to earn an academic scholarship to Providence College and to have a kind and generous Aunt, Mae Redmond, who gave me a thousand dollars every year. This along with my scholarship for $1,000 paid for my tuition and room and board. That number of $2,000 may be hard to believe today but it was true in 1958. Mom and Dad could not even swing the funds for incidentals and books, as things were very tight in the Redmond household. My uncle, Bud Morrissey, helped me find a job with the city of Columbus every summer enabling me to earn funds for the next school year. For three years I worked for the Columbus River Patrol out of Hoover Dam on the Scioto River and cleaned rather large outhouses, or if you prefer, latrines, in the park along the river. The fourth year I worked for Parks and Recreation as a recreation supervisor at Goodale Park on the edge of Fly Town not far from St. Francis Church and School, my home parish growing up and where I attended grade school.

I called the academic scholarship a "gift" even though I had very good grades in high school. I think the Dominican Fathers thought that I had the calling to the priesthood and would follow in the footsteps of my uncle, Father Stephen Francis Redmond, a Providence grad from the 1940s and his uncle, my great uncle, Father James "Jim" Walker. He was a lieutenant of Infantry, a decorated WWI veteran, who following the war went into the priesthood. Uncle Jim was historian of the Dominican Order in the USA, having been the Western Province Provincial, somewhat like a commanding general. They were both great men and worthy of emulating.

When I arrived at Providence, Uncle Francis had come to the college from New Orleans, a town he loved and where he was stationed at the time. I had some vision of going into the pre-seminary side of the college in a residence called Guzman Hall. Uncle Francis took me out to dinner and told me he thought I should spend the first two years in the regular college dorms and if at the end of that time I still wanted to enter the seminary, I could bypass Guzman Hall and go directly to the seminary. He took me through Guzman Hall which was like an old Army platoon bay (a wide open room) of twenty plus metal framed beds. Most were decorated with religious cards, rosaries and holy water bottles. Frankly it did not fit my style.

In the ensuing two years I enjoyed life at Providence and was decidedly engaged in the Reserve Officer Training Corps Program and many other campus activities. I even joined the United States Marines, well not quite, but almost! My family had many uncles and cousins in the Corps and I was drawn to that service. I enrolled in the Marine Platoon Leaders Course and had orders for Lance Corporal Lawrence A. Redmond to report to Quantico, Virginia in June 1960 for six weeks summer camp. In late May that all came crashing down when I was ordered to report to Chelsea Naval Base Hospital in Boston for an orthopedic evaluation of my left knee due to a high school football injury.

Taking the train from Providence to Boston, I made it to the hospital and had a Navy captain, an orthopedic surgeon, tell me I was not qualified for the Navy or the Marines. Not only had I had a previous knee problem but my left leg was $\frac{1}{16}$ of an inch shorter and my left thigh ½ inch smaller than my right. As I recall the Navy surgeon said, "It is my opinion that by the time you are forty you will have the knees of a sixty-year-old man; no way can I approve your joining the Marines." I was dumb struck, my dream shattered! Honestly, I cried on the train ride back to Providence. Although a disappointment it may have been in my best interest. Based on what I saw and experienced years later in 1968 on my first tour in Vietnam, had I been a Marine captain in Vietnam, I might not have come home at all. The Marines had a very high casualty rate among their officers in Vietnam.

I stayed in ROTC and at the end of two years Uncle Francis came back and took me out for a great prime rib dinner at a really fancy restaurant. When he asked me if I wanted to go on to the Seminary I told him, "No, I hope to graduate and serve my country in the Army." He smiled and said something like, "I knew that two years ago. Your mother had the calling, not you. I watched you grow up, play sports, drink beer, date girls, and the priesthood simply is not your calling."

The Providence ROTC Program was great and frankly more challenging than I expected. I was deeply involved in the Pershing Rifles—a military honor society. For those not familiar with that organization it was a must join for all truly gung-ho, committed ROTC cadets. We participated in drill meets and parades all over Rhode Island and New England. I was selected as regimental sergeant major my junior year and went to summer camp at Fort Devens, Massachusetts. My Pershing Rifles training and preparation for Marine Platoon Leaders Course held me in good stead. The first inspection in the barracks the drill sergeant, SFC Dustin, checked out my footlocker display, perfect; wall locker display, perfect; eyed my spit shined boots and flipped a quarter on my bunk. It bounced. He looked me in the eye and said, "Prior service, Cadet Redmond?" I answered, "No, Sergeant." And he moved on. I was nominated for Camp Cadet of the Week the first week and won! After that Cadet of the Week award I sort of "got over" (had it easy) like a fat rat and never pulled KP, or walked guard for the next five weeks of training. I think I came in second overall at camp but I can't swear to that; top five for certain. In retrospect I did "get over" with that Cadet of the Week Award. Maybe it was just the luck of a poor lad of Irish descent.

My senior year at Providence I was selected the cadet colonel commanding 2,000 rag tag ROTC cadets with about 200 committed and good leader cadets. Captain Paul C. Listro, West Point, was my mentor and the guy who made sure I didn't screw up. I was also the company commander of our Pershing Rifles, Company K-12, and we won Best Company in the Regiment that year. Captain Listro was our advisor and was very helpful.

About six weeks before graduation and a Regular Army commission (pending assignment as an infantry officer to either the 101st or the 82nd Airborne Division) I received, via Captain Listro, a directive from Department of the Army to report to Chelsea Naval Base, Boston for an orthopedic evaluation of my knees. Oh God, not again, I thought. You can well imagine my horror when the same Navy orthopedic surgeon walked in to do the exam. Luckily the doctor did not remember our earlier meeting. In short he said to me, "What's this for?" I responded the Army. He then said something to the effect, "The Army, I see. OK I couldn't qualify you for the Navy or the Marines. You aren't going to do any of that dumb stuff like jump out of airplanes or try to become a Ranger?" I told him no–yep, I fibbed; OK it was an out and out lie. He signed the papers qualifying me for my Regular Army commission and I returned gleefully to Providence not having a clue what I had just let myself in for.

About a week before graduation all of the distinguished military graduates who were to be commissioned in the Regular Army were called into a conference room and asked if we might be interested in joining Special Forces. I wasn't completely sure what Special Forces really was, or did, but I thought hell you're signing up for everything else, why not. We were told to sign on the dotted line, take a mental evaluation test of some kind, and that was the last I heard of it, for two plus years.

Redmond's Rule #1 – Lead, Follow or Get the Hell Out of the Way

My orders came through for the 101st Airborne Division and I graduated on 5 June 1962. My parents drove to Providence for the graduation. I honestly think that trip was the furthest they had ever been from Ohio. We traveled back to their apartment in Columbus where I spent one day and then I proceeded by train to Clarksville, Tennessee and my own "Rendezvous with Destiny" (this is the motto of the 101st Airborne Division, the Screaming Eagles, as stated by Major General (MG) William Lee in General Order #5 fall 1942).

2
BEING A NAP:
FORT CAMPBELL, KY, JUNE 1962

Now for the uninitiated a NAP is a non-Airborne person; a "leg" (one who walks to the battle rather than jumping in by parachute), a guy who, in other words, was not yet parachutist qualified. And there I was, a brand new butter bar (gold color bar) second lieutenant (2nd LT), NAP, in one of the two Airborne Divisions in our great Army at that time. Walt Werner, one of my closest friends from Providence, and also a Regular Army LT and fellow NAP had arrived at Fort Campbell the same day I did. We went together to in-process and we were both assigned to D Company, 506th Airborne Battle Group, known as the Currahees. We went to the Central Issue Facility to draw our gear. By the end of the day we had not yet reported in to our company.

I was sound asleep in my room, about 0200 that night when the phone rang. "Lieutenant Redmond, an alert has been called, report to your unit immediately." I thought it was a joke. It had to be a joke. This was something they did to all newbies. I stepped out into the hall. Walt along with two other LTs who reported in that day were also in the hall discussing if this was some kind of initiation joke. Suddenly, the light came on for all of us, this was real. Walt and I took a cab since neither of us owned a car at the time. Between us we had barely enough cash to pay for the ride having not yet been given a partial pay to cover our expenses for the remainder of June. We arrived at D Company each dragging two duffel bags of new equipment. Fortunately the cabbie knew the post and knew where the Currahees and D Company were located; neither Walt nor I had a clue.

The company commander was glad to see us; or so he said. He was a big, and I mean big, black captain, football player at Arkansas in the mid 1950s. To be a black player at Arkansas in the '50s one had to be tough and know how to play football. He introduced each of us to our platoon sergeants. I was very lucky. My platoon sergeant, Sergeant First Class (SFC) Arno C. Land, proved to be the epitome of a noncommissioned officer (NCO) and a mentor who quickly set me on the straight and narrow. The captain told him, "This is your new platoon leader. Take care of him and get his gear squared away." I thought to myself, well he might as well have said, here's a good case of smallpox, enjoy it!

Sergeant First Class Land, however, took me to the platoon headquarters and said something like, "Look, sir, we'll get your gear sorted out. I am not sure what's happening but if you just do what I tell you, when I tell you, this will be over shortly. We have these little call outs all the time; nothing to it." I am not sure what I responded but it was something close to a good Airborne School, "Clear, Sergeant. Yes, Sergeant."

He assigned a young soldier to help get me into my field gear so that I looked like a soldier who knew which end of the rifle the bullet came out of. Needless to say when that rascal finished with me he returned to the platoon bay and the word was out; hey guys we got a new "LOOOIE" and he didn't even have his gear put together.

About thirty minutes later I followed Sergeant Land downstairs and out to the company street where he told me to stand in the rear of the platoon. He said after he gave the report, he would move to the rear by the left flank and I should move to the front by the right flank and then just do what the company commander directed. In this case the order turned out to be, "stand easy men," to which I did not have to do anything. I was one relieved 2nd lieutenant. That also gave SFC Land some time to come speak to me and reassure me that all was OK.

About that time there was the unmistakable sound of 2½ ton (referred to as deuce and a half) trucks coming down the road; lots of them. Well SFC Land said, "Not to worry, sir, we do these little drills all the time. They are just making sure the Transportation Battalion drivers know where to report and can find the units OK."

Next came the command to, load trucks. Well SFC Land said, "Sir, we do this all the time. They will just drive us down to the airfield to make sure they can convoy properly. Not to worry."

Shortly the trucks pulled out and headed to Campbell Army Air Field. Well hello!

We off-loaded at the longest and largest airfield I had ever seen. This was definitely impressive stuff. At least it was impressive until the trucks all drove off and I got a funny feeling that something big was happening. SFC Land again told me, "Sir, we do this all the time."

Suddenly up came a stream of stake-and-platform trucks; now those are really great big trucks for you nonmilitary readers. There were twenty, thirty or forty of them. The trucks were loaded with what I was about to find out were things called parachutes. For a poor kid from the wrong side of the tracks in Columbus, Ohio this was getting pretty impressive but also a little scary. SFC Land said, "Sir, not to worry. We do this all the time just to check out the quartermaster riggers."

As quickly as the trucks with the parachutes parked, up came a second convoy of stake and platform trucks. They had all kinds of wooden boxes filled with what even a brand new NAP recognized as ammunition, real bullets, Tonto. You know the stuff you shoot at bad guys. Each truck had two Military Policemen (MPs) assigned to guard the cargo; yep it was the real stuff, live ammo for sure. At this point they had my attention, to say the least. Sergeant First

Class Land said, "Sir…" Well by now you get the idea of what he was saying!

I was reassured, a little. Then I noticed that many of the troops had jumped up from sitting or lying on the ground. You learn early in the Airborne that paratroopers all lie down whenever they can. They were all standing now and pointing off in the distance to these little specks in the sky. I don't know if any of you have ever been impressed by fifty or sixty plus Air Force C-130s in an air train coming in for a landing, all in trail, one behind the other, at forty-five to sixty second intervals. I was certainly impressed! Sergeant First Class Land said, "Sir…." About this time I was beginning to feel a little uneasy about what SFC Land had to say.

The captain called us both, along with Walt Werner and his platoon sergeant, over to his jeep and said something to the effect that, "Sergeant Land, this may be a go. I want you to get a parachute on Lieutenants Redmond and Werner, take them over to that C-130, and show them enough to keep them alive." Turning to us he said quite calmly, "You both may be about to win your jump wings the easy way." (Jump wings are awarded to any non-Airborne person who makes a combat jump.) Needless to say I was not impressed, nor was Walt. I was not terribly excited about what I was experiencing. Sergeant First Class Land said, "Sir…." At that point I am not sure what he said but I followed him.

Redmond's Rule #2 – Things get worse under pressure. Stay cool.

Sergeant Land got Walt and me into our parachutes, a contraption I had never even seen before and about which neither of us knew anything. We were totally engulfed with gear! The main chute, a reserve chute and our packs and weapons were all rigged and hung on our bodies in such fashion that moving was not easy. Heck, just standing was difficult. Walt then lumbered off with his platoon sergeant to another aircraft and SFC Land marched me up the ramp of our C-130. Then he said, and this I truly believed when he said it, "Look, sir, you will be number one in my stick (a group of jumpers). All you have to do is stand in the door. I'll hook you up to the anchor line cable (pointing to a heavy metal cable running down the interior of the aircraft). Don't worry about anything except keeping the body position I am going to teach you. When I tap you on the butt, spring up and out; your static line will do the rest." That was all not very reassuring to this non-Airborne twenty-two year old. He put me through the correct body position, and a quick orientation on the jump commands then marched me to the jump door. I really sort of waddled, being in a parachute with all that gear for the first time. He stood me in the door. I looked out at the forty-five men in my brand new platoon and saw them look back at me. I said to myself, "Oh Lord, if there are bad guys wherever we are going they are the least of my worries. These lads don't look very friendly." It didn't strike me at the time but Sergeant Land did not tell me what to do when the ground came up!

The good news is that about fifteen minutes later the ammo and parachute trucks cranked up and drove off. The aircrews all headed to the Clubs and we marched four miles back to our barracks. The exercise was terminated. Yes my almost "easy way to win my wings" was just a test, an exercise. Thus ended my first exciting day as a Currahee, Band of Brothers, you get the idea; and it did happen just as related. There were many days like this one to follow, some good and some not so good.

That was my first of many experiences I would have donning a parachute but it truly was my scariest. They really know how to welcome one to the Airborne.

Neither Walt nor I were jump qualified nor had we been to the Infantry Officer Basic Course. But there we were leading troops, doing the Airborne shuffle four miles around the Division cantonment area each day with the soldiers, pulling Officer of the Guard and going to the field with the Currahees. I must credit my later success at jump school to SFC Land who was a former Jump School cadre. The Fort Campbell Jump School had closed the end of April 1962 and I had missed the last class by just two months. He took me to the old jump school just down the troop line from our barracks and put me through about 90% of what I would experience, and endure, at the Benning Jump School. It was great preparation for what was to follow. He did teach me how to do a correct parachute landing fall when I reached terra firma. I was grateful for this training; it helped me immensely when I finally attended Jump School.

Two major field events in the "life" of D Company occurred while I was there as a leg.

The first event was a road march a week after I arrived. The company was supposed to march forty-four plus miles in two days to Kentucky Lake, bivouac and lie around drinking beer, eating burgers and hot dogs, swimming and just unwinding. After the fourth day we were to be trucked back to Fort Campbell. This was a Division directed training event but in this case the company timing was in conjunction with a three day weekend, maybe the Fourth of July, I have forgotten. At any rate the troops all requested through the chain of command that they be allowed to make the march in one day and then have a three day pass opening up the opportunity to visit Nashville, Tennessee and "E Town," aka Evansville, Indiana. The company commander got the OK and so we all started off on the march. At about the thirty mile mark we were all tired, soaked with sweat, our feet and muscles aching and most of us had blisters on our blisters. A lot of the troops were beginning to think that the cool water of Kentucky Lake sounded better than the flesh pots, booze and sin of those distant towns. At the forty-two mile mark, near a place called the Birdcage, a nuclear weapons storage facility on base run by the USMC for the Navy, the commander got a radio call saying that his replacement had arrived. I was selected to run into garrison in the commanding officer's (CO) jeep to pick him up and bring him out to finish the march with us. I commented that maybe someone needed the break more than me but was told to get my tail in the jeep and back to garrison to pick up the new boss. I will admit I was hurting but I wasn't the only one.

We all did finish this true exercise in pain and suffering and were turned loose for the next three days. Sore feet and aching muscles be darned, the troops for the most part took off for parts unknown, and whatever it was that paratroopers could get away with in those waiting dens of iniquity. Walt Werner and I spent the time with our feet elevated, airing out, and consuming large volumes of beer. No one to my knowledge ever suggested another 44 mile walk and a three day pass. The pain wasn't worth the reward.

The second event was during a field training week in the woods of Fort Campbell as the company prepared to go on Exercise Swift Strike II that fall. The platoon was ordered to dig in along a tree line with an opening of tall grass about 100 yards wide to our front. Everything was good until the opposing force came busting out of the wood line led by five M-48 "Patton" tanks. My son who served as an Armor officer will tell you that the M-48 was sort of like a mini tank. I agree when compared to the M-1 Abrams of today that he worked with during his time in the Army. But to a brand new 2nd lieutenant they looked like Hannibal's elephants coming at us. I ordered a retirement; no let's call it a retreat, back into the swamp behind us where the tanks couldn't go. Sound tactics I thought. Later we reoccupied the position after the attacking forces withdrew. Sergeant First Class Land and I had a little chat about Airborne soldiers and retreating. I never in the next twenty-four years backed away from a fight except for one incident I will report on later in this tale. "No retreat Redmond" became my mantra.

In those days, while being an officer brought certain perks and a level of prestige, it also brought some responsibilities that would amaze our modern day Volunteer Army lieutenants and captains. We leaders were required to be in the company mess hall each morning at 0400 when the sergeants rousted the troops; *Noblesse Oblige* (translation, Nobility Obliges). We drank coffee and discussed the upcoming day's activities and learned from the old hands. The troops knew when they got up we were already in the company area. Nice gimmick, maybe it was only the Airborne, I can't say for sure, but I was told it was standard up and down the troop line at Fort Campbell in 1962. I suspect it was a holdover from WWII. The really tough part was that you had to put on a clean set of starched fatigues, breaking starch we called it in those days, to go to the mess hall at 0400. Following our normal four mile run around the troop line at 0600 you cleaned up and broke starch a second time with a fresh set of fatigues. Then after lunch you were required to break starch a third time. Officers set the example with a clean, pressed uniform at all times when in garrison. The cleaning bill took up a good portion of my jump pay, once I qualified for and received jump pay.

One day in late July orders came through for LTs Redmond, Werner and Bonavalonto to proceed to Fort Benning for Airborne training, the Infantry Officer Basic Course and Ranger School. Jules Bonavalonto was another friend of ours from Pershing Rifles in New England and also assigned to the Currahees. Needless to say, after two plus months as non-Airborne soldiers in the 101st Airborne Division, we were ready. The three of us traveled to Benning in Jules's car. As I recall I slept most of the way in the back seat while Jules and Walt enjoyed the scenery.

3
BENNING SCHOOL FOR BOYS, 1962-1963

Fort Benning, Georgia is really a nice place, a great Army base. In August it is hot, sometimes very, very hot. Our first school was Airborne School and the heat was terrible. Each morning the instructors would double time us four miles then run us through a large outdoor shower and into the sawdust pit to practice PLFs, aka parachute landing falls. Needless to say we had sawdust stuck to every part of our body most of the day. The "Black Hat" NCO trainers loved it. One of the NCOs was a 101st veteran and he enjoyed nothing better than singling out Walt and me with our Screaming Eagle patches. In a rather loud voice he would ask: "Where are my chicken farmers in this formation? Drop and give me twenty [pushups]." His name was MUD (not really) and he retired as a sergeant first class and paraded all over Fort Campbell years later wearing first sergeant's stripes.

Sometime during the course, I can't remember exactly when, I had an interesting happening. One of my buddies, another Pershing Rifles Honor Society friend from Boston University, asked me to accompany him on a double date. Since we were in a small two seat sports car, owned by my friend, the lasses drove us in one of their cars. The evening and the ladies were really only so-so. After we had left the gals at the trailer park where they lived, and retrieved our wheels, we went to the Streamliner Diner on Victory Drive for breakfast. By that time it was about 0300 on a Sunday morning.

As we sat eating, a comment drifted across the restaurant about "officers trying to be paratroopers." We recognized two "Black Hat" instructors sitting across the aisle as the source of the comment. I was prepared to let it slip, eat and depart, but not my buddy. He walked over and got into a heated discussion with one of the Airborne Cadre NCOs. This evolved into a "Let's step outside and see who is the toughest." I thought, well here we go, my career is over after a lieutenant dukes it out with an NCO. My buddy was a little squat guy, ornery and hard as woodpecker lips. When we got outside he stood next to his little red sports car, convertible with the top down. The Airborne NCO took up a good karate stance and expelled a great and very loud AHHHH! My friend reached down behind the seat, pulled out a tire tool and hit the sergeant over the head. Now I knew my career was over for sure. We departed leaving the NCO, with a cut on his head bleeding sitting on the ground, being cared for by his friend. On Monday we saw the sergeant with his head bandaged. He ignored us and nothing was ever said. That was the old Regular Army for you.

After successfully enduring two weeks of physical pain and harassment, my first jump was from a USAF C-119 "Flying Boxcar" of Korean War fame. Not a bad jump but getting that puppy off the ground was a feat of amazing proportions. It did not seem to like to fly, at least it seemed that way to us sitting in the back. The other four qualification jumps came aboard C-130 Hercules aircraft. I would become very familiar with that bird over the next twenty-four years. All of my first five jumps were "night jumps," eyes closed all the way until the canopy opened. The fear of jumping from a perfectly good airplane at 1,000 feet is tough to overcome. Over the next few years that would change. At any rate I survived the training, made the five required jumps and was no longer a non-Airborne person. I had arrived. I was part of the Airborne fraternity, and could return to Fort Campbell as a fully qualified paratrooper.

Following Jump School the entire class attended the Infantry Officer Basic Course. While informative and helpful, my two months at Fort Campbell as a wannabe platoon leader had taught me most of what was being presented. The course was uneventful except for the colorful and special language from many of our noncommissioned instructors. In those days many of the instructors probably were not high school graduates. They were great soldiers, highly professional but not well polished. Every day was a hoot and a new experience. My vocabulary expanded exponentially over the next few weeks.

Two incidents do stick out in my mind from the Basic Course. One was during a patrol class where the guy in front of me stepped over a log and we all heard the distinct sound of a Georgia rattler. It was about six feet long and as big around as your forearm. Needless to say that one got my attention. I am not a big fan of "Jake the Snake" and after that happening I paid great attention to what was on the other side of any log. By the way, the LT who discovered Mr. Jake avoided a snake bite. Apparently Mr. Jake had been as surprised as we were and just slithered off. We sure did not pursue him.

The second incident was also during a patrol, this one at night. I was point man and we were heading back to base and still had to negotiate Upatoi Creek to reach the exercise end point. At any rate, I looked ahead, saw the creek, and turned and softly whispering said to the man behind me, "Hey, Upatoi CRRRRRREEEEEKKKKK" as the ground gave way and I fell about six feet into the water. Needless to say the initial whisper turned into a loud shout. Not a very tactical response. It was quite an experience and I was soaked from head to toe.

Being a brash young lieutenant, jump qualified, I decided it was time to get wheels. I proceeded down to Fourth Avenue in Columbus, Georgia to the Pontiac dealer. That evening I became the proud owner of a Pontiac LeMans, red and white. Darn I was proud of that car and kept it immaculate. It served me well for about three years when it was replaced by a maroon and white Oldsmobile "88."

After the Basic Course there was a five week delay before we were to start Ranger School. The Ranger classes before that were all filled and the brass figured they had to do something with us. No way could we just sit around and do physical training or heaven forbid chase "southern belles" and drink beer. The gang I was married up with were all Regular Army; most of them West Point graduates. The powers that be decided they would put together some things to keep us busy before the Ranger Class started.

As I recall the first new opportunity was a Jumpmaster Course. Very few "five jump commandos" get a chance at becoming jumpmasters but they did it for us. Unlike Jump School there was no harassment. This was deadly serious learning about donning a parachute; checking it out to make sure it had been put on properly by the troopers for whom you were serving as jumpmaster; and then actions and orders in the aircraft to ensure a safe exit at 800 or 1,000 feet. Walt Werner and I both passed and were awarded our jumpmaster rating. The day after we finished the course we were all ordered to report to a bleacher area for a "talk." Turned out the talk was a tail chewing from a Brigadier General (BG). It seems that out of 140 students only thirty-five of us passed the course. We were read the "riot act" in spades. The general was furious with all the Regular Army officers who saw fit not to put sufficient effort into the course to pass. The thirty-five of us who did pass wondered why we had been called to the "talk" along with the folks who failed. In fairness, being brand new jumpers is not the time to try to become a jumpmaster but the general wasn't hearing any of that. Frankly, I was just lucky and found all the mistakes on my jumper that I had to inspect for my Jumpmaster Proficiency Inspection (JMPI) portion of the final test. Passing JMPI was strictly a matter of luck for me.

They next sent us to an orientation on heavy weapons; .50 caliber machine gun, 4.2 inch mortar, 81 mm mortar, 106 mm recoilless rifle and I believe chemical weapons. That was a piece of cake, unlike the Jumpmaster Course; and they dragged it out twice as long as it needed to be. The language of the instructors continued to be something one did not forget.

The brass then did us a real favor, although it was a tough go. They gave us a chance to win our Expert Infantryman Badge (EIB). No easy feat let me tell you and in some ways harder to earn than the Combat Infantryman Badge (CIB). To get the CIB all you had to do was be in a direct combat front line area for thirty days and have some form of hostile contact with an enemy force at least once. For the EIB there were about forty different tests one had to take. These tests included a timed road march with heavy backpack, running the obstacle course in a set period of time and every variation of infantry activity you can think of from radio transmissions, to throwing hand grenades, to qualifying with rifle and pistol, and treating a wounded buddy. You were allowed to fail up to four stations and retake them the following day. I failed four, one being the hand grenade throw, but took them over and passed, so I got my EIB very early in my career. I felt very good about this and wore that badge proudly. Many Infantrymen serve a whole career and never earn that award.

After the EIB we had a couple of days off before our Ranger Class, Class 62-6, was to start. It was a Friday night and Walt and I were sitting in our BOQ room watching roaches crawl on the walls and floor. I told Walt that I had had enough of that and was going out for some bug spray. Honest, that's the gospel truth. It was a decision that would change my life, and perhaps one could say, made my future.

On the way back into post a Pontiac convertible with two ladies in it passed me. They looked interesting so I followed them to the Chute Snackette (now torn down) over by the jump towers. I struck up a conversation with the prettiest of the two and learned her name was Mary Elizabeth Devlin and she worked for the IRS in Columbus. Her father was the Deputy Provost Marshal (Deputy Chief of Police) for Third U.S. Army at Fort MacPherson in Atlanta. She also was an Irish Catholic and we both went to Mass at the Main Post Catholic

Chapel. I told her that I went to confession most Saturdays and she said she did too. The next afternoon we met at the chapel, fancy that little happening; and romance blossomed. That's how I met and started courting my wife. We saw each other daily after that until Ranger School started.

4
RANGER SCHOOL:
A SAGA OF PAIN AND SUCCESS

anger School is very challenging and something that must be experienced to be fully appreciated. Ranger training is a nine week sojourn in pain, sleep deprivation and harassment designed to stress the student beyond what he may encounter in combat. It is broken up into three phases of near torture. The first phase at Fort Benning, where each student is taught the rudiments of patrolling and the physical stresses are truly demanding, is aimed at weeding out those not totally committed to earning the coveted Ranger Tab on their left sleeve. Phase two takes you to the Mountain Ranger Camp at Dahlonega, Georgia where the focus is totally on patrolling and mountaineering techniques. The mountains are truly challenging physically. The third and final phase takes place at Eglin AFB, Florida, in the swamps. The swamps were known to be miserable in the winter. Ranger School works on a buddy system and you were always with a buddy who you would train with for teamwork and safety. In total the nine weeks are a time in purgatory; but they do feed you very well throughout the course. This simple explanation captures the essence of Ranger training in 1962. The following paragraphs attempt to capture a little of that experience as I endured it.

All I really remember about the Benning three weeks is that it was very physical; the weather was OK initially, but being December— even in south Georgia—during the Camp Darby patrolling phase it got very cold. I remember I shivered a lot. They truly tried to get the weaker, not totally motivated, to drop out. No one just quit that I can recall. Our class commander was the legendary Pete Dawkins of West Point football and First Captain of the Corps of Cadets fame. In my mind he was every bit as good a soldier and leader as folks said he was.

Sometime early in this phase, while at the Ranger training facility on Fort Benning I got one hell of an ankle twist and had a golf ball sized knot on my left ankle. This was the result of a bad fall doing hand-to-hand in the "bear pit" which was quite a grueling experience. I muddled through and gutted it out, sore ankle be darned. Rangers suck it up and charge on. For the first seven or eight days I was able to call Mary every night and chat for a few minutes. It reminded me of a Hollywood WWII movie where all the troops lined up to use a single phone. We couldn't talk long as other Rangers were always in line. The Camp Darby phase was where we really started learning patrolling tactics and techniques. It was not bad but Darby, at the far eastern end of Fort Benning, seemed to be located on one big beaver swamp. We were wet and cold the entire time. The patrolling training was super but the last activity is the thing that sticks in my mind. They closed the phase with an eighteen mile forced speed march from Darby back to Victory Pond and the rope drop. The rope drop was another of those tests designed to weed out the weak of heart. The Ranger student had to climb up a twenty-five or thirty foot tall pole, then walk across a narrow wooden walkway with no hand rail and at the end grab onto a rope and move hand over hand out over the water. Once in about the center of the rope, and well out over the lake, you had to request in a loud booming voice, "Sir, Ranger Redmond requests permission to drop." Well with Peter Dawkins as the class leader there was no doubt we were going to break the record for the speed march from Camp Darby to Victory Pond; and we did. My ankle was really hurting and I felt at times that I would not make it but just kept putting one foot in front of the other.

When we arrived at Victory Pond we were shocked; it was covered with ice, I repeat ice. Pete Dawkins had the privilege of climbing the pole first and requesting permission to drop. After he broke the ice we all did our thing. Darn it was cold. They trucked us back to the Benning Ranger Camp and turned us loose for the Christmas holidays. With my ankle the way it was this was a big break for me. I got as far as Battle Park and Mary's brothers' apartment, which she was sharing with her sister-in-law Marga. Her brother was assigned overseas in Korea at the time. I crashed on the sofa for one whole day; I slept close to eighteen hours. Then I said goodbye to Mary and Marga and drove to Ohio for Christmas and my first visit home since joining the Army.

Over that holiday the movie *The Longest Day* was opening and I took my dad to see it. This was a time before Vietnam when military men in uniform were admired and respected. There I was in my green uniform with jump wings, Screaming Eagle Patch, Expert Infantryman Badge and National Defense Service Medal sitting with Dad amongst a theatre filled with "feather merchants" (military slang for civilians) who were all goo-goo over John Wayne. Needless to say I was one cocky young lieutenant. The Christmas vacation went by much too quickly, but the break did allow my ankle to get almost back to normal. Mom and Dad were very proud of all I had accomplished in just seven months in the Army. I guess I was pretty proud of myself too. Neither of my parents had a clue what Army life was like, or all about, but they supported my decision to try it as a career. Also they couldn't believe I was making almost as much money as both of their salaries put together. I am not sure but I think that was pretty close. My salary was a glorious $222.30 a month, plus $110 a month hazardous duty pay when I was jumping. Compare that with today's salaries. *Wow!*

After returning to Fort Benning and the Ranger Camp, things got very interesting. They trucked us north to the Mountain Phase Training Camp near Dahlonega, Georgia. I will tell you flat out that this was the most challenging and toughest part of Ranger School; at least it was for me. I hated the climbing and rappelling training and especially disliked the free rock climbing. One of my classmates fell and shattered his arm on the free climb. That was an eye opener! This mountaineering stuff was dangerous! The patrolling exercises were good learning experiences but the mountains seemed to get steeper and more challenging with each patrol. Once the patrolling started our food ration was doubled, no holding back on the chow. Want two steaks? They were there. Second or third helping of spaghetti? It was there. We burned up the calories like there was no tomorrow. As I mentioned earlier they sure fed us well. We would finish one patrol, clean our gear, eat a huge meal, crawl in our bunks and then be rousted out two hours later and told to report for the next patrol briefing. It was brutal and at times we were moving like zombies. I was selected patrol leader for various segments of the patrols and always got "satisfactory" (SAT) ratings. I think one needed to have at least three of five patrols with a rating of satisfactory to earn your Ranger Tab. By the next to last patrol I had four SATs and no UNSATs so I felt pretty good about things.

Our last patrol in the mountains was the longest and most challenging. As we moved through friendly front lines the weather was balmy and the sun was out. The patrol took us from Greasy Mountain north to near the Toccoa River. The patrol started off well but then it began to rain. The temperature dropped sharply; definitely a change from the balmy temps when we moved out. Just after dark my Ranger buddy and I were sent out on flank security for a road crossing. Danger areas like roads, trails and streams always required flank security on both flanks of the crossing site. We did our thing; then crossed over and lo and behold we could not find the patrol. They had moved out without us.

It was still raining, getting colder and black as pitch. We decided that we should continue on and try to find the rally point that would be used for the final planning for the assault on the target. We moved about four hours and were so tired we both decided that rest was required. Cold, wet and dead tired we bedded down next to one another with two ponchos and our own body heat. I did rest but not sure how good the sleep was. We woke up just at dawn and started moving again.

My buddy and I had not moved more than 100 yards when we ran into the patrol. They had been moving all night with no rest. We smiled at each other and decided getting lost had not been such a bad thing. In fact, we had not been missed. That is not a good thing on a patrol. Someone had screwed up not recognizing that two Rangers were missing for probably the better part of six hours. The attack went off well as I recall but the temperature continued to fall as things unfolded. It was getting darned cold and the wind was howling through the trees.

The patrol returned to the objective rally point. The time was late afternoon. It was really cold and the wind was blowing fiercely. As we looked across the Toccoa River we saw a large number of 2½ ton trucks just sitting there. It began to snow, gently at first then harder. We all decided with the change in weather the cadre had decided to truck us home. No way, that's not in the Ranger creed. The lane grader appeared in the rally point and told us that we had to "escape and evade" with our buddy to Greasy Mountain and friendly front lines. This was the normal wrap up of the last patrol. My Ranger buddy said, "Look we have about an hour and a half of light left, let's make tracks." We took off running and continued up and down those bloody hills until it was so dark we were running into trees and undergrowth. After that we continued at a steady pace as fast as we could. If I remember correctly we got back to friendly front lines about midnight, passed through the check point and were trucked back to the camp and our hootch. I was dead tired, and after cleaning my rifle, stripped off my clothes and fell into the rack. At about 0400 the lights came on and a team of cadre and one of the camp medics came through the hootch and had us all get out of bed and take off whatever clothes we had on. If they found even a tinge of pink or red skin you were immediately ordered to dress and report to the aid station. I had a small red spot on the side of one foot and was sent to the aid station post haste.

When I went inside it was truly unreal. The place was packed with frostbitten Rangers. It reminded me of some of the aid stations we saw in the Korean War movies. It was a mess with Rangers lying or standing everywhere. There were guys there with feet that were ice blue all the way above the ankles. The Ranger instructors and medics were definitely not happy campers. The camp commander, a Distinguished Service Cross winner from WWII, was standing stoic off to the side. He was definitely concerned about the situation. He had over sixty cases of frostbite among his Ranger Class 6 West Point and Regular Army students. Definitely this was not a good thing. He was later relieved as camp commander and his career shattered.

I am not sure if we were trucked or flown by chopper back to Fort Benning but somehow I ended up in Martin Army Hospital. My frostbite was truly a mouse turd compared to many of the injured but I was treated royally. I never realized how many general officers' sons were in the class until the time I spent in the ward at Martin Army. When I was released it was for limited duty with the Airborne department to recoup and get ready to continue, I hoped, with the Ranger course.

When I had fully recovered from my very mild frost bite I would normally have been sent back to Fort Campbell. As a special exception for those many frostbitten Regular Army lieutenants from Class 62-6 (aka Frost Bite 6) some ranger candidates were being allowed to continue on and finish just the last phase of the course. I knew if I went back to Fort Campbell the chances of getting back to either finish the last phase or repeat the whole course were slim to none. Also the thought of going through the whole course again did not appeal to me at all. I went to see a "little old lady in tennis shoes" at the Assignments Division and she agreed to let me stay at Benning and finish the last phase at Eglin Air Force Base in early May. That was when I fully realized who really ran the Army; the little old civilian ladies in tennis shoes. I was one happy lieutenant. For two months I spent my days working odd jobs for the 44th Company where all the Airborne students were assigned. I took a lot of physical training with the students and saw Mary almost daily. By this time we were engaged to be married in July at Fort MacPherson near Atlanta, Georgia.

In April, along with about twenty other "Frost Bite 6" classmates, deemed recovered from that night in the mountains, we were trucked with a new Ranger Class to the Florida Ranger Camp. All I really remember about most of this phase was that it was warm and a lot more enjoyable than the mountains. At that point I had four satisfactory patrols on my record and I felt it would be impossible to get four patrols all of which I might fail and then not get my tab. This proved to be correct.

Two patrols in Florida stand out in my mind. One was the Yellow River patrol where we paddled in rubber boats down the river and then moved inland to attack a guerrilla base and rescue hostages. I remember being absolutely beat and beyond tired, actually sleeping as we walked in Ranger file through the swamp with the water anywhere from knee to waist deep. At some point they changed patrol leaders and I was called forward and the new leader told me to take the point. So there I was, dead asleep on my feet and out front by maybe fifty yards. I woke up quickly enough when I heard my first gator bellow. It was a frightening sound I would never forget. I had no trouble staying awake after that. I remember the sun had come up and suddenly I was walking on solid ground. Just ahead,

300 yards across a relatively open area of trees and Florida scrub brush, was our target. To this day I could not tell you how I was lucky enough to have navigated to, and come out of that swamp, right on the objective but it happened that way.

They picked a new patrol leader and we hit the objective killing the bad guys and saving the prisoners. At that point we also had two wounded (simulated) who were going to have to be carried back through the swamp to our boats. I had four satisfactory patrols at that point and was totally relaxed when suddenly the word came back, "Send Ranger Redmond up." I couldn't believe it, not point again! No, not point man; I was the new patrol leader. Why me? I was golden. I had more successful patrols than I needed to get my Ranger Tab and some guys could have been hurting for SATs in order to pass the course and get that tab on their shoulder. Regardless, there I was patrol leader again.

My role was to plan the return march. Well stumbling back through the swamp was not my idea of fun so I took a completely out of the box approach. There was a road that led us back to friendly front lines, so…. My plan was that we would make stretchers for the wounded and walk back on the road with security to the front, flanks and rear. Since our mission was also to find and kill guerrillas, if we were attacked we would fight it out and kill the bad guys. As I briefed the new order to the element leaders I saw some dismay and incredulity cross their faces. Rangers never walked on roads. They avoided them like the plague. I figured one unsatisfactory would not hurt my record nor cost me my tab. I was certainly not keen on going back through that swamp particularly carrying wounded. Surprisingly the captain who was acting as our patrol Lane Grader gave me a big "attaboy" for being innovative and I got my fifth satisfactory patrol. To this day I laugh about that. For all I know walking the road may have been the school solution. We did walk back on the road leaving the boats tied up on the Yellow River. I am not sure those rubber boats aren't still tied somewhere along the river bank.

Redmond's Rule #3 — Do the unexpected, it will likely work.

The only other patrol that stood out was the raid on Santa Rosa Island. After disembarking from a Landing Craft Medium (LCM) well off shore in the gulf we paddled in on rubber boats. We then crawled across the white sand with dirty semi-white sheets for camouflage and successfully attacked our objective. The water was warm, the night balmy and my last patrol in Ranger School was absolute fun! And I was not designated patrol leader for any phase of the raid.

Ranger School ended and I was awarded my Ranger Tab. I said goodbye to Mary with our wedding seven weeks away. I returned to Fort Campbell sporting that great black and yellow Ranger Tab on my left shoulder. I was a proud and happy soldier.

5
LIFE AS A SCREAMING EAGLE: BACK TO THE CURRAHEES

Upon return to Fort Campbell in late May 1963 I was assigned to C Company of the 506th Airborne Battle Group. This was the same parent unit I had left almost nine months prior. I was now one building over from my old D Company lash up. My company commander was a great soldier, Captain (CPT) Bob Crittenden, a bachelor, and all Army. He was a truly great leader who was destined to retire as a full colonel. He assigned me the Mortar Platoon to lead and a fantastic soldier platoon sergeant in Staff Sergeant Herman Trent. Herman went on to be a command sergeant major in the 101st before he retired. We were preparing for the Division Best Mortar Platoon competition and Sergeant Trent taught me volumes about mortars. We won the Battle Group competition and came in near the top in the Division. This success can be directly attributed to Sergeant Trent and the troops. We were both pleased with the men and their performance.

In addition to the mortars the platoon had two sections of 106 MM Recoilless Rifles. I can tell you those guns were some darned good tank killers and bunker busters. (NOTE: During the Vietnam War an anti-personnel flechette round was developed for this weapon and it proved devastating in countering mass attacks by the bad guys.) One of the 106 section sergeants, a staff sergeant, was a WWII veteran who served on the "other side" in the Luftwaffe. He was quite the disciplinarian and one heck of a soldier. He spoke with a distinct German accent. One day in the field the subject of WWII and discipline came up. He told me that we Americans did not know what we were doing spit shining the toe of our boots. He stated, with a slight German accent, that in the Wehrmacht and Luftwaffe they used to shine the bottom of their boots then walk on them. "That vas discipline, *Loytnent*, good German discipline."

Later in my career I had a pair of Cochran jump boots that were spit shined all over. They were beautiful and had double soles which made me appear a little taller. I shined the instep of those boots to the point of being able to shave in that portion of the sole. As a battalion commander in the 82nd I would administer Article 15 justice/punishment wearing them. I sat with my boots up on my desk. The first poor lad who came before me was horrified to see the instep. He knew he was dead; this lieutenant colonel had to be crazy. The word spread throughout the battalion that the "Old Man" shined the bottom of his boots. It was a great gimmick and the senior NCOs loved it. By the way, was I crazy? Maybe, but I was fair in dispensing punishment.

The wedding was rapidly approaching and Walt Werner, who had agreed to be my best man, and I proceeded to Fort MacPherson to link up with other friends, all lieutenants, who were in the wedding party. Dave Russell who had been my roommate my senior year at PC, Jack Kennedy also a PC classmate, and Fred Caristo from Boston University, were all there as ushers. My parents arrived with several of my aunts and my grandmother Redmond. The wedding was super and all went well with my uncle, Father Francis Redmond, officiating. My only problem came when, after the ceremony and reception, as we were leaving I found my car had been trashed. I had hidden it, but they had found it and did a job on it. At any rate Mary and I finally started on our honeymoon, two whole days. We spent the first night at Rock City/Lookout Mountain, Tennessee and then went on to Fort Campbell, Kentucky.

The company had to go to the field the next day with the entire Battle Group. Yes to the field, and so I left Mary in a guest cottage at Campbell. It was an old WWII officer's quarters with a small living area, one bedroom, with bunk beds in the living room and twin beds in the bedroom. There was also a small kitchen jammed into a corner for cooking and washing dishes. Oh yes, there was a bathroom too. We were preparing for Exercise Swift Strike III and my mortar platoon was to be used as a rifle platoon; don't ask me why but it was. I was gone from day three of our married life until day eight training for Swift Strike III! Some honeymoon, huh?

Just after returning from the field I was selected to be the officer-in-charge of a funeral detail. Funerals are, of course, sad events and the Army takes them dead serious, no pun intended. Funerals had better be done correctly and according to the book. I got the word on either a Friday night or Saturday morning and rounded up the best available NCO to be my assistant. He would organize the firing party, the flag detail, the vehicles, and other aspects of the service. The sergeant had experience with funeral details and told me he would handle all the administrative stuff and brief me, not to worry. But he told me we had one small problem; no blank ammunition for the firing party to practice the twenty-one gun salute. The last thing you need is a ragged sound to the volley fire right before taps is played. I was at a loss as to where to get ammo on a weekend. Then the NCO said, "Hey, sir, contact LT Buyle, he's the assistant supply officer. He'll have ammo but don't tell him I told you."

Although common practice in those days, it was a violation of Army regulations to have a cache of illegal ammunition, even blanks. Most units did keep blank ammunition, smoke grenades and explosive simulators to survive in a training crisis. Getting ammo from the ammo dump was a major pain in the butt with the civilian bureaucracy. It did not happen over a weekend. I called LT Buyle at his home and was flat told he had no ammo, go away, and bother someone else. After much heated discussion and begging on my part, we hung up with no resolution to my problem. Ten minutes later the phone rang and LT Buyle told me to meet him in the company street just before dark. He pulled up, handed me the ammo through the window of his car and sped away. It was sort of like a drug sale. The troops rehearsed, and on Monday we carried off a great funeral detail. A major challenge had been answered successfully.

From this rocky introduction, Ken Buyle and his wife Kathy became great friends of the Redmonds and remain close friends to this day. While recently visiting with the Buyles I learned that Ken did not have any ammo. He wasn't kidding. After we talked on the phone he was given a bit of counsel by his wife Kathy on dealing with fellow officers with a problem. He called me back telling me to meet him later and then went to Headquarters Company, into the reconnaissance platoon living area (in those long ago days known as a platoon bay) and found a young specialist he knew. He told him he needed blanks for a funeral firing party rehearsal and he needed them "now." The trooper insisted they had no ammo but Ken ordered him into his car and started driving down Range Road. The trooper was nervous and told Ken that the recon platoon leader would reprimand him and he would be digging holes for the next month. Ken told the soldier to just tell him where he should pull off the road and that he was not telling the lieutenant anything. Finally the troop said "Sir, pull over here." The young soldier jumped out of the car and scurried into the woods returning about ten minutes later with several boxes of blank ammo. Should by some quirk of fate the recon platoon leader be reading this, it may all be news to him. Ken will figure in this narrative several more times as we followed each other around for the next twenty years.

We did a lot of socializing with the Buyles at Fort Campbell, most of it picnics and simple cook outs because neither one of us had money to do much else. I remember one instance where I was tossing Ken's son, two year old Raymond Buyle, up in the air and somehow dropped him right on his head. It couldn't have hurt him too much as he has grown up to be an engineer/builder of some renown in Kansas and has a lovely family.

One day Mary and I decided to invite CPT Crittenden over for a good home cooked meal. It was an experience for her; she did not yet know how to cook. Frankly I was lucky to be able to heat a C-ration (a military individual canned, precooked meal—a true culinary delight.) or boil water. This dinner with my commander would be an experience for both of us. I cooked chicken outside on a little grill. If I remember correctly I lit the fire with lighter fluid that imparted a distinct taste to the chicken skin. Trying to put a meal together in that tiny kitchen/guest cottage was a task of a major magnitude. Mary pulled it off, with little help from me. Captain Crittenden was a perfect guest and very appreciative of Mary's efforts. He and I spoke of it a few years ago when I visited him in Montgomery, Alabama where he had retired. He claimed that it was a great meal that he had never forgotten. That comment could go either way. He remained a bachelor for quite a while, and Mary always said she hoped her cooking was not to blame. I would blame my lighter fluid goof more than her dinner.

Our first home was a small furnished apartment in Clarksville, Tennessee, not far from the Cumberland River. Not bad for two newlyweds just starting out. Well it was OK for the two months we lived there. Well, it was OK after we got rid of the roaches.

The decision to use the mortar platoon as a rifle platoon for Exercise Swift Strike III turned out to be a true godsend. We didn't have to hump the mortars all over South Carolina in the summer heat. Our drop zone was near Saluda, South Carolina, and we jumped from C-123s. I am not sure if the birds were from the Regular Air Force or from the National Guard but I think they were from the Guard. Being a new jumpmaster I had to show off my talents for the troops. Our platoon was split between two aircraft. I was jumpmaster on one aircraft, and Sergeant Trent the other. Our company had its own drop zone a few miles from Saluda. We departed Campbell Army Air Field with a set flying time, an hour and a half, to the drop zone. The weather was perfect. We were flying in two sets of Vs, three ships per V, with the whole company in the six airplanes.

Two hours later, as I hung out the door of the airplane straining to see our DZ and looking at Staff Sergeant Trent in the aircraft across from me, we both shook our heads and by our looks were saying, "These guys are lost." We had been given our ten minute warning about thirty minutes earlier, and gone through all the jump commands and had been standing by for over twenty minutes. There was no DZ visible to our front. Suddenly the plane did a very hard left turn almost throwing me across the plane and out the opposite door. When the airplane righted itself and leveled off I looked down and saw jumpers in the air below me and suddenly the red light turned green, I yelled, "Go," and jumped. It was an automatic reflex after jump school. I landed in a scrub pine woods just off the intended drop zone; so much for Air Force pilot accuracy in those days. Fortunately no one was injured and our assembly was perfect.

I really remember very little about Swift Strike III except that we had a good time. Honestly, dirty, hot, smelly and tired we did have a good time. The troops liberated watermelons from folk's melon patches as we trudged the roads. At one point we were given the mission to establish a road block on a major highway; try that today even in military friendly South Carolina. While manning the road block we lived in a wooded area behind a very nice family's home. The mother brought us lemonade and let us run the hose from the house to the woods so we could all take a cold shower. It was great. South Carolina remains a military friendly place still today.

The only other thing that sticks in my mind is a convoy move I messed up, or almost messed up. We had four or five segments (serials in military parlance) of trucks and I was the officer-in-charge of serial three. That meant there were two more elements, maybe ten, twelve truckloads of troops behind us. Somewhere along the route I fell asleep and woke to the truck jolting over something and no trucks in front of me, none, zero, zilch, nada! Ouch, in my midget mind there went my career before my eyes. After driving several minutes and making several guesses as to where to turn, with my heart in my mouth, we rounded a bend and came up on the lead two elements in the convoy. Needless to say I was one relieved lieutenant. To this day no one knew of this little, almost major error.

Upon return to Fort Campbell we settled into normal Battle Group activities and I performed the usual jobs of a junior officer. Also, Mary and I were offered quarters on Fort Campbell proper; a brand new home with three bedrooms, two baths and a very modern fully equipped kitchen. We lived on Kentucky Ave., about five minutes from the Battle Group area. They were really nice quarters for a 2nd lieutenant. Honestly it far outstripped anything I had lived in as a child. This Army was all right. We visited Fort Campbell in 2012 and those quarters still looked great and had been expanded and modernized since we lived in them.

One day I was selected to defend a trooper pending court martial who was sitting in the post stockade (aka jail). Yes, in those days every post had a stockade. He was up on charges for denigrating Old Glory. It seems he had made some very strong and vulgar statements about what type human waste should be placed on our flag. The lad had recently been tried and convicted of AWOL and other transgressions. He was a surly black troop who in my opinion had no business in the Army or even the USA. How he managed to make it through basic training and jump school was a mystery. After our first interview I came away very unhappy with the task of defending him. I tried to get out of the duty. The Battle Group personnel officer told me to suck it up and press on. About a week before the trial, a Special Court Martial, a sergeant mentioned to me that I should look up "stacking charges" in the Uniform Code of Military Justice. Basically it boiled down to the issue of trying a man for all known charges at the time of court martial. Checking the time line it was clear that at the previous court martial for being AWOL the issue of desecrating the flag was known. Uh Oh! The Perry Mason in me took over.

The trial judge, the Battle Group operations officer, a major, opened the proceedings. I stood and moved for dismissal on the grounds this was an illegal trial and charge based on UCMJ paragraph, such and such. The proceedings were closed, the court caucused quietly. When the Court Martial reopened the trial judge announced that the charges were dropped. I walked out of the court room and back to my office and the lad, who never thanked me, went back to the stockade. My opinion was he was a scumbag.

Redmond's Rule #4 – Always do what you believe is right, even if you don't like it.

About an hour later I was summoned to see the Battle Group commander, Colonel Richard Allen. I thought "Oh boy, here it comes." I walked into his office and he chewed me out for getting the lad off on a technicality and said something like. "That's the last soldier in this Battle Group you will defend, get out of my sight," or words to that effect. As I walked out of the office I was handed orders appointing me as prosecutor for the Battle Group. That was the last soldier I ever defended. However, as the Battle Group prosecutor I did send a few deserving lads to the stockade in the months that followed.

The 506th Battle Group was selected to participate in a test of a new system the Defense Advanced Research Project Agency (DARPA – the folks who really invented the Internet) was developing; a tool called the "People Sniffer." Walt Werner and I both participated in checking out the backpack device as well as the helicopter mounted version. The idea was that in the jungles in Vietnam (that war was heating up at this time) these devices would tell you if there were people up ahead. Hence you could possibly avoid ambushes. We never felt too comfortable with the backpack sniffer but I do believe the helicopter version was later used to fly over the jungle in Vietnam. I have no idea how effective this thing ultimately became or how many people, or families of monkeys it erroneously detected. I would encounter and test an improved version of the "People Sniffer" again in about 18 months.

Sometime in the early fall Mary announced that we were going to have a baby. She was expecting to deliver the next summer. We were both thrilled. In those days they were not quite so sophisticated in determining whether the baby was to be a boy or girl but we both readily agreed as long as the baby was healthy we would be happy. The next summer seemed light years away. Sometime in the fall I was promoted to first lieutenant and donned a silver bar.

Colonel Allen had this thing about education for the troops and getting as many non-high school graduates as possible to earn their General Education Development Certificate. He had even set up a library and counseling center in the Battle Group area to help them. Well, guess who was selected to be the officer-in-charge for this lash-up; yep, me. I hated leaving my mortar platoon and "Choppin" Charlie but I had no choice. This was not my idea of what an Infantry lieutenant should be doing.

Shortly after taking over the Currahee Education Center, word came down from Division that the Battle Group Pentomic unit organization was being changed. The Division would be re-organized into brigades with three battalions each. Hence, I escaped the education business and went back to soldiering. Well not quite, I first became the adjutant (S1, personnel officer) of the 1st Battalion 506th Airborne Infantry working for a crusty old WWII lieutenant colonel (LTC). The LTC was a WWII, Korea and Vietnam veteran, who was married to a Vietnamese lady who was still learning English. This was the start of one of the most memorable periods in my career.

6
MY FIRST COMMAND, 1964

was sitting at my desk working on a report for the colonel when the executive officer (XO) stepped in and said, "Redmond, get your hat and go to C Company." I looked up and said something to the effect that I was working on a report for the boss and needed to finish it as he wanted it that morning. The major frowned and said something like, "You don't get it lieutenant, go to C Company NOW! You are the new company commander." I was stunned. No explanation, just go to C Company.

I walked down one side of the street toward C Company (aka Choppin Charlie) and the fired commander, a West Point graduate, on the promotion list to captain, walked down the other. We exchanged glances but no words were spoken. That was our change of command. That was the old Regular Army.

Arriving at C Company I went immediately to the office and asked the first sergeant, John Moore, to explain what the devil was going on. He and I went in the commander's office and I heard: "Well, sir, do you know Private Jerome (not his real name), the kid that has been AWOL a number of times?" I responded that I did as he was notorious for his disappearing tricks. First Sergeant Moore then said, "Well, sir, we found Jerome chained in the platoon arms room this morning. Seems the platoon sergeant has been going out to Jerome's trailer looking for him and visiting with the missus. They got friendly, quite friendly. When Jerome showed up this time the platoon sergeant didn't want to stop visiting with Mrs. Jerome and so he has been keeping him chained in the arms room. The colonel relieved both the commander and the platoon sergeant and you are the new company CO, Sir." This tale may be hard to believe but I assure you it happened. First Lieutenant Redmond, two months in grade with a still new and shiny silver bar, was the company commander of C Company, 1st Battalion 506th Infantry, aka Choppin Charlie. That was the old Regular Army, for sure.

First Sergeant Moore and the platoon sergeants were lifesavers and made my job almost easy. The only senior NCO other than the first sergeant whose name I can remember is Staff Sergeant Herman Trent my mortar platoon sergeant from the old Battle Group. When I took over "Choppin Charlie" there was only one other officer in the company, the XO, a second lieutenant. He was a nice enough guy and a hard worker but he was a little quiet and reserved compared with other Airborne lieutenants around the battalion. He proved to be a great help to me and many times kept me out of administrative trouble.

I remember a number of interesting, and that is an understatement, happenings during my days commanding "Choppin Charlie." As you read on, please remember, I could not make these stories up. In some cases the truth that follows is hard to believe.

For example the day First Sergeant Moore came into my office and said that the Division Psychiatrist wanted to see me and one of our troops, Private Jones (again not his real name) in his office that morning. When I asked the first sergeant what this was all about he could only tell me that Jones had been a frequent visitor at the Division shrink's office over the last three to four weeks. Jones and I went in my jeep to see the shrink. First I went in alone and was told by the psychiatrist that Jones was in real medical trouble in addition to having serious mental issues. The doctor showed me a picture of what looked like a burnt hot dog. He told me it was Jones's manhood after he had circumcised himself with a razor blade in the platoon latrine. He then visited his girlfriend. Apparently she told him he would enjoy her more if he was circumcised. He was in a hurry and did not wait until he was fully healed from his personal surgery. She had a sexually transmitted disease. We medically boarded Jones out of the Army.

Another day the first sergeant brought Private Sam Smith (again not his real name) into the office. Sam was shaking and crying like a rat eating onions that had a bad case of diarrhea. When I asked him what had happened he told me that his squad leader, a former jump school instructor who did 250 pushups every morning to get his blood flowing, had beat him up, pushed him down some stairs and stomped on him. The sergeant, who was also present in the room, stated that he had only laid hands on Smith to correct him, but yes the lad had fallen. Smith insisted that he had been assaulted and wanted to press charges. I told Smith that I didn't see any blood, and no bruises. It would be hard to prove assault. We talked for quite a while and I convinced Smith that no court martial would convict the sergeant and that he should go back to the platoon bay, straighten up his act, and soldier on. To my surprise he bought it. Once Smith had cleared the area I chewed out the squad leader for being an idiot regardless of how much Smith needed a pounding. Fortunately the lack of bruises and blood saved the day. By the way, both the squad leader and Private Smith were black as the ace of spades. Hence no bruising was apparent on Private Smith. He actually squared himself away and I later promoted him to Specialist Fourth Class. I think he was terrified of his NCO squad leader.

Speaking of black soldiers let me make an observation for you. When I took over C Company, the company had approximately 39% black troops. You read that right, better than one in three of my troops were African American. I will tell you the NCOs were all top notch and good men as were most of the troops. Seems the black lads volunteered for Airborne for either the prestige of jumping out of planes, for the $55 extra a month hazardous duty pay or for the bloused jump boots. Whatever the reason, the 82nd Airborne "All Americans" and the 101st "Screaming Eagles" had a high percentage of black troops in those days.

The Army was an equal opportunity employer for sure in the early 1960s and our black citizens gained from it. Among the troops they ran the gamut from PFC Jones who we boarded out for his little medical experiment to Specialist Charlie Norman. Norman was a fantastic soldier and a recruiting poster quality trooper. I tried like hell to get him promoted to sergeant but the old blood stripe system, where the company commander could reduce an ineffective sergeant and pass his stripe on to someone in the company who was a good leader and more deserving of the rank, was gone. The best I could do for Specialist Norman was promote him to "two stripe" corporal. He was outstanding and did a great job for me. He was part of the informal chain of command that exists in every unit. I learned a lot about leadership watching troops like Charlie Norman and I was not shy in seeking their counsel when it seemed appropriate.

One Saturday, just after lunch, First Sergeant Moore knocked on the door once again and announced that there were two ladies there to see me. I told him to bring them in but stay in the room with us. The girls, not much over nineteen or twenty, were very attractive, and obviously nervous. They were ladies of the night from Nashville and had been regularly "dating" some of my troops. They seemed at a loss for words until one of them said, "Heavens you can't be the "old man" the guys talk about! You're not much older than us." After some hesitation on their part it came out that the gals were missing a stereo and a radio that they believed two of my troops had appropriated from their apartment.

More discussion followed and one of them dropped the comment that the lads involved had produced drugs, they claimed came from the unit! They stated that the drug was morphine. The first sergeant looked at me and we both immediately thought of the nuclear attack emergency kits, one on each floor, that had morphine stored in them. We said nothing to the ladies but assured them we would find and return their audio equipment.

After the girls were gone, the first sergeant and I along with the executive officer went and inspected the nuke emergency kits. All appeared in order until the XO, smart lad that he was, said, "Sir, why don't we tip them over and check the bottom." Bingo, we saw a big hole and found no morphine syringes. All the nuke emergency kits in the company had been cleaned out of morphine. The Post Criminal Investigation Division had a heart attack as did the entire Division Chain of Command. It seems these two gals had inadvertently revealed an ongoing problem throughout the Division and post. Numerous courts martial followed in various units around Fort Campbell. Oh yes, the girls got their stereo and radio back. But they did lose several of their better clients who marched off for an extended period at the Fort Leavenworth, Kansas, Disciplinary Barracks.

In those days the Army paid its troops in cash as there was no such critter as "direct deposit." Payday was basically a day off, one of the few the troops or for that matter we leaders could count on. There was none of this three and four day weekend stuff that the Army has now. Some commanders acted as company pay officer and others delegated the duty to the unit XO or other company officer. For me it was something I wanted to do and the first sergeant agreed. It gave me a chance to see every one of my troops, at least those present for duty on pay day, once a month. Some companies paid early and others paid later in the day. Regardless of what time he was paid, once a soldier had his pay he was released to his platoon. Unless he had screwed up, and owed his platoon sergeant some time, he was off the rest of the day. Trying to help the troops, with the Top Sergeants' assistance we paid early, very early in the day. I went to the Division Finance Office at 0400 to pick up the pay along with an armed guard; I also carried a loaded .45 pistol. Armed guard you probably question. There had been several instances where the pay officer had been robbed right on Fort Campbell while returning to his unit. When I returned, the executive officer and the first sergeant had envelopes in alphabetical order and the troops standing by lined up alphabetically. We normally could start paying by 0630 and would finish by 0800. Woe be it unto the troop who wasn't in line at the correct place when I called for him. The troops appreciated this little effort to get them out and off early with cash in their pockets to do whatever they had in mind for pay day. Nashville, Tennessee and "E Town" (Evansville, Indiana) waited with open arms for these lads with all that jump pay.

Redmond's Rule # 5 – Take care of the Troops and they will take care of you.

The Division was scheduled to deploy on Exercise Desert Strike One, out in California that replaced the Swift Strike series of exercises that took place in the Carolinas. This was 1964 and someone already realized that the Mid-East and desert areas were going to become of strategic interest. Our battalion was to stage out of Camp Pendleton, California and deploy into the Mojave Desert. I spent a good deal of time convincing my paratroopers they needed to look better, run faster and march farther than the Marines we were going to be billeted among for almost three weeks before the exercise started. Once we got to Camp Pendleton you can't imagine how fired up the troops were and how great they looked. The USMC was not going to outshine the Screaming Eagles. The first sergeant and I were quite proud of our men.

We flew into a Marine Air Station near Camp Pendleton, California. I think it was named El Toro, and what an experience that was. I had been invited to ride up front in the cockpit for the last segment of the trip from Campbell. I had never been in the cabin of a C-141 and was enjoying the ride as we began our approach to the runway. When we were at about 1000 feet, as we were descending, the copilot suddenly shouted that there were aircraft taxiing on our runway. Sure enough two F-4 fighters were on the runway we had just been cleared to land on. The pilot pulled us up and turned out of the traffic pattern as he gave the Marine air traffic controllers one hell of a chewing out. On the next approach the runway was clear.

Camp Las Pulgas, aka "The Flea," where we were billeted was a WWII Quonset hut cantonment area (normally a temporary site with billets for troops-the Army and the Marines both had lots of WWII temporary facilities still in use.) in much need of repair, at least by our Army standards. For three weeks we trained, ran the hills and relaxed a little before the exercise. As I recall a great deal of beer was consumed at the local enlisted club every night but we never had a problem with the Marines. Mutual respect, because we all thought we were elite soldiers. The difference was that we knew we were elite and jumped out of perfectly good airplanes to prove it.

While at Las Pulgas one of our frequent AWOL troopers came back. The first sergeant told me the lad had potential in spite of his frequent disappearances. I gave him an Article 15 Company Punishment and before dismissing him told him he was the new company guidon bearer and my driver. Talk about seeing a kid shape up, he proved to be a model soldier. During the exercise he acted almost like my batman (basically a valet), and of course the days of an officer having a batman were long gone. I liked the trooper. He really took good care of me and I never wanted for hot coffee throughout the exercise. Later I heard that after I left the company he reverted to his old ways.

The troops appreciated Fort Campbell after about a week at the "flea." Walking and running up the surrounding hills was a real smoke-bringer experience. Seemed like no matter where we marched or ran it was all uphill. Our admiration for the gyrenes (aka Marines) who lived and trained at Las Pulgas knew no bounds. I kept telling the men in pep talks that we were going to see the "Elephant"—an old Civil War term meaning go into combat. We were scheduled to jump into the Mojave but that was changed to an air landing with no explanation as to why. We were an unhappy bunch of paratroopers.

C Company was to land and move to a position up in the New York Mountains, yes the New York Mountains in California. We landed on a dry lakebed and started moving toward our objective, quite a walk by the way. At that point we only had five jeeps and a few mechanical mules (a small flatbed cart like vehicle) to move the mortars. It was hot, dusty and dry. I walked with the troops.

Two hours after landing LTC Collins rolled up in his jeep with a change in orders. By the way, that was the first contact with anyone from battalion since we landed in the exercise area. We might as well have been on the moon as in the Mojave. The colonel explained that the OPFOR, opposing forces, had already seized the New York Mountains. LTC Collins asked what I thought we should do and where my company could best be employed. He asked me? A much seasoned combat soldier was asking me? I think I had about six months in grade and four months in command at that point.

Looking out at the desert I saw what looked like a real honest to goodness "pass" in the hills about four or five miles further ahead. We did a quick map check on the hood of his jeep and I told him that I thought we should occupy that pass and keep the bad guys from coming through until things sorted out. He agreed and told me to get there as soon as possible policing up any stray friendly units I found on the way. That sounded like a plan to me. He then drove off. I don't remember the next time I saw him. It seemed there was a lot of confusion at that point; a true Clausewitz "fog of war" situation.

Redmond's Rule # 6 - No plan survives the first contact with the enemy.

We got to the pass and it was a classic, just like the cowboy movies – narrow passage with steep sides. After blocking the pass and occupying the hills we settled in. We had added several self-propelled anti-tank guns, a battery of artillery, a signal unit and some other miscellaneous troops before the sun went down. It was quite a nice task force. After dark all seemed in order and we bedded down for the night, with plenty of early warning security I thought. I was awakened by shouting just at dawn and found a member of the 5th Mechanized Division, part of the opposing forces, standing over me with a rifle pointed at the command post troops and yours truly. Suddenly my neat little world and our grand defense of the pass were coming apart.

Just as quickly I heard more shouting and the trooper took off back up the hill from which he had apparently come. I saw the opposing folks milling around on top of the hill and I determined that there was no retreat, only attack. I hollered for all available troops to follow me and up the hill we went. We probably had about forty troops charging up that hill by the time we reached the top. At this point we were totally intermingled with the attacking force. A controller/evaluator, umpire to a civilian reader, was on scene and he sorted us out. Both commanders were allowed to explain what we had done and what fire power we had at our disposal. I am not sure, maybe I talked faster, lied better, whatever, but we were awarded control of the hill and the attackers were required to withdraw. About three hours later, after we had been reinforced with a platoon of tanks, the 5th Mechanized Division attacked again. It looked like a reinforced battalion of armored vehicles. It was something to watch them come at us across the desert. Unlike that incident at Fort Campbell when the M-48 Patton tanks came at me, this time we were not moving. We were on the high ground and had the pass blocked and mined. We won the engagement, at least in the eyes of the controller/evaluator, and the pass was held.

Redmond's Rule #7 – Never back away from a fair fight, or one where you have a tactical advantage.

Life in the desert can be very dirty and the dust gets into everything; men, weapons, machines whatever. There were a number of cross country movements in any vehicle(s) we could beg, borrow or steal. I worked hard to keep the walking to a minimum as the temperatures reached close to 100 every day. Cross country movement in the desert without wheels is not fun. One interesting aside was the mechanical mules described earlier. These machines just kept running, in some cases with only three wheels. We made one move with jeeps, several ¾ ton trucks, two deuce and a half trucks and four mechanical mule transport vehicles. There were paratroopers hanging all over those machines. I rode a mule that traveled over twenty-five miles with only three wheels. I don't remember much about the exercise proper except for the dust and dirt. I do recall that at the end of the exercise we were nuked, simulated of course. Nice way to end the show.

We were very near Searchlight, Nevada and moved into a tent camp to regroup, get some real food and beer, and oh yes, clean up. A hot shower after those dusty days in the desert was a real gift from heaven. One morning in the mess tent drinking coffee with the company NCOs we had an unwanted visitor. A "sidewinder" slithered right under our table and out the other side of the tent. Needless to say we all paid better attention from that point on. There were lots of scorpions and some tarantulas there also. One had to be very careful to shake out your boots in the morning before you put them on.

After the third day word came down that each company could send one platoon to Las Vegas at noon; they would return the next morning. Needless to say the troops were thrilled. In those days soldiers could only go into a town in Class B (khaki) or Class A (green) uniforms, no fatigues. Our B-bags with Class B uniforms had caught up with us there in the desert and the first group of paratrooper studs got cleaned up for a visit to "sin city."

The next morning about 0800 the trucks came rolling back into camp and the noise was raucous and deafening. The troops were yelling and shouting. At first we could not make out the words. Then suddenly it became clear. They were shouting, "We have seen the 'Elephant.' We have seen the 'Elephant.'" The first sergeant and I assumed they referred to Sodom and Gomorrah in Nevada and thought no more of it. We did decide that perhaps we should accompany the next platoon into that den of iniquity. We got ourselves squared away and jumped into my jeep for the trip. As we came over the last hill before Lost Wages, there on the side of the road was a huge pink elephant. We both laughed our heads off at that one. Last time I was in Vegas going to Fort Irwin for General Dynamics, that pink elephant was still there. Seeing that elephant was quite a way to end Exercise Desert Strike One. As a comment I do recall that I left sin city with less money than when I entered. No Irish luck on that trip.

After returning to Fort Campbell we were designated Division First Ready Company (DRF 1). In those days the DRF 1 in the 101st and the 82nd Airborne were locked in the barracks for two weeks at a time and on a two hour string to deploy anywhere in the world. I had been sleeping in the office for several days; it was July 3, 1964. Sergeant Moore came into the office and said something along the lines of, "Sir, why don't you go home tonight. You're only five minutes away and your wife is due any day now. Go spend the night at home. If anything comes up we know where you are. The troops will never know and they would not think less of you anyway." I went home. At about 0200 Mary woke me and said it was time. I rushed her to the hospital and informed the first sergeant where I was. In the early morning I became the happy father of Lawrence Edward Redmond on the Fourth of July 1964. And the Top Sergeant was right, no one questioned where I had been that night.

Shortly after the birth of their grandson both sets of grandparents visited Fort Campbell. My parents were overwhelmed by the quarters the Army had provided a mere first lieutenant. I truly think, before they visited, they thought we were living in a tent. LTC and

Mrs. Devlin were impressed with everything, especially the fact that as a junior first lieutenant I was commanding a company in one of the Army's premier units. But without a doubt, both sets of grandparents really had eyes only for young Larry.

Without warning the "bird" I had launched back at Providence College just over two years earlier came home to roost. Orders directing me to proceed within a month to Fort Bragg for the Special Forces Qualification Course landed on my desk. The test I had taken and paper I had signed in May 1962 had caught up to me. When the levee for Special Forces and Spanish language school came down I was not alone. Ken Buyle and Walt Werner were on that same list. We would all gather again in Panama. I was about to embark on another phase of Army life that would prove unique and challenging. That is an understatement, as you will see.

All in all my time at Fort Campbell was quite an introduction to the Airborne community. I left Fort Campbell with enough jumps to qualify as a senior parachutist but at this point I never was comfortable with jumping. I did it, but I didn't really like it. Most of my jumps were from C-130s and C-123s and some were decidedly exciting; like the jump on Swift Strike III described earlier. Also I remember one C-130 drop on Los Banos drop zone when I was C Company Commander. We had the whole company (well almost the whole company) in two C-130s. The families were invited out to observe; it was to be a grand time with refreshments to follow. The pilots proceeded to put all but about ten of my men in the trees along the side of the drop zone where the families were gathered. Fortunately there were no injuries. I was still not enthralled or totally comfortable with jumping at this point in my career. Did I mention at that time officers got $110 extra a month hazardous duty pay? That kept us from starving.

7

SPECIAL FORCES SCHOOL, FORT BRAGG, NC

Mary and I, along with young Larry, aged four weeks, traveled to Fort Bragg for the three month Special Forces Qualification Course in September 1964. I had orders from there to Monterey, CA to the Defense Language Institute to study Spanish and then on to the 8th Special Action Force at Fort Gulick Canal Zone. That further travel assumed I successfully passed the Special Forces Qualification Course and Spanish language training.

Mary's brother, Captain Eddie Devlin, and his wife Marga, were also at Bragg as Eddie was assigned to the 82nd Airborne Division. They lived in Corregidor Courts in a small but nice brick home. We thought we would find a furnished apartment. There were so many troops cycling through Fort Bragg at that time that we were wrong in that thought. No apartments at any price were available. We finally rented a three bedroom trailer down a country dirt road in Spring Lake just off base. It was clean, and had three bedrooms but ended any thought that we would ever live in a trailer again, at least in Mary's mind.

When the course started I began meeting a whole new group of folks. The most colorful being LT Harry Jones, a former Green Beret staff sergeant who claimed he went to Officer Candidate School because he couldn't get promoted to sergeant first class. Harry and I quickly became fast friends. We were in the same student "A Detachment" for training. (The A Detachment is the basic SF operational organization comprised of twelve personnel. Two were officers and ten were highly skilled NCOs. In the school training environment we were all officers.) Harry became "Uncle Harry" to all his classmates because he was older than most second lieutenants by quite a few years. He taught me a "college degree" worth of knowledge about Special Forces (SF) operations and living in the field. His guidance and counsel held me in good stead throughout the next two and a half years in Special Forces (SF) and later in Vietnam. Harry was also slated to attend Spanish Language Training and be assigned to the 8th Special Forces (SF) Group in Panama. (From this point on I will use the acronym "SF" or the name Green Beret interchangeably to refer to Special Forces.)

A neighbor of Mary's from Battle Park in 1962 at Fort Benning, Captain Bo Baker, was in our training A Detachment and quite a stud. Major Joe Lutz was also in the course. On several occasions I would encounter both Bo and Joe (Major General Lutz) later in my career.

Our A Detachment cadre evaluator was a Captain Bobby Davis. Bobby and I would meet again at Infantry Branch and then once in Vietnam on my second tour to that war torn country. During our qualification training we had a number of parachute jumps, all from C-130s. I was getting used to jumping from that bird. None of the jumps were a problem but I remember one night we jumped out at Camp Mackall (a WWII training base west of Fort Bragg) and I was the only one who made the drop zone. The other team members landed in short pine trees just off the DZ. Gathering up the chutes in those pines was a slow, tedious job. It took forever to assemble the twelve of us and Captain Davis.

The school was tough but physically nothing like Ranger School. With the help of Uncle Harry Jones and a neighbor of Mary's brother, who was an instructor in the SF School, I did OK. Actually better than OK, I did well. That neighbor was a major named Bo Gritz and he was a dynamic and caring instructor. He was quite the performer and soldier on the teaching platform and the best of a great group of teachers. Bo, Harry and I would sit in Eddie's living room and talk about what it all meant, and of course tip a beer or two. The concept of SF, guerrilla warfare and counterinsurgency, and working with indigenous people was not what I had learned at Fort Campbell with the Screaming Eagles. Major Gritz was a treasure trove of information and insight, particularly information about the final Exercise, called Robin Sage, up in the Uwharrie Forest. The civilians in the forest played this guerrilla game to the hilt and each group of locals had their "side" that they supported in the exercise; either the SF and guerrillas or the 82nd Airborne opposing forces. This civilian involvement added a degree of real world operations to the exercise.

Major Gritz gave Harry and me the name of a particularly friendly restaurant owner who loved supporting the guerrilla role players and aspirant Green Berets. One Saturday Harry and I, dressed in redneck attire, journeyed up to the forest in an effort to make contact with this person. We found the restaurant and sat down at the counter for a late breakfast. The owner was there, courteous and OK but initially aloof. When we quietly dropped Bo Gritz's name he became overly friendly. That was the first time I ever had North Carolina "white lightening" with bacon and eggs. The white lightening was super but the overall effort to establish contact with a friendly asset proved not worth the effort. He had friends and vehicles which he readily agreed we could use so we were getting some good information for the exercise. But when the exercise finally kicked off our guerrilla operating area turned out to be on the other side of the Uwharrie Forest. Our trip gained us little except the idea of recruiting indigenous support; a chance to practice some "spook" tradecraft techniques and the experience of making contact with the indigenous underground.

If the name Bo Gritz rings a bell, it should. Bo retired from the Army as a lieutenant colonel then made a heck of a name for himself trying to find and bring back from Vietnam a group of POWs that he said were there, and alive. I don't know enough about what Bo really did or did not know, but he created a heck of a firestorm. Google Bo Gritz, I did; lots of controversy there. Read about him and make up your own mind. I liked the gentleman.

At some point during the course Mary and I decided to trade our Pontiac LeMans in on a new Oldsmobile "88." It was a great car, much bigger than the Pontiac and it would accompany us to Panama and serve us well. It would actually get involved in a clandestine SF operation.

Academically the course wasn't too hard but there was a lot of theory and SF tactics and techniques that had to be mastered. The physical side could be taxing at times. I always completed runs and rucksack marches. SF puts great stock in being able to walk forever with a sixty pound or heavier rucksack, usually heavier, on your back. At this stage in life I was good at that. One almost funny incident, much to my chagrin, sticks out in my mind. It happened one day when we were playing organized athletics; in this case flag football. Normally one would characterize flag football as rather tame; not this day. I lined up opposite Bo Baker and in the ensuing play I clipped him. It was not intentional I assure you. Next play he lined up opposite me and when the ball was snapped he hit me like a ton of bricks, knocking me out for a minute or two. He then helped me up with a grin on his face. Bo was a college football player from somewhere in the south and a big guy. I never clipped him again. We became friends after that and he became one of my mentors later in my career.

It came time for the field exercise, in those days it was called Robin Sage. Mary and the little guy went to stay with her parents in Atlanta. This saved us a few dollars and got her out of the trailer. It also gave Grandpa and Grandma Devlin a chance to spoil young Larry and they did just that.

We were to jump in near our area of operations but the jump was cancelled due to bad weather. We ended up jumping off the back of a 2½ ton truck along a dirt trail. I really don't remember much about the Exercise in the Uwharrie except for a couple of ambushes I participated in. The ambushes were text book perfect and good learning experiences. We actually attacked the 82nd troops on North Carolina Highways and simulated blowing up a couple of bridges. SF pretty much had free reign in the Uwharrie Forest in those days. The locals who came upon ongoing ambushes or attacks loved it and enjoyed playing the game. Throughout the exercise I acted as the assistant team radio operator and carried (or in SF parlance humped) a much too heavy, hand cranked generator for that radio all over the forest. Using Morse code we reported our activities with the guerrillas we were training. In those days SF still used quite old, not state of the art gear, and our success rate on making radio contact was abysmal. Speaking of state of the art equipment I clearly remember a signaling device, like a big flashlight for signaling airplanes. I carried that puppy throughout the exercise and never used it. It had a manufacture date of 1944 stamped on its side. SF communications has come a long way since 1964.

The exercise ended and I was out briefed by CPT Davis telling me that I had passed and qualified for my SF beret and half flash. In those days you did not automatically get your SF Group flash. Each SF Group had a distinctive flash, or unit symbol, that members of that unit wore on their beret. In 1964 you started with a half flash known as a "candy stripe" to be worn on the beret right below your rank. You had to earn the right to wear the full flash by proving yourself in the unit to which you were assigned after SF School. I was a proud soldier at that point and said goodbye to CPT Davis assuming I would never see him again.

8
LANGUAGE SCHOOL, MONTEREY, CA

Mary and young Larry came back to Fort Bragg for my graduation. We visited my parents in Columbus, Ohio and then drove south to Atlanta and spent a few days with Mary's parents. After enjoyable visits with family we began the long road trip to California and language school starting in December 1964.

The trip out west was uneventful. This was my first trip west of the Mississippi by car and Mary and I both enjoyed playing tourist and seeing some beautiful country. I do remember one interesting experience. We stopped in Las Vegas. I told Mary I was going to take her to a Casino Show. We hired a babysitter and off we went, I think to the Stardust. I wore my dress blues. At the casino I slipped the head waiter a $5 bill, in those days not a bad tip, hoping for a good table. He promptly gave me back the "sawbuck" and then took us to a front row table. The Vietnam War was really heating up at this time and I think the uniform got us special treatment. That would change over the next couple of years.

There were no student quarters at the Presidio of Monterey, site of the Department of Defense Language Institute West Coast Branch, so we rented a nice apartment in Pacific Grove not far from the Presidio. A limited number of student's wives were allowed to attend school and learn the lingo of the area to which we were being assigned. Little Larry went to day care and Mary became a full-time student. Classes were small and wives were not allowed in the same class as their spouse. I don't remember my instructors but they did a pretty good job teaching me. All the instructors were native speakers and several were Cubans who had participated in the Bay of Pigs fiasco. We were immersed in Spanish for six months, six hours a day, five days a week, forbidden to speak a word of English. The technique worked. I am convinced to this day that given time they could teach a monkey to speak Spanish. Well that may be a bit of an exaggeration, but it isn't far off.

Then came a defining moment burned in my psyche that I will never forget. One evening about halfway through the course I went down to the pool to get away from the "lingo" study for a while. When I reached the pool I was the only one there.

A few minutes later I was joined by a West Point captain, on the list for promotion to major, whose name I can't, and don't want to remember. We had met several times previously at the apartment complex and at the school. He was studying Vietnamese with follow on orders and an assignment in that country as an advisor. He was married to a very attractive German blond who was built like a Teutonic Goddess. After a few minutes in the water swimming I suddenly felt his hands on my thighs. He said, "Let's wrestle." I am not sure what I responded but I know I was not into wrestling, not with a guy anyway. I pulled away and kept swimming. A minute later it happened again. I figured it was time to retreat. Yes, never retreat Redmond "retreated." This was the retreat incident I mentioned earlier in this tale that I said would be addressed. Junior lieutenant versus a senior captain on the promotion list to major and I was a possible loser.

I was in a state of shock when I got upstairs and told Mary what had happened. Her response was something like, "Oh it's nothing, just playing around. You're just imagining something and making more of it than there is." I put it aside, but determined I would steer well clear of the captain from that point on.

The following Saturday morning another apartment neighbor, a *Columbiano* named Camillo Santander, knocked on the door.

(Santander by the way is a very famous name in Columbian history and Camillo was from that family.) I invited him in for coffee. As we sat around the kitchen table talking he suddenly said, "Larry do you know the captain in apartment 8?" My antenna went straight up and so did Mary's. She came and joined us at the table. I responded yes I knew him and why did he ask. Seems the captain's wife and Camillo's wife were both back in their respective countries visiting their families. The good captain had seen Camillo in the complex parking lot and asked him up to his apartment for a drink. Camillo saw no reason not to go. He related that after pouring drinks and sitting down across the coffee table from him his host calmly announced, "Well we might as well get comfortable," or words to that effect and stood and dropped his pants. Camillo fled the apartment, literally in a panic. He was not sure how to react or what to do, but since we had spoken a number of times and I was also in the Army he decided to confide in me.

After my head stopped spinning I asked Camillo if he would be willing to tell all this to the Army Criminal Investigation Division. He agreed. We were interviewed separately. We both told our tales and waited. After the Army Investigators did a short but thorough investigation the captain, married, on the promotion list, was suddenly gone from school and the apartment. He had been thrown out of the Army. The whole process took about two weeks. Old Army justice was swift and unmerciful.

I tell this story because it is an incident burned in my psyche about homosexuals. From this experience comes my deeply ingrained mistrust of most homosexuals. "Don't ask, Don't tell" is as far as I am prepared to go with gays in the military; and as you know that is now history. If this West Point captain was willing to jeopardize his career, marriage and future, knowing that I was married with a child not more than a hundred feet away, how far would he go with some young soldier? The gay community in large part has an agenda, and a willingness to push their gayness much further than

I am willing to agree to. I do know and am friends with several gay men who are not that way at all in terms of being pushy with their lifestyle. However, I disagree with gays serving openly in our military as is now allowed. I had one other gay happening that at the time it occurred I was not aware of the gay aspect. But that incident comes much later in this story in Alaska at well below zero, no swimming pools.

I remember one Saturday when we went down to the pier in Monterey to see the sea lions and other attractions. Keep in mind that this was early 1965 and the anti-war fever was just really getting started. There was a fairly active but small group of protestors working the pier and I was pretty disgusted with their signs and chanting slogans about Vietnam and Ho Chi Minh. Then I noticed a Catholic priest in the bunch, Roman collar and all. That floored me. I went over and said something like, "Father let me shake your hand. I have never met a dumb Catholic priest before." I don't have a clue what his full reaction was as he stood there speechless. I walked away and did not look back.

Following language school, Mary, little Larry and I drove across country to Atlanta and her parent's apartment. We were told the wait to have families join us at Fort Gulick Canal Zone was anywhere from eight to twelve months. Needless to say neither Mary nor I were too happy about that, but there it was. Mary and our son would live with her parents until she could find a nearby apartment. We shipped our car and I then marched off to Panama and one of the most intriguing episodes in my career.

I departed for Panama from Charleston Air Force Base, South Carolina. While waiting for my flight I was making a pit stop when the captain next to me, by the little white depository, asked if I was going to the 8th Group in Panama. He had seen the half flash on my beret and already knew the answer to that question. At this point I was a little skittish after the experience in Pacific Grove but answered yes, keeping a wary eye on the speaker. After washing his hands he introduced himself, CPT Kelly O'Malley, en route to an assignment in Italy after attending his sister's wedding. He told me his brand new brother-in-law was Florencio Berumen a captain in the 8th Group. The newlyweds would shortly be living in the Canal Zone. We had coffee and then went our separate ways to catch planes. Our paths were to cross several times in the years ahead but not again beside a little white depository.

9
8TH SPECIAL FORCES GROUP, 1965

Walt Werner had arrived in the Canal Zone about two weeks before me at the 8th SF Group. Amazing how the Army pulled that one off. He had gone to language school on the east coast in Washington, D.C. versus Monterey, California. We were both assigned to A Company, not the best choice for us as I will describe later. I was assigned a very nice Bachelor Officer Quarter right next to Walt. When I reported in for orientation at Group HQs it was quite weird. I was told, "Lieutenant Redmond, welcome to the Group. You won't see Colonel Simons, very few do. There is to be no 'backdooring.' OK, got it? Get out of here and get to your company," or words to that effect.

I walked out and over to A Company wondering what the hell that was all about and what was "backdooring?" I quickly learned that backdooring meant no visits with the wives of other officers or NCOs when their husbands were deployed out of Panama on Military Training Teams. Apparently such conduct was rampant in the Group – well hello, "Peyton Place" in Panama.

As for Colonel Arthur D. "Bull" Simons, (the 8th Group Commander) he was a legend in SF and a truly great soldier but terribly secretive. He was almost worshiped among most of the troops and was known as a leader who supported his men totally. But watch out if you were the lad who screwed something up. I regret that I never met him while he commanded the 8th Group.

But I would eventually meet him one night at Fort Bragg during a Delta Force exercise many years later. In the interim he had led the Son Tay Raid into North Vietnam to rescue prisoners of war held there and also the Iran hostage rescue for Ross Perot. You may remember reading about both those operations in the papers. Those two happenings further added to his special activity glory roster. He was a great soldier.

The 8th Special Forces, or 8th Special Action Force, was a unique unit. It was comprised of two SF companies each with a Command and Control Element called a C Detachment, 3 Command and Control B Detachments (each controlling 4 A Detachments) and 12 A Detachments. Additionally there was one each Military Police, Engineer, Intelligence, Psychological Warfare and Signal company as well as some other small elements. I believe only the 1st SF Group on Okinawa was constituted in a similar manner. With this mix of capabilities there was very little in the way of support to the nations of Central and South America and the Caribbean that the Group could not provide. We were big into nation building and counterinsurgency training and had military training teams (MTT) deployed throughout the area. It seemed that no matter what the topic of an MTT and the qualifications needed to provide the training, we had them. There were licensed noncommissioned officers ready to use and/or train locals on heavy engineer equipment, radio repair, newspaper printing, water purification, medical issues, teaching school to building darned near anything you could think of. It was an amazing talent pool and sure lived up to its title of "special."

Initially I was assigned as the XO of Team A 11. This was a normal assignment for a new lieutenant even one who had not been fully certified as a true SF soldier. My boss was CPT Ed Fricke, another well-known Green Beret and already a veteran of Southeast Asia operations. The Team welcomed me but it was clear that I was a "new guy" and had to prove myself. At this time the 8th had a large number of former members of the Laotian Operation "White Star."

Most of these folks were concentrated in A Company to include Ed Fricke. If you were not a Laos Project White Star veteran you were considered a second class citizen by quite a few of the Southeast Asia hands, to include the "Bull" who had served in Laos with the White Star Team.

A few days after arriving I was called into the B Team commander's office and told I would be participating in a guerrilla warfare exercise out in the Mojinga Fault/Fort Sherman area. It was a training test for elements of the 20th Special Forces Group, part of the Florida National Guard. I was to be a sub-guerrilla chief and would have half a dozen guerillas working for me from the Panamanian *Guardia Nacional.* The A Team from the 20th was to act as trainers for myself and the *Guardia* troops. This would be my first real test of whether or not I had learned enough Spanish to survive. As I was about to leave his office the B Team commander added, "I hope lieutenant, that you aren't going to mind but you will be working for Master Sergeant Dick Meadows who will be the overall chief controller and guerrilla chief." I told him that was OK by me. For those readers who may not be aware Dick Meadows was a true legend in SF at that time and later as part of Delta Force. His reputation was faultless. He could have put on senior officers rank, walked in a room anywhere in the world and no one would have been the wiser. There is a statue to Dick in the plaza in front of SF Headquarters at Fort Bragg. It is a well-deserved honor.

I knew nothing of the terrain and area of the Mojinga Fault or Fort Sherman. I decided a terrain orientation of the area was needed. This was a very dumb stunt. But if I was going to play the role of the local guerrilla chief I had better know the terrain, at least a little. On a Saturday morning I drove out toward Fort Sherman stopping at the Mojinga Fault trail; about seven or eight kilometers from Fort. Sherman. The name Mojinga Fault came from the fact that eons ago the terrain, probably earthquake induced, jumped up in an almost vertical manner about 100 to 150 feet high all the way from the road

I was on to a perfectly round hill out along the Chagres River. The jungle did not look bad, in fact it looked inviting. That was a false judgment on my part. But being a new guy I was not fully aware of all the many dangers waiting just beyond the cusp of the green. I was about to learn a few things.

I began moving along the trail at the base of the fault and was observing all I could to include spots for possible base camps, drop zones, of which there were few, and water sources. About halfway to the Chagres River I came upon the most beautiful waterfall, perhaps an eighty foot drop, and pool for bathing that I had seen up that point in my life. The water was crystal clear and I refilled my canteens. Good thing as that was the last "good" water I saw till I got back to Fort Sherman later that evening. There was a trail up the fault at this point and on the map it showed that it led to a road near Fort Sherman and Fort San Lorenzo.

As an aside Fort San Lorenzo was a 16th century Spanish ruin and quite interesting to visit. The Buyles and Redmonds went there several months later for a picnic and for a few anxious moments we lost track of little Suzy Buyle in the ruins. Fortunately while Ken and I were scurrying around in a near panic looking in a number of cisterns, little Miss Suzy was strolling the grounds and enjoying herself in the care of the 8th Group Surgeon. We all breathed a sigh of relief that day when the surgeon showed up with Suzy.

At any rate I managed to wander through the jungle oblivious to what might be around me, as I said above, a dumb stunt. I did find several good sites which we later used during the exercise as base camps, and one suitable drop zone. Just as I neared a small clearing I heard rustling in the trees above me and the most unnerving screeching as a family of howler monkeys fled at my approach. Needless to say that got my attention, at least for the moment. The monkeys weren't the only frightened critter at that moment along that trail.

I wandered down the road from Fort San Lorenzo toward the big hill at the end of the Mojinga Fault. As I did I suddenly got the strange feeling that I was not alone. Looking to my right across the road about 15 feet away slithered the biggest snake I had ever seen, except in a zoo. I assumed it was a python. I sure hoped it was not a Fer de Lance, a very poisonous snake. Well we both decided we had better places to be and split company, like immediately. I did go on to the hill and found the trail down that linked to the trail at the base of the fault.

At that point I decided this had not been such a good idea, and with the afternoon light fading, headed back down the road to Forts San Lorenzo and Sherman. On that trek I saw no more slithering critters or tree hanging monkeys but I had a very wary eye out now. I picked up a ride at the Jungle Operations Training Center Headquarters at Fort Sherman back to my car that was parked next to the trail where I had left it. I finished the day pretty cocky and satisfied I had accomplished my terrain orientation but fully realized that what I had done had been dumb and dangerous. As a new guy I should never have gone alone. After several beers that night Walt and I laughed about it. It was still dumb.

Redmond's Rule # 8 – Think it through, don't do dumb things.

I don't remember much about the exercise except that the A Team was pretty good during the couple of days of training they provided the *Guardia Nacional* guerrilla role players. The National Guard SF troops Spanish was probably better than mine. Admittedly, two of them were native speakers. Led by the SF lads from Florida our *Guardia* soldiers conducted several ambushes and successfully pulled off a parachute resupply drop. The drop zone was terribly small and the bundle landed in some tall trees. Fortunately the *"Guardia"* playing the role of guerrillas had little trouble extracting the chute and bundle from high up in the trees. They were great climbers. We did go down to the waterfall and the crystal clear pool to bathe about midway through the exercise. At the end I still stunk to high heaven. This was my first encounter with extended jungle living; it would not be my last. My language training paid off in that I not only got by with the *Guardia Nacional* troops, who spoke no English, but they even seemed to like me. I really think the effort on my part to speak only Spanish when talking with them created a quick, soldierly bond. The 20th SF troops did well and I awarded a passing grade to the team I evaluated.

The only point that I clearly remember was at the "hot wash up" at Fort Sherman when a lieutenant colonel from the 20th SFG and I were talking. He said, "I really want to talk with Colonel Meadows, WOW is he ever a great soldier!" or words to that effect. I told him to prepare for a major shock. Colonel Meadows is actually Master Sergeant Meadows. The look of disbelief was not really dispelled until Dick told him his rank. Meadows was every bit as good as his press clippings; more about Dick later in this tale.

Following the exercise I was granted full status as a Special Forces soldier and allowed to remove the candy stripe from my Green Beret and put on a full 8th Group flash. Needless to say I was proud of that flash. Special Forces was, and remains today, a great outfit and one I am proud to say I was part of.

Also my circle of friends continued to expand beyond Walt Werner, Ken and Kathy Buyle, and Harry and Marge Jones. I soldiered with and became friends with Flor and Rosemary Berumen, Joe and Pat Peden, Joe and Kathy Jaworowski, Tom and Marge McAndrews, Steve and Darlene Perry, Johnny Gilbert and many others. We were all new to SF and sort of on the outside since we had not served with Project White Star in Laos. White Star veterans were definitely in the ascendancy at this time in the Group but particularly in A Company and they occupied the bulk of the leadership positions in that unit.

Through Ken Buyle, and the informal grape vine, I learned of a gimmick to get your family to Panama quicker. It was called Pan Canal Vacation quarters. The Zonians, as those who lived and worked in the Canal Zone were known, received lengthy vacations back to the States, three plus months in some cases. They rented their homes completely furnished to military or incoming Canal workers. Mary and I discussed it via telephone and decided we would try to get a vacation home which would allow she and Larry to come down before we actually got quarters. It appeared that once you had your family there you magically managed to be assigned quarters; not always but in most cases.

In the meantime we got a new Group Commander and Bull Simons departed without my ever laying eyes on the guy. Two days after the new commander arrived we had an alert and reported to our companies somewhat befuddled. The 8th Group was not like the 101st Airborne and alerts were not often conducted nor were they very popular. It seems the new commander, COL Magnus Smith, wanted to see us march. So with eighty pound rucksacks on our backs we trundled off toward the Gatun Locks about nine miles one way. The march out was OK but the temperature was soaring. We stopped at the locks and rested then started back and the march turned into the stuff of legend. Later dubbed the Gatun Death March, we had folks dropping out like flies. It was not a good day. I must admit I was hurting but made it back through the gate and to the company area. An awful lot of troops had to be trucked back. Needless to say a more aggressive physical training program was immediately implemented.

I identified a nice set of vacation quarters in a Pan Canal Company village called Coco Solo and set the paperwork in motion to get Mary and Larry down to Panama. In the meantime Ken and Kathy Buyle had escaped vacation quarters and moved into housing out at France Field, an old WWII Navy PBY Seaplane Base not far from Fort Gulick.

I was selected along with a bunch of other newbies to attend Air Force Tropic Survival School just before Mary and Larry arrived. The school was on the Pacific side of the Zone at Albrook Air Base and lasted seven or eight days. Not terribly hard but you got damned hungry I can assure you of that. Good training on how to live off the land that was for certain. Two days of training at Albrook in the classroom then off to the jungle way up the Chagres River and deep in the jungle. We had an indigenous guide with our group of seven or eight trainees from the Army and the USAF. We foraged and found lots of edible plants and critters. We had even less than minimal rations so our main fare had to come from the jungle. Our group managed to find a python, a capybara (world's largest rodent, aka rat), and lots of plants, grubs and small fish and crawdad like critters. It all went in the pot. Smelled terrible but it was the best we could do. Yes, I did eat it python, rat and all. It was disgusting but warmed and sort of filled the stomach. It did keep us going.

The finale of the course was an escape and evasion float down the Chagres River with water wings. One of the challenges was to keep your hat. The local indigenous Indians were awarded a dollar for every hat they collected. If there were 100 students the Indians ended up with $100. It was their terrain and they knew it cold. We departed the camp site individually, each with our survival floatation device and choosing our own route down to the river. I think about ten minutes after leaving the camp site heading toward the river my hat disappeared in the paw of an Indian who sprang from behind a very large tree. The float down the river was fantastic, truly beautiful. There were a few areas of rough water and rocks but nothing too rough or dangerous. It was a once in a lifetime experience. As we floated down the river, over time we came together in groups of three or four trainees. People pay to do similar stuff today and here I was enjoying it free, compliments of the USAF. Just at sundown we were waived down by a guerrilla guide standing on the bank who took us to a small grass shack. We were then given instructions on the rest of the exercise. They also gave us a ball of rice and a mango. I devoured them both like a concentration camp inmate. I was going to regret that in about 36 hours as you will learn.

The idea at this point was to continue to escape and evade from the shack through the jungle and back to friendly lines at Albrook Air Base. It was a similar episode like the Indians getting the hat routine back in the jungle. Here the Air Force troops playing the bad guys staked out all the roads and easy to move through jungle areas and caught 90% of the students. If you were caught you were subjected to several hours of what would today be termed near torture. It was described by some other folks back at Fort Gulick as, "not fun." No water boarding but other unique events. One such experience was, I had been told, a metal trash container, totally dark, with six inches of water and lots of scurrying little crabs. Getting captured was not high up on my list of priorities that night. I had been linked up with an Air Force enlisted man, who had even less jungle smarts than me. Uncle Harry had given me the secret to not being caught. He said, "Go directly through the worst of the terrain and use a flashlight. The aggressors won't be there and the light will let you move pretty fast." Harry was correct. Breaking trail for several hours through the jungle was tough but we avoided capture and didn't see a single creepy-crawly. We probably made so much noise that we scared away any sane animal or critter in our path. We were the second team in that night and back asleep by 0100 in the morning. I readily admit the use of the flashlight would have gotten me an UNSAT back in Ranger School, and was not in any SF manual that I ever saw, but it was relatively painless and got the job done nicely.

Well the good news was the training was over and Mary and Larry were due to arrive the next afternoon. The bad news was the mango I had eaten. Seems mango skin is not the thing to eat and can cause a real outbreak of swelling and rash. My lips were swollen and red and very sensitive when I met the family at Tocumen International Airport. I had splurged and we had a room at the Panama Hilton in

Panama City that night. It was great to have them there. The next day we moved into our Pan Canal vacation quarters. Those quarters were not far from Fort Gulick just inside the Canal Zone. The décor was a little questionable but the house held all that we needed to survive.

A lot was happening in the Group in those days throughout South and Central America. Training teams were constantly departing and returning. We did everything from build bridges and schools, to dig wells, to train troops on counterinsurgency, to train snipers, and a myriad of other subjects. We all were just having fun but each of us wanted to go on a training mission anywhere. We were "gung ho" SF soldiers and wanted to be part of the ongoing crusade to stop the spread of Communism throughout the region. At this point about twenty lieutenants, me included, were all promoted to captain over a period of two weeks. As a captain I was transferred from Team A 11, as XO, to be Team Leader of Team A 10. It took me a while to really get a handle on the team for whatever reason. That could have been because I was new, not a White Star veteran or maybe because I had too many really veteran Green Berets. They can be unique and difficult to handle at times. I learned a lot about soldiering from them and did earn their respect over time.

I am not sure of the timing on a couple of incidents that followed but I was sent to Marksmanship Training School over at Fort Kobbe, a post on the Pacific side of the Canal Zone. It was a fun time but shooting can try one's patience and be quite boring especially when you are sitting around under cover waiting for the rain to stop so you can shoot. I did well learning how to train folks in long distance marksmanship. Launching bullets down range is easy. Just point the rifle and pull the trigger. Making sure that bullet reaches its exact target, at long distances, and scores high is another matter entirely. The idea was that at a future time I would go on a marksmanship training mission to a country in the region and teach their military Rifle Team how to shoot better and make a good showing at the

Annual Pan American Rifle Competition. There was strong spirit of competition among the armies throughout South America and the Pan American shoot was high visibility.

About this time my Team Operations Sergeant and I planned a little survival exercise. Or at least I thought it was to be a true survival exercise. We left Fort Gulick in a large rubber boat and crossed Gatun Lake. We then dragged the boat through the jungle and up over a hill and across an old railroad bed to the Chagres River. Paddling down the river to the vicinity of Fort San Lorenzo was a piece of cake as the Chagres at this point was a fast flowing river known to sweep boats out into the Atlantic. It was certainly different than the inland Chagres I had rather gently floated down during Air Force Tropic Survival School. Making landfall short of the Atlantic was not a problem for us. I later learned that the Gatun Dam spillways were closed that night; a fact that made it easier for us and reduced the current quite a bit. We set up a base camp in the jungle well away from the roads and settled in.

Just before dusk the Team Sergeant came to me and said, "Sir, come on we're going to get some lobster." Well that sounded quite interesting, it was part of the training plan and a new experience for me. We had all brought our lobster lights with us. We moved past Fort San Lorenzo and to the Atlantic Ocean about 200 feet down a steep cliff. Once in the water the lobsters were everywhere. In very short order we had almost more lobsters than we could carry. We moved back to the Fort San Lorenzo area and as we crossed the road heading to our camp one of my NCOs flashed a light and car lights blinked back from up the road. The team sergeant and two of my troops disappeared down the road reappearing shortly with ears of corn, butter, chili sauce and beer; lots of beer. This was not in the plan but it sure made for a fun eating experience in the jungle and a great story. The NCOs apologized for ambushing me with the corn, beer, butter and chili sauce but I had a good laugh over it. This was one super survival exercise and helped me bond with my team.

Out of the blue my A Detachment/Team was selected to support a U.S. Army Limited Warfare Laboratories (LWL) Test of what was reputed to be a new device. There were only seven members of my twelve man A Team present for duty. The other five troops were deployed around Central and South America; that was normal for the 8th Group. The seven of us proved more than enough in terms of test support. We were briefed on this new technological marvel called the Man Packed Personnel Detector. Well what do you know; it was a newly packaged version of the "People Sniffer" that Walt Werner and I had been involved with at Fort Campbell in early 1963. When I explained to the team from the LWL, and my team members that I was somewhat familiar with an earlier version of this system they were impressed. More importantly my standing and credibility with my troops jumped quite a few points. The LWL wanted to test this new version in a jungle environment and had chosen Panama for the test. We would be the bad guy guerrillas hidden in the jungle that the device was to alert on. As I recall the repackaged tool worked about sixty to seventy percent of the time but of course it could still alert on a pack of monkeys or any warm blooded creature out there (think elephant, tiger, et cetera). The Team got a glowing letter of thanks from the Director of the Limited War Laboratories for our support and the Man Packed Personnel Detector marched off to the war. I never saw the device when I served in Vietnam.

There were lots of jumps out at Gatun Drop Zone near the base. The area was a cane field with the Chagres River on one side, the Gatun Locks of the Panama Canal on another and Gatun Lake at the far end. Sounds scary but the Air Commando pilots never put me anywhere but right on the drop zone. Although I left Fort Campbell rated as a senior paratrooper I was still not really comfortable with jumping. The time in Panama changed that and I actually started making some day jumps, eyes open when exiting the airplane. I learned to enjoy parachuting in Panama.

Then came the infamous night when Mary almost divorced me. You may recall a few short pages ago I was promoted to captain along with about twenty other lieutenants. Well we planned a big promotion party at the Fort Gulick Officers Club. It was quite the social event. I have no idea what happened after the first hour or so. Fellow officers later recounted that I danced with a captain buddy and perhaps drank 30 manhattans. I cannot believe that latter point; 30 manhattans would have killed a horse. I admit I was drinking manhattans and more than was good for me.

Somehow Mary got me in the car after the party started to break up. I remember being sick and hanging my head out the car window as she drove me back to our vacation home. I seem to recall crawling up the stairs, really crawling up the stairs on my hands and knees. I know Mary was furious because she had to drive the babysitter home in the bowels of Colon which was not a very hospitable place at 0300 in the morning. Heck Colon in those days wasn't very hospitable in daylight. The next day was a Saturday and it was a complete blank. On Sunday I was shamed and dragged to church but remember nothing about the service. By Sunday night I had almost rejoined the ranks of the living. Mary was still not speaking to me. In fact I did not want anyone speaking to me as the feeling in my head was beyond description.

On Monday morning I went early to the coffee shop next to A Company. I was still one sick puppy but had straightened up enough to look halfway presentable. The first person who came in was a friend, Captain Johnny Gilbert. He sat with me and we had coffee. After about five minutes he asked me what he had done on Friday night! His evening and the weekend had been a total blank also. It is fair to say that all the celebrants had similar experiences. Mine was truly more than I had expected. You would think it would be a long time before I would make that mistake again; well, just wait a couple of pages.

Another unique experience about this party that remained unfathomed was how $5, $10 and $20 bills managed to get pinned to the ceiling of the club that night. It had to be thirty feet up to the vaulted part and there were bills everywhere and no way to climb up there. As far as I know this mystery remains unsolved to this day.

Shortly after this episode we were assigned quarters on Fort Gulick. I recall it as quarters 34A and was located just down the hill from the Officers Club. This was a very nice three story concrete home with three bedrooms and two and a half baths. The first floor was parking and a maid's quarters next to the laundry. It was really nice once I got rid of the roaches. I became known among our friends as Real Kill Redmond. I literally poured bottles of Real Kill down every nook and cranny that I could find. It worked! We got rid of the roaches.

Sometime after moving into our quarters I was selected to go with another captain on a Marksmanship Training Team to Bolivia. This would be my second visit to what was then a third world country, the other being Panama. Bolivia was a true composite of the old and the new. On one side La Paz and Cochabamba were very modern and up to standard. But just outside beautiful homes and haciendas, impoverished Indians lived in mud hovels built against the walls of the haciendas. The Spanish descendants of the original colonizers still held power. It was a marvel. At nights in La Paz the cars drove without lights because they thought it saved the batteries. At least that is what I was told. Our hotel was nice and very clean but somewhat on the modest side. The elevator operator wore a pistol under his black coat. The food was good, and inexpensive, but the potatoes were almost solid black. They tasted like Idaho bakers once you got over the color.

The Bolivians we were training were a great bunch. We had a LTC, MAJ, two CPTS, three LTs and several senior sergeants. They were attentive and fast learners. The previous year they had come in next to last at the games in Panama. They did not want that to happen again. The range we used was a simple known distance range out to 400 yards. For long distance shooting beyond that, out to 1000 yards, we shot across a very deep gorge. The winds made adjusting and hitting a target at 800 to 1000 yard range a major task. They proved quite skillful with their M1 Garand Rifles, concentrated hard on what we taught them, did well, and quickly improved. I think it is fair to say that I hit it off with all of them and my Spanish improved. I had no trouble at all with, *"Una cerveza fria por favor"* – A cold beer please.

About two weeks into the training I came down with the Inca "revenge" and spent three days closeted in my hotel room visiting the bathroom. Each day one of the officers, all lieutenants as I recall, visited to see how I was doing. On the first day the lieutenant brought me a rifle and a bayonet as a *presento* (present). On the second day another lieutenant brought me an old set of breast armor; not in the greatest shape but still very nice. On the third day I was again visited and given a beautiful carbine, 1876 vintage. I was flabbergasted. Although we had talked about history and old weapons I had not expected these gifts. Maybe my Spanish was not as good as I thought? I determined that I had to repay them in some way. I sent a letter to Mary telling her that I was going to invite the whole team to the house for dinner during the matches. I mailed the letter and promptly forgot it. That proved to be mistake on my part.

I mentioned the other officer on the Training Team with me. He was a good trainer to be sure, but also a classic ugly American. We had not been in country more than twenty minutes, having been met by a Bolivian Army Colonel and a U.S. Army master sergeant from the Embassy, when he began lobbying for a follow on HALO (High Altitude Low Opening) Parachute Training Team. Of course it would be led by none other than himself. "This is just what you need to make the people happy," he said or other such drivel. I was embarrassed. He never gave up pushing for that HALO training team. To my knowledge the Bolivians never took him up on the idea.

I saw quite a bit of La Paz in my off time and at the insistence of the Army sergeant from the embassy, who greeted us on arrival, one Saturday I took off for Lake Titicaca up on the Peruvian border. I thought that would be fun till I noticed he had placed a .45 caliber pistol on the seat next to me. He said quite nonchalantly, "Its loaded, Captain, just a little insurance policy." I did not have to pick it up all day. It was an enjoyable drive through very high desert country. There were lots of impoverished Indian villages and many a beautiful old church with massive wooden doors going back three to four centuries. The stone steps leading up to the doors were worn down from thousands of feet and boots treading them over the centuries. The interiors were beautiful and well maintained and the altars magnificent. A stark contrast from what lay just outside in the village squares. Lake Titicaca was quite beautiful. The trip proved to be memorable for the scenery. By the way an American in uniform was a bit of a shock to some of the Indians along the route.

As we packed up to leave I was pretty well satisfied that the Bolivian National Rifle Team was going to do better this year at the Pan American games. Our return trip was on the Embassy shuttle bird that traveled all of South America. For some reason we did not make any stops after departing La Paz and hence arrived back in Panama much earlier than we were scheduled. Mary was not expecting me early and I thought I would surprise her. When I got to our quarters it was about 0300 in the morning. I unlocked the door and stepped into the living room to be greeted by the snarling teeth of a 110 pound German Shepherd Police dog! Larry, meet Nina your new family member.

I knew Nina. She had lived in the house next door and was a beautiful animal, very well trained. She was however a military police dog and could be aggressive toward someone she didn't recognize. I had told Mary one day that if the dog was ever available I would sure love to own her. Well while I was gone there had been a suicide in the family and the husband and kids were reassigned to the States. Mary had purchased Nina as a surprise for me. It surely was a surprise when I opened that door unannounced! Fortunately Mary had heard the commotion and rushed downstairs calling Nina off. I loved that dog and she was a fantastic watch dog; took very good care of little Larry. She was, however, totally loyal to Mary. If I had ever raised a hand toward Mary or young Larry I doubt I would have had that hand very long. Nina was very protective of the family. She didn't like our car wash boy but got along very well with our maid and gardener.

I reported back into A Company and turned in my after action report to the Commander and said I was heading back to the A Team room. He told me not to bother that the Team was not there and the room was empty. "Your A Team is deployed to Bolivia." I responded something to the effect that I had been in Bolivia. He told me that in my absence most of my team members had, under another commander, deployed on a classified mission. No further information was given me and I was told to stand by for another assignment. A couple of months later it became clear that members of my old A Team with several attachments from throughout the Group had gone to Bolivia after a guy named Che Guevara. This composite Team was led by Major Ralph "Pappy" Shelton. They, along with Bolivian Army Rangers, caught him. I can tell you honestly I had nothing to do with the capture or death of *Senor* Che Guevara.

The well-known Mr. Guevara, by the way, a close confidant and brother in arms to Fidel Castro was not a nice man. In my mind his death at the hands of Bolivian Rangers was good for all of South America.

.

10
THE SECOND AND PERHAPS LAST 8TH SF INITIATIVE TEST

My next assignment was as the B Team Operations Officer. My duties directly relating to that position were basically uneventful but my activities beyond that job were quite challenging and unusual.

I was summoned to the Group Intelligence (S2) Office along with a buddy from A Company, whom I will refer to as Captain John Doe. We were told by the S2 that we had been selected for an 8th SF Group Initiative Test. This was apparently something the S2 dreamed up and COL Smith agreed to try. We were told we had a mission: figure out how to assassinate a political prisoner held in the Panama Canal Prison at Gamboa Canal Zone. We were given a phone number and told should we be apprehended by the Military Police, Pan Canal Police, or the Panamanian *Guardia Nacional* that we were to tell them nothing. We were instructed to pass the phone number to them with guidance to call that number immediately. The paper we were given had these instructions on them printed in both Spanish and English. The number would be manned twenty-four hours a day for the four days we had to complete the mission.

John and I went to his quarters to think this through and come up with a plan. After about two hours we had an idea. We would approach the prison officials with a cover story that we were graduate students from Loyola University in Chicago. John was a graduate of that institution. Our story was that we were working on master's degrees in Penology and were here visiting his parents who were military assigned to Fort Gulick. Flimsy cover at best but that was what we came up with. I called the prison and spoke to the Deputy Warden and made an appointment to meet with them the following morning. John and I both just knew they would be waiting for us with handcuffs.

Au contraire, they met us with coffee and donuts. We talked for about half an hour and then they gave us the grand tour of the prison. Amazing what we learned. We were provided information on the guards, half U.S. and half Panamanian; information on power, water, and backups for both those systems. We also were shown the extra secure lockup where they would keep any "high value" prisoner. They even showed us the yard where such prisoners would be allowed to exercise one hour a day. We observed the emergency generator location as well. We left feeling like we had escaped a major ambush. We had also gained a lot of sensitive information about a Federal facility.

That night we went to a hill overlooking the prison surrounded by all the sights and sounds of the jungle; lots of bugs and creepy-crawly things as well. The yard where important prisoners would exercise was readily visible even brightly lit at night. It was an easy 400 yard shot for a sniper from where we were lying. We spent about five hours there and observed a changing of the guard. We then decided to get some rest and proceeded to the Fort Clayton Bachelor Officers Quarters. We felt we had accomplished our mission and could easily write a report on how to deal with a prisoner and escape at least immediate capture.

After breakfast one of us had a brilliant idea. Why not try to get engineer drawings of the prison as well as drawings of the water, electricity and sewer systems. Those drawings would be the capstone to a successful mission. The Pan Canal Engineering Offices might just have them. I called and spoke to a gentleman, passing myself off as a Peace Corps worker from Bolivia. Having just come back from

Bolivia I could talk with a semblance of authority on the country. I told him I wondered if I could get engineering drawings of the Gamboa Federal Prison. I explained that the prison in Cochabamba, near where I was based, had been built in the late 1700s and was a disgrace. We hoped to get the Bolivians to build a new one and the drawings would be of great assistance. He agreed to help and told me to come by about 1300 to pick up the requested blueprints. John and I sat around all morning thinking that we were about to be arrested any moment.

At the appointed time John dropped me at the entrance to the Pan Canal Headquarters, a most imposing and impressive building flaunting our colonial power. He then drove to a parking area where he could watch the entrance and waited while I entered the "valley of death," or so we both assumed.

Once inside I walked directly to the Engineering Division, met the gentleman I had spoken with earlier and was presented with a four foot long cardboard tube stuffed with architectural and engineering drawings and blueprints. I asked the employee how much I owed him. He responded, "Not a thing, that's our contribution to peace in Latin America. Is there anything else you might need?" At that point I knew I was probably toast, but being a little cocky I said, "Well there is one thing. Their sanitation is pretty rudimentary. You don't happen to have plans for a privy do you?" The answer was something like "....two hole or four?" After getting plans for both latrines I thanked him, turned and exited the building expecting to be arrested by the Pan Canal Police at any second. As I left the building John pulled up in his little convertible sports car with a truly amazed look on his face. Frankly I was more than a little amazed myself. We made a credible James Bond exit and returned immediately to Fort Gulick. The rest of the day was spent writing our report.

The following morning we reported to the S2 with our "stuff." He was flabbergasted and after reading the report went immediately to see COL Smith leaving the two of us cooling our heels. The

Colonel came in and told us he was impressed, liked what we had accomplished and told us to keep the whole event under wraps as more initiative tests were being planned. We departed feeling pretty cocky and quite satisfied with our achievement. Later we were both presented Certificates by COL Smith stating that we had successfully completed Initiative Test #2. There had been a Test #1 given to some troops that we were all completely unaware of.

About three weeks later John and I were called back to the S2's office and told our exercise was now "classified" and to keep our mouths shut for sure. It seems Colonel Smith had told the Commanding General of Southern Command our tale at a cocktail party at the Tivoli Guest House. The commander asked what the Pan Canal Company had said when you told them you were going to run this little operation and what they thought of what we had been able to learn. When Colonel Smith told him that no one in the Pan Canal hierarchy had been consulted in advance and to that point no one knew but five people; the SF Group S2, the general, we two captains and himself. The general went ballistic; the operation was classified at that point. To my knowledge that was the last Initiative Test the Group conducted.

That was 1966 and to this date in 2014 I don't think anyone other than the folks mentioned above know of this episode except a couple old SF buddies with whom I shared it after many years. I am sure that after forty-five years and with us being out of Panama and the canal business that this is no longer classified. The key point for us to note today is how gullible we Americans can be. God bless those Pan Canal employees who helped us accomplish what we did. They thought they were helping two graduate students get degrees and the Peace Corps in Bolivia further democracy. The fact is our covers were so thin it is amazing we pulled off what we did. We had no student IDs from Loyola and I sure had no Peace Corps ID from anywhere. We were never challenged. Bottom line is if two brash young captains could blunder through something like this successfully what can determined, patient terrorists do today? Scary thought.

Redmond's Rule #9 – People are gullible, Americans more so than most.

About this same time, while assigned as the B Team Operations Officer, I spent about three months working part time as a lane grader in the Jungle Operations Training Center at Fort Sherman. The school there needed to be augmented with instructors because the number of students had grown exponentially with an influx of troops and battalion sized units heading to Vietnam. This effort qualified me as a Jungle Expert. I didn't truly earn it but sort of stumbled into it as a cadre of the school. Lots about the jungle I never learned.

One incident that hangs in my memory related to a Marine battalion that came through for two weeks of training on the way to Vietnam. The Marine units were overall very good by the way. One evening my NCO lane grader partner and I were sitting in the jungle heating C rations when we heard a heck of a ruckus on the next hill over. A lot of yelling, hollering and laughing could be heard. This was not normal behavior for Marines. We ran down the hill, jumped a small stream and up the next hill. There to our amazement and horror were a half dozen lads teasing a twelve to fourteen foot long Fer De Lance, one of the world's deadliest snakes. The NCO promptly killed the critter with his machete and gave the Marines a remedial lesson in identifying poisonous reptiles. His language was most colorful as I recall. The Marines had no trouble understanding his words.

11
BECOMING A LOGISTICIAN AND OTHER SPECIAL EVENTS

My next duty was as the Assistant S4, Logistics Officer of the Group. I could not even spell logistics. I was not happy but the job proved to be a great learning experience. Seems I was learning daily as a young officer.

As an aside, let me make an observation at this point about life in Panama in those days. You would have to have been there in Panama and experienced the time to appreciate life in the Canal Zone. The Zonians, Americans living in the Canal Zone, and the military stationed there, lived like the British did in India in the 1800s. We had every amenity from clubs and churches, to restaurants, to golf courses, to Olympic sized swimming pools. You name it we had it and it was all first class. The mostly impoverished Panamanians worked for very low wages. But for the most part, at least on the military front, they were treated with respect and a little extra when needed. Our maid was named, Ester. Little Larry couldn't say Ester and he called her Ah Zhu. She had a bedroom and lavatory on the first floor next to the laundry area. I thought it was sort of primitive but it was clean, bright and well painted. Turned out that her primitive quarters on the first floor of the Redmond hacienda were much better than her family home, which was literally a palm frond and refuse *bohio*, aka hut, in the jungle. I remember one day when she asked me if it might be possible to get a roll of what we called 100 mile an hour tape. When I asked her why, she said, they would use it to cover cracks in the walls of their *bohio*.

The rainy season was coming. Since I was the Assistant Group Supply Officer, Ester got her tape. She stayed overnight at Fort Gulick only when we were going out. Our gardener was named Leon, a very nice man who kept us in bananas from the many trees in the yard. The car wash boy's name I can't recall but he came every Saturday to wash the car and once a month waxed it. When we left Panama the car had to have a new paint job. He had literally waxed the paint away. Life in the Canal Zone in those days rivaled the best of the British Raj in India.

I had been back from Bolivia for about three weeks when I received a call from the lieutenant colonel who commanded the Bolivian Rifle Team. They were in Panama on the Pacific side for the Pan American Games shooting competition. You may remember that before departing Bolivia I had invited them to Fort Gulick for dinner. I told Mary that these nine soldiers were coming for dinner and she looked dumbstruck. I asked her, "What's the matter?" She said, "What visitors for dinner?" Seems international mail was quite slow and the actual letter arrived a week later. I was in deep trouble for several days.

But when the smoke cleared we had a great meal and our Bolivian guests enjoyed themselves immensely. Mary struggled with her Spanish throughout the dinner but did fine. Never a word of English had been spoken while I had worked with them in Bolivia or during dinner that evening. As they were leaving our quarters, in thanking Mary for a great American meal, they revealed that most of them spoke very good English. As an aside Mary spoke pretty good Spanish from her time at the Defense Language Institute in Monterey, and our visitors were most impressed. To my delight, the team jumped from a bottom third to a top third finish at the games. Guess we accomplished something positive while in Bolivia.

We did have a surprise encounter with three of the team a year later when we were staying at the Tivoli Guest House as I was leaving for Vietnam. The Bolivians were back for the games that year and also staying at the Tivoli. My LTC friend had seen and recognized young Larry playing in the hotel with his baby sitter while Mary and I had gone out to dinner with the Buyles. The LTC and two other members of the team waited in the lobby to see us and to wish me well in Vietnam. I was flattered they would go out of their way like that. The LTC and I communicated via mail a couple of times but eventually lost contact.

Shortly after becoming Assistant S4 it became very clear that logistics accountability in the 8th Special Forces was, I hate to say, next to nonexistent. Accountability was not a top priority in the Group. The S4 was an old SF hand, Captain Cliff Jordan and also new to the job, as was the Property Book Officer, Warrant Officer Sam Atcherley. The three of us were facing an Inspector General inspection with less than well maintained property books. We delved into setting things straight forthwith. It was a daunting task. WO Atcherley and I inventoried warehouses of "stuff" and slowly got a handle on things. It was not fun. The scope of the problem can be summarized and made clear in several sentences and one example. We found that we had two printing presses for the Psychological Warfare Company. But only one of them was on the property book. The value of these machines was $500,000 each. Talk about loose accountability. I learned about logistics and property accountability from Sam Atcherley who now resides just outside Fort Bragg, North Carolina. Property Book Officers are great people to have on your team, especially if they are scrupulously honest, which most are. We passed the inspection with a good rating; the effort was worth the reward.

Redmond's Rule #10 - Stay on top of your equipment accountability, it is a career breaker.

About two days into my new job I was going through my safe and when I opened the bottom drawer and was surprised to find a small, square wooden box. It was the only contents of the drawer. The markings on the box and the color of the lettering gave me some concern. I unscrewed the nuts holding the top in place and found that it contained twenty items. Or it should have contained twenty items; two were missing. I went to see the Group XO and told him what I had found. He was baffled by the find, or at least he stated he was. After inspecting the box he was also troubled by the missing items. He gave me a telephone number on the Pacific side to call. Next day a rather nattily dressed gentleman in civilian tropical attire came to my office, flashed his credentials and claimed the box. It disappeared and I was happy. Enough said.

Rioting broke out in Colon the main city on the Atlantic side of the isthmus where we were based. This was a Communist inspired outing and for some reason the Panamanian Government let it go on for several days. One night at about 0100 I got a call from the Group S4 and was instructed to pick up four boxes of ammunition, various calibers from the ammo dump and take it to a corner just inside the Republic. I was told I would be met by several members of the DENI, the Panamanian Secret Police. It seemed the rioters were targeting DENI Headquarters and the police were running dangerously short of ammunition. I was instructed to use my personal car for the delivery. With a drop off around 0300 I thought nothing of that. Wrong!

The S4 Ammunition Sergeant met me at the ammo dump and we loaded the four cases of ammunition in the trunk of my car. At a side street in Colon I was met by three members of the DENI who were very glad to see me. The streets appeared empty and the drop went perfectly. I returned to the Canal Zone none the worse for the effort; or so I thought.

The next day we got the word that the Panamanian Government had decided to end the riots that morning and if we wanted to see the show we should go to Coco Solo to the Masonic Lodge building and watch from the roof. As I recall the Masonic Lodge was the tallest building in both Coco Solo and Colon at the time. It looked directly down into one of Colon's main streets where the rioters were frolicking.

Several of us made the trip to the lodge and were imbibing of a second brew when a 2½ ton truck pulled up about two blocks from our observation point. From the roof of the lodge we had a perfect view of what then transpired. There were perhaps twenty to twenty-two *Guardia* troopers and a lone lieutenant in the truck. They unloaded, quickly assumed a wedge formation and calmly stood loading shotguns while the rioters watched and taunted them. The lieutenant ordered *"Adelante"* (forward) and every time a left foot hit the ground he yelled *"Fuego"* (fire) and they fired a shotgun blast, which I assume was birdshot; waist high down the street. I say bird shot because the rioters fled vice collapse grievously wounded had the ammunition been buck shot. It was instant riot control and a technique we would do well to remember. The Communists called the rioting off for the foreseeable future.

Two days later our S4 *Guardia* Liaison came to my office and presented me with an Eddystone Model 1917 U.S. rifle and a *"Cooperador de la Guardia Nacional"* card made out to "Captain Redmond, U.S. Army." Mary called it my "get out of jail free card" and it did work when I was stopped once by the *Guardia* for speeding in the Republic. Our liaison officer also informed me that for the foreseeable future whenever our maroon and white 1964 Oldsmobile sedan entered the Republic we should call a certain number and tell them at least 30 minutes in advance. Seems when I made the ammunition drop to the DENI it had been observed. For the next couple of months whenever Mary or I drove into the Republic we were shadowed by a *Guardia* car or truck.

On another occasion the Redmond's phone rang one night just before midnight. It was the Group Commander, Colonel Smith. The S4 was back in the States hence at that point the Colonel called me direct. Several cargo aircraft were inbound to France Field from the

Dominican Republic where the 82nd Airborne, supported by some 8th SAF troops, were deeply involved. The Colonel told me those planes were to be met and we would receive unspecified cargo; "Get two trucks and some help and meet the planes about 0400." That was the mission.

Putting it all together with the help of the S4 senior NCO we arrived at the airfield about 0300. France Field at this time was basically nothing but a landing strip with no tower, no lights and no emergency equipment. We had no radio frequency or call sign to talk to the birds but we were there. At approximately 0350 hours we lit #10 cans filled with sand and gas along both sides of the runway and waited. Promptly, just a couple minutes after 0400 we heard the planes approaching. As they rolled down the runway we turned on our truck lights and the aircraft taxied to a stop not far from us. We backed one truck up to each aircraft as the jump doors opened. At each plane a man in civvies waved and started throwing weapons off and into the trucks. The planes, both WWII C-47s, did not shut down their engines. It took perhaps eight to ten minutes to off-load all the guns. They ranged from WWII Mauser rifles to U.S. M16 rifles to M60 machine guns and all sorts of other weapons. When they were finished one of the civilians gave my NCO a note, waived us off, closed the door of the plane, and both birds began taxiing for departure. The note was passed to me and had only a phone number on it. The next morning I passed the note directly to the Colonel. Later that afternoon several men in civilian clothes came to the S4 Office. We proceeded to the motor pool where the trucks had been parked and placed under guard. The weapons were loaded into a large civilian van and disappeared; another successful SF operation.

A truly significant event in my life then took place. It was a farewell dinner at the Tivoli Guest House that helped me get back to the Screaming Eagles; this time in Vietnam. Flor Berumen was being reassigned to the 5th Special Forces in Vietnam. I had tried to get reassigned to Vietnam twice before but my 1049 paperwork requesting reassignment was turned down each time. It seems I owed the Army more time in Panama speaking Spanish. The Buyles, Pedens and Redmonds joined Flor and Rosemary for a farewell dinner at the Tivoli on the Pacific side. The Tivoli Guest House was a class act, all quite proper; shades of the British Raj. During the dinner we all discussed getting to the war and Ken said, "Wouldn't it be great to get back to the 101st." I agreed but explained again that both my previous 1049s had been rejected. Flor said, "To bad you don't have one now, I am going to Infantry Branch and would drop it off." At that point Mary jokingly said, "Well if you want to go that bad here's a napkin, write a 1049 on it." I took it and wrote something to the effect that I was a past Screaming Eagle and requested reassignment immediately to the First Brigade 101st Airborne Division in Vietnam and signed it. It was a Tivoli Guest House napkin with the Guest House name and seal of the Canal Zone embossed on it in nice gold lettering. We all laughed. Flor pocketed it and was off to the States the next morning. I would see that napkin again.

12
EXERCISE SEABREEZE
SAVAGE TRADE, 1967

The Group Commander had an idea to run as close to a real SF guerrilla exercise as could be done. Seems he had quite a few good ideas, like the Gatun Death March and that second, and probably last, Initiative Test. We would organize a complete and realistic Isolation Area with all the SF trimmings and prepare one A Team for what would look like a "real" go to war commitment against an enemy country. I was designated the S4 planner for the event. This proved to be a challenge but also an awful lot of fun. I mean I had to get a Rolex Watch, Johnny Walker Black Label Whiskey and small ingots of real gold (gold was not $1200 an ounce in those days) and several small roles of U.S. dollars to provide the Team to give to the guerrilla chieftain. That loot was to convince the team members this was not just an exercise but the real thing. And they would go in with live ammo, grenades, and the whole shebang! That was a decision we almost regretted later in a Puerto Rican cane field.

To begin we had to find a site for the exercise and it was decided, in the comfort of Fort Gulick, that the place was certainly Puerto Rico. Wasn't that a U.S. island? And there was a big Navy Base at Roosevelt Roads near the rain forest where the exercise would be held. The Navy would welcome us with open arms. The operation planner and I flew to Puerto Rico in a C-47 that the Air Commandos, who were as crazy as us, had signed up for dedicated exercise support. The pilot, a major, was every bit as totally committed to "Sneaky Pete" things as we Green Berets. We landed at Roosevelt Roads Naval Base and proceeded to base headquarters. There we were sternly told by the Chief of Operations, one captain, Navy type captain, "four striper," that we Special Forces types were not welcome on his base and "…good day." We were very unceremoniously shown the door and told goodbye. The captain was certainly not impressed by our credentials or intentions to possibly operate from his facility. We were all dumbfounded and snuck out of town as quickly as we could. Obviously Special Forces and Air Commandos did not have a good reputation with our Navy brethren.

There was a B-52 base on the western end of Puerto Rico named Ramey. The Air Commando major said that we would be welcomed there. It was further from the exercise site but it would work. So we took flight in that direction paralleling the south coast of the island. After about twenty minutes the pilot called us forward to see something. He made a low pass over what looked like a grass airstrip and a WWII Army training area. Sure enough that is exactly what it was. It was pretty big; more than big enough for what we were planning. We had to make two very low passes over the field scattering the cattle in order to land safely. Upon taxiing to the orange wind sock, the closest thing to a tower that was visible, we were met by a jeep load of very excited Puerto Rican Army National Guard personnel. They were the caretakers of this base. It was called Salinas Army Training Center. It is now called Camp Santiago, and is still operational. After a reconnaissance of the facilities which included everything we would need we made a couple of phone calls to San Juan. In short order we were authorized unlimited access to the base. The Puerto Rican National Guard folks were very helpful and made all our logistical preparation for the exercise pretty easy. They also helped us locate a suitable drop zone for the insert of the A Team. The drop zone was a cane field near the south coast and very close to where the Team was to operate in the Luquillo National Rain Forest. The exercise was coming together quite well.

Back at Fort Gulick we continued preparing and going through all the rituals for a major real world deployment of an A Team on what appeared to be a true SF guerrilla war operation. I was not involved in the situation or operations end of this activity but it sure had the appearance of a real mission from the logistical side. The isolation facility was superbly handled by the operation planners and the A Team moved into the facility. The Group Signal Officer and I were to deploy the lead elements early and set up the Special Forces Operations Base at Salinas Army Training Center ahead of the exercise. We were to depart from France Field near Fort Gulick in a C-130. When I got to the airfield I was appalled at the amount of gear we were taking. I told one of the NCOs that there was no way all that stuff was going on that plane. An old hand sergeant major quietly told me to go get coffee, and he would make it happen. Well an hour later the plane with lots more stuff than I believed possible, to include a jeep and trailer and a ¾ ton truck, lifted off for Puerto Rico and what was called Joint Operation Seabreeze - Savage Trade; never underestimate Special Forces sergeants.

I don't remember much about the operational side of the exercise as my concern was logistics and accountability of some very expensive trinkets. I mentioned before that we had provided the A Team some very special goodies to give to the guerrilla chief. That is part of the game. Well the night of the insertion we were all gathered around the drop zone waiting for the drop and enjoying some very nice weather. Things had been going smoothly thus far. The plane came over and the drop went off just as planned. After the team hit the ground things started going "sort" of bad.

To begin with, the Colonel got on a bull horn and calmly announced, "Team A-3 you are in Puerto Rico, not where you think you are. This is COL Smith the Group Commander. Come out and assemble on the strobe light you see to the south of the cane field;" or something approaching that message. The next thing we were all hitting the dirt as we heard several loud "kerchunks" as rounds were chambered in M16s. These lads were hyped up, and loaded their weapons, figuring they had been compromised. Several of us in the reception party started yelling out who we were and trying to convince them that this was an exercise not the real thing. We slowly cajoled one, two, and finally the entire team out of the cane. That was bad enough, but then things really got worse.

One trooper had lost his rucksack when it broke free from his web gear when he released it just before landing. No big thing, we would find it in daylight. Well it became a big thing when the sergeant calmly announced that his "ruck" held not money, not a Rolex, not Johnny Walker. Oh no, it contained four live hand grenades and the ruck had been found. But it had split open upon landing and three of the grenades were missing. Oh damn, or whatever words came to our minds. At this time there was a strong anti-U.S. group espousing the overthrow of the current island leadership. Leaving three hand grenades in that cane field just was not about to happen. You have not lived till you have seen two dozen SF types led by a full colonel crawling on their hands and knees in a Puerto Rican cane field. We did finally, just after daylight, recover all the grenades.

When the A Team finally assembled lo and behold who was the Team Commander but my neighbor at Fort Gulick CPT Tom McAndrews. Over the years, talking with him I learned that the overall exercise had been quite successful in the Team members' eyes. They were initially skeptical that it was for real. In the isolation area back at Fort Gulick they tested the system to confirm that it was a training exercise. Every special request they made for such items as exotic demolitions, foreign weapons and other normally not available items was granted post haste. But in spite of all the expensive goodies they were given, gold, money, booze, several Rolex watches they still were not sure it wasn't just training. But then, while en route to their drop zone, one of the wily NCOs on the Team went forward to the cockpit to check things out. He casually glanced at the charts on the navigators' table. Tom told me the real thing was lying there. The pucker factor for the Team just went to "this is for real." The Air Commandos had played the game to the hilt with the actual charts needed to comply with the scenario of the exercise being exposed to view. That explains why, after they had landed we were greeted with disbelief and the loading of M-16s in response to the colonel's bull horn announcement that they were not where they thought they were.

Within the last year (2014) Tom, over a drink, told me more about the mission from an operational side which I had not been read in on. I will try to capture his ideas if not his exact words. "The mission was to jump into a select site in Cuba, meet an asset (with whom we would later work in a guerrilla war mode), capture a key military official and extract him using the Fulton Extraction System. We had to sign away our U.S. citizenship in the event we were killed or captured. When we hit the silk (read jumped) we thought we were entering Cuba. The pucker factor was out of this world. Realism? Indeed, it was the best ever for peacetime and great preparation for spec ops in Nam." If I had been on that mission, I think I would also have been slow coming out of that cane field.

Having some things to buy in San Juan for the exercise I did not get back to the Special Forces Operating Base at Salinas until the following day. When I returned and walked into our cabin one of the other officers said, "Well if it isn't Mister Airborne." I had no idea what prompted that little greeting until I got to my bunk and found 75 sets of orders assigning me to the First Brigade Separate, 101st Airborne Division, Republic of Vietnam, reporting in May. That was just three months off. Flor Berumen had delivered my Tivoli Guest House "1049" and someone at Infantry Branch decided to honor it. I was going to see the "Elephant" for real. By the way, that bar napkin was in my file when I was later posted to duty at Infantry Branch assigning lieutenants to Vietnam and Korea.

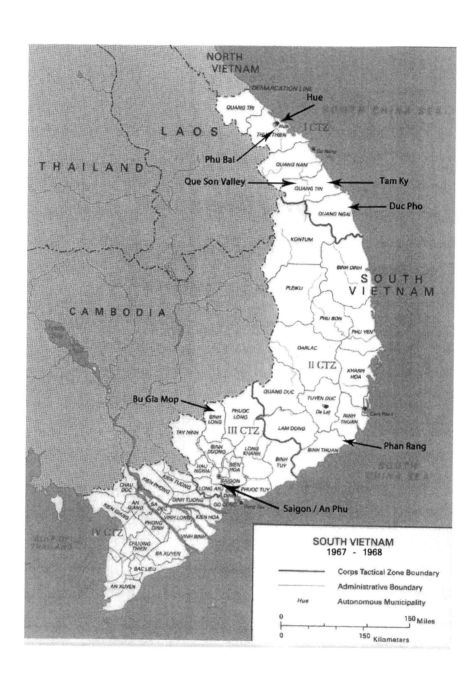

13
MY FIRST TOUR IN VIETNAM, 1967:
SEEING THE "ELEPHANT"

In preparation for a year at war Mary and I along with little Larry returned to the USA and I rented a nice little brick house in a new area of Columbus, Georgia. Mary wanted to spend the year we were separated near Fort Benning. This was an area she was very familiar with. Marga, her sister-in-law, would be there while Mary's brother was also in Vietnam; and it was only 110 miles from Atlanta and her parents. While I was deployed I wrote often. She more than me but I did write as often as I could. I think Mary has saved some or all of those letters.

I departed from Travis Air Force Base, California, on a Flying Tigers commercial charter and landed in Cam Rahn Bay. It was a long and very tiring trip. At the replacement facility at Cam Rahn I remember little except it was hot and dirty and we were lectured on the country and the Vietnamese people ad nauseam. They promised I would be going to the 101st Airborne First Brigade Separate and they kept that promise.

Phan Rang, the rear Detachment and home base of the brigade, was just up the road from Cam Rahn Bay. We made the trip there by helicopter. Once at the sprawling Phan Rang base camp I was in-processed and sent to "P" Training. The P stands for Proficiency. There we were refreshed on weapons, grenades, calling in artillery and Viet Cong and North Vietnamese Army booby traps and lots of other meaningful, lifesaving stuff. We also were given additional training on Vietnam, its culture and people. The only person I met in P Training that I remember was Doctor Richard Ignatius Porter, known affectionately as RIP, or Doc Porter. We were destined to be assigned to the same battalion, the 2-327th Infantry whose motto was "No Slack." Doc was later to be dubbed, again affectionately, the No Slack Quack. We became good friends and remain so to this day.

The First Brigade had been nicknamed the "Nomads of Vietnam," the "Fire Brigade" and several other sobriquets. Each name related to the fact that since their arrival in Vietnam they had been sent hither and yon wherever there was a problem and the fighting was intense. The brigade as a whole had never been back en masse to Phan Rang after they had first established the base camp two years earlier. The unit was on jump status and we received parachute pay but due to the circumstances in a combat zone jumping every three months for pay had been waived.

I got the bad news that I would not be going to a battalion initially but was being assigned as the brigade assistant G1 or personnel officer. At the time the brigade was up in I Corps at a place called Duc Pho. I flew by C-130 from Phan Rang direct to Duc Pho and had a chance to see the Vietnamese countryside. It was truly beautiful but full of bomb craters having been fought over since 1946 when the French failed to stop the Viet Minh from taking over the north.

At Duc Pho I met my new boss, Major Dick Kupau, a Hawaiian, and a great guy to work for. The brigade Commanding General (CG) was Brigadier General Salve Matheson a WWII 101st Airborne Division paratrooper and a great combat leader. He was affectionately known as General Matt. His deputy commander was Colonel Oscar Davis. He was another true soldiers' soldier whose language could sometimes be very colorful and intimidating.

The first night there I was invited to attend dinner in the CG's mess, along with Major Kupau, who introduced me to the rest of the staff. The mess was in a large tent and pretty rustic as general officer messes went; sort of World War II paratrooper hardcore no frills motif. It was an eye-opener watching the ritual in the mess as the general and Oscar Davis worked at humbling the staff for one thing or another. They seemed to get a real kick out of it but some of the recipients were obviously uncomfortable with the repartee. Although an esprit builder and done in good fun the banter could make a thin skinned person uncomfortable. Since I was designated to fill in when Major Kupau was not there I determined to be sure to keep a low profile and be prepared to deflect any spears that might come my way. On the first visit, as the new guy, I was required to drink an "after burner," aka a burning shot of cognac. I managed to get it all in my mouth in one gulp, and swallowed, quenching the flame and pretending to enjoy the experience. There was another new guy there who fumbled the toss down and spilled flaming cognac on one side of his face. Didn't really hurt him but he took a lot of ribbing from the other staff members.

After dinner that night I decided to head down to the shower point on a stream not too far from my tent. The shower was not terribly crowded but after a few minutes I noticed this one soldier staring at me as we both washed. Well based on previous experience in Monterey, California with the captain I was a little uncomfortable with this. After I completed my shower and was getting dressed the man came ambling over with nothing on but a towel. He opened the conversation with, "Excuse me but I think I know you. I am Captain Roland Torer, the brigade Catholic chaplain and you sure do look familiar." Good heavens, talk about a small world. I responded, "Oh my God, Padre, yes you do know me. You were my assistant pastor at Our Lady of Peace Church in Columbus, Ohio about ten years ago." Father Torer was one hell of a priest and soldier. He medically retired as a full colonel. Years later I visited him in his apartment in D.C. and held his hand as he was dying of cancer.

The job of an assistant S1 was not terribly challenging. Hence I decided to try to win an air medal by flying door gunner on the nightly security flights around the Duc Pho camp perimeter. To earn an air medal you had to spend a certain amount of hours flying in direct support of operations. This was the first and last time I ever chased a medal. They never meant that much to me. Later, without trying, I would qualify for a half dozen additional awards of the Air Medal. While at Duc Pho an Army Commendation Medal from the 8th SF came in for me. I did not know I had been put in for it.

About a week into my new job Major Kupau called me into his office, at the back of the tent and told me we had a little problem. This comment about having a little problem almost defies description and needs some further explanation. As the Personnel Office we were responsible for Morale and Welfare items in support of the troops. At this point the brigade had been at Duc Pho for about three weeks. We had relieved the USMC at this base camp and they had moved further north to confront a growing Viet Cong/North Vietnamese Army presence around Danang and Hue. When the Marines departed they had left us a "beer yard" full of canned beer from various manufacturers. Now in Vietnam at that time every troop in the field was entitled to two beers a day. Problem was they could only get them on resupply day. So woe be to the supply sergeant who did not get the brew to the chopper and hence the field. Major Kupau told me and I paraphrase here, "Larry, it seems they are having trouble getting beer from our beer yard out to the field on the resupply helicopters. Will you get down there and sort it out." Well I thought OK, what can be so tough about this. I can straighten this out, no problem.

When I arrived at the beer yard I was shocked. This place was huge, probably an acre and a half in size. Pallets of beer were stacked five and six pallets high and most were falling apart. Cardboard to hold the pallets together and the metal bands to keep the beer neatly contained were either missing, washed away by heavy rain or simply rusted away. Thousands of cans of beer littered the ground. I do not exaggerate there were beer cans everywhere, most still full but rusty and muddy. There was a real danger that moving pallets could cause whole stacks to come crashing down and injure folks. It was certainly a bigger job than a couple of us could handle. The word went out to the battalion rear areas to send help. Initially some of the troops were reluctant to dig into this task but the promise of a blind eye and some extra brew to take back to the unit area soon had a whole lot of hands moving beer cans and forklifts moving pallets. I recall that it took us about three days of slave labor to fix up the yard to the point that it could operate efficiently. I often wondered if our sister service lads had sabotaged the beer point or if they just muddled through somehow and got the beers out to the field by brute force. You have not lived until you have imbibed of a warm Pabst Blue Ribbon or Carlings Black Label from a rusty can in the middle of the jungle, and enjoyed every ounce.

Not long after the "battle of the beer yard" we had another attention getting experience. Just down the beach from the brigade base camp, was an ammunition point called Task Force Gallagher. It was a huge complex. I was walking back from lunch when there was the loudest explosion I had ever heard. The ground shook and the explosions continued to rumble through the air. I turned and looked toward the sound and saw a huge plume of smoke streaming skyward. It actually resembled a nuclear cloud. The ammo dump was going up. That place blew for two days. It seems a soldier had run a fork lift prong into a pallet of 155 artillery ammo powder charges and set off the fireworks display. Unfortunately his error killed not just himself but several of the other troops at the dump. This site provided all the munitions for the units, to include the Vietnamese Army troops, in the area. Things were a little tight for a while until another ammunition ship arrived and the ammo dump could be reconstituted. The explosions, as I said, went on for over two days and made quite a show at night.

We had one decidedly funny incident that took place over a period of time relating to COL Davis, the Generals' Mess and the S4 Logistics/Supply team. Finding a topic to harass the staff about was part of the game in the mess as I mentioned earlier. Well the fickle finger of fate moved around from staff section to staff section. One of my friends, the Assistant S4 Logistics Officer, Captain John Miller, provided the nightly briefing on logistics status for the brigade. Our forward support element set up a small forward ice cream plant to provide ice cream to the troops. John began briefing the ice cream status at the evening brief. After several days of ice cream statistics COL Davis announced, "Oh crap, most of it is milk by the time it gets to the troops." So John commenced reporting on how many gallons reached the field hard and how many were soft. Well COL Davis, not to be outdone, asked "Well what kind of flavors are we giving the troops?" So John then began briefing the flavors, chocolate and vanilla, as well as the consistency when the ice cream reached the field. After a couple more days the Colonel turned to the S4 and asked why they only had chocolate and vanilla? "Can't you logistics pukes make some other flavors?" The S4, a really great soldier, LTC Bob Elton, turned to him and asked what kind of ice cream the Colonel wanted. Somewhat taken aback by the question Colonel Davis said, "How about pistachio ice cream?" The S4 responded, "Yes, sir, we will see what we can do." He turned to Captain Miller who now had the mission without a clue as to how to produce pistachio ice cream. But salvation and solution came from a trooper, as usual.

The very resourceful Specialist Four who ran the Generals mess got the mission from Captain Miller to help come up with pistachio ice cream. There were no pistachio nuts to be found anywhere but the mess steward did manage to find some green cake coloring and a can of stale walnuts from God only knows where. He then proceeded to make pistachio from the daily ration of vanilla. The next evening, without comment, the new creation was served at dinner. Colonel Davis upon receiving his portion asked, "What the heck is this?" As he tasted it no one said anything but then he said, "Well I'll be darned, it is pistachio! How the devil did you guys ever do this?" No one said a word. The harassment over ice cream at the evening briefing ceased. I believe the Colonel did not know pistachio from tutti-frutti! We underlings had a laugh on the "Good Colonel" and kept the secret. And the story lives on. I am indebted to Lieutenant General (RET) John Miller for providing me the full facts concerning this little event.

Several weeks after I had settled in as the assistant S1 personnel officer, Colonel Davis stopped by to speak to both Major Kupau and myself. Seems that General Matt was expecting a new captain to report in and he wanted us to be aware of his background. I will not refer to him by his real name but will call him Vlado Davidovic. He proved to be a little eccentric and was one of the most unforgettable characters I ever met. He was an Eastern European aristocrat who had fled his country after WWII. He attended St Cyr (French West Point); been commissioned in the French Paratroopers; served in Indochina; was captured at Dien Bien Phu; then served in Algeria and was part of the paratrooper revolt against General Charles de Gaulle. He fled to the USA and obtained a commission in the U.S. Army. He was an in-country transfer from some other unit in Vietnam. The capstone to this list of achievements, given us by Colonel Davis, ended with, "Oh yes, his next of kin is General Morris (not his real name), the commander of all U.S. troops in I Corps which includes Duc Pho and our brigade." Major Kupau and I got the message this was "super trooper" and very well connected. We had better take care of him.

Several days later as I sat at my desk I looked up and saw the entrance to the tent partially filled with a short, squat, overweight, round faced, older individual in jungle fatigues with his baseball cap bill twisted to the right, fully extended over his right shoulder. This gent sort of waddled down to my desk and announced in a decidedly French accent, "I am Davidovic." Needless to add, this was not the troop I had been expecting to meet. Thus began my experience in the saga of Vlado Davidovic, a decidedly unique and different character.

Let me summarize my impressions of him. He did do everything he was reputed to have done, as far as St Cyr, Foreign Legion, Dien Bien Phu and all the rest of his bio stated. He never had cigarettes, always bumming them from others. Major Kupau had trouble assigning him within the brigade and rumor had it that General Matheson asked LTC Ed Abood to take him as a favor to him. Colonel Abood did so and made him his S2 Intelligence Officer. At one point, when a company commander was wounded LTC Abood sent Vlado down as the interim commander. After a few days the company was almost in open rebellion and LTC Abood had to move him back to S2. I was told he did not operate well in the jungle. In hindsight it is questionable how he survived the first Vietnam War with the French.

After Vietnam Vlado would pop up occasionally and be at a reunion or call me at home. He was a social animal who had an ability to throw out generals names like we change socks. He called my house in Tampa one night and left a voice mail asking that I call him. He stated that he was staying with Ollie North and left a number for me to call. When I returned the call, sure enough, Ollie answered. Vlado was not bashful about approaching people who could help him. I will say one thing, when the weather in Nam was cold, wet, and totally miserable he would always come around with a small flask with cognac and give us a shot. That was after he asked if we had any cigarettes.

At one point following the war, I was approached by a fellow officer asking if I would sign a statement for a Silver Star for an action during which Mr. Davidovic was said to have been very heroic. I was unable to help since I was not on the hill at the time of the action, and said, "No can do" to the officer who asked. The last I heard Vlado was alive and well and living on the Champs de Elysee in Paris. He was in contact with the 101st Association National Headquarters in early 2011 and asked that they pass on his regards to me; he was a truly unforgettable character.

One day General Matheson called me to his tent and told me he wanted me to go to Saigon to the United States Army Republic of Vietnam (USARV) G1, Brigadier General Cole. He handed me an envelope and told me to give this to the general, and only the general, and tell him "I want this guy moved out of the brigade <u>now</u>." He provided no further information but being a good soldier I saluted and moved out smartly like Sir Galahad on a quest. Frankly I was bored working the personnel business and the idea of a plane trip over Vietnam was somewhat appealing. Getting a look at Saigon, "the Paris of the East," also sounded interesting. As it turned out I was to see darned little of Saigon on this visit.

I flew first to Phan Rang to our base camp on the scheduled shuttle from Duc Pho. Vietnam, war and all, was still a beautiful country. At Phan Rang I fell into the clutches of the Rear Echelon M@$%&# F*%#@$& (REMF an acronym best left unexplained for the more delicate readers of this tale. It will appear a few more times in this writing.). They set me up for a flight on to Saigon very early the next morning. Then they announced that a front line trooper, not so at this point in my tour, needed a night on the town and a chance to unwind. We ate at the on-base dining facility then adjourned to the Officer's Club. It was a major mistake on my part allowing me to be troop led by these REMF "heroes." We drank an awful lot. Nay, we drank way too much. I did not get to bed until about 0200, and got up at 0430, to make the 0500 C-130 flight to Saigon. When I got to the plane, I was not in good shape, and sicker than a dog. I told the crew chief unless he wanted to clean up a very messy airplane he better open the jump door and let me lie next to it. I think the other troops on the plane had a heck of a laugh watching me barf most of the way to Saigon. I was the senior guy on the plane at the time and too darned sick to care or be embarrassed.

After arriving in Saigon, Ton Son Nhut Airbase, I got a lift to USARV headquarters, which was located not far away at Long Binh. I found the G1 Office and walked in and told the Administrative

Assistant that I had an appointment and wanted to see General Cole on behalf of BG Matheson. About that time a booming voice hit me from the side with something like, "Captain, you look like hell. Come here." I couldn't argue with that comment about not looking so good and turned to see the G1 sergeant major eyeing me closely. It was not a friendly eye. As I turned he read my name tag and in a more subdued tone said, "Are you the same Redmond who commanded C Company 1-506 in 1964 at Campbell?" I responded that, "Yes, Sergeant Major, that was me." He then said something to the effect "Well my name's Seago and I became first sergeant of that lash up after you left. I replaced Top Moore. The NCOs told me about you. Hell, they thought you were good. You aren't seeing my general looking like that. Come with me." He took me to his hootch out behind the office and told me to undress, lie down, sleep, and when I woke up to come back to the office and he would get me in to see General Cole. When I woke late in the afternoon my uniform had been washed and starched and my boots spit shined. I cleaned up, dressed and went back to the G1 office. The sergeant major said, "Well Captain, you are a little more presentable and look like the officer the NCOs told me about."

He took me into the generals' office and I failed in my mission. The General read the note from BG Matheson, looked at the file and calmly said, "Go back and tell Matt that I won't, and can't do this." He resealed the package and handing it back said, "That's all Captain, you're dismissed." I was terribly dejected, I had failed. UGH, I would rather face a tiger than General Matt with this response. As I departed I thanked the sergeant major for his help. Between the Choppin Charlie NCOs, who apparently liked Lieutenant Redmond, and Sergeant Major Ben Seago my career may well have been saved from the error of my overindulgence.

I started the return sojourn to Duc Pho via Phan Rang. This time I avoided the REMFs, hiding in the BOQ from arrival until departure to Duc Pho. On return I reported my failure to General Matt and his only comment was, "I expected that." To this day I don't know what was in that package.

Shortly after returning to Duc Pho COL Davis, the deputy commander, called me to his tent and told me that another officer was inbound to the brigade and that he was a personal friend of General Matheson's from the 10th SF Group at Bad Tolz Germany. His name was Captain Othar Shalikashvili and what flashed through my mind was "Oh no, another Davidovic." This fear turned out not to be warranted. Several days later as I sat at my desk the entrance to the tent was blocked by a rather tall and imposing figure who came down the stairs, walked up to my desk and announced in a strong Russian or Eastern European accent, "Captain Shalikashvili reporting for duty." He was an in-country transfer from Special Forces and he proved to be a super soldier.

(NOTE: This officer was a class act and we have met off and on since at various reunions. One night over a beer at a gathering in D.C. he asked me if I had been to the "Wall." When I sheepishly answered no, he responded that he also had not been there. I had always feared going and seeing the names of men there that I had led into battle and had been killed. Then he said, "Larry, would you go with me tomorrow?" We went the next day and it was a very moving experience. I have returned to the "Wall" every Memorial Day for the last fifteen years and during other visits to Washington.)

About this time I received a roster of inbound officers and on that list appeared the name, Buyle, Kenneth CPT. I quickly contacted the personnel folks down at Long Binh and requested Ken not be diverted to some other unit. Frankly I saw him as the lever to pry me off staff and out to a line unit. Ken did arrive and actually was my replacement although I had already been reassigned to a battalion when he arrived.

14
THE 2ND BATTALION
327TH INFANTRY:
"NO SLACK"

The "No Slack" Battalion Firebase and Tactical Operations Center (TOC) were almost overrun one night in the summer of 1967 and the S3 air/assistant operations officer wounded and medivaced. I was sent down to be his replacement. I was finally in the field and about to see the real "Elephant" up close and personal. The battalion commander was LTC Edmund P. Abood whose call sign was Black Panther. He was a slim, swarthy, Lebanese-American Christian and the smartest tactician I ever met. He was also held in high regard by all on the brigade staff as well as General Matt. I was happy to be going to his battalion. He should have been a general but his attitude toward Israel when he was on the Army staff later in his career was public knowledge and the powers that be saw to it that no stars were forthcoming for him. He retired and went to work on special black, covert, projects for the Army in the bowels of the Pentagon. I often visited him in his office and stayed at his condo when I was in Washington on GTE and General Dynamics business (my second career). He was quite a man, a real American patriot.

During my time with the 2-327 I met some unforgettable characters, such as MSGT Harvey "Paratrooper" Appleman and SFC Eugene "Hardcore" Perry. Both these super NCOs worked in the S3 operations shop of the battalion. They proved to be great mentors and I valued their friendship. There were many fantastic troopers in that battalion, some of whom I am still in touch with. I consider them friends, and have an opportunity to see them from time to time: Jess Myers; John Lawton; Bob Crosby; Doc "RIP" Porter, the No Slack Quack; Ed Dube, my first sergeant in A Company (now deceased); my tunnel rat, Rich Luttrell (now deceased); and Terry Wren, who later became my radio telephone operator and helped medivac me the day I was wounded—to mention only a few.

My time as the assistant S3 was interesting but not terribly heroic. Oh I got shot at a few times and mortared with too much frequency but not a lot of direct combat for me. There were however some very memorable moments. I will relate some of them in no particular order.

I recall the day in October when John Lawton's company command post was overrun as I sat on a hill watching the fight down in the Que Son Valley about three kilometers away. At that distance there was nothing we could do to help but call for artillery and air support. I remember Captain Tony Mavroudis and C Company moving to rescue the remnants of A Company. I remember listening to Specialist Terry Wren, the A Company command net radio operator hiding in the nipa palm and whispering very softly that the North Vietnamese (NVA) were moving through the rice paddy killing the wounded. Terry described how an NVA soldier reached down, looked CPT Lawton over but did not shoot him. Apparently they thought, given his many wounds, he was as good as dead and why waste a bullet. Once C Company closed on the remnants of A Company CPT Lawton was medivaced and survived his wounds retiring as a colonel.

One evening just before dusk we received a report that a booby trap had detonated in the Command Post of C Company. Both First Sergeant Henry and Captain Tony Mavroudis the company commander were wounded along with a number of other troopers. A medivac helicopter was immediately dispatched to pick them up. A later report stated First Sergeant Henry had been killed in the blast. Captain Mavroudis appeared slightly wounded and he directed that the other troops be evacuated first. Before a second chopper could get in to pick him up he died having a much more severe wound and internal bleeding than he or the company medic realized. Tony was a great soldier and we all mourned his passing.

We were in the mountains overlooking the Que Son Valley for about eighteen days. The last time any "friendly troops" had been there was in 1954 and they wore French uniforms. The bad guys, the Viet Cong, Mr. Charles, whatever you want to call him, did not like our presence. Starting on day four or five they began shooting at us with a mortar and also what we deduced was a 57 mm recoilless rifle. They shot at us a couple of times a day with that recoilless rifle and we could never locate or silence that "puppy." We fired a lot of artillery trying to end the harassment but never succeeded. After about eighteen days the vaunted, highly regarded, "No Slack" Battalion, at the direction of Brigade HQ, was to be withdrawn for another mission. We had seen plenty of action out there; that was for sure, to include the A Company contact that almost cost John Lawton his life.

As the assistant S3 I ran the extraction off the hilltop sending out the troops, artillery and equipment via the incoming helicopters. "Huey" helicopters for troops, and "Chinooks," heavy lift birds, for the artillery, ammunition and other equipment. All went well until we were almost finished clearing the hill when the weather closed in on us. The fog was thick as pea soup. I looked around the hill and almost choked. We were down to eight folks, mostly command post types, not front line grunts. We had weapons, but eight soldiers would not be able to keep the bad guys off that hill and survive. Once we cleared out the VC always came to check out the area for goodies we might have left behind. So we had a problem; no we had three problems. First, there were too few of us to be anything like safe. Second, there were too many of us for a single aircraft. The Huey had a lift capacity of six troops at our current altitude. And third, the weather was zero visibility. This situation was my fault. I had screwed up allowing us to be too few and too many. My heart was in my mouth thinking we might have to start trekking out of the Que Son Valley on foot in that weather. This was not a good area for an eight man patrol, too many bad guys between us and Highway 1; good guy land. Things were looking rather dicey. Highway 1 was about an eight mile walk over some very inhospitable terrain with a lot of not so friendly folks along the way.

Suddenly the radio crackled and a voice said something like "This is Dancing Horse 4 coming in for pickup, pop smoke." Well hell, I had no idea who that was but we popped smoke and a Huey materialized out of the fog and landed directly to my front. I ran to the chopper and told the pilot we had too many men for a single lift. He told me to "load them anyway" because nothing else was coming in, the weather was getting worse – it was now or face that walk out of the valley. We quickly loaded, I was the last man to board the chopper. When he lifted off he veered left over the side of the hill and gave that bird all the power it had. We started dropping like a rock and I thought, "Oh God, here I come. I hope Lord I have led a decent life." We continued to lose altitude but slowly that young warrant officer got the bird to level off and we made it back to Highway 1 flying under the clouds and on into the brigade base camp. If I knew who that young warrant officer pilot was flying Dancing Horse 4 that day I would buy him a beer, no, I'd buy him a truckload of beer! He probably saved eight lives! I hope he received an award for his actions; he deserved it.

One day we came under heavy mortar fire up near Chu Lai. The tactical operations center (TOC), which had been dug in and heavily sandbagged, took a direct hit. I was off shift during this attack as was Jesse Myers, and we were both hunkered down trying to sleep in a foxhole nearby. One of the 8 by 8 inch roofing timbers in the TOC came crashing down hitting Sergeant Perry on the head. He was medivaced but in his own inimitable fashion showed up back in the field the next day. He was sporting a very large white bandage, a purple heart and a very sore head. Gene was a great field soldier and a man you could count on in a pinch. He was very outspoken and you never knew what he was going to say next. This did not sit well with some of the other officers. But in fairness it was just his way. I learned a lot from him.

We went through a typhoon up around Chu Lai while out on a firebase. I really thought we were going to be washed away. The rain was unbelievable coming down in sheets night and day. I recall one night CPT Davidovic visited my foxhole to get some of my cigarettes. I saved my sundry pack smokes for him. This night it was truly cold, wet and miserable. After I gave him my cigarettes he politely offered me a shot of cognac. Damn that was good. Somehow we weathered that typhoon for over two days, and the war continued once the weather cleared.

Redmond's Rule #11--The worse the weather the more you will be required to be out in it.

We moved frequently all over the northern part of Vietnam but always south of Danang. At that time the area around Danang and north was Marine country. At one point the First Brigade became attached to, then Task Force Oregon, the initial element of the Americal Division, of later Mai Lai Massacre infamy. We were authorized to wear the Americal patch with Airborne tab in lieu of the Screaming Eagle patch. Not one soldier changed patches. Eventually we were detached from Task Force Oregon and returned for the first time in several years to Phan Rang for a brigade stand-down. It was the first real stand-down for a good many of the troopers.

Lieutenant Colonel Yerks, who had replaced LTC Abood as battalion commander, decided we should have a party before we went back to the field. The appropriate food stuffs and booze were prepared and a whale of a party took place that night. The following morning most of the battalion officers were sick as dogs. They claimed bad shrimp caused the stomach problem. I was OK as were several of the company commanders and lieutenants. The planning was all done and everything was set for an insertion one day after the party. We assumed the combat assault would be delayed till the battalion staff and a couple of the company commanders recovered; wrong assumption.

We were moving to the Central Highlands area, quite a distance from Phan Rang and a longer than normal flight. Helicopter assets from all over the area had been prepositioned to do the insertion rapidly. The planned insertion could not be slipped because the helicopters were required back at their normal bases. So, brigade sent LTC "Ranger" Ralph Puckett down to command this insertion and he and I called in the artillery preparatory fires on the new fire base and in several different Company LZs. It came off as planned with no problems and all was well. The sick officers all returned to duty within twenty-four to forty-eight hours. Colonel Ralph Puckett by the way was a great soldier, a legend from the Korean War who won the DSC for actions there. He is retired in the Columbus, Georgia area and is very active with the Ranger Regiment at Fort Benning.

Sometime in October we were informed the rest of the 101st Airborne Division would be coming to Vietnam. We would rejoin them and cease being a separate brigade. The first element to come over in early December was the 3rd Battalion of the 506th Infantry commanded by LTC John Geraci. He was another legend from Korea and a great soldier. The 3-506 leaders were married up with the No Slack Battalion leaders for an orientation on how operations were conducted and to get a feel for what "the Nam" was like. It worked out well.

I remember one fire base that we were opening just before Christmas; it was near the ancient Imperial summer capital of Bao Loc. The artillery and air preparatory fires went in as scheduled and the LZ was cold; clear of bad guys. Shortly after the perimeter was established someone found a 250 pound unexploded bomb up near the top of the hill. It was decided to have the engineers detonate it in-place. We all moved down to the edge of the perimeter and safety, or so we believed. Well when that bomb went off we all thought it had to be at least 500 pounds because the whole hill shook and dirt and debris rained down on all of us. We were lucky no one was killed or injured.

Several incidents that occurred around this time while we were up in the Central Highlands stand out in my mind. The assistant brigade engineer and I, representing the 2-327, were sent with several other officers to Song Be to survey the next brigade base camp area up near the Laotian/Cambodian border. The First Division had a firebase there and it reflected a totally different approach to fighting the VC from the way we operated. The "Big Red One" troops built fighting positions that were low and round. Too difficult to explain but one issue was that from the fighting position you could not see to your front, only to the left and right meaning that you had to totally rely on the fighting positions to your left and right to protect you. It was OK as long as those positions were not taken out. If the fighting positions to your left or right were neutralized then the next thing you could expect was an NVA or VC hand grenade coming in through your firing slit. I was glad I served with the 101st where we dug conventional foxholes.

The reconnaissance team from the Screaming Eagles was bedded down in a large tent across the runway from the First Division Firebase. We were outside any real perimeter or wire barricade except for the local Regional Force/Popular Force troops providing some degree of security. There were lots of engineers and earth moving equipment scattered around but no formal line of defense that I could see. Not the best solution in my midget mind. We conducted our reconnaissance of the area and divided up terrain for each of the battalions. The assistant brigade engineer and I were walking one particular piece of ground and there were engineers and huge bulldozers nearby clearing land for our new base camp. Suddenly two Vietnamese in black pajamas came around the corner of a trail carrying U.S. carbines. We were about to open fire when I saw that they had yellow scarves or bandanas around their necks. I grabbed my buddy's M16 before he could shoot and told him to hold fire. The Special Forces camps put those scarves on their strike force troops as a means of recognition. Those scarves saved two Vietnamese troops that day.

That evening we were getting ready to clean up and in came a couple of new troops, one a major, Public Affairs Officer. It was his first time in Vietnam and he had been in-country maybe a week. To the best of my knowledge he had never heard a shot fired in anger. We were sitting around talking and finally I told the group, there were probably twelve of us in the tent, I was going to go take a shower. Yes, but not the kind of shower you picture. It was a collapsible canvas bucket called an Australian shower. It held a couple of gallons of water and had a nozzle via which you could control the water flow when it was suspended above you. I had just lathered up when we all heard the distinct pop of mortars being fired. I ran, nude and soapy, and jumped into a trench nearby as the first round impacted on our side of the airfield. The enemy fired about ten rounds walking them across the airstrip toward the fire base. After the sounds of mortars being fired stopped, I waited about a minute got up and started back to the shower. The new major asked, "Where the hell are you going?" I told him, "Well, sir, I am going to finish my shower. Charlie has taken his mortar and gone home for the night." That was their normal method of operation, fire a few rounds and run like hell. That pattern of shooting and running would change in about four weeks.

15
A NEW ERA:
THE DIVISION IN CHARGE

Sometime in mid-January 1968 I was told, as I recall by the executive officer, I would take command of A Company. That was what I had wanted for seven months, a command. I was a happy camper. I don't remember exactly where we were but I am pretty sure it was near Song Be. The first sergeant was Ed Dube, a good man, and a great field soldier. (Ed, following retirement, fought a valiant fight against cancer before succumbing in January 2012.) Every leader had a personal call sign for radio traffic. I took "Exterminator" for mine.

About five days after I took command I got wind somehow that the Division commander was coming to visit us. We were undergoing a resupply at the time. Then I was told he was coming to relieve me of command. I can't say for certain but think the source of that info was Sergeant Perry back in the Tactical Operations Center. The new CG was known as a wild man who did things on impulse. Sure enough he landed and walked over to me and said, "Captain, you're relieved." I picked up my rucksack and started walking to the helicopter. Having heard his reputation for impulsive things I thought what the hell, I had nothing to lose at that point. As I moved away he told me to stop and asked me what I was doing. I told him I was getting on the helicopter and that it was his company, he could command it. He then said in a very sarcastic and challenging tone, "Well, Captain, can you explain to me why your company has the highest malaria rate in the Division?" I did not know that fact at the time but I did know that the incubation period for malaria was about twenty-one days. I told him that, and that I had been in command less than a week. The General turned, didn't say a word, walked to his helicopter, departed, and I kept command of the company.

Shortly after my encounter with the General we had one incident I regret. We were somewhere west of Song Be and held up for the night near a wide river. We set up our night defensive position back away from the river and put out ambushes to the flanks and rear. My communications sergeant, good man and a heck of a communicator, asked if he could man an observation post down on the bank of the river. I told him OK and he, along with several troops, went down to outpost the river for the night. This area was a free fire zone, no friendly Vietnamese moved from 1800 until 0700. The night passed quietly, but just after dawn we heard fifteen or twenty shots from down at the river. I looked at my watch and it was 0703 hours. I moved down to the outpost after receiving a radio transmission that they had just engaged a sampan. This was a type of canoe prevalent all over "the Nam" and a primary mode of transport for the Vietnamese. When I got there I was informed that they saw the sampan coming down the river a few minutes before 0700. They tried to hail it but the lone occupant ignored them, so they fired him up. We assume they killed him. The sampan floated away down the river and we were not able to search it for weapons, ammunition, rice, et cetera. Was the traveler a bad guy or an innocent Vietnamese who had just broken the curfew? Did he die? We never found out. He had definitely broken the curfew and that error likely cost him his life.

Shortly after this we were informed that elements of the brigade were going to conduct a parachute assault on an old SF camp called Bu Gia Mop. It had been overrun about two years before and had been under enemy control since that time. Well needless to say for a bunch of paratroopers the idea of a parachute assault was greeted with a great deal of enthusiasm as well as fear! Although we were on jump status at the time, and being paid jump pay, we had not jumped in Vietnam. Most of the troops had not jumped since they qualified as paratroopers at Fort Benning; a good reason to be more than somewhat frightened. Parachuting requires frequent practice or it can be very dangerous. When we leaders were shown aerial photos of the old camp and airstrip it was surrounded by what looked like anti-aircraft positions: lots of them. Not a good thing. Before planning really got going, the idea of a parachute assault was abandoned and we were told to standby to air assault short of Bu Gia Mop, establish a fire base, and move there by foot.

We air assaulted, along with the entire battalion, minus C Company that had set up and was guarding a fire base that provided artillery support to our assault. We inserted without enemy contact into a cold LZ near a *Montagnard* village called Bu Blim, perhaps ten kilometers from Bu Gia Mop. About three weeks earlier North Vietnamese Army (NVA) regulars had occupied Bu Blim and killed over 300 *Montagnards* using flame throwers. The bad guys really were not nice folks. They were an equal opportunity killing machine; men, women, children, the village animals all were burned to death. The tale of Bu Blim had made the Pacific *Stars and Stripes* and many of us knew of it. Not a pleasant story but it happened. Once on the ground things started heating up.

This was my first major operation in command of A Company. We had about 100 troops in the field at that point. The battalion commander had picked a fire base to establish and support the move to Bu Gia Mop. We moved without incident to that point and set up the base and brought in artillery to support the pending move to the old Special Forces Camp. There was no contact up to that point but we did find an abandoned Viet Cong base camp with two dead enemy; one lying in a hammock with his leg gone. A Company was assigned the area of the fire base on the far side away from Bu Gia Mop. B Company was assigned the portion closest to the old SF camp. We started patrolling and probing the close in area around the firebase. A Company had no contact but B Company could hardly get outside the wire moving toward Bu Gia Mop before they were in contact with the enemy. "Charlie" did not want us going to the old SF camp that was clear. C Company moved overland and established a defensive position outside the fire base and did heavy patrolling at a distance from our location. They had contact daily and suffered a number of casualties.

I remember one night after we had set up the firebase, I had put out a listening post about 200 meters down a finger of land that led up to our position. About midnight I was sitting in my company command bunker when we got a radio call from the listening post. "We are surrounded, the "dicks" (enemy) are all around us. We are going to blow our claymores (anti-personnel mines) and come into the fire support base." I got on the radio and asked them if they had been discovered? "No, but the SOBs are all around us." I told the sergeant to lay low, don't move, don't make any noise and give us a communication check every fifteen minutes by breaking squelch on the radio twice. When you pressed the radio hand set push to talk switch you put out a small sound that could be heard at the receiving end. We would answer by breaking squelch once. Well needless to say the whole firebase was on 100% alert all night. Nothing happened. The next morning I led a squad down to the outpost to check the area out. They had been surrounded all right, by a herd of ten to twelve water buffalo. The area was littered with piles of buffalo feces. The whole firebase had a good laugh on that one. But for the most part we all did miss a night of sleep.

We never did get to Bu Gia Mop which it turned out was a major, heavily defended North Vietnamese Army supply dump in preparation for the 1968 "TET" (Vietnamese New Year) offensive. They were using the old camp and airstrip as a supply distribution point and actually bringing in helicopters with gear and people from Cambodia. Yes, the bad guys also had some choppers. Additionally, a road that trucks could use had been built through the jungle from the Ho Chi Minh Trail directly to the old Special Forces camp. That pretty much explains why John Miller's B Company had contact every time they left the firebase and headed for Bu Gia Mop.

16
THE TET OFFENSIVE, 1968

The 1968 TET New Year Truce was upon us and we were about to start 48 hours of ceasefire. Late in the afternoon the day the Truce began we were ordered to dismantle the firebase and prepare to move out the next morning. No information on why this change. We tore down all the bunkers and cleared the area of anything of value and settled in for the night. We had no idea what was going on except that early in the evening we were told we were going back to Song Be. Battalion did not know what was happening but certainly something was up. Sometime in the middle of the night the firebase was heavily mortared. One round landed directly on a former fighting position that had been dutifully filled in and sterilized. The two troops who had occupied that position were both killed. They were my first casualties. I had seen dead and wounded before this, of course, but these were "my" guys and it was a tough loss. Unfortunately they would not be the last. This did not appear to be much of a truce. Prior to TET starting it was possible for a unit to spend two or three weeks with no contact except an occasional sniper, a fleeting glance of a fleeing black pajama clad Viet Cong or an encounter with a booby trap. Once the offensive kicked off it became almost constant fire fights for every unit in Vietnam.

A Company was the first unit pulled off the base and upon landing at Song Be there was no one from the battalion to meet us. I was instructed by a major from Division to put my troops on a C-130 that was inbound. A second bird was also inbound for any portion of the company that did not fit on the first aircraft. I received no other information and still had no idea what was happening. We did an engine running on-load and I got on the first aircraft. We did get the entire company, weapons, rucks and all on one plane. The plane wasn't on the ground more than two or three minutes as it appeared they were worried about mortar attack. There were no seats and we just sat on the floor jammed in like sardines. This was not the normal Air Force mode of operation. I asked the crew chief where we were going and what was happening. He said. "Sir I don't know what's happening. We are going to Ton Son Nhut Airbase outside Saigon. The last guys I put off there went off the ramp shooting." Needless to say I was taken aback by this information and a little doubtful of this tale. However, I had the troops load and lock their weapons as we prepared to land. I passed the word to the men over the roar of the engines as to what little information I had, but expect to be in a fight upon landing.

When we landed I was the first one down the ramp and was met by an Australian Major who said, "Captain, take your company over there (pointing) to the perimeter and occupy as much as you can. Relieve the Air Force personnel there." We moved about 300 meters to the perimeter where I met an Air Force lieutenant who was very glad to see us. The ground to our front was littered with bodies of North Vietnamese Army (NVA) regulars. That observation was made, based on their khaki uniforms and pith helmets with red stars. They were definitely not local Viet Cong in black pajamas. The Air Force troops had done a great job of killing a bunch of them. They were policing up the bodies and throwing them on 2½ ton trucks as we occupied the foxholes and took over defense of a fairly large chunk of the perimeter. The attackers had come close to breaking into the base. I remember that there was a dead North Vietnamese captain with the top of his head missing lying in the hole next to our command post. The Air Force engineer clean up teams removed that mess just after we moved into position. War is not a pleasant business. Throughout the day other elements of the battalion arrived and took up positions to our left and right.

We were not at Ton Son Nhut very long; two days at most, as the TET Offensive gathered steam. The enemy, however, did not return to attack Ton Son Nhut. One event does stand out in my mind during the time on that perimeter, because it cost a young man his life. The first night there one of my platoon leaders, call sign "Little Beaver," whom I will call LT Riddle, came to my foxhole and asked to speak to me. He was new to the company having joined us, as I recall, at Song Be. He sat down and we shared coffee. Then he broke down and said I needed to relieve him. "I'm not qualified, I'm too fat, I don't fit in, I can't do anything right, I shouldn't be in the Airborne, all you do is chew me out!" We talked for quite a while and I bucked him up. I counseled him that my correcting of him was to help him get his combat legs and was nothing personal nor any reflection on his leadership ability. Gave him quite a pep talk and told him how good he could become. Told him "the Nam" would take off that little extra weight. He thanked me and we parted company that night with him in much better spirits.

As I recall the day after that, 5 February, we were airlifted from Ton Son Nhut to a place called Nha Be which was about ten kilometers south of Saigon on Highway 1. The Landing Zone (LZ) was cold and secured by Vietnamese Regional Force/Popular Force (RF/PF) troops. Nha Be was an oil transshipment point on the Mekong River where large tankers put in to offload crude oil and refined products. It was old, having been built back in the early French Colonial era. The houses and buildings were all very nice compared to the villages with thatched huts we were used to seeing. Initially there was no contact with either VC or North Vietnamese Army (NVA) forces.

I was directed by the Battalion Tactical Operations Center to move north along Highway 1 to the village of An Phu and link up with the

American District Advisory Team and await orders. At this point no other battalion units were in the area. We moved up Highway 1 to An Phu without incident and linked up with the advisors there. They were very glad to see us as heavy fighting had been raging just north of An Phu in Saigon/Cholon for several days (Cholon was the Chinese enclave of Saigon). Around noon I received orders to move north and block and engage suspected enemy (mostly NVA) reported to be evacuating the city. The Advisory Team provided us a platoon of RF/PF and together we moved toward Saigon with the RF/PF well to the front leading the joint force. There were no American Advisors with this RF/PF element.

We moved about two kilometers when we had a meeting engagement, unexpected contact, with an enemy force of unknown size. As we moved up a road leading west toward Cholon I received a radio transmission from Sergeant First Class (SFC) Niche Alonzo, call sign Lonely, with the lead platoon. He stated something was wrong. The doors on all the hootches were closed and the RF/PF to the front had disappeared. This was definitely not a good sign. As I was calling SFC Alonzo to tell him to hold up and check the hootches firing broke out just ahead. This developed into a pretty good fight. One of the troops near me yelled, "Captain Redmond there's a 'dick' over there." Without checking I simply said shoot him. Well that was an "awakening" moment. The trooper was armed with a 40 mm grenade launcher, not a rifle. The bad guy was not more than twenty-five or thirty yards away in a hootch. Needless to say when that 40 mm grenade round exploded it got my attention. It also killed at least one bad guy.

At that point I was still directing things from the center of the road, not smart, but it was the only high ground around from which to observe; the area being all rice paddies left and right.

Redmond's Rule #12 – Where you sit determines what you see.

We had been receiving rifle, machine gun and 51 caliber fire from a concealed enemy force. Looking down the road I saw an NVA mortar squad setting up right in the middle of the road. This was not a small enemy unit since it had 51 caliber machine guns and mortars. It had to be at least a battalion sized force of maybe up to 500 men. I got down into the rice paddies, where I should have been all along. I assure you the command post troops appreciated that decision. We had several walking wounded but no one killed at this time. Artillery fire was coming in and I called for gunships or fast movers with big bombs to join the fray. I directed LT Riddle to take his platoon around to the right and attempt to flank the bad guys.

A pair of helicopter gunships came up on the company radio net and I directed them as to where to fire and what we were up against. It was a no brainer for the gunships as there was a distinct and large canal just north of our position. We had orange panels displayed prominently on the south side; and we were well back from the canal. The bad guys were on the north side. Wouldn't you know it, the first gun run came in on the south side of the canal. Fortunately no one was hit and I called off any further strafing runs by that pair of gunships. That kind of help we did not need. We continued bringing in artillery on the enemy to our front. That artillery fire pretty well silenced any fire from the bad guys just ahead.

About that time I received a frantic call from LT Riddle's platoon sergeant who stated that the LT was dead, hit in the chest with a 51 caliber machine gun round while leading his platoon in an effort to flank the enemy. He died instantly. The platoon was pinned down and had several wounded. By that time the bad guys had unleashed mortars, 57 mm recoilless rifle fire and 51 caliber machine guns on us although firing was now sporadic and ineffective. I directed SFC Alonzo to break contact and bring first platoon back through the Headquarters element and 2nd Platoon. When he reached us in the rice paddy I told him to go to the right and take over the pinned down platoon and bring them back. He did just that finding the platoon disorganized and the platoon sergeant a basket case. SFC Alonzo had two Distinguished Service Crosses (DSC), several Silver Stars and numerous Purple Hearts. To say he was a great field soldier would be an understatement. I later put him in for a third DSC for his actions that day. The result of that you will read about in a few pages. We broke contact with support from artillery and helicopter gunships, which I vectored in well north of us to avoid any more gun runs on the south side of that canal. I don't remember any fast movers, jets, but there may been some in the distance behind the area of engagement closer to Saigon.

We pulled back to An Phu and I was ordered to set up a perimeter and hold. Battalion then inserted a second company, B 2-327, commanded by my buddy, John Miller, to strengthen the position. Intelligence now indicated a large force trying to move from Cholon in the direction of An Phu. At that point we didn't need some intelligence "weinee" to tell us there were lots of bad guys headed our way. As the senior captain, I took charge of the Army troops on the perimeter. We set up with the An Phu Advisory Team and they were very glad to have us.

Late in the afternoon, I was directed by one of the Assistant Division Commanders, to place a platoon with the Regional Force/Popular Force (RF/PF) element in a fort just south of town. I believe this was in response to a request from the Province or District Senior Advisor who felt reinforcing the fort was necessary. The fort was about 150 to 175 yards outside the town but had a good commanding view of the rice paddies around the village. I sent LT Ed Kowski's platoon for several reasons: they were good; he was a former Special Forces enlisted man with a previous tour in Vietnam and the most reliable lieutenant in the company. I had only been in command about three weeks at this point and the company was, and most of its personnel, were, new to me. I went with LT Kowski to the fort and got him linked up with the RF/PF and settled in along one side of the perimeter. At that point all seemed OK.

Throughout the evening there were periodic shots fired, mostly outgoing but some were incoming. The bad guys were out there and definitely probing our positions. Sometime around 0230 a big firefight broke out near and around the fort. Up to that point we had good radio contact with all elements in and around An Phu throughout the evening. With this large scale fight we lost all contact with LT Kowski's element. We moved the company radio around the area but could not establish contact. From the main street we could see flashes and explosions from around the fort. After about twenty minutes the RF/PF reported that the fort was under heavy attack but holding. I then had the Advisory Team ask for a check on my platoon and to get them another radio if necessary. It was reported that all was OK; the Americans were in the trench fighting but that they could not be reached because the center of the compound was under heavy small arms and rocket fire.

We continued getting reports to this effect about every fifteen minutes throughout the night. Firing at the fort continued sporadically off and on for the next two hours or so, as did incoming at various areas around the village proper. As I recall B Company was probed several times during the night but no major ground attack materialized in their sector.

At about 0530 the radio crackled and a 2nd Platoon trooper in a panicked voice stated that the North Vietnamese (NVA) had broken in and were killing all the Americans. Somehow they had lost radio contact at the time of the first assault and had finally managed to get a radio working. I organized and led a relief element down the road by moving in the paddies. As we left An Phu moving to the fort all firing had ceased. We reached the fort just at dawn. At that point the platoon had eleven dead and six or seven seriously wounded. I don't believe there was a man out of the approximately twenty-five in the platoon who was not awarded a Purple Heart.

There were several NVA bodies in the fort, one in the block house where they apparently first penetrated the fort and several more in the wire. Lots of blood trails where other killed or wounded had been dragged off. We also found an abandoned NVA machine gun in the middle of the fort that had been firing into the back of the trench where our men had been resisting the assault. We immediately began taking care of the wounded and getting things sorted out. We medivaced most of the platoon with wounds requiring more attention than we could give them. Shortly after that we began getting more help than we needed. The battalion executive officer flew in and in a huff told me in no uncertain terms that I had cost the battalion commander his career. I should have decked him. But instead quietly told him I had work to do as we stood there on Highway 1 with 11 bodies covered with ponchos. (NOTE: I could not have done too much damage to the commander's career as he went on to retire as a lieutenant general.)

Finally the other assistant division commander, BG Richard Allen, whom I had worked for back with the Currahees at Fort Campbell, flew in. He walked past the commander and the executive officer and came directly to me and gave me a hug and asked for a briefing. I told him what I could from what I knew. He looked around the compound, looked over at the village 150 yards away and said; "Looks like this platoon saved the fort and the village. If they had gotten this place they would have come right in your back door. They obviously weren't expecting to find Americans here; great job. What award are you putting the lieutenant in for?" or words to that effect. Frankly, at that point, awards had not even been a slight blip on my radar. I told him I guess a Silver Star. He responded something to the effect that possibly a Distinguished Service Cross was called for.

We were pulled off the line along with B Company and, I was later told, replaced by a brigade of the 9th Infantry Division. I can't vouch for that tale of a whole brigade replacing us, but the 9th Division folks were coming in on the same choppers that we went out on. I had about forty troops still on their feet, several slightly wounded.

We were flown to Bien Hoa, the 101st base camp, and I was directed to report to the Division chief of staff, COL Larry Mowery. He told me that BG Allen had briefed him on the action. He told me I had done a great job and that the company would be reconstituted with replacements. I did not feel like I had done so great, 11 men had died. When I later talked over the action with some of the officers and sergeants they all agreed that had we tried earlier to take a relief force down to the fort we would have been ambushed and lost a lot more men. In retrospect they were likely correct in that observation. I know one thing from this experience. For the rest of my time in command, and on my second tour in Vietnam, and when commanding the 1-505 Infantry at Fort Bragg I was absolutely wild about maintaining radio contact. Lots of young radio operators did not quite understand the "old man" going ballistic when they did not answer my first radio call. When they heard the story of An Phu they learned quickly.

While getting the company reorganized at Bien Hoa and the new troops integrated we came under rocket fire every night. There was a nice secure bunker not far from my hootch and I occupied it whenever the rockets started coming in. First Sergeant Dube and my XO, LT Norm Fretwell, were absolutely a godsend in getting the company back on its feet. They took care of all the administrative actions for me and together we made rapid progress. We put a lot of troops in for awards. Sergeant First Class Alonzo and LT Kowski were both put in for Distinguished Service Crosses. I do not know about LT Kowski's DSC but you will read about SFC Alonzo's in a few pages. We were up to about 120 troops on paper with around 100 present for duty. By Vietnam standards, especially during Tet, we were fat with troops. We continued training for several more days at Bien Hoa, mostly zeroing weapons and orienting the new troops on booby traps and company standing operating procedures.

Sometime about late January 1968 the battalion motto, which had been "No F'n Slack" for over two years, was changed. The F word was dropped because, we were told, several female officers based at Bien Hoa objected to it. There was no effort made to fight the change. Then word came down that the battalion commander's time in command was over. His replacement would be the Division G2 Intelligence officer, LTC Charlie Beckwith.

17
"CHARGIN CHARLIE" TAKES COMMAND

Yes, this was "Chargin' Charlie" Beckwith, aka "Charger," of later Delta Force and the Iranian Desert One hostage operation fame. About two weeks earlier, Command Sergeant Major (CSM) Bull Gergen who had been my first sergeant in Delta Company of the 506th Currahees at Fort Campbell in 1962 had joined the battalion. Both these soldiers were what one would call real hard asses. I knew of Beckwith from his exploits in Special Forces in Vietnam when he commanded a special SF project named, ironically, Project Delta. He was a big Ranger type with a "travel light, freeze at night" mentality. He took "Charger" as his unit call sign. Bull Gergen was cut from the same cloth. They would make a tough pair. Word came down the day after LTC Beckwith assumed command that he would inspect each company the next day and he wanted a full rucksack showdown. I read that to mean a lean and mean rucksack with more killing instruments and ammunition than goodies! That was a good thing in my mind but something that was already standing operating procedure (SOP) in the company.

I assembled all the platoon leaders and platoon sergeants and told them to get light, really light. The platoon leaders were instructed to reinforce the buddy team concept with essential comfort items being carried by every other man. No extraneous personal stuff, be ruthless, think like a Ranger. First Sergeant Dube oversaw the preparations and when the inspection was over I was told by LTC

Beckwith that the company looked "pretty good." For him that was some accolade. I really expected the inspection to be a reason to relieve anyone who did not measure up to his exacting standards and replace them with his friends from the Florida Ranger Camp. Lieutenant Colonel Beckwith did take this opportunity to transfer SFC Alonzo to Battalion Headquarters as the recon platoon leader. I truly hated to lose him but could not object as Niche was a great field soldier and would serve the battalion well in this new position.

One incident stands out in my mind that relates to Charger and it happened at Bien Hoa around this time. We received a group of new replacements and several of the company commanders including me went up to Battalion HQ to pick up our troopers and hear LTC Beckwith greet them. Well the greeting was something else; that was for sure. No, that's even an understatement. Charger stood in front of his tent, beer in one hand, his jungle fatigue jacket open showing off his torso with the scars from wounds he received two or three years earlier leading his Project Delta troops in the rescue/relief of an embattled Special Forces camp.

Charlie had a distinct way of speaking and tended to repeat himself and say, "sergeant, sergeant" or "boy, boy." He liked to refer to the troopers as "boy." I recall that his speech went something like this, and I won't get it right but I am trying:

> Gentleman, my name is Charlie Beckwith, Lieutenant Colonel Beckwith, and I am your battalion commander. Boy, boy, you are here in Vietnam under my care and leadership. You're not back on the block now, that's your buddy back there dating your girlfriend, eating pizza, drinking beer and enjoying your girlfriend's charms. You are here to fight Mr. Charles and his North Vietnamese buddies. Your ass belongs to me now. Some of you aren't going to make it home, pay attention boy,,,boy, and you

may go home on your own two feet; or you _will_ go home in a body bag. You got that boy?

He would go on like that in his gruff, southern twang voice and with lots of expletives thrown in. The new troops would be almost terrorized. But he was right!

At this point the TET Offensive continued to rage throughout Vietnam. Within a day or two, A Company was alerted for air move from Bien Hoa to Phu Bai. Phu Bai was up in I Corps and the Marines were in one hell of a fight at Hue a few kilometers to the north. I suspect you may remember the battle of Hue during the TET offensive. It was one big and very tough fight. The North Vietnamese wanted to take and hold Hue as a symbol of their success in the offensive. The Marines were doing a great job of seeing that it never happened. We boarded one C-130, packed in again like sardines sitting on the floor. The entire battalion was going but I believe we were first. I had no guidance from battalion except get up there and that they would all be following shortly.

We arrived at Phu Bai about 2300 at night in a truly pouring rain storm and it was much colder than down south. There was no one there to greet us, no one. It was darker than the inside of a cow and the rain was coming down in sheets. I told First Sergeant Dube to move the troops into a fairly dry but dark and empty hangar. I would see if I could find someone and determine what was going on. I started walking and sort of feeling my way because the rain was pelting me and it was black as pitch. Suddenly I got a sense that the ground around me was moving, no joke, the ground was moving. I froze and tried to determine what was going on. A door flew open at a nearby building and light flooded the area to my front. The area was filled with stretchers with wounded Marines lying in the rain. I had stumbled into the U.S. Navy/Marine Hospital at Phu Bai.

Suddenly I felt a tug at my leg and a voice said, "Hey buddy you got a cigarette?" I told him no, but standby I'd get him one. I went back to the hangar, got a pack of cigarettes and a pack of matches and made my way back to the wounded Marine. I lit his cigarette and asked him if he had been in Hue. He responded in the affirmative and I asked if it was bad and again got an affirmative answer. I then asked how he got wounded. He said that his platoon had been ordered to attack a house and in the ensuing action everyone in the platoon had been wounded or killed and the wounded were lying nearby somewhere. He then said, "Yeh, all four of us were hit. That was all that was left. I was the acting platoon leader." I then said, "Well sergeant, that's some story." His response was, "Oh, I'm not a sergeant, I'm a lance corporal [the Army equivalent rank being PFC]." Semper Fi, God Bless them! The medics came out at that point to take him in for triage and I wished him luck. He never knew my rank or even that I was in the Army.

I don't remember how the battalion came together at Phu Bai. It is all a jumbled blur. I do remember we were billeted in old Marine hootches and Charger and the battalion staff were there and operational. The weather cleared, that was a blessing. The day after we arrived we were called to the Battalion HQ and an operations order was issued. B Company was to advance to the north toward Hue on the east side of Highway 1 and A Company, was to advance on the west side with the same mission. Objective, get into Hue and help the Marines trying to recapture the ancient Citadel there. I cannot recall what C Company was to do but I suspect follow behind and be ready to reinforce or support our efforts. About an hour before we were to move out Charger came down personally to see me with a change of orders. Putting his arm around me (honest, no kidding) he said something like, "Boy, boy, I want you to take your company over to the Perfume River, turn north and move along the river till you reach Hue and link up with the battalion along Highway 1. Get me some body count boy, you got that? There are 'dicks' out there and I want some body count." That was it. No intelligence on the enemy, just "get me some body count."

We crossed the line of departure on time heading due west toward the river vice north directly toward Hue. The area west of Phu Bai at that time was rolling hills with some forest area of small trees and some secondary jungle growth but most of the area was cleared. At the time we had about 110 troops in the field. For Vietnam that level of troop strength was quite high but the men were mostly new replacements. I had three lieutenant platoon leaders and a lieutenant artillery forward observer; all but one were newly assigned. Sadly the only names I can recall are the artillery lieutenant, Neil Martinson (a pseudo name), and one platoon leader, LT Miller. In a moment you will understand why LT Martinson's name is embedded in my mind. The company executive officer, LT Fretwell, was a former West Point first captain and a great soldier. He remained at Phu Bai to sort out the establishment of the company rear area. First Sergeant Dube was with me along with my radio operator Terry Wren, who had just returned from the hospital. Our company interpreter, Sergeant Thuan, Vietnamese Army, was also with us. Thuan was a good man and he spoke fair English.

The last minute change in mission and route of march left little time for a detailed map reconnaissance. We moved almost due west out of the Phu Bai base camp and headed slowly toward the Perfume River. About an hour and a half after moving out I got a call from the lead platoon to come forward they had something I should see. Well we had drifted a little north, about half a kilometer from the azimuth I thought we were moving on. I should have paid more attention but movement was easy and it was in the direction we were ordered to move. The lead platoon had come upon a huge complex of buildings to include a large church with what looked like a monastery building attached and numerous other structures. There was a saw mill, furniture factory, *nuoc mam* production plant (a very stinky fish sauce used as a condiment by all Vietnamese) and numerous other structures to include gardens with fruits and vegetables. It turned out to be a Benedictine monastery run by

French priests. It was my intention when I saw the built up area on the map to bypass it but we had drifted north a little too far. A good map reconnaissance and discussion with the platoon leaders might have avoided this happening. The point man and platoon may have been drawn toward this site based on the sheer size of the complex. No idea why, but the fates and my lack of attention had led us there.

When the command group reached the site the platoon leader was already talking with three of the Benedictine priests. There were numerous other young Vietnamese priests standing around in black cassocks. I questioned the French priests. Only one really spoke decent English. He claimed that there were no Viet Cong or North Vietnamese soldiers there, they were all north around Hue. They did tell me that they had several hundred refugees in the church; locals who had fled the fighting in the city. Had I been half as smart as I thought I was I would have dug a little deeper into the Vietnamese priests standing there but I was trusting and did not do that. Perhaps being a decent Catholic cost me at that point. Sergeant Thuan came over to me and half whispered, "*Dai Uy*, bad place, I no like, we go, bad place." (*Dai Uy* being Vietnamese for captain and pronounced Da We.) He gave no further elaboration on why he didn't like it there. I was faced with a decision, search the place and check it all out, or trust the old priest and continue on my mission. Given the size of the place, the mission Charger had given us and the number of refugees reportedly there, as well as the lateness of the hour, I chose to move out to the west.

We moved only a short distance, just outside the built up area, and stopped in a pine forest that may have been part of the monastery grounds. From the west edge of the perimeter we could see the Perfume River and the highway on the other side. First Sergeant Dube and I walked the perimeter and saw to it that we were tied in and no gaps existed between platoons; at least we thought we were tied in and secure. Lieutenant Martinson called in our night defensive position protective fires and shot a few pre-registered missions north in the area we would move through the next day. We bedded down for the night in this pine woods; the last good thing that would happen over the next 36 hours or so.

About 0100 I received a call from the platoon on the west side of the perimeter that there was truck traffic on the road on the far side of the river. LT Martinson and I crossed the hill to that area and sure enough trucks with their lights on were proceeding north toward Hue. The LT called in a fire mission on the road but it was denied by battalion who stated that the trucks were Marine vehicles. Sometime after 0600 the next morning we got another report that the trucks were heading back south, lights blazing. When that report reached battalion we were told that they were not Marines after all and that we had permission to fire. By that time it was too late, they were all long gone.

Just after 0700, as we were rucking up to move out, one of the troopers yelled out, "Captain Redmond, there's an NVA soldier over there." Quickly looking to my right, sure enough a North Vietnamese soldier in khaki fatigues, pith helmet with his AK 47 slung on his shoulder was walking toward us. He did not know we were there. How he got inside the perimeter is a mystery. We shot him dead. About two minutes later as some of the troops were searching the dead enemy the platoon closest to the monastery came under fire. Within a few minutes we had two platoons in contact and moving into the built up complex. Things heated up quickly and in short order, although we had no wounded or killed, we did have five or six enemy killed on the ground. We could see bad guys firing at us from the second and third floors of the monastery. One of my troopers put a LAW (shoulder fired light anti-tank weapon) directly into a second story window. The resulting explosion must have made for some very unhappy enemy in that room.

LT Martinson was adjusting artillery ahead of the attacking platoons. I was standing next to him along with Sergeant Dube. I heard his call for fire moving the rounds closer to the monastery proper. When that adjustment came in, the round burst in the trees almost directly over the command group. The noise was deafening. Fortunately only one of my men was slightly wounded with a piece of shrapnel in his forearm. Minor miracle I thought. We called for a "check fire" and in the resulting "who shot John" radio traffic the artillery battery blamed my forward observer for the error. That was pure BS; the call for fire properly moved the next round away from us, not toward us. At that point we had other fish to fry as we were in a pretty good fire fight.

Out of the blue, battalion directed that we break contact and move immediately north to Hill 39 to relieve a Marine unit in deep trouble. I again reported that we were in heavy contact and had a North Vietnamese force of undetermined size there in the built up area. Again I was told to break contact and move north as fast as we could. When I hesitated for a minute or so the battalion executive officer came up on the net. He repeated the change in mission and restated our orders to move to Hill 39. He calmly announced over the radio, "Exterminator, either you move now or Charger will relieve you." My commo sergeant, good man that he was said, "Sir, tell them we can't break contact. We got the bad guys here and the Screaming Eagles never run from a fight." I looked at him and told him if it were us up there on Hill 39, and in trouble, would we not want someone to come to help us out. He shrugged his shoulders, nodded affirmatively and picked up his rucksack. We broke contact, pulled back a couple of hundred yards and started north. Our only casualty to that point was the troop wounded when the 105 round went off in the pine tree overhead. A successful engagement in that we left six confirmed enemy dead at the monastery and no idea how many may have been killed or wounded when that LAW went into the monastery upstairs window.

We moved north as rapidly as we could without totally throwing security to the wind. I kept the battalion operations center informed of our movement. They reported that the Marines were watching and waiting for us. My lead platoon started up the hill, reported that they could see a big tracked vehicle with three recoilless rifles (RR) on each side and asked that we again tell the Marines we were approaching. I responded that the big vehicle was a Marine ONTOS and yes it had six RRs mounted on it. Before we could send a call to battalion to alert the Marines, firing erupted. The lead platoon LT came on the net and screamed to have the Marines cease fire. Then just as quick he came back with, "Aw shit, the tracers are green, bad guys up there." The Russian ammo that the enemy used had green tracers where our tracers were red. The lead platoon point man was down and the LT used fire and maneuver to retrieve what we hoped was a wounded paratrooper. Unfortunately when they reached him he was dead.

Using artillery to help break contact we pulled back about 300 meters and set up a perimeter for the night in an area of heavy undergrowth. Darkness was rapidly approaching. Just after dark I called all the platoon leaders to the command post. I told them we were moving out in thirty minutes, Ranger file; belly button to butt, and we were heading back toward the monastery, no talking, no noise and no lights. Whatever you do, do not break contact as we move. One of the new lieutenants, and I do not remember his name, argued with me. "Sir, we don't move after dark, it's too dangerous." He kept insisting and I calmly said, "Lieutenant, you're relieved." I do not know what happened to the LT after that as you will understand in a moment. He may or may not have ever been relieved. This was the third time in my military career that I pulled back from a fight, but it was not a retreat, it was a tactical repositioning. I just did not like being at the foot of Hill 39 all night. The place was obviously crawling with NVA.

Battalion came up on the radio net and said "Charger" agreed with my decision. We moved out in Ranger file and moved about three kilometers to a hill not too far from that damned monastery. When we were about a half a mile away, the site we had just left was mortared very heavily. Sergeant Dube came up from somewhere in the column where he had been seeing to it that we kept moving and did not break contact. He whispered, "Sir the men think you are a genius. They would follow you to hell. That was a great decision to move." I chalk that decision up to a sixth sense, gut feeling and luck. Unfortunately my luck was about to run out. We formed a perimeter and settled down in tombs that covered the hill we stopped on. Up around Hue there were lots of tomb areas and they were fairly deep round circles with a hump in the middle. They provided pretty good instant foxholes. We had no contact during the night, all was quiet. The troops performed like true paratrooper professionals.

The next morning the fog was hanging directly above us. You could almost reach up and touch it. I was on the radio talking directly to LTC Beckwith explaining to him what had happened the previous day and evening. The information was all in the battalion log but I wasn't sure if he read it or not. I explained that we had one KIA, whose body we had carried half the night, and that we were almost out of ammunition for the machine guns. He roger'd that information and said sit tight. As soon as the fog lifts enough he would send in a helicopter with ammunition and would extract our dead trooper. Almost as quickly as the handset was passed to my radio man we all heard the distinct "whump" of mortars being fired. Everyone took cover immediately having no idea what the target was or where those missiles of death were about to impact.

I jumped in the little tomb we had as a fighting position and company headquarters and LT Martinson lay on the outside edge of the tomb next to me. As totally incredible, nay downright impossible, as it may sound the first round impacted in the tomb between the LT and me. The distance could not have been more than three or four feet. The blast went up and out of the hole catching my whole left side; shrapnel penetrated my side and collapsed my left lung. The explosion and concussion stunned me and wounded a number of troopers. SGT Thuan was killed, but I only learned of that much later. I stood and looked over the hill to see the second round impact in the second platoon area and the third impact in the same general location. They had us pinpointed. In addition to the sucking chest wound I had numerous other open wounds on my legs, back and arms but at that point was unaware of any of that. Adrenaline had kicked in and I was oblivious to the extent of my injuries. We had no idea of the location of the mortar due to the low lying fog. Well, when you are under effective mortar fire you have two choices, remain and take it, or clear out of the area. I chose the latter in whatever state of trauma I was. Still on my feet, I yelled for the company to move off the hill and down into a draw away from the monastery. I somehow got out of the hole and started down. I was in such a state of shock that I left my carbine and rucksack and just wobbled off the hill. That's when a second round hit a few yards behind me. This time I was down for the count.

I woke up laying in that draw surrounded by command post personnel; including First Sergeant Dube and Terry Wren my battalion radio net operator. I told the first sergeant to have LT Miller take over the company as he was senior. Don't ask me why that thought entered my mind but it did. The first sergeant told me that had already happened and the mortars had stopped when we pulled off the hill and they did not know exactly where we were. The bad guys did fire at random after that and Terry Wren was wounded by a mortar round that landed nearby shortly after helping put me on a medivac chopper. So much for the mortars having stopped. I remember nothing of the flight back to Phu Bai.

Over the years at various reunions and gatherings of veterans from the unit I learned of a couple of controversies surrounding my medivac. First, Sergeant Perry got in hot water for clearing a number of artillery fire missions in support of the company that were called in to try to stop the mortar fire. Artillery ammunition was in short supply and Charger had directed that artillery was only to be used in situations where troops were in direct contact with the enemy. "Hardcore" Perry approved the artillery mortar suppression missions on his own. The whole of A Company appreciated that. Second, as mentioned earlier the fog was quite low and thick. The medivac helicopter made several attempts to land but could not make it in. The pilot reported that visibility was still zero–zero, he couldn't see the ground, and that he would have to abort the mission. Jesse Myers was the battalion duty officer at the time and he begged the pilot to make one more pass because several men would die if he could not land and extract the seriously wounded. On the next try the fog thinned enough that the pilot made it to the landing zone. I owe Jesse for that one as well as the pilot.

When my eyes opened in the Phu Bai U.S. Navy medical clearing station they were looking up at Captain Doctor "the No Slack Quack" Richard Ignatius Porter, our battalion surgeon. He was holding my hand and crying. We exchanged words but I do not have a clue what we said. A few minutes later two big burly Navy corpsmen manhandled me to a standing position in front of an X-ray machine to get a picture of my chest. They had me so doped up that I felt no pain when they moved me. The next thing I recall was waking up and looking at the rather large frame of COL (later Brigadier General) RIP "Cottonmouth" Collins, then our First Brigade commander. Again I have no idea what we said to one another. I was still really doped up. As I tried to roll over I saw LT Martinson in the next bed. The entire right side of his face was gone and he had numerous tubes going into I don't know what. He survived, his face was rebuilt and he now lives in the great northwest.

18
HEADING HOME
THE HARD WAY, 1968

blacked out at that point and awoke in the U.S. Air Force Hospital in Danang. I remember very little about that stay as they definitely had me in dreamland. I do remember they had a chest tube in me draining the area around my collapsed lung. I was in intensive care and they kept giving me shots of Demerol for the pain. I quickly realized how nice narcotics could feel. After three days the docs felt that I was able to be transferred to a better equipped hospital in Japan. They removed the chest tube and I was prepared for transfer on a U.S. Air Force C-141 medivac aircraft. Initially I felt OK and actually slept most of the trip. The Air Force nurses on the flight were great.

After landing we were put on a bus, I remained on a stretcher, and moved to the Camp Zama Hospital. Lying on a gurney in the hallway for quite a while I began to feel bad, really bad. I do not know if they forgot me or were just very busy; most likely the latter. Finally I threw my arm out in the passageway and stopped a "candy stripe volunteer." I told her that I really felt bad and that I thought something was wrong. She disappeared and a minute later a doctor hovered over me, read my diagnosis, listened to my chest and yelled, "Move that man into that room across the hall, right now." Once out of the hallway he literally climbed on the gurney and jabbed a scalpel into my chest. I have no idea where he got that knife. Blood shot three feet into the air and all over the place. The doctor had saved my life. They had removed the chest tube too early and I was bleeding to death internally and did not know it. The indentation where he jabbed the scalpel in my chest is still there. I was put in intensive care at Camp Zama for three weeks and I slowly weaned myself off the Demerol. It was too good.

While at Zama two troops from the company visited me. They had both been wounded after me. One was the company lead medic from the command group and he told me that my heart stopped once on the ground and he revived me. Doc Porter, years later, told me that he had met the helicopter crew that brought me in and that my heart had stopped on the flight to Phu Bai and they had again resuscitated me. The Good Lord did not want me at this time. The troopers seemed genuinely glad to see me as they thought I was a dead man when they saw me going out on the medivac. They told me that the company had a number of wounded during the mortar attack but that the only death had been our interpreter, Sergeant Thuan. He was a good soldier and loved his country. His loss figures little in the course of the war but to me it was as sad as any of my American troops who paid the ultimate price.

The lads did tell a second tale worth sharing. It seems that after the mortar attack, with an interim company commander sent down by battalion, the company went back to the monastery. The mortar fire had come from near the church. It was determined that the monastery was an alternate command post for the North Vietnamese Army fighting in Hue. The French priests had lied, fearing for their lives. The young Vietnamese priests were obviously NVA, probably officers. I have no specifics on what all happened when the troops swept through the monastery but was told that some religious articles disappeared: chalices, communion patens, several items for use in benediction and other religious items. Division got a report on this and the pilfered articles were sought out and returned after the fighting in Hue subsided. The sad part about this is that all those refugees in the church had disappeared when the company went back and they may have been butchered by the North Vietnamese. Over 2500 people from Hue, leaders from the community of all walks of life, were killed and buried along a road about 1 kilometer north of the monastery. They are known as the Martyrs of Hue. I have often wondered about the fate of the "refugees," or were they "hostages," who were there the first day we got to the monastery. Had we stayed and fought it out, would we have saved all or most of them? Were they just everyday folks, real refugees, or were they part of the leaders who became victims of a massacre? I will never know. I understand that there were three or four French priests among the martyrs.

After three weeks in intensive care I was up and walking a little. I still had a lot of pain and was not running any races. The doctor who was treating me said that they would send me back to Vietnam in a few days to my unit to complete recovery. The hospital was full and frankly I think they needed the space. At this point it was late March of 1968. When I told the doc that my tour was up on 5 May he changed his mind and I was programmed to return to the States. In mid-April I flew on a medivac flight with other wounded troops to Travis Airbase, California, and from there on to Andrews Airbase, Maryland on another medivac aircraft. None of the flights were bad but I really do not remember much. I was not anywhere near even 70% recovered at that point and slept a lot. In retrospect a return to Vietnam to recuperate did not make sense. Good thing the doctor changed his mind.

I do remember sitting on a bus at Andrews waiting on my next medivac flight to Fort Gordon, Georgia and the hospital there. Suddenly the front door opened and a COL in a grey overcoat, flying saucer hat and gloves stepped on board. It was cold that April night. I recognized him immediately as COL Frank Dietrich from the First Brigade. We had met in May 1967 when I first got to the brigade. He called out for CPT Redmond and I raised my hand. He said he was the Pentagon duty officer that night and saw my name and unit on the inbound medivac roster and wanted to come see how I was doing. We chatted for a few minutes about the old brigade, General Matheson, Colonel Davis, Colonel Collins and LTC Abood. Then an airman came on the bus and stated that those going to Fort Gordon should follow him as our flight was ready. I never saw Colonel Dietrich again. He was a 101st Screaming Eagle from WWII and another legend in the Airborne. After retiring he lived in a little town in South Carolina called Clemson.

When we landed at Fort Gordon I was taken to the hospital and spent most of the day sleeping. Early that evening, CPT "Uncle" Harry Jones suddenly walked into my room with a six-pack of cold beer; shades of Special Forces. The head nurse, a major, stormed in and promptly announced that no beer was allowed on her ward. Uncle Harry explained the facts of Special Forces life to her and that he was the Fort Gordon Headquarters Company Commander and she should take a hike. Not sure what else he told her but she departed and let us enjoy our beer. Leave it to Uncle Harry.

Over the next couple of weeks Mary drove several times from Fort Benning, not an easy drive, to visit me. At some point the doctors cleared me to leave the hospital for short periods and I would visit Harry and Marge at their quarters. We relived old times and shared war stories. On one visit Mary brought young Larry along and I began to get reacquainted with my little trooper. I kept harassing the doctors to release me to go to Benning for continued recovery. They began by clearing me for four day passes and I drove to Fort Benning relieving Mary of that problem. I was driving our Oldsmobile from Fort Gordon to Fort Benning every few days which left Mary without a mode of transport. We purchased a second car. It was a ten year old VW *Karmann Ghia* sports car for Mary to drive. Finally the doctors cleared me for release and Department of the Army, Infantry Branch, issued orders assigning me to Fort Benning pending attendance at the Infantry Officers Advanced Course. I said a fond farewell for the moment to Harry and Marge and drove home to Mary and Little Larry. I was still not anywhere near 100% ready physically.

19
BENNING SCHOOL FOR BOYS, AGAIN

After an evaluation at Martin Army Hospital I was assigned to the Airborne Department for duty with the Tower Committee. It seems I could not escape the Airborne; maybe I asked for that but I don't think so. My duty consisted of taking physical training every morning and doing what I could of the morning four mile runs. It seems my left lung was much reduced in size and it took me awhile to get it sort of returned to normal. I was short of breath, sucked air for the first couple of runs. After about four weeks I was doing pretty well with the running and was definitely on the mend. In August the doctors released me from training with the Airborne Department and I started the Infantry Officer Advanced Course along with about 180 classmates.

The class work was easy and I did well in the course. I continued working out and running to get my body back in full working order. The body was progressing. At some point that fall the Majors Promotion List came out and I was on it. Then sometime around November I was informed I had been awarded the Silver Star for Gallantry in Action near An Phu. I never felt gallant and would have gladly traded any award for the twelve men whose lives were lost during those thirty-six hours of purgatory. To make the issue even more unappealing, to me at least, an SFC named Niche Alonzo, aka "Lonely," stood just down the line from me in the formation. He was also awarded the Silver Star, his Distinguished Service Cross (DSC) having been downgraded by some REMF weenie at Division back in Vietnam. That was a crime and a travesty as I saw it. When the ceremony was over I went to Sergeant Alonzo and told him so in damned plain infantry language. He looked up at me and said, "No, sir, you earned that award. You did what they paid you to do and I did what they paid me to do and what you asked of me. Don't ever feel you don't deserve that medal." I still think he should have gotten the DSC for his actions that day. Niche is, I believe, a full blooded Apache Indian and was a fantastic field soldier. I never saw him again until Fort Campbell at a 327th Regiment Distinguished Member of the Regiment (DMOR) ceremony. I think that was about the year 2000. I had put him in for the DMOR designation and with the help of Sergeant Major (RET) Harvey Appleman, who lived at Fort Campbell, we made sure this recognition was not downgraded. Niche appreciated that award and was quite proud the day he received it.

The defining moment in my career, at least to that point, happened as I recall in January 1969. I had been promoted to Major just before Infantry Branch came to Benning to give us all our next set of orders. The war was still continuing in Vietnam at that point. I stood in line an hour with my classmates waiting to be told my future. Most of my classmates were heading back to Vietnam. When I finally moved in front of a short, chunky, cigar chewing LTC named Johnny Johnson he said, "Oh you're Redmond, go stand over there I'll see you in a little while." I moved off to the side and waited. I thought, well they have finally found you out, you're about to be cashiered. About an hour later LTC Johnson walked over to me and handed me two envelopes. He told me, "There are two sets of orders there, one for Vietnam as a District Senior Advisor and one to Infantry Branch Washington D.C. as a Lieutenants Assignment Officer. Go home to your wife, talk about it and decide which set you want. I will be here tomorrow morning in the coffee shop at 0800. Let me know your decision." Then he turned and walked away. I didn't know what to think.

When I got home that afternoon I told Mary that we needed to talk. I made coffee for us. In those days I seldom made coffee so I think she smelled a rat. When we sat down at the kitchen table and I explained what was going on she was not terribly happy. Her first response was, "They can't do that. They can't send you back to Vietnam so soon; it hasn't been a year since you were released from the hospital! That's not right." Now at this point Mary was five months pregnant with our second child. She was adamant that Washington was better than Vietnam and I had to agree with her. But they wanted me in D.C. soonest as a lieutenants' assignment officer. They were looking for a recent Vietnam returnee who could relate to the problems of LTs being assigned to a very unpopular war. Someone who would have some empathy for the lieutenants, at least that's what LTC Johnson had told me. Mary's response to that was something like, "Relate to the lieutenants, and be understanding, and have empathy? Are they serious? Well they are getting the wrong guy for that." She was partly right in that statement. But we both decided that a tour at Infantry Branch beat another trip to Vietnam so soon.

At any rate the next morning I saw LTC Johnson and told him I would like the assignment at Infantry Branch but went on to explain that my wife was five months pregnant and due to deliver about the time they wanted me up there working. He replied that I should not worry, they would move me early, and I wouldn't have to finish the course. I was at that time the number two man in my class academically. The school gave me constructive credit for the remainder of the course and I effectively graduated number two. The irony of that is that I missed all the tactics instruction and tests. Perhaps it is more than ironic, perhaps humorous, but four years later I would return to be the lead instructor in the Offensive Tactics Division of the Brigade and Battalion Operations Department. A somewhat strange twist wasn't it? Also, in an interesting quirk, I would be working for COL Larry Mowery who had been the chief of staff of the 101st in Vietnam who entered this story just after the fight at An Phu. His son, Captain (later Major) Jim Mowery, would enter my life in 1979 at Fort Bragg. It truly was a small Army.

20
INFANTRY BRANCH:
THE ASSIGNMENT BUSINESS

We moved from Fort Benning to Washington D.C. in early 1969 and as an impoverished, truly poor, newly promoted major we could not afford to purchase a home or townhouse. Oh if only we had bought one of those totally out of the question townhomes for $27K and somehow gutted it out. We would have made a bundle over the years. Instead we rented a two bedroom apartment in a place called Spanish Village in District Heights, Maryland. It was a nice apartment complex then, and a fairly easy drive to D.C. We drove by the place in 2006 and decided it sure would not do today. The neighborhood and the apartment complex had deteriorated markedly.

When I reported for duty at the old WWII Tempo "A" Buildings in Washington, that housed Army branch assignment offices just outside Fort McNair, I got a rather unexpected surprise. I was not going to be the overseas Vietnam and Korea lieutenants' assignment officer but was to work in the Infantry Aviation Assignments Division. I would be working for LTC George Newton. LTC Newton was a great guy and he was assisted by two ladies, the little old ladies in tennis shoes were in D.C. also! My orientation was to be pointed to a desk and told to pay attention to the ladies. After about two weeks of listening and learning I was allowed to not just review files and direct that orders be cut, but also to conduct interviews. I cannot tell you how many times visiting officers who had come to review their files sat there stunned to see their assignment, career counseling officer was not an aviator. I never had a problem dealing with that however. And I judge 90% of the aviators I dealt with left happy. I was as honest with them as I could be and laid out, as best I could, what potential they had for further advancement.

As part of our duty all the officers did file reviews for the Order of Merit List (OML) for the next promotion, schooling or command list. We would each take home five files a night and review, evaluate and fill in the information that would make or break an infantryman's career. I would spend perhaps three or four hours, five nights a week, looking at files of senior infantry aviators and scoring them while we were going through the OML process. Mary would swing by after she put young Larry to bed and open each of the files, look at the picture, and give me a number (max was 1000 total points). It was uncanny; her guesstimate of an individual's OML score, based solely on a cursory look at the picture, was never more than fifty to sixty points off! I would spend hours working on those files and she would spend seconds and was so close, it was amazing, and given the time I put in somewhat disheartening. Pictures are important. I was always glad when the OML cycles were completed because then we had some time together and time to do a little sightseeing around D.C.

There were many incidents that occurred while at Infantry Branch that are chiseled in my mind. The first and truly most joyous and important was the birth at Andrews Air Force Base hospital of our second child, and first daughter, Katherine Marie on May 8, 1969. She was a truly fantastic addition to the clan and we all welcomed her. She was a great baby. Little Larry took to her immediately and they shared a bedroom without a problem.

Sometime in the summer of 1969 some of my relatives from Columbus, Ohio came to D.C. to attend the presentation of a chalice that Uncle Francis, Father Redmond, had created. It was to be presented to the Catholic Cathedral at a special mass. Uncle Francis was a true artist, and seeking diamonds, rubies, garnets, opals, whatever people would donate, he then created some beautiful and almost priceless works of art in the form of chalices. I am not sure just who all came from the Redmond clan but I know several of the Walker girls (great Aunts), Aunt Florence (who was very close to her brother Father Redmond), Grandma Redmond, and Aunt Blanche and Uncle Phil and others. There was a gaggle of them. After the service we invited them all over to our apartment for a brunch.

Among the attendees was Mr. Bill Gulley a cousin by marriage. Bill was a former Marine who won the Navy Cross on Guadalcanal. He was a "Mustang," promoted from the ranks, former major, forced out, or back to his enlisted rank, following Korea. He chose to stay in the Corps. Bill ended up a sergeant major White House aide. When he retired, President Lyndon Johnson hired him as Director of the White House Military Office. At the time of the chalice dedication, standing in our kitchen, he told Mary and me that he worked in the basement of the White House with no mention of a title or what he did. It was odd because he kept getting beeped and calling someone. For years we thought he worked in the White House mail room or some such place. Following his retirement from that job, just after Jimmy Carter was elected president, he wrote a book entitled _Breaking Cover_. The book is well worth a read, but also pretty disturbing in some of the things he revealed that went on in the White House. Suffice to say, he did not work in the mail room.

One morning about 1000, LTC Newton stood up at his desk and said, "Larry, you're in charge, I am going over to the Pentagon." I asked when he would be back. His response stunned me. He calmly said, "I won't be back, I am the new executive officer for the Chief of Staff of the Army. Good luck, you will be OK until Major Claude Ivey arrives." Claude was an inbound aviator scheduled for assignment to the Aviation Division. And with that a non-rated infantryman became the Chief of Infantry Aviation! No joke, it happened just like that. I survived the next six weeks supported by those two little old ladies in tennis shoes.

I did create one minor incident that brought me to the attention of the Chief of Officer Personnel Directorate (OPD), who at that time was an aviator brigadier general. A paper had been prepared in the Pentagon about some aspect of an increase to aviator pay. It came to my desk for comment. After reading and thinking it through, with my paratrooper mentality, I wrote a comment and sent it on. In rough terms I non concurred with the thrust of the paper and added that aviation pay should be tied to actual flying similar to jump pay; "No fly, No pay!" Well I was summoned to the Chief of Officer Personnel Directorate's office to explain my non concurrence. When I went in the general went ballistic. He initially looked at my blouse and said something like, "Major you aren't an aviator." I explained that I was surely aware of that fact but it made my comments no less germane. Well then the real tail chewing began. The facts of life concerning aviator pay, whether a pilot flew or not, was rapidly explained in enlisted man fashion and I was asked point blank if I was trying to sabotage the war effort with tripe like this. How could we expect to keep aviators if we didn't pay them? I thought to myself that the answer was, like paratroopers, they would stay because they loved what they did; but I wisely kept that comment to myself. Eventually I escaped and returned to my office but on the way went by to warn the Chief of Infantry Branch to stand by for a call. Colonel Newman only smiled and thanked me. I think he may have wondered how my non concurrence got out of the office without him seeing it. I heard no more about this incident and continued as Chief of Infantry Aviation for about another three weeks.

Once Major Ivey arrived and got his feet on the ground I was directed to move to the lieutenants' assignment desk (Vietnam and Korea). Literally, it was about ten feet across the hall from Aviation Branch. My desk mate was Major Steve Arnold, a West Point grad who had been with me at Benning in 1962 as we were being trained on the finer points of being a lieutenant. Steve handled lieutenant assignments to Europe, elsewhere in the world and back to the U.S.

Our desks abutted each other. Steve and his wife lived in an apartment not too far from us and we rode back and forth together to the office every day. I was about to get my baptism by fire for a second time. I cannot tell you how many LTs thought they were too smart, or had mothers who were dying, or some other reason that would preclude them from riding to the sound of the guns. I probably answered four Congressional inquiries every week, some weeks more. Each inquiry demanded to know why their constituent could not have a job at Fort Podunk issuing tennis balls and basketballs. I got pretty good at churning out responses to Congressmen and never had an LT's orders rescinded. Rescinding orders seldom happened and only in real hardship cases.

I sent several hundred new lieutenants to Vietnam every month. Many more officers than when I had been in Aviation Branch. I tried to send them to whatever training they requested prior to going to the war. That included Ranger, Airborne, Heavy Weapons and Jungle School in Panama. Many were sent to two or three schools. Later in my career I crossed paths with numerous officers who survived "the Nam" and stayed in the Army who thanked me for those schools. I probably conducted three to four career interview/counseling sessions with lieutenants going to Vietnam every day. Most were very patriotic and willing to serve, but a few were the recalcitrant, "I don't want to go, antiwar types." Frankly I did not like dealing with them. As Mary had said back at Fort Benning I was not prone to show much sympathy for troops who did not want to ride to the sound of the guns. I remember one lad who was quite outspoken and truly an antiwar peacenik. He stormed out of our interview and, I thought, off to Vietnam. Ten months later Steve assigned him from Vietnam to Europe for follow on duty. Steve later had an inquiry from Europe as to where the rascal was? He had not reported to duty there. Seems he had never gone to Vietnam either. Later we found out that the lad was living comfortably and quite peacefully in Canada; so much for the Army keeping track of the troops. Once an order was cut, no one really knew what happened. How many others never reported to Vietnam? I have no idea but suspect more than a few.

There were a hundred staunch patriots for every antiwar type that I encountered. One such soldier I clearly remember was First Lieutenant Robert "Bob" Howard, a former Special Forces NCO who had received a direct commission. During a trip to Fort Benning interviewing Advanced Course students I met and talked with Bob who at that point was attending the Infantry Officer Basic Course. He was a very highly decorated soldier with several Distinguished Service Crosses and a handful of Silver Stars, Bronze Stars with Valor Device and Purple Hearts. He had, I believe, over two years in Vietnam serving with various Special Forces units and going to places that our Government said we did not go. At any rate I told Bob that he was being assigned to the 82nd Airborne Division for his troop leading time. He stated that he wanted to go back to SF at Fort Bragg not the 82nd. I convinced him that service in the 82nd was just what his career would need. That was true.

I thought no more about it until five months later when Bob called me at the office. He stated that since he now had the four months troop duty time (at that time all LTs had to have at least four months with troops before going to a combat assignment) he wanted to be reassigned to VN. In the interim since our first meeting at Fort Benning one of Bob's DSCs had been upgraded to the Medal of Honor. MOH winners were not to be reassigned to combat. He was not a happy camper when I told him no orders to the war. Immediately after we hung up I called the 82nd Division Chaplain to check and see if Bob had any problems that might have prompted that request. The Chaplain called me back and said that Bob had no issues; he was doing well as a troop leader, was liked by the chain of command and had no family issues. I did nothing, as the regulations dictated. About three days later Infantry Branch received a message from the Commander of U.S. Military Assistance

Command Vietnam (MACV), General Creighton Abrams. The message requested First Lieutenant Robert Howard's immediate assignment to General Abrams office at HQ MACV for duty in a noncombat position. Needless to say Bob got reassigned to MACV. I don't know what he actually did on that next assignment. He went on to be a full colonel and a great advocate of the Missing in Action and Prisoners of War. He was a true patriot and hero.

I had been at Infantry Branch about five months, when, one day, going through files and efficiency reports of other officers, some of them my peers, caused me to question why I was there. I came to this questioning attitude based on seeing the numbers and potential "block" ratings on the efficiency reports of a bunch of my contemporaries. They had, in some cases, higher ratings and were blocked higher than I had been for potential value to the service. An old friend and Special Forces School classmate, LTC Bo Baker, worked at Branch as the Command and General Staff College Selection Officer. I went to see him and posed the question, "Sir, what the heck am I doing here. My efficiency reports are not nearly as good as a lot of my Regular Army contemporaries. Why did I get picked to be here?" LTC Bobby Porter, later MG Bobby Porter in the 82nd Airborne, worked the Senior Service College Selection Desk about ten feet away. Before Bo could reply, Bobby, and I use that name with the greatest respect and admiration, stated, "Larry we read the words. We ignored the numbers and blocks for potential. We looked at the quality of the seniors you worked for, and by the way SF rates notoriously low. The words told us you were the right guy." Well at that I assumed my next job would be commander of a Division or Chief of Staff of the Army. Before I could celebrate those nice words and really internalize them, my bubble burst as Bo said, "Yes, and you were available."

Redmond's Rule #13 – Being smart and persevering is good, but nothing beats dumb luck.

Yes, like a picture in your file is important, availability for assignment plays a role. My good fortune at being available for assignment to Branch played a major role in the rest of my career as you will read in the pages that follow. As I turned to leave LTC Baker added, "Don't worry, you will be early select for lieutenant colonel." I let that go in one ear and out the other; my mistake on that point, as I would learn a few years later. But being worried about promotion to LTC was not even on my radar at this point. Heck, I only had ten months in grade as a major.

I believe it was around the 1st of December 1969 when I received a call that my Father had passed away in his sleep. He was only 59 at the time. He died of a brain hemorrhage. Mary and I packed the car and the two little ones and took off for Columbus, Ohio and the funeral. By the time we got there most of the funeral arrangements had been made. Mary took Little Larry and Kathy to Chuck Gorder's wife Jane in Wapakoneta, Ohio, and then returned to Columbus for the funeral. Chuck and I had been friends and neighbors in the Advanced Course at Fort Benning. Our Ohio roots had kept us in touch. The service for my Dad was at St. Patrick's Church, where Dad had at one time been the sexton, and the burial itself at Holy Trinity Church in Somerset, Ohio. Thanks to the good graces of Father Redmond (again) Mother was given priority for an apartment at Nazareth Towers, a brand new senior living facility in downtown Columbus. The apartment was very nice with an eat-in kitchen, living room, bedroom, walk-in closet and bath. We settled Mom there and it turned out to be one of the best decisions ever made on her behalf. She loved the place, had any number of "girlfriends," played bunko, bingo, canasta, did the race track in season, went to lunch and dinner and the movies and visited all over downtown. My two surviving Walker family Aunts also lived there. Mom really had a blast at Nazareth Towers. We closed out the apartment on Henderson Road, said goodbye to Mom and with the children in tow returned to D.C.

Then an incident occurred that should not have happened. It was totally my fault. Colonel Abood called me from the Pentagon where he was then assigned and asked if I could help ensure the assignment of a major friend of his back to the First Cavalry Division. The major was already on orders to that unit and it seemed like a simple enough request. I sent a telegram (TWIX in military parlance) to my counterpart at United States Army Vietnam (USARV) G1. We knew each other from the Advanced Course. It was an "eyes only" TWIX for my buddy by name. With that parameter no one else should have seen the message. The officer at the receiving end in Vietnam was also from the 101st in the 1967-68 timeframe and knew both me and Colonel Abood and his call sign of Black Panther. The TWIX was simple enough; "Black Panther requests assignment of Major Jimmy Jasper inbound First Cavalry Division not be changed. Flag as "do not divert." Exterminator 6 sends." Well, all hell broke loose over that neat bit of encoded language. Seems the intended assignment officer on the "eyes only" line was on two weeks leave. The officer who did get the message went ballistic. The First Cavalry was having a rash of fragging incidents (hand grenades thrown into living quarters) carried out by disgruntled U.S. troops. Guess who got a call direct to his desk from the USARV G1 himself? After explaining the whole story I was still called to attention and read the riot act. The General did not think my effort at coded messaging was the least bit funny or cute. The major did get to the First Cavalry Division; mission accomplished, albeit with a major hiccup.

Steve Arnold was my LTs assignment desk mate and a fantastic guy. I truly believed he was a future chief of staff of the Army. He did retire as a three star general. He was quite a soldier and I tried to emulate him in many ways. One Friday about 1600 the deputy chief of branch, COL Aubrey Norris, came into the cubicle area and told us to get our blouses and go over to the Fort McNair Officers Club. There was a reception for some big shot and they needed "potted plants" to fill space. Steve and I trudged through the snow to the club. We then stood around with drinks in our hands being served canapés by ladies in black dresses with white aprons in a beautiful grand ballroom with high ceilings, twenty foot high windows and fantastic, expensive looking draperies. The room was packed with generals and colonels and a few wives. I want to say there was a grand piano with pianist adding a real class act flavor to the gathering. As I stood there a thought hit my mind; what in blazes was I doing here? I turned to Steve, another former 101st Airborne First Brigade Vietnam boonie rat and said, "Steve, this just isn't right. We shouldn't be standing here in fancy uniforms, in these grand surroundings with all these bigwigs. The whole setting reminds me of a WWII movie with a room filled with Nazi generals. Hell buddy, we should be busting through those windows in jump suits with our Thompson submachine guns blazing killing all these Nazi SOBs." We both laughed, but I was pretty serious. This wasn't what I had joined the Army to do. The Washington scene was not my idea of what soldiering was all about. I still hold that opinion.

An old college classmate, roommate, and friend stopped by Branch sometime in late 1969 and asked for me. Although he was a major at the time he wanted me to do his interview and file evaluation. The Majors Division assignment officers both agreed that it would be OK for me to do the interview. When we went in to the interview room the first thing he said to me was something like, "I asked for you buddy cause I had a problem and need a gut level evaluation of what I should do." When I went through his file it was very good, exceptionally good with the exception of one recent Special Forces report, from Vietnam. The report reeked of personality conflict with his boss. My Providence classmate confirmed that such was the case. There was nothing there truly derogatory, just a lot of damning with faint praise and innuendo. But his rater had done a real job on him. I felt it was beyond recovery unless he could find grounds and gather statements to get it pulled from his file. I left for a few minutes and took the report to LTC Bobby Davis (Yes, the same Bobby Davis who had been my faculty advisor in SF School.) for another opinion. Bobby agreed with the analysis I had given my classmate. I told my friend the facts and that unless he could get the report deleted from his record he would never make LTC. He thanked me for my candor and departed. Shortly thereafter he left the Army and settled out west. He has a horse ranch and is enjoying retirement. We talked in the fall of 2011 and I asked him if he was going to return to Providence College for our 50th Class Reunion. His answer was, "No way, too much concrete and macadam for me." Same old troop I had known since 1958.

One afternoon in January or February 1970, the Deputy Branch Chief walked into our cubicle area and calmly announced. "You two have been selected to attend Command and General Staff College (CGSC), where do you want to go? The Navy and Air Force Schools are available." We both thought he was joking. Steve however was quicker on his feet and replied, "Sir, I'd like to go to the Air Force College in Montgomery, Alabama." That's how I got selected for the Navy C&GSC at Newport, Rhode Island, by being slow; got a great year at Newport (Rhode Island) by default.

Shortly before we were to move to Newport I was sent on a trip to several western Army bases and Fort Leavenworth to brief officers there on what was happening career wise. By this time all my interviewing and speaking at various events had enhanced my public speaking ability to a pretty high level. Hence they trusted this mere major with the right to ride into the valley of death and spread the word. Or perhaps I was expendable and they were sending me out to be "bayoneted," so to speak. Before I left Washington the news was not good, it was "back to Nam" for 90% of the Infantrymen. While at Fort Lewis I received a phone call telling me to change my pitch; only about twenty-five percent of them would go back to the war. The U.S. was starting its drawdown. The war would wind down for us. Needless to say this news made my presence and presentation a lot more palatable as I toured various Army bases around the country. It turned out to be a fun trip. When it came to public speaking my assignment at Infantry Branch truly honed a God given talent for shooting the bull. Later in 1983, while a student at the Royal College of Defence Studies in London, the family traveled to Ireland and we all kissed the Blarney Stone. That sealed my speaking skills.

21

THE NAVY COMMAND AND GENERAL STAFF COLLEGE

Newport and the Navy proved to be an exciting and fun year for the Redmonds following the blistering work pace and pricey living of eighteen months spent in the Washington area. We found and rented a nice house just outside the main gate to the College on Dudley Ave, one block off Admiral Kalbfus Street, a main drag. It was nice but I recall the entire home was paneled; every wall and every ceiling in every room. This was rather depressing and dark during the winter months. And boy winter in Newport on Narragansett Bay was cold, snowy and usually dreary. Our next door neighbor was a Marine Major; he and I would walk to class except on the snowiest, coldest days.

I do not remember many of my classmates except for Major Owen "OB" Seaton who was also in Command and General Staff College, the "Junior Course," and LTC Tim Gannon who was in the War College, the "Senior Course." Later in Tampa, Florida, Tim would become a lifetime friend and neighbor. My Navy Classmates were all good guys but we never got to be overly friendly and following the course I lost track of them. That was a shame.

Being new to "squid land" and naval things, and the associated terminology we "foreign service types" all arrived a week early and were put through a very well done orientation so that we appreciated both the Navy and the lingo a little better. There were some impressive and memorable moments during that week. We learned about Navy terminology and why certain classes of ships had special designations. In all honesty it was baffling to many of the green suit types. Several of us decided that rather than try to keep DDs, DDGs, DEs, CVs, CGs, SSBs, SSNs et cetera, straight in our midget grunt minds the easiest thing to do was call them all LGBs (Large Grey Boats).

As part of the orientation we were taken on several cruises which were remarkable for different reasons. We were given a ride, and what a ride it was, on the USS *Basilone*, a DD (aka destroyer). If the name Basilone strikes a chord in your memory it is because Sergeant Basilone USMC, for whom the ship was named, was a key player in the first two episodes of the HBO Mini Series, "The Pacific." He was awarded the Medal of Honor for his actions on Guadalcanal and later died on Iwo Jima. I think, but could be wrong, that the rule that MOH winners not go back in combat may stem from his death. The skipper of the *Basilone* at the time was the "star" of the Atlantic Fleet and a quote, "Admiral in the making." He took us out a few miles into the Atlantic and then showed off his ship going all out and doing U turns and circles at flank speed, it was quite impressive albeit an old vessel. We started back in to port and being a good commander he turned the bridge over to a young Ensign to dock his ship and get some seamanship training. The young officer brought her in a little too fast, just a bit too fast mind you. But we did ram the pier doing a real nose job on the bow of the ship. In the days that followed we heard that the skipper was going to survive that error but I don't know if he ever made admiral.

The second cruise was a real attention getter. It was on an old WWII diesel submarine. We left the dock at Quonset Point with several of us on the bridge. Once into Narragansett Bay proper we all went below and I immediately realized that the silent service of WWII was not for me. The ship was cramped to the extreme, smelly and somewhat dirty. Running submerged there seemed to be more than a few creaks and groans that caused us land lubbers to question if we were ever going to surface again. The sights, smells and sounds of a diesel boat were something else. We sailed/cruised, whatever, down to New London, Connecticut where we transferred to a nuclear attack sub for the trip back. WOW, what a difference. The nuke was bright, airy, large and very modern. The trip back was a tad more relaxed in terms of concern for ever seeing the surface again. My admiration for the submariners of our Navy was and remains deep and abiding. They are a special breed. Sailing below the surface of the water was not my gig.

One other nautical incident sticks out in my mind from these school days. There was a small harbor just below the main building, Mahan Hall, and it contained about twenty sailboats of various sizes. Many of us trained on, and were awarded licenses to sail up to, a twenty-six foot vessel. I think I went out twice skippering a boat before the second Titanic occurred; well not quite the Titanic and an iceberg, but close. One of my classmates was a Coast Guard lieutenant commander and an America's Cup "registered official" judge. Now among sailing-yachting enthusiasts that is like being a four star general; well at least a two star general. One Saturday he took a crew of us out for a sail on Narragansett Bay. It was really enjoyable and the wind was up and the bay rather rough. After about three hours of cutting the waves we headed back in. He was at the helm as we approached the dock, well inside the breakwater. Somehow he got disoriented and ran her aground on some very rough rocks. Fortunately he had slowed us down a great deal before the impact. Needless to say it was not what any of us expected. No one was knocked overboard or hurt but it was a heck of a jolting stop. It also convinced me that if an America's Cup judge could run a boat aground, then sailing was not going to be my gig. I wanted a motor boat that "stopped on a dime" when you cut power. The word around school was that we had done about $6,000 worth of damage to the copper bottom. There was a Report of Survey done to determine who was at fault but the results exonerated the skipper and crew from culpability and hence from having to pay for the repairs. I never went out in a sailboat again, except once many years later with Mary's uncle, George Devlin, up at Cape Cod.

As part of the War College, George Washington University in D.C. ran a program leading to a master's degree (MS) in International Relations. In those days having an advanced degree was a real discriminator for senior rank and so I availed myself of the opportunity and did get an MS in International Relations. By the way, a master's degree still remains an assist to further advancement in the military.

The school itself was remarkable in that it certainly opened my eyes to strategy above the foxhole level. For that I am eternally grateful. The culmination of the course was excellent. We had a one week Command Post Exercise that included moving a task force to a fictitious nation where we were to invade. I was designated the USMC Landing Force commander, three star general for the war game, and presided over the high level planning. Also that role gave me the privilege of issuing the order to "Land the Landing Force," but beyond that the staff did all the work. It was a piece of cake, and different for an old paratrooper ground pounder.

The real culmination of the course came with a two week symposium called Global Strategy Week. Yes, two weeks long called "GS Week!" Only the Navy could come up with that one. We were broken down into eighteen to twenty man groups and augmented with senior civilians and military types to help focus our discussions and findings. One of the things I remember was getting in a rather heated discussion with an Air Force brigadier over social issues; specifically whether citizens on welfare should be required to work in some capacity to earn their payment. I said yes and he said I was advocating a national garbage collection corps. I told him if that was what it took, so be it. There were to be no free lunches on my watch. Not often an Army major had the liberty to argue with a sister service brigadier.

Another facet of this symposium was that I was assigned duty as escort for Dr. Lyman Kirkpatrick, a former Deputy Director of the CIA. Doctor Kirkpatrick was wheelchair-bound after a bout with polio. He was an adjunct professor at the College and I had taken one of his elective courses. The rumor was that he was the person after whom "Dr. Strangelove" was modeled. I can only relate that he was a class act and a brilliant mind. In WWII he had served with the Office of Strategic Services and later with the CIA. Perhaps there was some truth to the Dr. Strangelove rumor. It was a delightful time squiring him around and I remember him to this day.

Mary's Mother and Father came up for a visit and we had a wonderful time. Grandpa Devlin liked fried clams and we saw to it that he got his fill and then some. He was in a wheelchair by then having lost one leg to a number of strokes and that somewhat inhibited his visit but overall it was a good time. His brother, George Devlin and his wife Pat, came down from Dover, Massachusetts to visit at the same time. Newport was an enjoyable year particularly after my time at Infantry Branch with the long hours and displeasure associated with the cost of living in Washington.

In late spring 1971 our orders came out, and mine, no surprise to me, took me back to Vietnam. Having sent Infantrymen for second and third tours, some of whom were killed, I felt obligated to go on a second tour. My orders called for assignment back to the Screaming Eagles and I was quite happy about that. Mary wanted to return to Fort Benning to stay while I was deployed. I flew down and bought a house under construction out St. Mary's road on a street called Gettysburg Way. It was small but adequate I felt, and Mary was pleased. It was the first home we purchased and I was not happy to be so in debt; about $26,000!

When we arrived in Columbus via Fort Monmouth, New Jersey and Fort Bragg we found the house on Gettysburg Way only half finished. Needless to say Mary's pleasant demeanor changed instantly. With my departure pending in less than a month we decided to get out of the contract and find another house. We were successful and ended up in a nice home in the Holly Hills development closer to Fort Benning and overall a better area. We were now $27,000 in debt.

22
RETURN TO THE NAM, 1971

My second trip over, to what at that time was, "my generation's war" was uneventful. I was most pleased with the attitude and pleasant manner of the flight crew; particularly given the prevailing attitude in the U.S. at that time. The antiwar sentiment was truly bad. Maybe the stewardesses were being kind to the lads going over to fight a very unpopular war. I remember the gals were all cute.

Upon arriving at the 22nd Replacement Detachment at Long Binh I was informed I would be going to the United States Army Republic of Vietnam (USARV) staff. No way could I accept that. I called my old friend LTC Bobby Davis (my instructor in Special Forces School and also a buddy from Infantry Branch) who was then working in USARV G1 Officer Assignments. Sometimes who you knew and soldiered with previously helped solve problems that would otherwise be insurmountable. He told me all the U.S. combat units would be out in about six to eight months and that I should come to the G1 to work. I told him flat out that I wanted to go back to the 101st and stay with them as long as I could. I reminded him that I had sent Infantrymen for their second and third tours, some of whom had been killed or seriously wounded. Bobby knew that only too well. I told him that as long as there was a Screaming Eagle or a combat unit in Nam I wanted to be there with them.

As you are about to read, that was the opening to a period in my career I would much rather not write about, but feel I must. The war had become very unpopular, drugs and racial problems were rampant both in the military and our country.

Bobby made the assignment back to the 101st and I flew from Ton Son Nhut north to Phu Bai. By this time the old base at Phan Rang had been turned over to the South Vietnamese and the entire Division was located at the sprawling Phu Bai base in northern I Corps. I don't remember the in-processing but there was no going through "P Training" like 1967. The first night I was invited, I think because I was a field grade officer, to have dinner with the Commanding General (CG) in his mess. That was my first indication that times had changed in the 101st and Vietnam. The mess was not terribly fancy, but certainly not a general purpose medium tent, like the old First Brigade. The tables were covered with white linen and we were served by mess stewards in white jackets; silver candelabra adorned the head table and we ate off real china. This was quite a change from my first general officer dinner at Duc Pho in 1967. I was not impressed with the CG.

Redmond's Rule #14 - The degree of civilization is inversely proportional to the proximity to combat.

The next day as I was finishing in-processing, COL Ed Abood, my old battalion CO from the 2-327 in 1967, looked me up. He was back for a second tour and was the Division Support Group commander. We went to dinner that night at the Phu Bai Officers Club. Nice dinner and a decent club considering we were in a combat zone; or at least I thought it was a combat zone. Mostly we talked about the old First Brigade but Ed also gave me a word of caution. He said, and I paraphrase here, "Larry things are not like 1967. Do not be surprised by anything you see or what you may encounter. There are real drug and racial problems." Ed turned over command shortly after that and I was not to see him again until I had retired and he was working as a civilian in the clandestine/covert operations office in the bowels of the Pentagon.

I was assigned to the 1-502nd Infantry Battalion as the S3 operations officer, the job I wanted. After a brief day and a half orientation in the battalion area by the executive officer who was an acquaintance from the Advanced Course, I flew out to Firebase Barbara on the edge of the A Shau Valley. The battalion had relieved a Vietnamese Army battalion at the firebase so that they could go north to support one of the Lam Son operations into southern Laos. The Lam Son operations were incursions into North Vietnamese base areas along the Vietnam/Laotian border undertaken by the South Vietnamese Army supported by U.S. Army aviation assets. They generally were failures and cost us a lot of helicopter assets. Barbara was an old firebase, had been attacked a number of times but never overrun; except by the huge rats that occupied almost every unoccupied inch of terrain. One slept with his mosquito net strung tight and tucked in all around the air mattress. It was not unusual to wake up and find the net sagging close to your body with the top part being occupied by several large critters. It was somewhat unnerving although I do not think I ever heard of anyone being bitten.

I met the outgoing S3 on the helipad as I jumped off the helicopter. He was a senior captain who had been the S3 for almost six months as they had no incoming majors. He shook my hand, welcomed me, grabbed his rucksack and jumped on the bird and waved goodbye. Not much of a turnover or briefing of the situation or of my duties.

I was directed to the operations bunker and there met the battalion commander, a West Point officer getting his "command time" ticket punched. We talked for a few minutes. He had obviously seen my file at some point before I arrived. Very little was asked about my background. After perhaps ten minutes of chat he stated that my first order of business was to get the reconnaissance platoon out in the bush. "They have been here on the firebase two days and need to get back out patrolling," he told me. I saw the S2 Intel Sergeant who briefed me on the area of operations and what the recon lads had been doing. He gave me some ideas on where I should send them next and I readily agreed. I went to the operations bunker and sat down and wrote a fairly extensive operations order with all kinds of emergency plans should they lose communications given the surrounding hills and valleys; also what to do should they get in deep trouble with the NVA. Guess I put all my SF training and experience into writing an order that covered all the contingencies. There were plenty of bad guys out there but the S2 sergeant had pointed out to me that they were trying hard to avoid contact with American units. They knew we were leaving soon and were just biding their time.

I sent for the recon platoon leader and was rather surprised when a Staff Sergeant entered the bunker and stated he was reporting as directed. Normally the recon platoon was commanded by the best, and senior, LT in the battalion or a soldier of the caliber of Niche Alonzo from my first tour. No matter. I was taken aback when he told me that he had been the platoon leader for almost eighteen months. He was a Fort Benning "shake and bake" NCO sort of like the WWII "90 day wonder" LTs that Benning turned out by the boxcar load during the big war. I looked him over, now on his second six month extension in Vietnam, and frankly liked him. I told him to take out his pencil and paper that I wanted to give him an operations order (OPORD). He looked at me rather strangely and said, "Sir, excuse me I will be right back." He returned maybe three minutes later with the standard Army green note pad and a pencil and sat down across from me. He had tears running down his cheeks. When I asked him what the hell was wrong he responded, "Sir, no one has given me a complete OPORD in almost a year. Normally we are told to go in some direction and be back in three days." I was surprised by this response and frankly shocked; what was going on? After I went through the whole five paragraph field order and especially all the contingency plans on how we would regain communications if it was lost; and all the appropriate signals and rally points; and other contingency information he stood, saluted and departed. I sat there awhile and mulled over the thought in my mind, "just what the dickens had I come back to?" It was only going to get worse.

I do not remember much that happened while we occupied Firebase Barbara but there was no contact with the enemy. Oh yes, there were lots of rats. After three days we resupplied the recon platoon on site in the jungle and gave them new orders on where to patrol next. This saved them a long walk back and up the hill to the firebase. There was no contact by any of our companies while we were there on the edge of the A Shau Valley. The S2 intelligence sergeant's assessment that the enemy was trying to avoid contact was looking accurate. Lam Son ended and we were helicoptered back to Phu Bai turning Barbara over once again to the Vietnamese First Division. By the way, those were some first class soldiers in spite of what our news media said about the Army of the Republic of Vietnam (ARVN). They were as good as the ARVN Parachute Division and that was top notch.

We did not stay in Phu Bai long but began occupying old firebases in the Piedmont area west of the Division base camp. There was little contact with the NVA or VC who really were doing their best to avoid contact with us. Then several of us in the S3 operations shop determined that we were part of the reason for that lack of contact. I would send companies out with orders to break down into four platoon elements and set up several mechanical ambushes each night saturating the area with kill zones for any bad guys moving in the area. Somehow one of the NCOs in my shop pieced together from contradicting reports that at least one company commander was setting up a company sized perimeter (it was safer-that was true) instead of sending out saturation platoon ambushes over a larger area. I forget how the battalion CO handled it but the company commander was not relieved.

One night, about 2200, I was called back to the operations bunker from my sleeping area and informed that a mechanical ambush had gone off. The platoon in the vicinity could not, or would not, try to check it out until daylight. The battalion CO said to wait but I felt it needed a look. He told me I could fly out and see what happened, if I could get a helicopter. We had so little contact I think I really thought it had to be an animal that had tripped the ambush. I wanted to know.

We called for a helicopter with a floodlight and shortly one appeared. Maybe the pilots were bored that night; I am not sure. As I recall one of the S3 sergeants volunteered to ride along. We found the site OK and sure enough there were a bunch of bodies strung out along this trail through three foot high jungle grass. Heck it may have been six feet high. Viewing from a hovering helicopter can be very misleading. I asked the pilot to get down closer for a better look and a good count of the bodies. He hovered about 15 feet above the ambush and we counted and confirmed eight dead North Vietnamese troops in khaki uniforms. We were unable to get an accurate count of their weapons but saw at least five rifles. The claymore mines that had been daisy chained together alongside the trail had ripped hell out of the site. Suddenly a light came on in my brilliant mind, what if this wasn't all of them? Who and how many might be hiding just off the trail in either direction. I yelled at the pilot through the intercom to get the hell up and out of there right now. Hovering over that ambush site was a very dumb move on my part. Not sure I ever pulled another stunt that dumb. Well maybe I did as you will read shortly. One thing that going down close showed was that one of the dead was quite big unlike 95% of the Vietnamese. Was he a Chinese advisor or just a big NVA? We never found out. When the company that set up the mechanical ambush searched the site the next day the bodies and most of the weapons were gone. Bloody equipment and several destroyed rifles were left in the tall grass but otherwise the site had been sterilized by the bad guys. Someone had been out there and not too far away.

Being an S3 at this time in Nam was actually fun as we moved companies around from one area to another. I got to put in a lot of air and artillery preps on landing zones with just the artillery fire coordinator. We got pretty good at it. The boss did not seem to like flying that much unless it was an insert of more than one company, and operations of that size were rare. We also kept getting the same aviation support from a Major Dick Pack an aviation lift company commander. His copilot on most flights was his Operations Officer Tom Sewell. Tom would be a student of my mine in the Infantry School several years down the road. Major Pack's aviation company later flew my troops at Fort Bragg when I commanded the 1-505 in the 82nd Airborne Division.

I will never forget one particular incident that may have helped save my life. I flew to the rear to accomplish some coordination with the brigade S3. After getting off the chopper I was walking past the recon platoon area. We had pulled them back to Phu Bai the morning before from a week long mission deeper in the jungle than normal. The troops were there drinking beer and cooking steaks on a grill. They called me over for a brew. I truly appreciated that. But as I looked at them I was struck by the fact that they had been in base camp over twenty four hours and still had not showered; and they were wearing the jungle fatigues they had patrolled in for a week. I gave them hell and told them they were the best troops in the battalion and needed to look like it. They were special and needed to stand out, better than the average boonie rat. By the way that term is used in sincere respect and admiration for the men who walked the boonies. I gave the recon troopers "what for" in grunt infantry language. One young sergeant looked at me and said, "Sir, you are the first officer who ever said they give a shit what we look like. We will take care of that problem. We also appreciate the OPORDs you write for our missions." I think within two hours I saw several of the recon lads showered, haircut and in fresh washed fatigues. How this little incident may have saved my life will be clarified shortly.

23
LIFE IN PHU BAI
WITH THE REMFS

fter three months as the S3 I was reassigned to be battalion executive officer (XO) back at Phu Bai proper. I do not remember who replaced me as S3. I went to the rear and spent one day with the current XO who was returning stateside. All, according to him, was fine in the rear area, no problems. Well that was to show itself as not exactly correct.

My first night as XO was to prove momentous and scary. Accompanied by the battalion S1, personnel officer, I walked through the area. Initially all seemed pretty good and everything normal. As we approached the mess hall about 2200 the place was ablaze with lights and lots of chatter could be heard. The S1 and I entered to be confronted by about 200 black soldiers. We were the only white faces in the place. The silence was deafening. One specialist fifth class cook from our battalion came up and saluted and I asked him what was going on here; who were all these troops? He told me that they were brothers from all over Phu Bai who just came together to talk and relax. I told him that was great but that they were not welcome in the 1-502nd mess hall drinking our "kool aid" and coffee and eating our cake. They could relax and talk in their own mess hall. I also asked him if I had been a white PFC would I be welcome there. He assured me I would be welcome, of course, but there was a rumbling of discontent as the 200 began to sullenly file out and back to their own units. I had just made my personal discovery of the tip of a terrible racial iceberg floating through the entire Army in Vietnam.

The next night I was again walking the area and heard very loud music coming from one of the hootches. I asked a young troop who was sitting on the step of a nearby hootch what that was all about. After popping to attention he shrugged his shoulders and said something like, "Well, sir, we just leave those guys alone." I sought out the first sergeant of C Company to whom the hootch belonged. He stated that that hootch was filled with druggies and field refusals white, black and Latino. These were soldiers the troops did not want to have with them out in the jungle. He went on to say, "We just let them do their thing; it is best that way." I told him that was unsatisfactory and that he was going to bust that hootch up and he would do it in the morning or I would get someone who would. I then went and briefed the battalion sergeant major as to what was happening. He claimed he had not been aware of the hootch in question.

As an aside, let me say that many senior folks in Vietnam at that point were marking time, like the enemy, till we withdrew. Many of the senior NCOs were on their third or fourth tour in Vietnam and no one wanted to rock the boat or be the last man to die in a cause that we were in the process of abandoning. I can only say that I could not blame them for that attitude. I hate to write those words but they are the reality I experienced.

The next morning the hootch was untouched and I confronted the first sergeant and told him to bust the hootch now and send the troops to the field or I was going to get someone who would. He still refused. I called the commander, who was out on a firebase, on the secure radio and explained the situation. He agreed something had to be done and arranged for the senior sergeant in the field with C Company to be flown back to Phu Bai. I waited at the helicopter landing pad. The delight in my face must have been observable by all when the biggest, meanest looking African American sergeant first class I had seen in years jumped off the chopper and came over to report to me. When he heard what needed to be done he only commented, "This should be fun." Well he gathered up about a dozen really big lads from the battalion rear contingent, and backed by the sergeant major went about tearing the hootch down; literally plywood sheet by plywood sheet. The empty vials of heroin that fell from the ceiling numbered in the hundreds. There were about six troops in the hootch when it began to come down and they offered no resistance. I am not sure what happened to each of them but the majority went directly to the field. I don't know how they fared out in the bush. The sergeant first class became the immediate new C Company first sergeant. Our battalion sergeant major had the recalcitrant first sergeant reassigned somewhere else in Division; I never saw him again.

Word spread that the new XO had been less than kind to the "brothers" and to the druggies. One day a young black sergeant stopped by my office and asked to talk with me. He told me he had heard about the confrontation in the mess hall with the brothers. He went on to advise me that maybe I should look into the actions and attitudes of our battalion drug rehabilitation counselor. The drug counselor was a "Mr. Milquetoast," wimpy looking sort; a specialist fourth class and a loner who ran his own drug rehab and counseling shop. Obviously he was not making much headway with that endeavor. When I inquired of his whereabouts I was told he was off on R & R (Rest and Relaxation leave) and would be gone for another week.

I went to the battalion sergeant major and gave him the info that I had and together we went to this lad's office and sleeping area. He actually had about half a hootch all to himself. The door was padlocked. But, lo and behold, the hinges were screwed in from the outside. The sergeant major left and a few minutes later returned with a screwdriver and we did a little unauthorized entry. Once inside we were astounded by what we found. Very little drug counseling material was there but a whole bunch of literature that knocked our socks off. This lad was deep into black radical issues and propaganda. There were stacks of propaganda flyers and broadsides trumpeting black revolution. One broadside was titled something like "The Liberator." The headline read "Black Brothers Score Great Victory" and went on to tell a fictional story describing an attack on a car in the Mississippi Delta about the year 1980. In the article a white family had been wiped out the night before by the glorious black forces. This was really grim and intimidating material. We took samples of all the bad stuff making sure there were no signs of our entry and then re-secured the door and left. The literature we found was shown to the battalion CO and then passed to the Army Criminal Investigation Division Office at Phu Bai proper. We were told to keep quiet about our find. We did that but kept a wary eye out for signs and indications of further even more serious discontent.

There was so much happening that I am sure I am not going to get all the rest in proper sequence but I am going to do my best. Shortly after the rehab counselor incident the battalion commander left on R & R and I became the acting battalion commander. When he returned he became the acting brigade commander as the brigade commander then went on R & R. So I ended up leading the 1-502nd in a combat environment for a full month and a couple of days. This was to prove in most ways a challenging but rewarding month. I did not get a report card (Officer's Efficiency Report) for that thirty day period in command; thirty days being the magic number for which an OER was supposed to be submitted. My service as battalion commander was not mentioned in my efficiency report for serving as the battalion executive officer either. The battalion commander sensed, I am sure, that I did not have a lot of respect for him.

At any rate I spent the next thirty days pretty much in the field on various firebases and loving the chance to command. It was interesting to say the least.

One of the first things that happened was that we were sent to Firebase (FSB) Rifle to relieve a battalion of the Division that was back filling for an Army of Vietnam unit up north on another Lam Son operation in southern Laos. I remember walking up the road and entering FSB Rifle while LTC Kenny Leuer, who had been with me at Infantry Branch, led his battalion off the base and walked down to waiting trucks that had brought us there. We exchanged a few words and he informed me that all had been quiet while his troops had been there. Rifle is significant in this tome for one reason. I will not try to describe all that went on there but will insert here three pages from a book entitled *The Sentinel and the Shooter* that pretty well sum up the significance of our time at FSB Rifle.

Extracted from *The Sentinel and the Shooter*, by Douglas W. Bonnot, with author's permission pages 283 to 285:

> ...One exception was FSB Rifle occupied by the 1/502nd Infantry Battalion (AMBL) when a three man team deployed there in late October in support of a second Brigade initiative. A new acting Battalion commander, Major Larry Redmond, had assumed command of the Battalion two weeks earlier. By the end of his third day on FSB Rifle he had completed a thorough inspection of the FSB defenses, organic and supporting weapons and communications elements.
>
> Major Redmond had settled into the Battalion TOC and gathered his staff to brief them on the results of his inspection. As the details of the items to be addressed were prioritized, discussed and the action items agreed upon, the discussion turned casually to the action on the hill a few months earlier when the base was overrun by NVA sappers.

"Yeah, I heard about that. Wasn't there a Chaplain that took part in the assault to regain the hill," asked one of the junior officers.

"Took part? I heard he led the assault with only an SFC from the 326th Engineers and a medic backing him up," offered another.

"Young was his name a Captain with the 1/501st if I recall," added yet another.

"Pardon me Sir, there's a young man here who insists on seeing you about something important," one of the Battalion RTOs interrupted from the doorway.

"What is it about, Sergeant?" asked the major?

"He wouldn't say, sir, but he says it is really important and will speak only with you."

"Curious. Ok gentlemen, if there are no further questions, let's get to the tasks at hand. Sergeant, ask the soldier to come in." The major rolled up the map he had been using during the briefing, rose and handed it to the RTO to be secured.

"Come in young man. Tell me who you are and exactly what is so important that you had to interrupt my staff meeting?"

"I can't tell you that, Sir, but you must come with me now," insisted the soldier.

"You can't tell me who you are?" The major's voice raised an octave, his eyebrows rose noticeably and he seemed to rise on the balls of his feet, his head cocked slightly to one side.

"Please, Sir, it's imperative."

The major surveyed the young soldier before him. A rather nervous sort he thought, no name tag or insignia of rank, although he was wearing the Screaming Eagle shoulder patch of the Division. It wasn't unusual for soldiers to become unkempt in the field but even the few amenities available on the FSBs were usually enough to...

"Sir! Please, we haven't much time. You must come with me now!"

The young soldier was very insistent and never before having heard a junior enlisted man use the word imperative, Major Redmond's curiosity was piqued. He decided to learn what the excitement was all about, "Lead on soldier," he said.

They stepped quickly outside the TOC and the Battalion Commander was only slightly surprised that darkness had fallen since his staff meeting had begun more than an hour earlier. They made their way along the trench line until they reached the young soldier's bunker.

Major Redmond paused and looked around. Even in the darkness he was certain he had not previously visited this bunker. He had thought that he had inspected them all.

How had he missed this one? He looked around again to orient himself to a known reference.

"In here, Sir." The young soldier, holding a blackout curtain aside, beckoned the Battalion Commander inside.

Major Redmond entered and took a moment for his eyes to adjust to even to the dim lights of the interior. "What is this…?"

There were two other men in the bunker. One rose and assumed what could only be described as a modified position of pseudo attention. The other sitting with his back to the entrance was bent forward, his left hand pressing a set of headphones close to his ear. His right hand, clutching a pencil, shot up in an unmistakable gesture requesting silence. It dropped abruptly as he began to write furiously on the back of a C ration carton. The soldier, the three man team leader that had led the Major to the bunker, quickly spread a map on a small table, glanced at the soldier who had just removed his headphones and turned to see who had arrived. Unimpressed he went back to his radio.

"Major," the Team Leader said, "At this moment, there is an NVA Regiment massing on this hill some four kilometers away. It is their intention to occupy FSB Rifle before morning. I can't tell you how I know that and I don't have the authority to even tell you what I just have. However, I do know this: I can't do anything about that Regiment but you can. I also know that whatever will be your fate come sunup, will be mine also."

The Team Leader glanced again at the radio operator who nodded his head and said, "Tonight for sure."

He folded up the map, handed the major a slip of paper with the grid coordinates of the hill he had just indicated on the map.

"We've still got work to do here, Major, but thanks for listening. I think you can find your way back to the TOC, right?"

Major Redmond turned to go and with one quick backwards glance, shook his head and exited the bunker.

"Sergeant" he called as he reached his TOC. Get Brigade on the secure net and see if we have any Air Force in the area that we might be able to divert an Arc Light (a trio of B-52 bombers) onto these coordinates in next couple of hours. Tell Brigade to check that out as quickly as possible and I'll give them a SITREP later." He handed the slip of paper to the RTO. "And get the Company Commanders back here in fifteen minutes."

Half an hour later, and after several heated secure radio exchanges with the Brigade Operations Officer, S3, the Major had finally convinced them to talk with the parent unit of the "team" whose call sign the major had insisted could explain more. After bringing the company commanders up to speed on the real possibility of a major assault on the firebase that night everyone settled in to wait

Approximately 90 minutes later the RTO announced that Division reported they had succeeded in diverting a USAF B-52 strike, or Arc Light, and that gunships and Tac Air were also on alert.

The night passed without incident except for a rather loud and long rumbling accompanied by a noticeable shaking of the ground in and around FSB Rifle. At first light the RTO, rubbing his eyes with his free hand set a cup of hot coffee down in front of his new commander. He thought to himself, "curious, you don't often see a Battalion commander smiling."

"Sergeant, ask the sergeant major to join me immediately."

"Listen, Sergeant Major," he said, as the sergeant major, coffee in hand, stepped inside the TOC. "I know who those guys are and I want you to keep an eye on them. Let me know if they do anything strange."

"Could you be more specific, Sir? Seems to me that everything they do is strange."

"Roger that, Ummm, well just let me know if you see them packing and it looks like they are going to leave. I am going to get a couple of hours sleep; wake me if anything important comes up.

"Sleep?" The Sergeant Major glanced at his watch. "Sleep?"

"And peacefully I might add.......

The words written on previous page convey what happened that night. The gist of the story is true and happened as Doug Bonnot wrote it. I would add that in addition to the loud rumbling and shaking that accompanied the Arc Light bombing we observed flashes off in the distance. Doug got the information from his Team Leader who related it to him when he was researching operations and happenings from their time in Vietnam. He published it in his History of the 265th Radio Research Company. That unit was a unique and valued military asset that worked behind the "green door" (Army Security Agency radio intercept) with little recognition, where much recognition was deserved. I did not know this tale was being told until Doug sent me a copy of the unit history. It was quite a surprise to see it in print.

Not sure how long after this happening, but about five or six days later we were relieved by a battalion of the ARVN First Division and were trucked back to Phu Bai with no problems encountered. Rifle was not a terribly pleasing place to be situated as it had high ground on three sides. Not sure why we or the ARVN ever went there to begin with. It closely mimicked another SE Asia battle site called Dien Bien Phu.

(ABOVE) Fort Devens, MA.
ROTC Summer Camp, 1961.

(LEFT) Fort Benning, GA.
Jump School, August 1962.

Fort MacPherson, GA. The Devlin-Redmond wedding, 7-6-63.

The 'Old Man' Commander of Choppin Charlie 1-506 Airborne Infantry, Fort Campbell, KY, 1964.

(BELOW) End of Desert Strike One, the Mojave Desert, 1964. LT Redmond standing far left, with moustache.

8th Special Forces Group, Exercise Seabreeze-Savage Trade, Salinas Army Training Center, Puerto Rico, early 1967.

(BELOW) Larry and Mary, Canal Zone 1967, before he departed for Vietnam. 8th Group Commander Colonel Magnus Smith standing to the left rear.

(ABOVE) The S1 Team, Duc Pho Vietnam ,1967. *Left to right*: LT Luker, CPT Redmond, SPEC 4 Carrillo (Honoree), Major Kupua, SPEC 4 Hurley, SPEC 5 Herron.

Award Ceremony, Duc Pho, Vietnam, Army Commendation Medal for Service with 8th Special Forces Group.

"Exterminator 6"
commanding A Company
2-327, Airborne
Infantry. Vietnam,
1968.

Firebase in the not
at all hospitable
Que Son Valley,
1967.

Telefax — **western union** — Telefax

703A EST FEB 28 68 AA005
SPC58 CTA051 A CT WA035 XV GOVT PDB
WASHINGTON DC 27 1137P EST
MRS MARY E REDMOND, DONT PHONE
2617 RICE ST COLUMBUS GA
THE SECRETARY OF THE ARMY HAS ASKED ME TO INFORM YOU THAT YOUR
HUSBAND CAPTAIN LAWRENCE A REDMOND WAS SLIGHTLY WOUNDED IN
VIETNAM ON 25 FEB 68 AS A RESULT OF HOSTILE ACTION. HE RECEIVED
METAL FRAGMENT WOUND TO LEFT ARM AND CHEST. HE WAS ON COMBAT
OPERATION WHEN HIT BY FRAGMENTS FROM HOSTILE MORTAR ROUND.
HE WAS TREATED AND HELD AT THE 3RD MEDICAL BATTALION INVIETNAM.
ADDRESS MAIL TO HIM AT THE HOSPITAL MAIL SECTION APO SF 96381.
SINCE HE IS NOT REPEAT NOT SERIOUSLY WOUNDED NO FURTHER REPORTS
WILL BE FURNISHED
    KENNETH G WICKHAM MAJOR GENERAL USA THE ADJUTANT GENERAL
    (97).

FEB 28 1968

(ABOVE) Slightly wounded! A bit of a misstatement considering eight months hospital and recovery time.

Promotion to major, 1969, at Fort Benning, GA during the Infantry Officer Advanced Course.

Operations Officer
1-502 Airborne
Infantry. Phu Bai,
Vietnam, 1971.

Award of Joint Service Commendation Medal by Colonel Raney,
Headquarters MACV-J3 Operations, Force Development. Saigon, 1972.

24
A NEAR REBELLION:
THE PHU BAI THIRTEEN

We were not in Phu Bai long before we airlifted out to Fire Support Base Birmingham due west of Phu Bai and began patrolling in that area of the Piedmont. Shortly after beginning operations around Birmingham one of our companies that had spent the previous four months guarding the ammo dump located in Danang was sent back to Phu Bai and returned to our control. The Danang duty was pretty soft stuff, no humping rucksacks up and down the hills, through the jungle and across streams along with all the unpleasant aspects of jungle living. We planned to insert them in the Piedmont area near Birmingham. The morning of the insertion, into a cold landing zone secured by one of our other companies, the weather was good at Phu Bai and at the LZ. But at Birmingham the fog was like pea soup all over and around the firebase. We could not get airborne to over watch the insert. There was no critical reason to be overhead for a cold insert so the insertion went on as scheduled.

Shortly after the company had landed I received a radio call from the rear stating that 13 soldiers had refused the order to deploy and were now at Phu Bai refusing to talk to anyone except the "major." At that point I could get no further info and informed the battalion rear that I would be returning to Phu Bai as soon as the weather cleared. I called the company in the field to talk to the commander only to learn that his XO was in the field with the troops. The company commander had remained in the rear with the troops who refused the order to deploy. That did not sit well with me.

The weather cleared about an hour later and I flew to the rear battalion landing pad. Once there I walked immediately to the company area and found the company commander along with the Division Provost Marshal (PM), a bunch of MPs and a representative from the Division Judge Advocate General's (JAG) office. I spoke with the company commander who had no excuse for staying at Phu Bai while his troops were being inserted in bad guy land. As we talked it appeared he was pretty shaken by things. He had in fact placed all thirteen recalcitrant soldiers in the same hootch. Things really got dicey when he told me that they had not been disarmed and still had their weapons and ammunition to include hand grenades. At that point I was totally dumbfounded. This was a West Point officer who should have known better. Common sense dictated that at least the bad guys should have been disarmed. After a short conversation with the JAG representative concerning the Uniform Code of Military Justice violations facing these lads I turned to the Division PM and told him I was going to enter the hootch and said: "If I am not out in five minutes waste them all." I know, hard to believe. Do not ask me why I ever said it, but I did!

It was about a thirty yard walk to the hootch but it seemed like three hundred. I entered and was confronted by 13 black soldiers all talking at once about their grievances and that they had truly been wronged. I told them that I was not talking with any group of 13 soldiers, about their perceived wrongs. I explained that I saw green, Army green, and talked only with individual soldiers, they were not a union. I explained to them that they were at that point all guilty of a Federal Offense in refusing to go to the field. Their guilt was not negotiable in that they were in that hootch and not in the field. I explained they would have a choice of how they could proceed and that the Division JAG was coming in to explain their rights to them. I then told them I would call for each man individually to come out and we would talk. I turned and walked out expecting to be shot at any moment. When I came out, the JAG officer went in and explained their rights under the Uniform Code of Military Justice. I know that JAG was scared because I was terrified – honestly more frightened than any other time in my life; including several darned good firefights written about earlier in this tale.

While waiting for the JAG to finish his briefing, knowing what the mutinous troopers' options were, I requested and was immediately granted two helicopters. The choppers were positioned on the resupply pad not far from the Battalion HQ. One could see the helicopters from the office. I also did some quick research on what had prompted the incident and tried to formulate what I thought would be a correct response to what I believed I would be hearing. When the JAG finished he came by and again told me what he had passed on to the guilty troopers. When he finished, with several MPs surrounding the HQ, I called for each soldier by name. Surprising me, they all came out individually and were disarmed for our meeting. Each soldier was offered the opportunity to get on one of those two helicopters. One would take them directly to the field and their company and they would receive a Summary Court Martial from me at a later time. If they refused the Summary Court then the other chopper would take them to Long Binh Jail and a Special Court Martial that could dispense "really hard justice." By the way, Long Binh Jail was not a pleasant experience. Or so I had been told and the troops knew the same stories about, as they called it, LBJ. It was not somewhere you wanted to go.

I did give each of them the opportunity to explain their perceived grievances. I won't bore you with the full thirteen stories. They were basically all the same. In a nutshell the problem was out and out discrimination against a brother – at least that is how they saw it. Seems the wronged trooper had been in the field for the same number of months as the lad who got the job of company clerk. Nice reward for having humped the boonies; but also a very important job. Each soldier kept telling me the same story and a thread, and name, began to appear. After they talked I asked them if the aggrieved trooper had a High School Diploma, or, and even more important, could he type? In every instance the response was, "I don't know, but what difference does any of that make." I then asked them if they wanted their Combat Infantry Badge orders; promotion orders; pay kept straight; R&R processed on time and lastly their end of tour awards and orders back to the states. They all responded that they did. I then informed them that the aggrieved trooper did not have even a General Educational Development Certificate and couldn't type a word; probably couldn't spell typewriter. That was the truth.

All but one of the guilty soldiers opted to get on the chopper and rejoin their company in the field. The one recalcitrant individual who refused and opted for the trip to LBJ was the soldier whose name came up in almost every discussion as the prime instigator of this refusal to go to the field. It turns out that he was a former sergeant with a previous tour in Vietnam. After that tour he had returned stateside, left the Army, and then traveled via Mexico to Cuba. He had spent eighteen months in one of Castro's *Venceremos* brigades being thoroughly brainwashed and radicalized. He then returned to the U.S., reenlisted and volunteered to go to Vietnam. He was assigned to the 101st where he became a trouble maker of the first magnitude. He was very successful at that. He refused to go to the field and I had the Provost Marshal ship him off under guard to Saigon and jail.

Redmond's Rule # 15 – Forgive and forget, but first get even.

We only learned all the facts about his background after the fact. I am not sure what punishment was meted out to him but I hope it was time in Leavenworth and a dishonorable discharge. I later held

Summary Courts Martial for the other twelve guilty soldiers and took away all stripes and hit them hard in the pocket book. This was a case of revolt in the ranks and needed to be squelched hard.

A few days before Christmas while we were still operating around Birmingham the Bob Hope Holiday USO Show was coming to Phu Bai that night. At that point we were under the operational control of another sister brigade. Our Battalion Heavy Mortar Platoon leader told me that we were running low on high explosive ammunition for the mortars. I had the logistics officer request a resupply. That request, because it required a heavy lift helicopter to move the ammo to us, was denied by the brigade operations people in Phu Bai. I had the supply personnel request the ammo again. This second request was also turned down. Not to be denied I went directly to Division and requested an immediate "TAC E" (Tactical Emergency) resupply of the needed ammo. We got our ammunition but I also got a devil of a counseling on declaring a "TAC E" when not in heavy contact with the enemy. I was told the Bob Hope show came off without a hitch. Had the bad guys tried to launch mortars that night, at Phu Bai and Mr. Hope, we were ready to respond. I believe had we been under the control of our parent brigade this incident would never have happened.

Sometime shortly after this we were directed to move the battalion to Camp Evans, where the First Brigade had its base camp. The mission was to provide camp perimeter security as the First Brigade stood down, moved down to Phu Bai, and prepared for return to the States. This was the beginning of the Division's deployment home and exit from Vietnam. We basically secured the perimeter and did local patrolling for three days while the brigade moved south to Phu Bai lock stock and barrel. On the last day, about noon, word came down that the brigade was fully out of Camp Evans. They had pulled everyone out. The Vietnamese First Division had a battalion already on site and occupying bunkers as fast as we could vacate them. The brigade operations officer told me that he would be flying out with the commander but that there would be a helicopter up over Highway 1 to ensure we had radio communication to Phu Bai as we came down Highway 1. He then departed on a helicopter with the colonel and other staff officers.

About an hour and half later, around 1400, and as the last of the battalion arrived in the center of the camp to join up with our trucks, the S3 NCO came into the command bunker and said; "Sir you had better come see this, you are not going to believe it." When I stepped out into the semi dark, overcast, cloudy and chilly I Corps afternoon, I was horrified. There must have been, not just the trucks to move us to Phu Bai, but I estimate 100 plus more vehicles of all sizes and descriptions to include jeeps, three-quarter ton trucks, deuce and half trucks, a platoon of stake and platform trucks other support vehicles and perhaps 2,000 additional people! These were the brigade and Camp Evans support elements. But the operations officer had told me they had vacated the camp; and were all gone! This was a major issue. It was mid-afternoon, cloud cover was about 200 feet up and it would be dark in about three hours.

The S3 looked at me and I said something like, "OK we're going south. We have four rifle companies. Make up four serials, one company to secure each serial, front and rear security for each serial and we are getting out of here by 1600: questions? Make it happen." And he did. I turned and said good bye and good luck to the Vietnamese Army lieutenant colonel whose troops replaced us and I prepared to leave. I was not happy about moving this totally ad hoc gaggle down the infamous Highway 1, the *Street Without Joy*, made famous by Bernard Fall in his book of that name about the French Indochina War. It was quite an inhospitable place.

We started south a little late, but still time to clear Hue City before dark. Guess what? Yep, you got it; we had no helicopter relay up over Highway 1. We had no, repeat no, radio contact with Division till we were south of Hue and approaching Phu Bai. That trip down Highway 1 to Phu Bai had my pucker factor so high I am surprised

I did not have a stroke. We were totally on our own, no nearby help and no contact with any friendlies except those in the column. We made the trip without incident, not even a broken down vehicle. When I got to Phu Bai I was furious and tried to sort this out with the brigade staff. I was told to basically forget it. "You're here and all is OK". The next time I saw the brigade operations officer involved in leaving us high and dry he was a major general. He went on to get four stars. Enough said on that.

One morning just after resuming my duties as battalion XO I walked to the door of my hootch and upon opening it found two members of the recon platoon, armed, standing there. I asked them what they were doing here and why they were not out in the bush. They told me I needed to talk with their platoon sergeant. When I tracked him down I learned that the word was out that the brothers in Phu Bai did not appreciate me and that they were going to frag me. Fragging, as you may recall was when a disgruntled troop tossed a hand grenade into a leader's tent or hootch. Sadly this was still quite popular in Vietnam at the time. When the recon platoon got wind of that they asked the battalion commander to be allowed to return to Phu Bai and see that nothing happened to me. They had gone all over Phu Bai and told the brothers that if anyone screwed with me they would not like the message that would follow. For about a week they kept an element in the rear that basically guarded my quarters and me. I owe my commander and the recon troops for that one and possibly for my life as well.

Then things came to a real head with the black radicals. One of our first sergeants, an African American, who had just come back from R & R came to see me. He knew some of the things that the sergeant major and I had uncovered. Seems sitting in the C-130 heading north from Saigon he had been surrounded by brothers who talked freely thinking that being black he was on their team. He told me that they had been talking about the "Big Brother" from Saigon coming to Phu Bai and then things would really happen. I notified the Army Criminal Investigation Division (CID) of what he had told me and put it out of my mind. About two nights later I was lying in my bunk listening to Armed Forces Vietnam radio when a tune I had not heard before was played. It was titled "Hey Big Brother" and was apparently not just a hit in Vietnam but also back in "the world." The words hit me right in the gut. They smacked of rebellion in my mind. I could not remember the words exactly after forty-four years so I looked them up on the Internet to make sure I could remember them. They went something like: Hey Big Brother, we are tired of waiting, tell us what to do, no one wants to die, Big Brother is coming, what you gonna do. This whole thing sounded like a radical call to arms.

I couldn't sleep the rest of the night. Was I paranoid? Rebellion, revolt what was brewing? At any rate the next morning I called the CID again and an agent came to see me that afternoon. He listened politely and I thought he was going to tell me to go get some rest. But he did not. He calmly said to me, "Did you ever hear of the Sepoy Rebellion?" I responded, "Sure, India, British Muslim troops revolted in the mid-1850s. Real bloody mess, took a year or better to quell it." He said, without batting an eye that we were on the cusp of a Sepoy Rebellion by some of our black troops there at Phu Bai. He told me that they were tracking the "big brother" from Saigon and that things were going to happen. Later, before dark, I flew out to the field and briefed the Commander on what was going on. Or at least what I thought was going on. He was not surprised but added that I should watch out. I slept with a loaded .45 pistol next to my bunk for the next couple of days.

The Army then descended on Phu Bai with a bunch of CID folks and scooped up most of the leaders. It turned out we lost four or five troops in the roundup to include the Drug Counselor and the specialist fifth class cook I had confronted in the mess hall the first night I was XO. He was reported to be a main organizer at Phu Bai. Sounds like a good move by the Army right? Wrong. They did not court martial any of them but sent them to different units all around Vietnam. I guess the rationale was that since we were pulling out rapidly, and it would take some time for them to try to reorganize, that this solution beat a series of major court-martials with all the publicity that would entail. Frankly I do not agree, but there it is. At least as far as I know, that is what happened. It was not a good scene, nor one I would want to go through again.

Before I leave you with the impression that all our black troops were a problem let me set the record straight. There were some truly great troops out there especially the lads who walked the jungle and fought for their buddies of all colors. The young sergeant who first alerted me to our questionable drug counselor; the sergeant first class who tore down the drug hootch; and the first sergeant who told me of the Big Brother's pending visit to Phu Bai are only a few of the black troops/leaders who soldiered and soldiered well. Of the recon platoon troops who protected my hootch when the Phu Bai radicals were going to frag me about one third were black.

I recall also a happening one day near the mess hall. A black soldier walked past me without saluting. I saluted him and wished him a good day. He seemed a little flustered and sheepishly returned my salute—he had seen me, of that there was no doubt. Then I noticed that he had a slave bracelet about five inches long on his right wrist and forearm. Slave bracelets woven from boot laces were popular and ran the gamut from a small wrist adornment to a full up gauntlet running from just below the elbow down to and over the hand forming a gauntlet type affair. The Army had directed that all bracelets would be no more than one inch in width. I looked the lad in the eye and told him that the bracelet had to come off, a one inch bracelet was OK but that was all. He looked back and said, "Major Redmond, you an all right dude, sir, but remember, I have to live with my brothers." I looked at him and simply said, "One inch trooper, got it?" I saw him several days later near Battalion HQ and he threw me a super salute. The bracelet was now one inch wide. He smiled and I smiled back as I returned his salute. All he needed was to be pointed in the right direction. It was a true shame that those thirteen troops who were misled, well twelve troops since one of them was an incorrigible radical, did not get better leadership. There were a lot more good black soldiers than bad out there in Nam, even at this point in the war.

Our battalion received orders to prepare to stand down and redeploy to the States, in this case returning to Fort Campbell. They told me I would be going home with the troops. This was after just over six months into my second tour. I said no, I wanted to spend the next six months as an advisor with the Vietnamese Airborne Division. I was told that you just didn't get into the Airborne Advisory Team, the Red Hats; that they selected you. I looked at the Division G1 representative and said, "Send them my record. Airborne, Special Forces, Airborne Company Command in Vietnam, Silver Star, battalion S3—they will take me in a heartbeat." Guess what, they turned me down; didn't want me. I was one disappointed soldier; unknowingly I was also one lucky guy. When the Easter Offensive of 1972 started several months later the ARVN Red Hat Advisory Detachment took very heavy casualties.

The USARV G1 did get me a job at Long Binh in the IG Office so I would be able to finish my second tour in Vietnam. Although this assignment proved short lived it was to be an eye opener. I was given a small cubicle, a desk and two four drawer filing cabinets filled with case material.

I was told to review and get smart about the Article 32 Investigation the IG had prepared on Colonel David Hackworth. An Article 32 Investigation is the preliminary step conducted to see if a General Court Martial is called for based on an analysis of the facts available. "Hack" as he was known by those who liked him was quite a controversial and colorful character. He entered the Army at the end of WWII at the age of fifteen, fought in Korea, and served almost five years in Vietnam. Lots of controversy surrounded his career. In his book *About Face*, as a battalion commander in the 101st Airborne First Brigade in 1966, one could get the impression that he had hand grenades bouncing off his body before breakfast and again before dinner. He had a chest full of awards.

In the spring of 1971 he had given an interview to the media in which he stated that the "war" was lost and that we should get out now. The military hierarchy was not at all happy with him. Late in 1971, he had been allowed to retire in lieu of court martial and had, by this time settled in Australia where he became a very successful businessman. I was not sure why I was tasked to look through his Article 32 files. Was someone considering reopening the investigation? I was not to find out. I was only there a little over a week and had waded through two file drawers of statements, reports, allegations, exhibits and whatever. All I really remember was that if even ten percent of what I was reading was true; then this Screaming Eagle, and well known hero, combat leader was a great disappointment to me.

My boss, the Deputy IG, walked in one morning and said. "Redmond, who the hell do you know? I am in receipt of a message from the Office of Personnel Operations, Infantry Branch to get you reassigned to a meaningful job." The Infantry Branch mafia had struck again. I was reassigned to Military Assistance Command Vietnam (MACV), J3 Operations Force Development Branch. It was a joint, all services, assignment and supposedly more career enhancing. This ended my short, less than two week stint as an Inspector General.

Frankly I think it would have been fun to continue working COL Hackworth's Article 32. I do know that it is correct that he was never court-martialed but retired from the Army and after a few months in Spain had settled in Australia. Rumor at MACV, and I stress rumor, was that part of the deal was retirement and not returning to the USA; the quid pro quo being no court martial and all that might come out at such an event. Fact is that "Hack" did return to the States to retire and then spent a few months in Spain; or at least that is what his book states. Hackworth lived in Australia for a number of years and became a successful restaurateur that much is certain. Then he came back to the States where he became an outspoken critic of the upper echelons of the Army. There was nothing good or proper about the "Perfumed Princes," as he termed them, running the Army. He had a following in the junior officer ranks and among the enlisted troops that bordered on worship. In many eyes he could do nothing wrong and everything he said was gospel. For a while he was a "talking head" on military matters for various TV network news programs. He always wore a black turtle neck and a black sport coat; in my mind he did not look like the professional soldier he claimed to be. He died several years ago. In his book, in the last chapter he verified much of what I had read in the Article 32 Investigation files. But the admissions were cast in a light that certainly did not merit court martial and reflected well on Colonel Hackworth. We will never know the whole story.

As a side bar to my sojourn at USARV IG let me add a short tale worth relating. One afternoon I had returned after lunch to my BOQ (Bachelor Officer Quarters), only a block or so from my office. Lo and behold who should come down the hall but Major Fred Caristo! Fred had not changed a bit. We greeted each other with a big hug, like long lost brothers. The last time I had seen Fred was at my wedding in July 1963. There in the BOQ he stood in dirty rumpled tiger stripe fatigues, camouflage on his face and mini hand grenades, the real thing, hanging from his load bearing equipment. He was a sight. We talked for a few minutes and he gave me some cock and bull story about who he worked for without divulging any real info and told me that he had just returned from a recon but could not say where he had been. I have not seen Fred since that chance encounter, but have recently learned that he is a real hero. He served in MACV Studies and Observations Group (SOG, really clandestine operations) and won a Distinguished Service Cross for actions on a failed Bright Light (prisoner rescue) Mission. I was not aware of this until I read a really intriguing book, *SOG*, written by Major (Retired) John L. Plaster. Talk about heroes! There were many unsung heroes who worked SOG reconnaissance missions. Their exploits are legend in the Vietnam Special Forces community. I have nothing but great respect and admiration for those men who crossed the borders and sought out the North Vietnamese in their sanctuaries. But, of course, none of that cross border stuff ever happened.

I did have some interesting times at MACV J3 Force Development. I moved from a BOQ at Long Binh to the Missouri BOQ in downtown

Saigon. Not a bad deal and I shared a room with an officer I would meet again at Fort Bragg. His name was Raphael Hallada, a senior artillery major. He worked the night shift in the J3 Operations Center so we really saw each other very little. Basically we each had an almost private BOQ room. I saw Raphael again when he was COL Hallada, the Chief of Staff of the 82nd Airborne Division when I was the XO of the Third "Golden Brigade" on Ardennes Street at Fort Bragg. He went on to become a two star general; a good guy and solid soldier.

When the Spring Offensive of 1972 started I experienced several happenings that are of interest. One morning early, as I was taking a shortcut through the MACV Command Center, on my way to the office, I heard a briefer telling GEN Abrams that "Hiep Duc in the Que Son Valley continues to hold out." Now as a point of reference you may remember during my first tour with the First Brigade 101st Airborne that we were out in the Que Son Valley. That was the place that A Company had a platoon and the HQ element overrun and where the recoilless rifle shot at us every day until we pulled out. Well Hiep Duc was now a District HQ that when we were out near there had not been occupied by friendlies since the Viet Minh chased out the French in '54. I waited till GEN Abrams had moved on to the next Corps area map for his continued briefing and then approached the briefer and challenged him on the tale. He told me that the Vietnamese Army had reoccupied the area about two years earlier. They had established a District HQ, an ARVN element, a battalion of Regional Force soldiers and a battery of 105mm artillery was located there. I was amazed and impressed. Each morning on my way to work as I took the shortcut through the command center he would give me a thumbs up signifying that the base at Hiep Duc continued to hold out. After about five days the thumb went down. I stopped and he told me, "They haven't been overrun but are coming out with all the guns, the families and all the livestock from the area. They cannot be reinforced and so they are giving up the place but they are coming out proud." At that point I honestly thought that the South Vietnamese might yet have a chance to survive.

Shortly thereafter for some reason I was in the command center when GEN Abrams was being briefed on the big fight up at An Loc where the NVA were locked in a house to house fight with the Vietnamese Army (ARVN). The ARVN were resisting mightily but they were hard pressed by, reportedly, a large number of tanks. The J2, Chief of Intelligence, was insisting that no tanks had come down the Ho Chi Minh trail so the staff position was that tanks in An Loc was not possible. It had to be a bad report. The next morning the *Stars and Stripes* front page heralded the battle with a picture of a burning T34 tank in the center of An Loc. So much for the J2's monitoring of the trail. Turns out no tanks had come down the trail, that is, none under their own power. The North Vietnamese had transported them down the trail on "low boy" flatbed trucks. Hence no tracked vehicles were ever reported as reaching Cambodia since the sensors, vice human eyes, reported vehicles with tires coming south. So much for the ballyhooed hi tech sensor based intelligence gathering. Nothing replaces human intelligence and eyes on the target.

A few days later the USMC Advisor to the Vietnamese Marines in I Corps was brought to Saigon to meet with GEN Abrams (aka Abe). We thought he was brought down to be chastised for requesting that the U.S. Fleet, off shore, "Land the Landing Force" (a reinforced battalion of U.S. Marines) to support the Vietnamese Marines at a key bridge north of Hue. I was not privy to the conversations but through the grape vine heard that Abe, who could be very hard core, was pretty gentle with the Marine and told him he admired his courage but landing the USMC back in I Corps was not politically acceptable.

A major confrontation then took place in the Force Development Office. The original Chief of Force Development returned to the U.S.

and was replaced by COL Frank Garrison, an old 101st Screaming Eagle and a good man. His best friend, it turned out, was the Senior Advisor to the ARVN Airborne Detachment and he came to see COL Garrison. In the course of the conversation, which we in the outer office could all hear, a comment was made to the effect, "Yeh, now with the big battle on we can't get any replacements for our wounded. Everyone is afraid to come where the fight is!" I sat there as long as I could take it and finally stormed into the boss's office and unloaded on the good colonel about my efforts to join his damned outfit two months before. I flat stated that I did not appreciate being called a coward, in so many words. The two colonels looked a little dumb struck and I just turned and walked out. The ARVN Airborne Advisory Detachment Commander departed shortly thereafter, without so much as a fare-thee-well. Colonel Garrison later told me that I was right in what I had said.

We in Force Development were active in bringing back to Vietnam some special U.S. assets that were key to helping the South Vietnamese stop the NVA invasion. I got in real hot water with the J3 lieutenant general over the movement of some Tube Launched Wire Guided (TOW) anti-armor teams from Fort Bragg, 82nd Airborne Division troops. They were being sent to Pleiku up in the Highlands. The NVA, with tanks, that again had not come down the Ho Chi Minh Trail, but were there in the highlands by magic, were pressing the South Vietnamese hard. For some reason the J3 wanted the TOW teams from the 82nd to come to Saigon and then be flown up to Pleiku from there. I wrote a dissenting paper saying send them directly to Pleiku. My non concurrence pointed out that we could save a day and half and get the TOWs into action faster by sending them directly into Pleiku and the airstrip there was safe.

The J3 XO, who went on to be a three star general, initially refused to send my dissenting memo to the J3 since he had told GEN Abrams that the TOWs were coming to Saigon first. OK, just tell Abe that there had been a change in plans. Uh, that wasn't too likely. The J3

XO and I got into it and I said some nasty things, major to major. He finally did send the memo in to the J3 who refused to discuss the matter with GEN Abrams. My name was mud. The TOWs came to Saigon first and I kept a low profile around the J3 for quite a while. Later, when the TOW Teams did go into action they were of great service and there was a picture of one in *Stars and Stripes* taking out an NVA machine gun up on a water tower near Pleiku. Bringing those U.S. Airborne troops back into Vietnam was one hell of an issue. I was told, the final approval came from President Johnson himself; but I cannot swear to that. Fortunately none of the troops who came over were killed and as the NVA offensive died out the teams were quietly returned to the USA. Since the story made Stars and Stripes, and identified the TOW teams as part of the 82nd Airborne, it would seem that this information is no longer classified.

That pretty well sums up my time in Saigon, except that I did find a great French restaurant with superb French Onion Soup and rolls. It was called *Le Bon Fouchette* and they served fantastic food and the coldest *Ba Muoi Ba* beer in Saigon. I passed a few nice evenings there and on the veranda of the Hotel Continental watching the traffic stream by. My orders back to the States came in assigning me to Fort Benning where I had left the family; another example of the Infantry Branch Mafia taking care of its own. I was pleased and looked forward to whatever awaited me at Benning. Having completed a second tour, half of it directly in harm's way, I could look any Infantryman in the eye and feel I had also done my part.

26
TRAINING INFANTRYMEN,
1972

The assignment to Fort Benning, and the Infantry School, was something I looked forward to. Mary and the children were settled there in a nice home and it made my transition to the school environment and teaching easy. I was posted to Brigade and Battalion Operations Department (BBOD), at that time the premier element in the school. The director of BBOD was COL Larry Mowery, the former chief of staff of the 101st Airborne Division from 1968. (It was he who told me I would have a new company the day after the engagement at An Phu during TET.) I was assigned to the Attack Committee as a battalion offensive operations instructor. My direct boss was to be LTC Guy S. (Sandy) Meloy. I was slated to be the replacement for the most highly regarded instructor in BBOD at the time, Major Ray Wagner, who was on orders to Korea. Ray was great with the students and always got high marks on the course critique sheets the students filled out

First, if I was going to be an instructor I had to attend and pass the Instructor Training Course (ITC) which was very challenging. There really were no freebies in ITC. If you failed to meet their standards you did not teach at the Infantry School. The key was to do what they called Vs and Ws (moving backward and then forward) as one walked around the teaching platform. You also had to have a good delivery, an in depth knowledge of your subject and the ability to think on your feet. The time at Infantry Branch had ensured that I could speak and think on my feet, so the rest was just paying attention to what one had to do to meet their stringent requirements. While I waited for the next ITC Class to commence I lived in the classroom with Major Wagner learning all that I could from him about offensive tactics and operations. He was a great mentor. ITC was not that hard for me but I put in long hours. My graduation test class was a thirty minute presentation on the Principles of War. I could not look at a note and had to present the entire class from memory while also V'ing and W'ing around the classroom. I did better than OK and was the ITC Class Honor Graduate. Later as the lead Offense Committee instructor I presented the Principles of War Class to each new Advanced Course. It was fun.

Then I got down to the real test, learning eight different blocks of instruction ranging from eight hours to one hour in length. I was also given responsibility for the eight hour Command Post Exercise and an eight hour tank/armored personnel carrier attack "problem" out in the field. Ray Wagner departed after about ninety days and I became the lead instructor for battalion offense. In the ensuing months I became Ray Wagner reincarnated garnering great praise and lots of kudos from most of the students. I was either hated or loved. The hate stemmed from our battalion offense test portion of the instruction which was a four hour "write for your life" (as termed by the students) exercise. Students had to justify their attack order in minute detail explaining why they chose their given course of action based on the key letters METTTS. Those letters stood for Mission, Enemy, Time, Terrain, Troops and Space. The student couldn't just pick a solution without explaining how each of those words had been weighed and thought through in coming up with their solution. It was a difficult test and no matter how hard we pressed and stressed use of METTTS, some of the students never got it. Grades were habitually not much above a C+ with some truly outstanding and some truly sad solutions. Seems in BBOD it had been that way for quite a while.

There were three standout instructors in BBOD after Ray Wagner left. One was Major Steve Siegfried who taught Defensive Operations; another was Major Ben Legare who taught Operations Orders (and later was young Larry's mentor when he was a student at the Citadel) and myself. One of the other great instructors was in the Support & Logistics Activities Department (that is not the correct name, my memory fails me on this) and whose claim to fame was that one test question always had twenty six trucks as the answer. I cannot tell you why each test had a question with twenty six trucks as the answer but it gave the students a lot of laughs as the story spread from class to class.

I tried to make my instruction both solid and entertaining. I had many semi-patented phrases and jokes that I used, like my 16th Redmond's Rule which was:

Redmond's Rule #16 - Shame on you if you don't love killing! Think attack.

I also had a lot of gimmicks to keep the students on their toes. We taught classes with seventy-five to one hundred students. It was hard to get to know so many students but Ray had taught me a few tricks. I would memorize twenty names in each class. When I wanted to call on a student for his solution to the previous night's homework, or an in class problem, I would stroll down toward the front of the classroom, turn my back to the students and call on CPT Hoobotts to give us his "Clausewitzian" solution. I would then turn slowly letting my eyes sweep to the, by then, standing stuckee. The students were amazed thinking that I knew their names and recognized them all. It really was a good bonding technique. Another gimmick was to call on CPT Persnakis, the other students all breathing a great sigh of relief. When CPT Persnakis stood I would ask him who the dashing, debonair rascal was who was seated one row in front and two seats to the left or right; that officer would provide us his answer. When a student was slow to answer I might hit him with, "What? Not paying attention in the major's class; stop having sex fantasies and get with the program." The studs loved it and it did help keep them all on their toes.

At some point along about now I made a decision to get another master's degree. Georgia State University had a night program at Infantry Hall (aka Building 4, or to the students Bunker 4) and one of the offerings was a Master of Education in Counseling with a minor in Psychotherapy. Do not ask me why, but I signed up. Mary and I discussed it and it opened a door to possible teaching as a second career after the Army. I enjoyed the studies and had no trouble keeping up with the course work once I had all my Offensive Operations classes down pat. Major Legare was also a glutton for educational punishment and joined me in this extra-curricular seeking of an advanced degree. We would both be successful in this undertaking.

I recall clearly the big snowstorm that hit Columbus, Georgia that first winter. We had sixteen inches of snow. It started snowing about 0800 in the morning and by noon the decision was made to close the school and send everyone home. Let me tell you, it took me three hours to go four miles to Holly Hills. Drivers in Georgia, for the most part, do not have a clue how to handle snow. We also lost electricity and hence heat in the house. I remember we bundled up the two kids and made our way across the street on a sled to a neighbor's home who had a fireplace. It was fun but somewhat inconvenient. The white stuff was pretty on day one and two but turned awfully ugly until it finally melted away about five days later. That spring Mary and I decided we wanted to live on post so we sold the house and moved into 106 Dial Street, very near Infantry Hall where I taught. It was really convenient for me getting to school and the whole family was happier on post. Our next door neighbors were the Sharbers (Pete and Faye) who had been with us at Fort Campbell in the 506th Infantry in 1963-1964. Pete had gotten out of the Army, gone to the Seminary and was now a Baptist Minister Chaplain. They were great friends and neighbors and we remain in touch with them to this day.

Before Ray Wagner departed for Korea I purchased his boat; a 16-foot runabout that we kept for quite a few years and enjoyed a great deal. I suspect my children, at least Larry and Kathy, remember it well. That was our first of many boats. Life at Fort Benning and the Attack Committee was good.

I liked being an instructor and frankly felt I was making a real contribution. Colonel Mowery was a great guy to work for and LTC Meloy allowed me to do my thing, to a point. I had a number of interesting happenings while walking the halls of Bunker Four.

One day COL Mowery, with LTC Meloy present, called me to his office and asked me to attend a briefing that was being given by the Army Deputy Chief of Staff for Personnel on the new Army Officer Efficiency Report (OER). OK, thought I, my past service at Infantry Branch should allow me to cut through the BS and see what is really new. It appeared this was a piece of cake. I went, listened and reported back to my two bosses, "Sir, nothing is new. If you want to kill an officer's career, do what the General said in his briefing. If the officer is worth saving, and advancing up the chain, keep giving him top marks." or words to that effect. Colonel Mowery seemed to accept that evaluation, but LTC Meloy was almost irate that I would contradict the General. I should have read the tea leaves better at that point but didn't. The report I would get later from LTC Meloy was not the top drawer rating I had advocated, but not a bad one either, sort of "Major Redmond was a very good instructor, among the best we have; here every day and the students loved him," but it would be there in my file forever. This was the first time in my career that, then LTC Meloy, later Major General Meloy, would impact negatively my sojourn in the Army. There would be another instance, in fact several.

For all who think they will advance and achieve high rank because they are good and deserving of being a general or attended West Point and are anointed, I can only say, "guess again." It is all based on luck and who you work for. An average or bad Officers Efficiency Report may well be luck of the draw based solely on who becomes your boss at any given time. It is the system. Oh yes, then there is the intangible and much misunderstood, "being available" that took me to Infantry Branch when all the cards said return to Vietnam for a second tour.

There was another learning experience that occurred one night while I was assigned to BBOD. One of the department directors had been promoted and was being reassigned. We all attended his farewell party at the Officers Club. When he got up to give his farewell talk it was obvious that he had imbibed a little too much. But he did a pretty good job of delivering his talk. However when he finished he started all over again from the opening salutation! Efforts by his lady to silence him failed and we all sat through the same talk for a second time. Later in my career when I was the designated speaker my wife was near my side and making sure I did not drink too much. When I was being introduced she would lean over and quietly whisper, "Remember, stand up to be seen, speak up to be heard and shut up to be appreciated." That counsel worked well. I never gave the same speech twice to the same audience

One day walking the halls on the first floor of Bunker 4 I ran into LTC Bo Baker from Special Forces School and Infantry Branch. He was there recruiting "studs" for the new Ranger Battalion they were forming at Fort Lewis WA. He had been designated the first commander; a well-deserved honor as he was a great leader. I just knew he would call to interview me as his S3. That did not happen. I was crushed. Bo went on to successfully command the 2nd Ranger Battalion and was later selected to command the 10th Special Forces at Bad Tolz Germany. Sadly Bo passed away, heart attack I was told, while in command of the 10th SF Group. He was a super soldier and destined for stars in my mind. Guess I just didn't meet his idea of who he wanted for a "stud" Ranger Battalion operations officer.

Colonel Mowery's replacement, one COL J. Ross Franklin, reported in to start the transition as Director BBOD. Colonel Franklin was a celebrity and hero who won the DSC for his actions at An Loc in 1972 as Senior Advisor to the ARVN Division fighting those tanks that weren't there; and had not come down the Ho Chi Minh trail. He had a reputation of being a real hard-nosed operator who attacked and intimidated juniors for little or no cause. One day while he was learning the ropes and sitting in the back of the classroom he approached me at a break and confronted me about something. I fired back at him with an answer about the fact that he did not yet understand and needed to listen more, or something like that. The colonel smiled and went back his seat; I think he was just testing me. After that one confrontation we got along famously for the remainder of my time in BBOD.

As I neared completion of my Master's Program from Georgia State, I decided to take the Industrial College of the Armed Forces National Security Management Course by correspondence. You might say I was a glutton for educational punishment. The Course consisted of, as I recall, 15 books on all aspects of economics, industry, grand strategy and a myriad of other topics. After reading each book you had to take and pass a test on the subject matter. Needless to say I was a busy rascal. I completed that puppy successfully in June 1975.

Then came the decidedly strange day, a Saturday in October, when the 1973 Yom Kippur War in Israel broke out. What was strange was the happening at Doughboy Stadium that defies explanation. Young Larry was playing on a local football team and I was working the chains on the sideline. Colonel Franklin wandered over and asked me if I had heard that the Israelis and the Arabs were at it again. I told him yes I had and that, "I am going to go over and observe that war," or maybe it was "I sure would like to go watch that war." We both laughed and forgot about the comment.

About a week later I was in the field with seventy-five Infantry captains, a company of armored personnel carriers (APC) and a company of tanks conducting a combined arms attack problem. The radio in my APC crackled and I answered the call to be told to turn over the completion of the problem to another instructor and to return in the APC directly to Bunker 4, immediately. I challenged the message and was again told to "Return to Infantry Hall immediately and report directly to COL Mowery." Now, as you may or may not know, one does not normally drive tracked vehicles on macadam roads except in special situations. Well I assumed that somehow the Army had finally woken up to all my inadequacies and I was about to be court-martialed or cashiered for sure. We took the macadam roads all the way to Bunker 4 figuring what the heck, there was nothing to lose.

Upon reaching Infantry Hall I went immediately to COL Mowery's office and he told me to go home and tell my wife that I was leaving for Israel tomorrow as part of a UN Peace Keeping Team (or something like that). To say I was stunned would be an understatement. I told him I did not have a passport, shots, nothing. He smiled and simply told me, "Major that will all be taken care of in Washington, now go tell your wife and pack your bags." I was dumbfounded but headed home to give Mary the news. Needless to say she was less than thrilled by this turn of events. This was particularly disturbing to her since she was expecting our third child in March of 1974 and we had no idea how long I might be deployed. I was, however, excited about the chance to see the "Elephant" one more time.

Eight days later I was still sitting at Fort Benning. As time dragged on I was trying to ascertain how or why I had been selected for this mission. I wondered if COL Franklin, following our discussion and my flippant remark at Doughboy Stadium, might have had a hand in this; that turned out not to be the case. There was a link to my past that explained it, and it wasn't Ross Franklin. Sometime during the wait I did get the word that duty was to be with the United Nations Truce Supervisory Organization–Palestine (UNTSO-P). I also was fortunate to talk with a LTC instructor at the school who had served there. That helped me understand a little about what I was heading into. He asked me what I thought of the Israelis. I told him I liked them, that I really only knew what I read in the NY Times from college days. He warned me to be ready to possibly change my opinion. My opinion did change, at least a little, as you will read.

After a week of waiting the word came to proceed to Washington and report to one of the major hotels in Crystal City. Not to an Army base and a simple BOQ, but to a very nice civilian hotel in Crystal City near the Pentagon. This surely was going to be a good deal! In the lobby was a desk with a sign, stating "UNTSO-P Designees Report Here." When I walked up to the desk Major John Shalikashvilli, the brother of Othar Shalikashvili from the First Brigade of the 101st in 1967, did my in-processing. If that name sounds familiar it is because Major Shalikashvili went on to wear four stars and become the chief of staff of the Army and the first foreign born chairman of the joint chiefs of staff. When I checked in he had a note for me to call Major O.B. Seaton a former classmate from the Navy War College who at that time was the executive officer to the Army Deputy Chief of Staff for Intelligence. O.B. came to the hotel that night to have a drink and just chat. There had been a roster of possible officers for this mission that had come across his desk. My name was on it. He had circled it with a notation, "Good troop, send him." That was the link that got my name on the list and another look at the "Elephant." Luck again had a hand in my career.

There were 36 of us being in-processed and issued gear. We were given lots of stuff that did not at the time seem to make sense. For example, arctic hats and winter parkas, sleeping bags and overshoes along with large WWII artillery field glasses and other gear were among the items we were given. Heck, arctic parkas, I thought I was going to Israel and the desert. We received a briefing from our contingent commander, a ramrod straight, full colonel infantryman. It turned out that the eight day delay was necessitated by some very high level negotiations between the Soviet secretary of state and our own Henry Kissinger. The deal was that thirty-six each American and Russian "observers" were going to be added to the UNTSO-P force to help ensure that the truce that was currently underway would continue. Apparently, at the national political level the U.S. would keep the Israelis in line and the Russians would keep the Arabs in line. Those of us who were being sent over directly were sacrificial lambs if this diplomatic effort should fail. No, the "keeping in line" would be done by our respective Governments. We would just cook, look, and report and be sort of in harms-way. I will explain all that in a few paragraphs.

27
OFF TO THE HOLY LAND AND
THE "ELEPHANT": AGAIN

We left Andrews AFB in a C-5 Galaxy transport along with 75 Peruvian Infantrymen and a cargo hold full of trucks painted white with big blue UN markings on them. These Peruvian soldiers were being sent over as part of the deal between the U.S. and the Russians to do something. We never did find out exactly what. Talk about incredible troops. These kids from the Andes sat almost at attention with their rifles between their legs most of the trip. We did have one good deal on the flight to Israel that is worth relating. The C-5, while a great airplane when it flew, had a terrible maintenance history. The aircraft stopped in the Azores to refuel and got a warning light of some kind so we got an extra day there drinking some fantastic Portuguese wine. Several of us suspected that the crew wanted that "remain overnight" stop in order to pick up lots of good Mateus, but have no idea for sure. When we did finally take off for Tel Aviv there were numerous cases of wine in the cargo area. You make the call on the red warning light.

In that we were assigned to the UN, and arriving in a USAF aircraft, getting into Israel was pretty simple. We were met by UN representatives and whisked through customs. We were bussed up to Jerusalem and briefed at the United Nations Truce Supervisory Organization-Palestine (UNTSO-P) Headquarters in the old British Mandate building on the Hill of Evil Counsel; where Pilate passed judgment on Jesus. At this time I saw very little of Jerusalem. I must

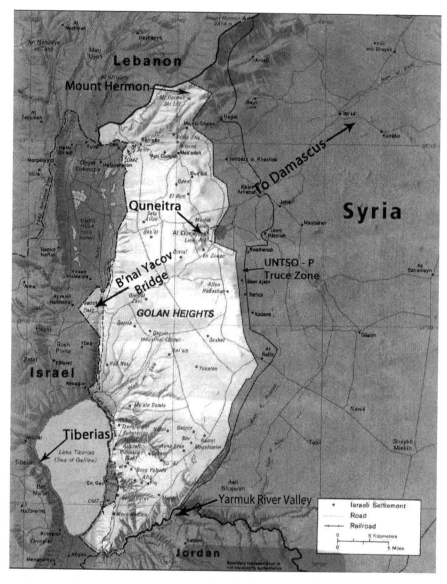

admit, however, it was impressive driving through the city. The feeling of history was around every corner. I was assigned to the Tiberias Patrol station up north on the Sea of Galilee. There were a number of Americans posted here as only a few were allowed in Damascus and Cairo. All the Russians were split between those latter two sites, as the Israelis would not allow Russians to be based in the country.

Dick Beltson, Tom LeBlanc, Billy Walters and I found a new semi-modern apartment consisting of a living/dining area, a kitchen, two bedrooms and a bath. There was no central heat or air and no furniture to speak of except a kitchen table and four pallet like beds. We had arrived in early November and we could already feel winter in the air. It gets darned cold in Israel in the winter and much colder up on the high desert. We all slept in our sleeping bags when we were not patrolling and I for one shivered on my treks to the bathroom in the middle of the night. The kitchen was adequate although about the only thing we fixed there was coffee and cereal. We ate out every night when we were in town. The bathroom had a sink, commode and shower, if you could call it a shower. It was a pipe coming out of the wall and there was no shower head or curtain. When one took a shower the water went all over the bathroom. Needless to say, lacking heat, those sleeping bags were a godsend. Not exactly what I had expected for living quarters but it beat a poncho on the ground in the mud in the jungle. By U.S. standards it was pretty grim. The apartment was owned by the Honorary Military Governor of Tiberias Province, an older, retired Israeli Army colonel; more about him shortly.

UNTSO-P was, I learned, a typical UN operation. The folks there ranged between extremely competent professional soldiers to reservist bank clerks serving for a year, and the money and perks that came with the UN job. I might add they were pretty good perks. For example booze in the UN Commissary was obscenely cheap; Johnny Walker Red went for eighty cents a fifth. Other foodstuffs to satisfy the palates of the UN troops were equally low priced. The mission of the UN observers in Tiberias was to patrol between and around the adversaries (Israelis vs. the Syrians, Jordanians, Iraqis and I recall a few other Arab brethren) up on the Golan Heights. Outside our patrol sites themselves we only went where the host country's occupying military allowed us to go. While on patrol we jokingly said our job was to look, cook and report.

The patrol system was pretty good. You patrolled one week, had one week off, completely off, and then went on a week of standby in case you were needed. So if you weren't called to meet some need during the standby phase you basically worked one week and had two weeks off. Then you started the cycle over again. When you patrolled you operated from a patrol base, located in no-man's land between the adversaries that normally consisted of a house like trailer with sitting area, radio communications area, kitchen and sleeping area. Outside latrines were standard. There was also a bunker reputed to be able to withstand a 500 lb. bomb. I am glad I never had to test that point. These were not bad bases and had several kerosene heaters that kept you pretty cozy even on the coldest night. Each patrol had an Israeli Liaison Officer (LNO) who met us at Quneitra up on the Golan and accompanied us all day. The LNO then returned to Quneitra before dark preferring not to be basically alone overnight between the lines.

Biggest problem I had was shopping for food and then cooking. Before this experience I could not boil water. That is still a major activity for me, boiling water that is. The patrols consisted of two officers and we took turns cooking for each other. Some of the Europeans were great chefs, or at least fancied themselves as such. I did have some superb meals and even better desserts and cocktails. Oh yes, as a complete departure from U.S. standards the UN drinks alcohol in the field. I had many a delicious Manhattan up on the Golan and bananas flambeau several nights. We were unarmed, not issued weapons of any sort. I did carry a USMC K-Bar knife, sort of against the rules, but what the heck.

I patrolled with a number of soldiers from different nations including, Australia (twice), Canada (twice), Ireland, Denmark, Finland, France, and at least one or two others. I never had a bad patrol mate but one, as you will read, who was less than a sterling soldier. Our method of operating and patrolling was a totally different happening: certainly not the same standards as the U.S. Army. By this time in the war things had changed from a war of movement to a static war of waiting while the two sides, working with the U.S. and Russia, sorted out full ramifications and rules of the truce. While they called it a truce, as you are about to learn that was not quite the case. It was officially a truce but there was still a lot of shooting. Seldom did a day pass when jets from one antagonist or the other didn't fly along the truce line taunting the other side to engage them so that they could return fire. I must observe that the Arab jets beat a hasty retreat when an Israeli fighter came up to challenge them. It is hard to describe all that I saw but let me relate a few of the major events that I can recall. Some were truly amazing.

On my initial patrol, day one, as I came up on the Golan Heights from the Jordan River the first Syrian tank was sitting burned out about two kilometers from the B'nai Yacov Bridge. There were maybe a dozen destroyed Syrian tanks and armored personnel carriers all around this area. This was the only way up to the Golan at that time and if the Syrians had taken that last two kilometers of ground, with even a small force, the Israelis would have played hell getting back up there. I am told that today there are several bridges and roads up to the Golan. The Israeli's only make a mistake once.

When we got to Quneitra, at one time a Syrian city of perhaps 50,000 people, up in the center of the Golan, it looked like Stalingrad in 1942. Quneitra had been captured in the 1967 War and was where the Israelis had their Golan Command Center. It had been overrun earlier in this war but recaptured in the counter attack. I mentioned that the town was devastated and my Australian mate told me, "Yes, quite a bloody mess; only about 5,000 people living here today. There was little fighting here in 1967, what you see destroyed is the result of Israeli live fire training in cities. They are systematically going block by block with unit training." I could never get a full answer from any of the Israeli liaison officers I worked with as to the truth of that one.

Also on my first patrol up on the Golan just after dark my Australian patrol mate and I were outside in the Observation Post (OP) "looking" and chatting, and trying to stay warm. Almost simultaneously we both observed headlights coming toward our OP from the Syrian lines. At first we counted maybe fifteen sets of lights but the number continued increasing until it was well over 100. We reported this happening and were told to observe and report but be prepared to seek shelter in the bombproof bunker. The vehicles just kept coming for about three hours. We were equally baffled that the Israelis did not open tank and artillery fire at the Arab forces. Artillery and tank fire was being exchanged daily somewhere on the Golan. The next day we were told that the Syrian Army moved a brigade forward to replace, I believe, a Jordanian brigade. It had been quite a sight and frankly I was not happy sitting there thinking those rascals were getting ready to launch a major attack directly at us. Since the Israeli's did not fire on this activity I believe they had been informed via political channels and had agreed to this relief in place.

On my third or fourth patrol a massive Israeli artillery barrage, that filled the desert landscape as far as the eye could see, erupted over the Syrian lines with the only warning being a low rumble from behind us. This barrage far surpassed anything I had seen in Vietnam. When it was over the Syrians came out of their holes and fired a massive barrage back at the Israelis, tit for tat; shades of WWI. Well it was a truce of sorts I guess. At least there were no tanks charging east or west.

We did some vehicle patrolling when the Israelis would let us. We had to get clearance from the Golan Command Center to move around by sending the route we wished to travel and places we wanted to visit one day prior to a roving patrol. I can tell you that the desert fight up here had been something else. We went past one burned out column of tanks, armored personnel carriers, transport trucks, jeep like vehicles and three or four fire trucks. Yes, I said fire trucks. This was about three weeks after the war of maneuver had ceased and the cease fire, such as it was, had taken effect. There were still some bodies on the ground and in the vehicles, all burned beyond recognition. It appeared that Israeli aircraft had caught the lead tank on a small bridge immobilizing it and the whole column. They then methodically strafed and destroyed what was sitting there in the desert. I noted that every dead soldier on the ground carried a chemical retardant cape/poncho and a gas mask. I would report that observation when I got home. Surely they had not intended to use chemical weapons; or had they.

You might wonder why they didn't just drive off and scatter in various directions rather than sit there like ducks in a shooting gallery and be butchered. Well, the Golan is an interesting place. Many areas are covered with rocks of all sizes, shapes and variants of sharpness, large enough to stop a vehicle from moving cross country and causing tank treads to break. Those rocks can puncture even the toughest tire. This choke point was such a place.

On another patrol we came across a half dozen Soviet T54 tanks all in a very small area and all killed with a rear shot to the engine compartment. The Israeli Liaison Officer told us that they had all been taken out by one "super Sherman." This is a WWII U.S. tank, originally of limited capacity, that the Israelis had upgraded with a larger gun and better armament. This single "super Sherman" had hidden in a gully, allowed the bad guy tanks to slip by, then came up and started shooting them from the rear. The destroyed tanks had all been buttoned up. One tank turret had been rotated ¾ of the way to the rear indicating to me that this tank commander realized what was going on, but too late.

Each of the vehicles mentioned just above were marked for recovery by the Israeli's with large white numbers. One tank still had the crew in it and a hand was sticking up from the driver's compartment and an Israeli troop had painted it white. The Israeli military had their own "draggin wagons" (low boy tank transporters) roaming the battlefield picking up even the burned out hulks. They recovered these vehicles and took them back to rehab and reissue them as Israeli Army tanks. It was strange to see Russian T54s with

Israeli markings but they had several operational battalions of these tanks. While I was still in Israel there was a parade in Jerusalem or Tel Aviv and the Jerusalem Post had a front page picture of a company of these captured and refurbished tanks passing in review. The Israelis are amazing people.

I remember one other instance where we came upon a column of six or eight "abandoned" tanks, not a scratch on them, with the weirdest camouflage design I had ever seen. It was circular, wrapping all around the vehicle and ending in a swirl at the top of the turret. I used to have pictures of me standing on top of one of these. They were Iraqi tanks. I climbed inside one and it had exactly eight kilometers on the odometer. That told me that they had been trucked on low boy tank transporters up to near this site and started to attack from there. Then, for whatever reason, their crews abandoned them. There was a message here for the battles in Desert Storm and the later invasion of Iraq but that message never surfaced. The message was simple; the Iraqi's were tenth rate chumps.

Speaking of camouflage the Israelis had the best camouflage system going. No painting, no pattern, they just let the equipment get dirty with the dust and mud of the desert and, "voila"—great camouflage. We spend a fortune painting and repainting our vehicles. I can tell you the Israeli system works pretty well. I do not know if that is still an Israeli practice or not. Of course, it would never suffice for the U.S. Army where everything must be in a particular pattern and freshly painted

On one patrol, when we were roaming the central Golan, I was with a Canadian captain named Rick Kane, a retired Princess Patricia Regiment sergeant major and a paratrooper. When he retired he was given what the Canucks called a "tombstone promotion" to captain in order to serve with the UN. Only officers could serve as observers. We stopped at a bar in this little Arab village, yep a bar in Muslim land, and we were on our second beer. The Arab barkeep even served our Israeli Liaison Officer (LNO); anything for a shekel or pound.

Suddenly around the corner near the bar a convoy of Israeli trucks came tearing by. Each truck had a full complement of soldiers all attired the same, helmets on and with rifles tucked neatly between their legs. These guys looked like real soldiers not like the Israeli Defense Forces we normally saw. As the convoy departed Rick turned to the Israeli LNO and said, "You bloody bastards are moving the Parachute Battalion or the 'Golani' Brigade. We weren't supposed to see that were we?" The LNO did quite a tap dance and you could tell he was totally flummoxed. We reported that movement and it was later confirmed by Tiberias control, as a repositioning of a Para Battalion. Our LNO may have gotten in trouble for inadvertently letting us see this unannounced troop re-positioning.

On that same patrol Rick and I came to a small walled area with the remnants of a house. Our LNO did not object to our walking around so we assumed there were no mines. Not very smart on our part, we both later agreed, but the assumption did prove correct. As we wandered around the area we came upon a mud/earth teepee-like construction with a thin wisp of smoke coming out the top. We approached the opening and inside found an old Arab man and woman who we assumed was his wife! This was absolute and unbelievable poverty. I am not sure how they survived. There appeared to be one blanket, one pot, one small kettle – all filthy and to say their clothes were dirty and ragged would be an understatement. No lights or candles were visible and the floor was dirt as were the walls; and not a window. To say this was pretty grim living would hardly do it justice. We both left them a few Israeli pounds. Our LNO just shrugged his shoulders and walked away. Talk about poor, we had just seen it. This beat anything I ever saw in Appalachia or on an American Indian Reservation. No welfare or social services support here. But I suspect these folks chose to stay there instead of trying to get to Damascus.

The weather had been downright cold as I have mentioned. About three days into one patrol I went out to spend some time in the base observation point. Things had been quiet and I am not sure what prompted me to go out. When nothing was going on, or we were not patrolling or cooking, we normally read books. As I stood there perusing the desert I thought "Gee, it's getting cloudy." Then I realized that it wasn't clouds, it was snow. It had started to snow! Well by the time it finally stopped we had close to eighteen inches of the white stuff and the Israeli Army engineers had to clear a road for us back to the main drag when our patrol ended. The Golan Heights was really something else.

Not sure how true it was but I was told that the area had been partially forested 1000 years earlier but that the Ottoman Turks had cut down the trees and sent them to Turkey to be used for construction. There was no reforestation. Talk about a lack of environmental sensitivity! At any rate from the base of Mount Hermon in the north to the southern extreme of the Golan at the Yarmuk River Valley the "Heights" were basically treeless. As I mentioned earlier there were so many rocks and boulders that movement off the roads was next to impossible. The Arabs forces had successfully launched attacks "off the roads" leading the advance with two and three bulldozers abreast clearing a path. When they had to deploy to deal with Israeli defensive positions or counter attacks things tended to go downhill. The use of the bulldozers was an innovation I must give the Arabs credit for. It worked, to a degree, and almost got them to the edge of the Golan and a stunning victory.

On another patrol several of us reported in to Tiberias control to pick up our vehicles and patrol mates. We were assigned a female LNO, a departure from the norm. Quite an attractive young lady we all thought. She led us up to the Israeli Defense Force (IDF) Headquarters on the Golan. It was not that we could not find our way to Quneitra on our own, but the IDF did not trust us to drive anywhere east of the Jordan River unescorted. We might see something they did not want us to see. In Quneitra each patrol was assigned a male LNO to go forward to the truce line. No females were permitted closer to the Arab lines than Quneitra. Believe me the pictures of attractive Israeli women marching with Uzi Submachine guns in parades that you see in the New York Times is just that, a parade. They did not fight. No self-respecting IDF soldier would let the gals near the front where an Arab might get them; at least that was the case in 1973. That has changed somewhat in the IDF today and women are serving in units where they would not have been allowed ten years ago. However, I must observe that Israeli women did fight in the 1946 War for Independence in order to survive.

(NOTE: Permit me an observation. Now thanks to our politicos and feminists we have young women with missing legs, arms, hands, blinded, and in some cases hideously burned. I doubt that any of our Congressmen/women or feminist advocates have a daughter who served and was maimed in Iraq or Afghanistan. Isn't Washington just wonderful? This is political correctness at its worst in my mind.)

I remember only too well one patrol where we went out to the furthest east position occupied by the Israeli Army. It was a hilltop, sort of like a Vietnam Fire Support Base with tanks, personnel carriers and artillery. The colonel in charge showed us around and took us to an observation point and told us to look closely, we could see Damascus. My eyes were pretty good in those days but darned if I could see Damascus. As we walked back toward our vehicles the colonel commented, "We could have taken Damascus. But that would be dumb. There are several million people there and our whole country has only just over 4 million." His observation was correct. Suddenly I was confronted by an Israeli private who, pointing his finger at me asked in perfect English, "Why does your country send us such shitty equipment. Your anti-tank weapons (TOWs) don't work. Henry Kissinger is awful." The colonel yelled at him in Yiddish and he sort of shut up. I responded as I walked away, "I don't know about any of that but I am sure Henry only sends what you ask us for." (By the way, according to the IDF colonel, our TOWs, Tube Launched, Optically Tracked, Wire Guided, Anti-tank Missiles worked very well.)

I think this may have been the patrol where CPT Joe Argentieri, Army Special Forces, and a USMC captain whose name I cannot recall linked up with us while they were also on patrol. Normally two Americans did not patrol together, only with a representative from another country. Something had happened and they let these two Yanks out together. The two of them were sitting in their vehicle along with their LNO flipping hand grenades like baseballs. Yes, I did say real hand grenades, or so it appeared. The Golan was littered with ordinance and also there were small ammo dumps all over the place. Whatever you wanted you could find, well almost anything you wanted. I asked Joe if he was crazy and he said, "No, sir, these are disarmed grenades, harmless. Want to know how to do it?" I said sure and they proceeded to show me how to disarm a hand grenade. There are now one each British Mills grenade and one Russian grenade, both disarmed, on my book case shelf maybe ten feet from where I sit typing this. No I am not going to tell you how to disarm a live hand grenade. However, it is not rocket science.

One night when back in Tiberias several of us went downstairs to our landlord's patio looking out at the Sea of Galilee for a brew with the old colonel. He told us quite a few war stories from the early days and the 1967 war. As the evening wore on he got very philosophical and made an observation that I have never forgotten. He calmly said, looking out over the sea at the Golan Heights, "You realize we really must have peace with the Arabs. Every time they go out on one of these little training exercises they get better. There are over fifty million of them and four million of us." He was correct. I agreed with him at the time and agree with him still today.

28

A VISIT TO DAMASCUS

One day I had the opportunity to visit Damascus during a standby week. Shopping in Damascus was a highlight and lots of the UN wives were always looking for a convoy over that they could tag on with. Individual cars were not allowed to cross the lines and families only made it over in UN sponsored convoys approved by both sides. Clearance for the trip through the lines was requested and granted. We all assembled at Tiberias Control and Rick Kane and I teamed up in a UN car. I was going to stay with the Americans who were assigned to Damascus. Rick planned to stay at the Canadian House. This proved to be quite an adventure.

When we departed Tiberias for the Golan and Damascus there must have been fifteen to eighteen vehicles all white with UN markings or private vehicles flying UN flags. The heights were covered in heavy snow until we got past Quneitra. Near the furthest most point of Israeli advance along the Damascus road they had a small "tin soldier" one man guard post (unoccupied normally) painted blue and white, the colors of the Israeli flag. The convoy halted and Rick and I sat there waiting. After about three minutes Rick, who was driving, observed that all the people in the cars ahead were out of their vehicles, standing in what was now two to three inches of snow and ice. Rick got out and walked down toward the front of the column. I followed about ten yards back. The lead Israeli Army vehicle had stopped at the shack and run up the Israeli flag. Now the Israeli Liaison Officer (LNO) was checking the IDs of everyone in the vehicles. Rick went ballistic. He read the LNO the riot act and rightly pointed out that everyone there was in a UN vehicle or civilian vehicle flying the UN flag and to make women and children stand out in the cold and snow was ridiculous. The LNO relented, everyone got back in the vehicles and we continued toward Damascus. He, the LNO, was an obnoxious SOB. Sorry to have to relate that tale.

The last of the snow now behind us, we approached another "tin soldier" hut painted red, black and white, the colors of the Syrian flag. A lone Syrian soldier standing at attention in the shack waived us on and we continued to Damascus; a small difference in our treatment there to be sure.

Damascus was quite a city; ancient, and modern at the same time. The outskirts were typical Arab mud construction but the center of town was modern, mostly European motif stemming from the French Protectorate following World War I. There is also a section that is very Biblical in construction dating back at least two thousand years. Large wide boulevards, huge roundabouts, parks and large modern apartment buildings and shopping areas brought one into the 20th Century from the narrow, dark, damp construction from the time of Our Lord. The American UN Military Observers (UNMOs) had a very nice ground floor apartment in a more modern section. Several of us from Tiberias stayed with them for our short visit, which was only three days as I recall. It was a busy three days.

The night we arrived from Tiberias all the Americans were invited to the Canadian House for a party with the Russian "observers." We arrived promptly at 1800 and there were no Russians. The reason for that was that the Canucks had laid an ambush for the Russians who were to arrive at 1830. We Yanks arrived early to be briefed on which bottles of vodka were watered down and which were pure vodka. The idea was to let the "Russkies" drink themselves into a stupor while the North Americans stayed semi sober. It worked well and as the evening wore on one point became clear. The Russians were not combat arms officers as they claimed they were. They were all intelligence officers who had not a clue about combat, combat equipment or field operations. As an aside the U.S. UNMO contingent of 36 troops did have two intelligence officers as their basic duty branch, but the bulk of us were combat arms soldiers.

On the first morning there we were invited to visit the Syrian Liaison to UNTSO-P in his office. His rank was captain but we all figured he had to be at least a colonel. First off, he had a very nice office far above what a captain would be expected to have. Secondly, he was too politically savvy and a little older to be just a captain. This was also the first chance the Damascus based U.S. Military Observers, there were four of them, had to meet the Senior Syrian LNO. One of the first questions they had for this guy was, why had their apartment and suitcases been searched? They knew it had been searched because they used the old hair in the suitcase edge CIA/SF trick to monitor if their bags had been opened. Without missing a beat the captain responded, "I am sorry about that. Give us some time and we will be as good as your CIA and you'll never know we were there." Can't make this stuff up, I lived it.

A second question was presented by another Damascus based UNMO to the effect, "Well tell us how much of the Golan you will accept back to ensure peace?" The captain, with only a moment's hesitation said, "If I came into your home and took it all from you, but then said, OK you can have one bedroom and we will share the kitchen and the bath, how would you react?" The U.S. UNMO responded he would want the whole house back. The captain then said, "Yes, and we want all the Golan back."

The conversation then took a decidedly strange turn. The comment was made that the Israelis could not give back all the Golan as that would allow you to see down into the Jordan Valley and shoot directed fire at the Israelis there. That would not be acceptable. The captain again responded to the effect, "But you must realize when the State of Israel was established we sat there and we did not fire at the farmers and others. But over time we watched their tractors take large chunks of land out of the 5 KM Demilitarized Zone and plant crops there. So one day we shot at them to stop this. They just kept taking another hundred yards here and a hundred yards there. They kept getting closer to the Jordan River. So every morning it became habit for our troops to shoot at them." Well I thought this whole story was apocryphal, but I kept my mouth shut. I will revisit the demilitarized zone story in short order.

Following the meeting with the Syrian liaison we visitors were taken to the Street Called Straight where St. Paul preached. Visiting the old Biblical portion of Damascus was quite a thrill. The shopping was pretty good too. I still have the inlaid chess board I picked up there and Mary has some very nice jewelry I bought her. There is also a replica Arab pistol with inlaid brass hanging on the wall in my study. It looks real enough up there and shines nicely. I think I paid $2 U.S. for it. It was truly amazing to walk streets going back 2000 years. In spite of the dirt and smells, it was interesting and a once in a lifetime experience.

That night several Americans and Canadians went to a very swanky restaurant to have dinner with a Russian major we had met the previous night. We were sitting having a cocktail being served by waiters in tuxedos surrounded by the high and mighty of Damascus society waiting for one last Canuck to arrive, Captain Rick Kane. Suddenly the Russian jumped up and hollered, "Hey Rick, over here you Canadian (expletive deleted)"– and then the stream of obscenities that flowed out was most embarrassing. We could not tell which of the ladies around us spoke English or even knew what the words meant. They were definitely not highbrow stuff. We told the Russian to shut up and asked him where he got that language. He responded something to the effect, "Yes, good American idiom. I go on patrol with Canadian captain, he teach me what to say." Needless to say it was a great joke, albeit somewhat more than embarrassing at that moment. To say that our Canadian allies did a job on the poor, naïve Russians is to somewhat diminish the full truth. And to my knowledge the Russki didn't have a clue.

On the last night in Damascus I was taken to the Swedish Embassy Bar. It was reputed to be the watering hole in the city. It was nice, very crowded and several of us managed to get seats up at the bar and were imbibing. One of the UNMOs, from Norway I think, leaned over and said, "Uh oh, here comes that Russian lieutenant, watch out, we think he wants to defect." We were joined by the young Russian and a lively conversation ensued. In the course of the discussion the Russian blurted out, "You know I go to Beirut for visit; very nice city; lots of shops. Shops with just ladies purses and shops with just men's shoes and shops, with anything you might want." He was much impressed with the glitter and westernization of Beirut. This was before the Civil War there and Beirut was still the Paris of the east. He went on to ask, "Is the entire west like that?" One of the Canadians at the bar said, "Of course you bloody fool the whole west is like that." The Russian then responded, "No you are the fools. In my country we have one store and it has nothing to sell." Being one of seven Americans in the whole country, and having not even a *charge de affairs* to turn to I didn't want to be the man this lad might try to seek asylum with. I quickly decamped the bar returning directly to the apartment. Departing the next day back to Tiberias I have no idea what happened to the young Russian. Maybe he did try to defect. If so I hope he was successful.

29
UNMO LIFE AND
OBSERVATIONS ON ISRAEL

After returning to Tiberias my next patrol was with a captain from the Irish Army. Nice guy and a very good soldier. His wife had accompanied him to Israel and lived in Tiberias; serving with the UN could be a really good deal. He came to me before the patrol and said, "We will be going up on the Golan together. There will be no need to worry about cooking for me. I'll be bringing my own food." I was not sure if he had heard about my two standard dinners, one of ham and one of pork chops, and decided he did not want any of that. Or possibly my meals were so bad that my culinary reputation had preceded me to the degree that he simply did not want to try my cooking. At any rate I took care of myself food wise for the patrol. When he showed up in the morning to go on patrol he had a small basket with cheese and bread and a few other items and seven bottles of Johnny Walker, one for each day of the patrol. He began drinking on the way up to the Golan and finished the last bottle on the way home. He was one of the best patrol mates I had the whole time with the UN. He insisted on getting up in the middle of the night when firing went on to render all "shoot reps" as the UN termed violations of the ceasefire. While chatting one day he told me the drink was to make sure that if the bloody Arabs snuck into our base and cut our throats at night that he wouldn't feel it. That was certainly a cheery thought. I never heard of such an event happening over there, ever. We did have one Italian UNMO killed down in the Sinai area when his vehicle ran over a mine. Being an UNMO could have its dangerous side.

Soon after that came the patrol and the incident that I still live with today. My patrol mate was a Danish Regular Army captain, good guy. We were exploring on foot not too far from our base, several days into the patrol, when we came upon a Syrian trench. He jumped over it and not to be outdone by a Danish captain I followed suit. The far side was a decent distance but also had a distinct raised berm, not a flat landing surface. When I hit the berm I led with my right foot and landed jamming the foot and the leg right into my spine. The jolt was jarring and I was stunned. Electric shocks can best describe the feeling and there was a great deal of pain. I stumbled forward and could hardly straighten up and walk. With the help of my Danish patrol mate I got back to the trailer and lay down. I did not get up for the next couple of days except to relieve myself from time to time. It hurt a lot. Just getting out of my sleeping bag to get up took maybe eight to ten minutes. I could only move in very small increments and sit up slowly.

Upon completion of the patrol I returned to the apartment and spent the off week and following standby week in my sleeping bag. My roommates brought me food and helped me a great deal or I never would have survived. The first week I was scheduled for patrol Captain Argentieri volunteered and took my patrol for me. Joe was really a savior. By the time I was well enough to go on patrol again, and my name came up for duty, two weeks later, I was moving around fairly well but still with lots of pain.

I gutted it out and went on this next patrol albeit far from 100% physically. One of my apartment mates, I cannot remember which one, did my shopping for me as there was no way I could navigate safely through the melee that was the food market in Tiberias. My patrol mate for this patrol was a Finnish bank clerk, reservist major, as I recall. A nice guy, but he was not a soldier by any stretch of the imagination. He had volunteered for duty with the UN for the money and perks. Our base for this patrol was the furthest north on the Golan right at the foot of Mount Hermon. It was a small caravan/trailer type facility and the only entrance faced directly at the Syrian lines. We were doing OK and sticking close to the base, with the Finn handling most of the cooking. I think it was about four days into the patrol, early evening, when we heard a heavy machine gun open up. I was wrapped up in my sleeping bag staying warm.

The Finnish major jumped up and opened the door to be greeted by a stream of green tracers coming directly at us from a Syrian tank about 500 meters to our east. After his scream died away he ran like hell for our bomb shelter. I lay there and watched the green tracers passing directly over the trailer. It was obvious the Syrians were not shooting at us but at that moment I could not say for sure what they were shooting at. I judged that if they were going to shoot at me, then it was "my turn to die" as Charlie Beckwith used to say. No way could I get up and move quickly to cover. So I just lay there, and prayed. Suddenly a tank main gun directly behind us, and slightly higher fired; there was quite a boom immediately in front of it. That turned on the light as to what the Syrian tank had been shooting at. The Israeli had baited the Syrian tank into firing at it and then tried to take the tank out with its main gun. They missed; both tanks withdrew. After sending in a "shoot rep," life at the base of Mount Hermon returned to peace and quiet; or what passed on the Golan in those days for peace and quiet.

My last patrol was at the farthest south patrol base on the Golan and overlooked Jordan and Syria to the east with Israel to the west behind us. The Yarmuk River Valley, a very deep gorge like area, was just to our front and south. While not quite the Grand Canyon it was, one impressive land formation. It was a very quiet area due to the terrain and I don't think we had even one incident (shoot rep) the whole week. To the best of my recollection this part of the Golan had seen only one major battle between the Israelis and the Arabs early in this war. The entire area had been scoured clean by the Israelis and there were no signs of this battle. My back was a little better. It was sunny and warm. I sat out and soaked up some rays and read; and of course had a few drinks at dinner.

Throughout my time in Israel, whenever I was off duty, I would team up with other Americans and visit the Holy places. Several of us spent a couple of days walking the streets of Jerusalem (before I hurt my back) and got a fantastic tour from an American Franciscan Friar who was very popular with the UN personnel. I saw most of the key places in and around the city to include the Way of the Cross, Church of the Holy Sepulcher, Calvary, Garden of Gethsemane, Mount of Olives and other places. One interesting point was, at that time, the Church of the Holy Sepulcher was in dire need of repair and I mean dire need. Problem was that the various Christian sects could not get their act together on what to repair next. They had the money but no agreement among themselves on how to make the repairs or what to fix first! I kid you not. I do not know if that issue has ever been resolved. The other interesting fact is that this Church, dating back to long before the Crusades, was hand grenade distance from the Wailing Wall (holiest place in Judaism) and the Mosque of the Golden Dome from which Mohammed is said to have been taken up to Heaven (third holiest place in Islam). Mohammed borrowed lots of ideas and customs from Judaism and Christianity to create his religion. That statement may not be politically correct but it is my opinion. I also visited Nazareth and Bethlehem as well as Canaan. There were lots of other biblical sites around Tiberias and the Sea of Galilee. You haven't lived until you have eaten St. Peter's fish at a restaurant on the shores of the Sea. St. Peter's fish by the way are carp. Not exactly a delicacy in the USA. Christianity was everywhere as was Judaism and Islam. On my book shelf is a pictorial tour of the Holy Land called *In the Footsteps of Jesus*. It is a book well worth perusing.

If you will permit me, a few observations about Israel may be in order at this point. First, as of 1973, in spite of what the *New York*

Times would have led you to believe back then, the Israelis have not yet turned the desert green. There is a lot of brown desert still out there. That is to take nothing away from what the Israelis have done in the matter of agriculture compared to the Palestinians who lived there for centuries before the modern state of Israel came into existence. The Palestinians accomplished nothing in the way of food production that can even compare. The Israelis are terribly smart and innovative. The Palestinians could not hold a candle to them. I realize that is not a politically correct opinion but it is what I observed.

Also, Israel is not a Little America and the people for the most part do not love us. They are their own nation and people. They also have internal disagreement among the Sephardic and Ashkenazi Jews that to me was shocking. The really Orthodox Jews are hard to comprehend; but they are dutifully faithful to their religion. I even witnessed ultraorthodox Jews throwing rocks at UN vehicles being driven on the Sabbath. The average Israeli, in 1973-1974, believed strongly that we meddle in their affairs. I agreed with them in that point and the current Obama administration has made it much worse. There is no such thing as queuing in a line for service. Anyone from a child, or teen, to a little old woman who speaks the language will cut in front of you at a store or shop. Tourist traps were an exception to that rule since there were few or no Jewish shoppers. I got waited on at the market by waiving a twenty pound note and yelling, "Who do I pay?" It worked.

In 1973 the Palestinians lived comfortably throughout the country, although perhaps not quite as well as their Jewish neighbors. In fairness many of the Palestinian businessmen and shop keepers lived better than a lot of Israelis. They were active in the political process of the nation at that time and I believe that is still the case today. Most of the Palestinians I met and talked with liked the USA. That has certainly changed in the last forty years, as has my opinion that both sides have a story and we need to be sensitive to both.

Radical Islam has changed my feelings on this issue. The radical Jihadist agenda to change the entire Western world and replace our way of life with a Caliphate and Sharia law, being the catalyst for that change in my attitude.

There is another key observation that could never be allowed in the USA, that I must make. The Israeli soldiers carried their weapons and ammo wherever they went; yes weapons and ammunition. You even found them in the discos and bars. I never heard of an incident or argument leading to a misuse of those weapons. Try that in D.C., Detroit, Atlanta, Memphis or Baltimore for starters. The Israeli Defense Force soldiers had great self-discipline in this regard. You could not but admire them for that.

One day in late February all the American UNMOs were approached by our colonel about the possibility of extending our stay to a full year. I told them I would consider it if they would guarantee me a trip home when Mary had the baby and if they would allow the family to remain in quarters at Fort Benning until I got back. The trip home was supposedly doable but no dice on the housing issue. That convinced me that I was going home and I wanted to go before the baby was born in mid-March.

As I recall, over half the U.S. UNMOs made the same determination to head home. And so in early March a gaggle of us departed Israel for the USA. I can tell you we were happy and ready to go. Our flight could not get into La Guardia due to bad weather. We landed in Hartford, Connecticut. Well let me tell you "little ole" Hartford was not prepared to process a whole transatlantic plane load of folks through customs and reentry into the USA. It was particularly cute when the customs agents got to the UNMOs. For example I had some gold and some silver jewelry, two disarmed hand grenades, a replica pistol, a 155mm artillery shell casing and a sword and I cannot remember what else. By the way, some of the UNMOs had more stuff, especially gold and a number of disarmed grenades. Needless to say the agents were horrified. The chief agent was summoned, looked over our customs declarations, checked our ID cards heard our tale of where we were coming from and said something to the effect, "These guys are OK, anyone willing to declare this gear and war trophies is good to go." Try to get away with any of that today! By the way, there is no more UNTSO-P, it has been renamed the United Nations Disengagement Observer Force (UNDOF). There were and still are several other observer elements in previous hot spots around the globe; Kashmir and Cypress to mention two such organizations.

Once through customs I then caught a plane to Atlanta. It was good to be home but the experience had been fantastic. The really good news was I was home just in time for the birth of my daughter, Patricia Ann on 19 March 1974.

30
BACK TO NORMAL IN BUNKER FOUR:
... OR SO I THOUGHT!

I was surprised that upon return I had gained a degree of celebrity. Rather than go right back to teaching I was tasked to put together a briefing as to what I had seen and experienced. Most of it is included in a less military form in the preceding chapter. While preparing this little "class," I was in the library researching more information when I came across a map. Not just any map mind you but a map showing the truce lines from the 1948 War of Israeli Independence. Guess what? There was a 5 kilometer demilitarized zone along the Jordan River up by the Golan. This added a degree of credence to the Syrian captain's tale about why they shot at the Israelis that I had not originally given it. We can all learn.

The briefing was fifty minutes in length and I sprinkled in lots of slides and pictures. It was a big hit for about six or seven presentations. Then someone in power noticed that I was saying things like, "Many Israelis do not really like us and feel we meddle in their affairs." That was what I experienced. I also said, "The Palestinians seem to like us." That was true in 1974. "The IDF looks good but really are a third rate power; they cannot project power and have limited staying power. We should not change our doctrine to be like them since they look good because they are fighting an eighth rate enemy." Well this was not a good theme to be playing because General DePuy, who at that time was Training and Doctrine Command Commander, wanted us to adopt all the techniques and tactics of the IDF. I spent a number of hours talking to the hierarchy of the Infantry School about this. Later General DePuy did change his mind on adopting IDF doctrine and tactics. I doubt my briefing or arguments against changing our doctrine had any influence on that decision.

Out of the blue one day I was summoned to Colonel Franklin's office. He told me that a team was coming to interview me about some of the things that I had been talking about. This was sort of surprising, but it got even better. A few days later two men in civilian clothes, claiming to be from the office of the Deputy Chief of Staff for Intelligence, showed up to talk to me. They stated that they had been interviewing all the folks who had come back and they wanted to discuss some of my observations. We talked for several hours. Bottom line, and what got their interest, was that 75% of the returned observers were saying the same things I was. That fact made me feel pretty good but had not made the Army hierarchy very happy. These intelligence officer types were particularly interested in some tactical issues and our attitude toward the Israelis. You may remember I went over pro-Israeli and came back judging that both sides had a story that needed to be heard. It seems that most of the returned observers had the same opinion of the Israelis. They tended to be arrogant, did not like us and felt we meddled in their affairs. Sadly the attitude and bearing of some of the Israelis had turned most of us off.

They were specifically interested in several tactical points I had been briefing. Among them; the use of bulldozers to clear the way for attacking tracked vehicles, the fire trucks among the lead attacking echelon and the fact that almost every Arab body I had observed had a chemical protective cape and gas mask. They asked me what I made of the fire trucks and the capes and masks. I responded that the only reason I could deduce for those facts was that they planned to employ chemical weapons and the fire trucks were there to decontaminate tanks and APCs. Why they did not employ chemical weapons, since they appeared ready to do so, I did not have a clue. It is possible they feared the Israelis would also employ them particularly if their attack was succeeding. Fortunately, to my knowledge, no chemical weapons were used by either side.

They also challenged how I could say the Israelis were a third rate power. I explained that I based that statement on the fact that the Israeli Defense Forces (IDF) had limited staying power and could not project power the way a first rate military would. Also they were blessed with interior lines of communication and could shift units from the Sinai to the Golan almost overnight thereby enhancing combat power and looking more like a first rate power than they really were. Plus there was little doubt in my mind, at least in 1974, that the Arab powers were 7th or 8th rate fighting machines in spite of having large amounts of fairly modern Soviet equipment. Their soldiers were just not well trained or motivated and made the IDF look better than they were. At least that was my opinion based on almost five months of observation. The Israeli Air Force in 1973–1974 was a first class military organization and definitely ruled the skies. The Arab air arm simply could not compete. My criticism of the IDF was sound in that too many U.S. Army senior leaders wanted to completely revamp our doctrine and tactics to emulate the Israelis. That idea was wrong then and it remains wrong today. The U.S. military has a much more complex and worldwide mission compared to the Israeli mission of defense and national survival.

Things got back on a normal track and I returned to the platform teaching and enjoying myself. I think over the four years (minus five months in Israel) that I was an instructor I must have taught 3,000 Infantry captains. Many of those lads crossed my path again in my career. They always remembered how hard I had been on them but they all admitted they learned a lot and I kept them entertained and on their toes. Sometime during this period I earned the nickname of the "Short Fat Major." Maybe it was deserved; I am not sure, HA!

In early 1975 I completed my schooling for the Master of Education that I had been pursuing through Georgia State University.

The last course I had to take was a practicum, one-on-one counseling at Martin Army Hospital under the supervision of a resident psychiatrist. I dealt with several patients but the one that stuck out was a retired first sergeant who, following retirement from the Army simply could not cope and was so depressed it scared me. The old NCO simply could not handle civilian life and had lost a number of jobs, the last being night watchman; not a terribly challenging position. He had a domineering German wife and she was certainly part of the problem. Cannot say for certain if I helped him; he really needed more counseling than I could give him. The day the practicum ended I went directly home and had coffee with Mary. I told her that never again would I practice psychotherapy. That was enough, and I have not plied that art again. Except let me say that many of the principles I learned helped me get along with and influence soldiers and people for the rest of my career. Fooling with human mental problems has remained off my radar screen.

In the late spring of 1975 my mother had a stroke and I flew to Columbus, Ohio to be with her. While I was there she had a heart attack and went into a coma. I had been with her all night in the hospital. About five in the morning I went to the nurses' station and told the head nurse that I was going to go back to my aunt's and clean up and that my mother would not be alive much longer. The nurse, a look of incredulity on her face, asked why I had said that. I explained that I had sat and watched men die in combat and that she had the death rattle I had heard several times before. While I was at Aunt Florence's showering and changing clothes the hospital called to tell me Mom had passed away without waking. It was peaceful. Mary and young Larry flew up to join me for the funeral. Our two daughters, both had the Chicken Pox at that time, and stayed with good friends, Betty and Monk Foley, who lived across the street. Following the funeral we sorted through Mother's belongings and rented a U Haul van to bring some of her treasured items home with us to Fort Benning. My parents are buried alongside many Redmonds and other relatives at Holy Trinity Church in Somerset, Ohio.

Shortly after getting back to Benning I received a call from Infantry Branch telling me that I was being reassigned to the Office of the Deputy Chief of Staff for Operations (DCSOPS) in Washington. I politely told the officer calling that I was not going to Washington and please find me another job. "Well I can't do that, the orders are cut," he said. I responded, "Revoke them. I am not coming to Washington. Been there, done that, filled in blanks on a computer printout just like you are doing. You can't promise me I will command, make lieutenant colonel, be a colonel, be a general, you can promise me nothing. Well the only thing you can promise me is eighteen hour days, five plus days a week, in the bowels of DCSOPS. I am not coming." The action officer was dumbstruck. I hung up. About two weeks later orders came through assigning me to a Special Forces job in Thailand with the Joint Casualty Resolution Center (JCRC). If the assignment officer thought he was getting back at me he was mistaken. I was quite thrilled going back to a Special Forces, aka snake eater, position. Career wise this was, however, a dumb move and almost career ending. I have not lost sleep over it yet. I was still with soldiers and not pushing papers around a desk and walking the halls of the Pentagon. For me duty in the Pentagon was the assignment I most dreaded. Another great adventure was about to start.

Mary wanted to stay at Fort Benning while I was overseas and we chose to move to Battle Park, a civilian apartment complex located on post near where she had lived when I first met her. At this time wives were not authorized to remain in government quarters when their sponsor was overseas. The apartments were quite small and several had been opened up and connected. We rented two connecting apartments. This enabled us to keep all our household goods, nothing went into storage. Since they were living on post the children remained in the same school and were able to use the military school bus. This also kept them close to their friends.

About a week before I left for Thailand the phone rang early one morning in our apartment. It was Colonel Franklin for me. "Larry, tell me your Social Security Number." I gave it to him and heard, "Well I'll be a son of a bitch, it is you. Congratulations you just came out below the zone for early promotion to lieutenant colonel." He was as surprised as I was. The comment made six years earlier by then LTC Bo Baker at Infantry Branch had come to pass: "Don't worry, you are going to get an early promotion."

I am sure the reference in this chapter title to *Hell in a Very Small Place*, a book written by Bernard Fall, about the French in Indochina and the battle at Dien Bien Phu, may raise a question in your mind. I will explain below.

The JCRC was, among Special Forces types, a true enigma. Many thought it was a CIA front and that they were running operations back into Laos and Cambodia as part of black/covert operations against the North Vietnamese. Nothing could have been further from the reality. But having heard the rumors, I did take out another $50,000 in term life insurance. I visualized myself paddling or swimming from Nakhon Phanom, Thailand, JCRC's location (when my orders were issued), across the Mekong River, and working the Laotian side of the border. Was I about to learn the truth!

I don't remember much about the trip across the Pacific except that it was on a commercial airliner with mostly U.S. soldiers going to Thailand. On the flight over I did meet Captain Dick Irby, Signal Corps, who would end up working for me at JCRC. He was as much in the dark about what really went on at JCRC as I was. Upon arrival we were met by a representative from the Army Attaché's office. He informed us that we would spend the night in Bangkok at the Chao Pia Hotel and travel on the next morning by plane to Samesan a U.S. Army Logistics Support Base down the coast to the south of

Bangkok. The JCRC had changed its base of operations since my orders had been issued. There would be no swimming across the Mekong River that was for sure. The Chao Pia was a nice facility and I stayed there whenever I traveled to Bangkok, which it turned out was a monthly ritual.

Samesan was an oasis of delight in what had been the periphery of the Vietnam War zone. It was unbelievable compared to what I had experienced during my previous two tours in SE Asia. The base had it all: very nice wooden air-conditioned BOQs, two rooms and a private bath with full time maid and laundry service. The Officers Club was on the Gulf of Thailand and was quite large, with good food, very reasonable prices and attractive Go-Go dancers. The walk from my BOQ to the club was less than 100 yards. There was a very large swimming pool, a bowling alley, golf driving range, large gym with every type of physical fitness equipment you can imagine and a large sauna. There was a running track around the base that clocked in at about three miles. There was a marina where you could rent boats and water ski. You name it and I think it was there. As I first looked around I thought to myself that while I was living in the dirt in 1967 and 1972, and being shot at, other Army types were enjoying this life. Charlie Beckwith had been right, "Life is very unfair."

Redmond's Rule # 10 - Repeated; The degree of civilization is directly proportional to the proximity to combat.

Headquarters JCRC, and its staff elements were housed in decent wooden office facilities that were fully air-conditioned. I was assigned to the J3, Operations shop as the Chief of Operations and Training Branch. My boss was a Marine LT COL, and a super officer. I had a Marine CPT (a mustang former gunnery sergeant) and Captain Dick Irby as my assistants. JCRC had been downsized somewhat in the move from Nakhon Phanom to Samesan but still had a full joint staff and a reinforced specially tailored A Team for Missing in Action (MIA) remains recovery operations. That A Team was under the command of Major Jim Grimshaw. Jim and I were to become a thing in the bars of Bangkok: more on that to follow. Our mission was to find and recover remains of U.S. MIA throughout SE Asia but particularly in Vietnam, and if there were any there, to recover live Prisoners of War (POW). This was August 1975 and Saigon and the south had fallen to the North Vietnamese in April of that year. The North Vietnamese masters were not about to let us poke around Vietnam looking for remains, or more politically explosive any live POWs. Operationally we were dead in the water.

The JCRC also had operational control of the Central Identification Laboratory Thailand, CILTHAI. This was a basically civilian outfit with several military types for oversight. The CIL's mission was to identify remains found, recovered by the SF Team or other sources, and brought safely to Thailand. The civilian anthropologists and forensic scientists who worked here were phenomenal. Give them a couple of bone fragments and a piece of skull and they could reconstruct a pretty good picture of what the individual had looked like, height, weight, race, and age. I was most impressed. In the CIL they had bones and remains waiting to be identified to include several badly burned but basically whole corpses. It was gruesome work in my mind but necessary. As I said they did amazing work and were very successful using DNA and bone structure in identifying many servicemen's remains. Their efforts brought closure, albeit sad, to families waiting for word on their missing loved one. I will return to this point in short order.

The commander of JCRC at this time was an Army colonel, a leg (a non-Airborne person, a NAP). There was considerable grumbling on the part of many, especially among the SF types, that the unit had been relegated to the leadership of a NAP. This was particularly true in that previous commanders like BG "Barbed Wire" Bob Kingston and BG Joe Ulatoski were both former Green Beret snake eaters and highly respected. The troops felt JCRC was being denigrated and made ready to be disbanded. They were not too far off the mark. The overall caliber of the Officers and NCOs was basically exceptional, especially the Army intelligence personnel who were outstanding. Our deputy commander was an AF colonel who was very good. We had a liaison officer assigned in Hanoi, at that time a major, working with the North Vietnamese, or whatever passed for working with them. He was a bit of an enigma. He had been up there from the time JCRC was first established. Some of us thought he might really be with one of our three letter agencies. We never found out, but I know he stayed there a long time and finally retired as a lieutenant colonel. Was he from one of the agencies? You tell me.

About a week after I arrived several members of the SF Team wanted to take me out to welcome me to Thailand. They were glad to see another SF soldier come to the command. We went to a club near Samesan and had a good meal. Then the entertainment started along with the really heavy imbibing. I stayed sober and when one trooper stood up and announced that they had plans for me for the rest of the evening (I won't go into that.) I stood and excused myself and returned to Samesan. The team never warmed to me after this snub on my part. They were to be a thorn in my side ever after but I never regretted not staying for the evenings planned "entertainment." Guess they thought I was a prude, or of a "different persuasion."

Once a month I flew to Bangkok for coordination at the Embassy. On each visit I was briefed by our local intelligence agents behind the green door and told that there were no live POWs in SE Asia. They encouraged us to continue looking for remains of MIAs and forget POWs. One little known tidbit they did pass on was that the French apparently were still paying $10,000 each for small boxes of remains supposedly from troops lost at *Dien Bien Phu* in 1954. The intelligence folks chuckled and added that in most cases no one knew if the remains were French, Vietnamese or monkeys. In my mind it was a criminal act on the part of the North Vietnamese.

After retiring from the Army I became part of an SF POW MIA group tracking info on possible POWs in SE ASIA. I wrote the following article in 1991 and it was printed in a couple of SF Chapter newsletters in Florida.

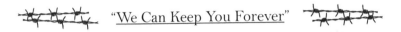 "We Can Keep You Forever"

The average Vietnam veteran, I believe, would probably tell you that the most controversial issue still remaining from our Vietnam experience is the question of MIAs. Did we leave American POWs languishing in enemy POW camps? If so, are any of them still alive?

This issue has not died in the 18 years since Operation Homecoming. Why? This is a very complex question and one that cannot be adequately addressed in a few lines. Books have been written about it; television documentaries produced about it; senior officers have "quit" over it; and unscrupulous opportunists have made money out of it, playing on the anguish and surely forlorn hopes of the families of the missing.

Having served with the Joint Casualty Resolution Center (JCRC) during 1975-76, I am closer to this issue than, quite frankly, I would like to be. During my watch with JCRC we heard, and received in writing from our North Vietnamese counterparts numerous disclaimers. They emphatically denied that they had any knowledge of even the location of bodies and or remains, let alone the thought of holding living Americans in captivity. As the

Chief of Current Operations in the J3 shop I was briefed monthly in Bangkok Thailand on all (at least that is what I believed), sightings of Americans in Southeast Asia. I returned from that assignment convinced, at least 90% sure, that there were no living Americans held against their will.

Over the last 18 years that opinion has changed. Not changed because of the return of a live American but by the persistence of the rumor that there are, or were, live Americans left in Southeast Asia. Also in spite of constant denials by the North Vietnamese that they held remains of our missing, there has been a constant trickle of "remains" since the late 1970s. No one has yet produced a live POW, and I do not believe a true, "live POW" is out there today. However, I now believe we did abandon POWs in Southeast Asia, particularly in Laos. Those brave men were left under the most trying circumstances, in which, in my opinion, only a few could possibly have survived this long. If there are still live Americans in Southeast Asia - and such a happening would not surprise me, the human spirit is indomitable and we had lots of gutsy men become prisoners - then those men have in some fashion accommodated to the fate to which our nation condemned them in the name of the "greater good" of putting the Vietnam war behind us.

Today it is my considered opinion, not arrived at rashly or without considerable thought, that there may well be living Americans, no longer POWs, in Southeast Asia. How they have survived, what accommodation they may have accepted to ensure their survival, we should not ask and should not care. They are not in my mind traitors, cowards or any other title you care to give them except heroes. They survived when our great nation abandoned them. If anyone still survives, getting them back (if they desire) should be a national priority.

If this short piece captures your interest and causes you to ask what led this writer to the above conclusions then I have accomplished my goal.

If you have not followed or kept abreast of the POW issue, other than casually, I urge you to take a few hours to look into such recent writings as *Kiss the Boys Goodbye*. All who served in Special Forces will recognize many a name we know and respect in that book. You will also not like what you read. Nor will you be convinced by the circumstantial evidence literally jumping out from every page. But remember that we have sent men to jail and in the past have executed them, based on such circumstantial evidence.

The letter of resignation from the POW desk of the Defense Intelligence Agency, and his explanation of this action by Colonel Millard "Mike" Peck, also makes outstanding reading. Copies of it are floating around the community. Some of us may question his decision, which he gave an eloquent defense of on *Nightline*, but don't question his motives nor sincerity.

If you would really like to be turned off, then I urge you to read, "An Examination of U.S. Policy Toward POW/ MIAs" written by the U.S. Senate Committee on Foreign Relations Republican Staff (available from any of your Representatives or Senators). What that document will tell you, unfortunately, is that we left our first POWs under Communist control when we pulled out of Siberia in 1919. The record gets sorrier after that, and I will let you read the appalling facts.

As a final offering, for those of you who have not seen it, I would recommend watching the BBC documentary "We Can Keep You Forever". That program, produced in 1986, truly convinced me of my position as stated in the preceding paragraphs. To hear Henry Kissinger say publicly that he now believes we might have left POWs in Laos--and I believe that is what he said--put my doubts to rest.

The North Vietnamese DID hold French troops as pawns after the 1954 Geneva Accords (according to the above mentioned Senate Report). It does absolutely no good to say that; "Such a thing is dumb!" "It makes no sense!" "No one in their right mind would do such a thing!" "What would it gain them?" Those thoughts, questions and ideas are the application of a western mind's thought patterns to a situation created and managed by the Vietnamese. I recall we spent fifteen (15) years trying to sort out a "Vietnamese" problem applying western logic. We all know how far that got us. I find it most probable, as the BBC reporter learned, that a North Vietnamese Lieutenant Colonel interrogator flatly told a POW, "Remember--we can keep you forever."

(NOTE: Sometime in the mid-1990s my phone rang one night about 0300. Mary answered and shook me awake and said, "It's for you." When I took the phone a voice said "Is this Colonel Redmond?" I responded that it was Mr. Redmond and that I was now retired and I asked who was calling. The voice stated, "Who I am doesn't matter." He went on to tell me that he was calling from California and in several short sentences gave me a POW tale that shocked me. He mumbled something about this being good and then hung up. I was still half asleep but it was not a dream. Based on this wild tale I determined at that point that I did not want to be involved in the POW issue any longer. Some things are best left alone. I backed away and I have had nothing to do with the POW question since that time. My phone has not rung in the middle of the night with such a message either. Now, let me get back to my JCRC experience.)

On several of my monthly trips to Bangkok Major Jim Grimshaw came along to do other coordination with the Army Support Group Thailand. Jim and I would stay at the Chao Pia Hotel and frequented the Bird Cage Bar across the street. We were usually in uniform during these water hole stops. On several occasions we were approached by other patrons about what we did down at Samesan and what JCRC was really all about. The two of us had a spiel down that rocked some French, Aussie and even expatriate (expat) American folks back on their heels. We would tell them that we really couldn't talk about what we did. When pressed we would look over our shoulders and glance around the bar and then whisper, "Have you ever heard of Hell in a Very Small Place?" To which most responses were "What? You don't mean you're going to…." To which we would quickly respond "Ssshhhhsh, of course not there." Jim and I jokingly referred to Samesan as "Hell in a Very Small Place." Not sure if all the victims of this charade realized they were being played or not. Honestly, I can assure you that I have never been to Dien Bien Phu. But the mystery and mystique that surrounded JCRC was enhanced with each telling of this tale. Jim rotated home after I had been there about four months. He was a good soldier and a heck of an SF operator. I missed him.

Since we were not welcome in Vietnam, now under Communist control, and Laos and Cambodia were off limits our operational activities were less than challenging. I had more free time than I liked. With the J3's approval my guys and I spent a lot of time working out and reviewing the files on over 2500 missing in action. We dug deep looking for possible leads that we could pursue and seek approval from the North Vietnamese to run a recovery operation against that file. We proposed a number of search operations through the U.S. Embassy in Bangkok to the folks in Hanoi. They were all turned down. Needless to say it was quite frustrating. But I will say after a year I was in great physical condition; swimming half a mile each noon and running three to four miles most days and pumping iron in the evenings. During the tour I won Presidential Fitness Awards for both Swimming and Running. I was proud of those patches as I was never a big physical fitness type.

I did review nearly half of the 2,500 plus files of our MIAs. It was sad and disturbing reading. I worked with several Army intelligence analysts from the J2 Intel shop, really good guys. One, a young captain, came to me with a theory about a missing F-111. This plane had taken off from a base in Thailand and never reached a flight path electronic checkpoint just near the Laotian/North Vietnamese border. His theory was centered on the terrain following radar of the F-111, a really hot bird in its day. It seems that while the radar worked well when there was foliage and hard land beneath it, apparently it could lose relevance when it went over water. The flight plan called for a low level approach out of Thailand that would take it over a major lake. Just on the other side of the lake was a normally not relevant mountain. But with the lake breaking up the return from the radar the captain felt there was a good chance that the plane had crashed into that mountain. The J3 and I agreed and we put together a plan to visit the area accompanied by Thai Border Police. This effort would be good training for the SF Team that was, when not training, sitting idly by waiting for a mission. The commander approved the plan for execution and it was cleared by the Embassy and reluctantly cleared by the Thai authorities. The captain and several of our troops drove to the area along with the Thai Border Police to do a preliminary reconnaissance as a precursor to a full up recovery operation by the SF Detachment. The party ran into a group of guerrillas near the Cambodian border. The team was shot at and the effort was quickly abandoned. Now we understood why the Thai officials had hesitated somewhat in saying go ahead. SE Asia could be a very unpleasant place even in times of peace. We planned no further operations in eastern Thailand.

The JCRC assisted the Thai Military at Utapao Royal Thai Air Force Base (RTAFB) in administering a refugee camp filled with about 5,000 South Vietnamese refugees. The actual camp was near the beach at the Utapao RTAFB adjacent to Samesan. This was a Thai operation but the U.S. had a major hand in assisting and our SF Detachment oversaw the camp's day to day operation. One Saturday I took a drive over to the camp just to show the flag and see how things were going. When I got there I found no representative from the SF element was present. After quizzing a Thai guard I was told the SFC, supposedly on duty, was down at the beach at the Green Latrine Bar drinking. I called over to Samesan and directed that an NCO familiar with the camp get over there right now. I drove to the bar and found the NCO in question nearly dead drunk. His excuse for this behavior was that his best friend back in the USA had just died in a sky diving accident. I chewed him out and took him back to Samesan making sure before we left that a U.S. sergeant was on site at the camp. I deposited him with the Commander of the SF Detachment for appropriate punishment. Not sure what happened to him as the young captain was not very strong.

About this time we were called to assist several of Senator Ted Kennedy's staffers in recovering the bodies of the two U.S. Marines left at the U.S. Embassy during the frantic withdrawal from Saigon in April of that year. The basic arrangements had all been made through diplomatic channels and the staffers would use an Air France jet to fly into Ho Chi Minh City, aka Saigon, for the pickup. Our role was to accompany them with CILTHAI reps and bring the bodies back for positive ID and preparation for return to the United States for proper burial. This was accomplished without a hiccup. The two staffers as I recall were hard to deal with and quite arrogant.

Then a very unhappy incident occurred at the Marine Birthday Ball in Bangkok with lots of the glitterati of the Thai and U.S. military in attendance. Sometime during the evening's festivities a food fight broke out between two tables of our SF Detachment. This totally inappropriate activity was quickly quelled but this was a stain on the "Green Berets" record that was going to be hard to remove. My Marine mustang assistant never forgave me and after this incident he and I did not see eye to eye until he left. As the Senior SF guy remaining in the unit at that time he blamed me. I was not aware of what had transpired until it was over but that mattered little. I was counseled by my Marine boss and directed to severely chastise the Team Leader. The captain in question didn't seem to see the harm in it all, "just good clean fun" was his attitude. Later several of the NCOs came and apologized to me even though I was not in their chain of command, at least not directly.

It was alluded to several pages back that JCRC and the Central Identification Lab did a great job of identifying remains and bringing closure to families concerned over missing loved ones. Well that was only partially correct on two counts.

First, all MIA continued to be paid their base pay and allowances with the money going to their family or bank account for the family sustenance. Also every MIA got promoted with his contemporaries. Many had already reached full colonel or sergeant major rank, their next of kin being recompensed monthly a tidy sum. We had occasion to be visited by several families. One lady had her "escort" with her and was adamant that she would not accept a presumptive finding of death for her late USAF husband, now being paid as a full colonel. If JCRC declared someone presumptively dead based on an analysis of all the facts and reports, and it was accepted by the Department of Defense, then the pay stopped and the family received a lump sum payout of $50,000. This lady wanted none of that. Some of us wanted to puke but stifled our disgust.

Second, there was a whole cottage industry in Thailand based on finding MIAs and living POWs. This industry was made up of Thai, Laotian, Vietnamese and a few U.S. ex patriots living in and around Bangkok and northern Thailand up on the Thai/Lao border. It was not in the interest of these soldiers of fortune to see us positively ID remains or announce, based on all the facts in the case, a finding of "Presumptive Death." Such action took a pawn off the playing field. These lads were truly unscrupulous in milking cash from families seeking any word on an MIA. It was sad to see and hear about it happening. I sure hope none of these rascals are out there today but if there is a nickel to be made some degenerate will try to make it. Bo Gritz, mentioned earlier in this tale, was for a time, deep into the "rescue of living POW trade." I believe Bo was sincere and really tried to rescue what he thought at the time were living POWs. Unfortunately he was the exception.

We had one visit from a Congressional Delegation looking into the MIA-POW issue. There were several Congressmen and their hangers-on to include wives. The Intelligence and Operations offices cooperated on the briefing preparation. It was good. We also sent a message, back channel, to the State Department asking that the Delegation come to Samesan and JCRC before visiting Hanoi or Ho Chi Minh City. Much to our chagrin the D.C. gang chose to ignore this request.

The Congressional Delegation arrived from Hanoi and once in the briefing room announced that the North Vietnamese had no more bodies to turn over to us and surely there were no live POWs left in SE Asia. I was not in the briefing but my boss described to me what went down. Our Commander went on with the briefing in spite of the initial announcement from the Delegation. He laid out fact after fact showing where we had more than credible evidence of possible bodies being located that deserved a site search. Then he lowered the hammer. He unveiled a large photo of our Hanoi Liaison and a North Vietnamese lieutenant colonel standing together beside a cross with the name of one of our U.S. Navy prisoners on the grave marker. Calmly the commander said something like, "Gentlemen let me introduce you to the JCRC Liaison to Hanoi. He is the man you see in the photo next to the grave of an MIA whose remains we have yet to recover." When our liaison stepped to the front of the room you could have heard a pin drop. At that point the Delegation lead jumped up and declared that they had to continue on their itinerary. I hate to report they went shopping in Sattahip the village just outside Samesan. Sad, sad tale but it did happen and they did go shopping. It appeared to us that they did not want to know the truth.

Sometime in early 1976 we moved from Samesan to Utapao Royal Thai Air Force Base right next door (a Joint U.S. and Thai base). The facilities were good and I now had a whole USAF trailer as my BOQ. The AF facility had a craft/model shop and I began building lots of HO model train cars from matchsticks and other Thai wood. The model trucks and couplers I ordered by mail from the U.S. It was fun and many of those train cars remain on my layout today.

Utapao was a great base and the RTAF had a super Officers Club. One night Dick Irby and I and a couple of other troops were there eating Thai fried rice and drinking Singh Ha beer. Thai beer was laced with embalming fluid. Honest it had a good slug of formaldehyde, and tended to talk to you the next morning if you imbibed a little too much. I quickly learned that two of those Thai beers were my limit. Suddenly someone commented that there were some shadows moving along the floor by the wall about 15 feet away from our table. After a moment we all, almost simultaneously, realized that the shadows were rats scuttling along doing whatever rats do. Not to be scared off, we continued an occasional night out at the club. The food was really pretty good.

Then the news some of us had been expecting came. The JCRC was being "asked" by the Thai Government, along with all major U.S. activities, to leave Thailand within a year. The fallout from the loss of South Vietnam was beginning to bubble to the surface. The United States had become *persona non grata* in South East Asia. The J3 shop was tasked to come up with a list of possible sites we could move to. The principal criteria being that the site be in relative close proximity to Vietnam, so that we could still, if permitted by the North Vietnamese, undertake recovery operations with some degree of ease. The initial short list of possible new bases included Hong Kong, Formosa and the Philippines. The first two options were nixed by the State Department and also by the Formosan Government in a telegram to the U.S. Embassy Bangkok, info JCRC. It appeared our false reputation of being part of some covert operation was widespread and our presence not desired on Formosa.

At the direction of the J3 I took a four man team to the Philippines to check out Clark Air Force Base, Subic Bay Naval Base and a place up in the mountains, San Miguel Naval Radio Station. I must say that the Philippines is a great country with fantastic scenery. It is a charming country and the people seemed to love us. We are now long gone from there, but I would truly enjoy going back for a visit. San Miguel was our last stop and what a glorious tropical site it was; a Little America up in the mountains and jungle north of Manila. It had everything we needed; lots of open housing, facilities of all kinds and plenty of office space as well as an airstrip capable of handling C-130 aircraft. It was perfect. Clark AFB and Subic Bay Naval Base would have worked but all of us on the team felt San Miguel was the best choice.

We did visit Manila and had two days with some time for sightseeing. Quite a city and Americans were definitely liked by the folks on the street. We observed that the tourist population was largely Japanese with lots of cameras hanging all over their bodies. The Philippine people did not like them, at least not in 1976, in spite of the money they threw around. The Japanese occupation of the Islands during World War II was not forgotten.

Upon return to Thailand we were told that in our absence the State and Defense Departments had decided JCRC's and CILTHAI's next home would be Barber's Point USMC Air Station in Hawaii. Just wonderful, another three thousand miles further away from the area we were expected to operate in. The move would commence in ninety days.

(NOTE: The JCRC and CIL remain today in Hawaii at Joint Base Pearl Harbor-Hickham vice Barbers Point. It has been renamed the Joint POW/MIA Accounting Command with CIL HAWAII as a sub element and a brigadier general in overall charge. They now search the globe for Missing in Action bodies to include those from WWII and Korea.)

With a drawdown and departure date looming in ninety days, Dick Irby and I both called our respective assignment officers for orders to our next duty stations. Dick was handled well and in good order as I recall, but darned if I can tell you where he was next assigned. Possibly back to the Citadel, his alma mater. I had a bit of a problem with my assignment officer. You may be getting the idea that I could never communicate well with Infantry Branch. First the assignment officer got belligerent and told me I had called two months early. My return date was August and the timeline from Department of State had us out of Thailand shortly before that, so it really was not too early. He argued with me about such a drawdown taking place; challenging me on how I got such intelligence, "Infantry Branch had no such info." He was very argumentative and would not listen. The conversation ended with me a very unhappy camper.

I sent a letter to Infantry Branch laying out what was happening. About two weeks later I had a phone call from another major at Branch. What a difference a letter and two weeks made. He asked me where I wanted to go and I said to the 82nd Airborne Division at Fort Bragg, North Carolina. He told me that he had no openings at the 82nd for majors but could get me to Fort Bragg, XVIII Airborne Corps. I was thrilled and thanked him and said getting me to Fort Bragg was enough. His response was, "Hit the ground running, good luck." Totally different attitude than the arrogant know-it-all that I had first dealt with. Maybe I say that because he gave me what I wanted. I assumed that once at Fort Bragg I could affect a change from Corps to the 82nd with ease. Heck, the Assistant Division Commander was Brigadier General Guy S. Meloy whom I had worked for at Fort Benning in 1973. I thought, "Wow, this was made to order, just what I wanted." I sure got that wrong.

32
ANOTHER ADVENTURE:
FORT BRAGG, 1976

The flight home was commercial, fairly comfortable and uneventful. Unlike my second return home from Vietnam there were no protestors to contend with. By the way, I never was spit upon or cursed even when I was in D.C. at Infantry Branch at the height of the protests. That was certainly not true for too many returning Vietnam vets. Guess I was lucky. I traveled to Fort Benning where Mary had already made arrangements for our household goods to be shipped to Fort Bragg. We drove north to Fayetteville, North Carolina and a seven year stint in one place. What a change that was. And what an eventful seven years it was to be.

We rented a nice home in Cottonade just two minutes from Bragg. It was not fancy but really middle class nice in what was then a very pleasant community. Before I signed in to XVIII Airborne Corps I went to see BG Meloy at the 82nd and offer my invaluable services to the "Almost Airborne" Division. (Known jokingly as the Almost Airborne Division since the unit patch had two AAs on it stemming from WWI and the name All American.) Well getting reacquainted with the General was quite a disappointment. He said they did not need me and that I should go up to XVIII Airborne Corps and enjoy myself. Imagine that; me, yes me; being turned down for duty with the 82nd and by a former boss! Wow, no way Jose! But that is just what happened. Later, over time, I deduced that my three tours with the 101st Airborne Division and time in Special Forces did not "qualify" me for duty on Ardennes Street with the All Americans. I was later to prove General Meloy wrong on that count.

I signed in at Corps Headquarters and was posted to the G3 Operations Division as the Chief of Current Operations. I was working for a real hardnosed aviator lieutenant colonel and stern taskmaster but a super soldier. I learned a lot from him and respected him greatly. The G3 at the time was a West Point graduate and a super gentleman with whom I worked closely. As Chief of Current Operations I was responsible for monitoring everything going on at Fort Bragg and administering all "taskings" in support of activities on the base. This made me a well-known and in some cases a much disliked task master. Units did not want to give up people, vehicles, equipment, whole companies of troops to do this task or that thing; support to other units in their ongoing activities that could not be supported from internal assets. But the giver of assets this month became the receiver of assets the following month. The job, while demanding, did make me known throughout Fort Bragg. This was to prove very helpful to me over the next several years.

Another aspect of my duties included the setup, management and maintenance of the Corps Tactical Operations Center (TOC). This was no small task and took considerable time and attention. Also our commander wanted to make the Corps Advance TOC smaller and lighter for ease of deployment. The sheer size and scope of the TOC required considerable setup time and made moving it extremely difficult once it was established. I can remember Mary's dad, LTC Devlin, telling me about TOCs in WWII; how big and monstrous they were in the early days in North Africa. He went on to say that about two weeks after landing in Tunisia, the First Infantry Division TOC operated under an olive tree and they worked off the tops of C Ration boxes. The German Stuka dive bombers did a job on any large tent structure. Here we were forty years later with an even larger TOC and possibly facing the Russian Air Force. Not a pleasant thought. We eventually got a mobile jump/advance TOC established in two specially built huts that we mounted on two-and-a-half-ton trucks. It worked OK and could move around and still link back to the main TOC for operations. Oh yes, this jump TOC was also air droppable.

I had a terribly embarrassing moment on our first field deployment down at Bladen Lakes, NC for a Joint Army, Navy, Air Force Atlantic Command exercise. All was going great and on schedule until we started to erect the new ARFAB, Army Fabricated, no idea why they called them that, tents. Somehow the pins to hold the metal framework for the canvas up and in place had not been brought from Fort Bragg. It took several hours of frantic calling back to base and a new speed record on the highway to get those damned pins to us. All the while I was getting darts thrown at me via the eyes of my boss and the Corps Commander. The G3 took it all in stride, gentleman that he was. It turned out OK in the end. I survived and the TOC was up and running before sunset and the beginning of the exercise. Needless to say that was the last time we went anywhere without those pins. In fact, I believe, this near disaster resulted in an Army wide modification whereby the pins were affixed with a screw and small chains to the metal poles near the point where they were to be inserted to secure the structure in an upright position.

Sometime early in my tenure as Chief of Current Operations I was promoted to lieutenant colonel. That change from a major's gold leaf to a lieutenant colonel's silver leaf helped me greatly in my struggles with units that were reluctant to provide support through the Post Tasking System. I had as I recall about five majors and three senior NCOs to administer the taskings. We managed to keep the Post running efficiently especially thanks to the NCOs who knew all the ins and outs. Reserve Officer Training Corps Summer Camp support taskings were particularly tough and demanding. Woe to the unit that missed a required Summer Camp support action. Every morning was another challenge and more than once I posted before the Corps Commander to explain why such and such a task had been botched by this or that unit. Sometimes my shop had made the mistake and I ended up eating crow and getting a good counseling. But it was fun too, not all problems.

Early on in this assignment my boss and the G3 introduced me to bird hunting and I acquired my first shotgun. We spent many weekend mornings quail hunting and enjoying the bird fields around Bragg. The Corps Commander at the time, Lieutenant General Hank Emerson, was an avid bird hunter and the four of us passed quite a few Saturdays shooting quail and dove. I must admit not many dove. Those rascals are elusive, like scat backs in football always zigging and zagging; and very hard to bring down. I also began to get into deer hunting but only to a limited degree. We still had that sixteen foot Glastron boat I had bought from Ray Wagner back at Fort Benning. The family went boating, picnicking and fishing in lakes around Fayetteville as often as we could. Kathy and Larry became very good water skiers.

The Army had just constructed new quarters, very nice, on post and we were offered the chance to move there. It was a little closer to Corps Headquarters and would make my commute a bit shorter. Mary and I checked out the housing area and we're quite impressed. The house we took was quarters 111 Watts Court. It was large, four bedrooms, two and a half baths and a den that looked out on woods where the children could play. It was quite satisfactory. We moved; and in the next six years paid the Government via our Housing Allowance what it cost them to build that place. But the house was big, brand new and close to everything and we enjoyed it. We especially had some great neighbors in the court; our closest friends there, "Heavy" and Jean Morris, remain friends to this day.

At some point in the winter of 1977 we were scheduled to deploy to Europe on a NATO Exercise called Able Archer. This exercise was designed, among other things, to test our ability to work the nuclear release system and employ tactical nukes via artillery. This was not an easy mission. There was a very complex and difficult nuclear release system that had to be learned and understood completely. The entire system was one that received detailed inspection and attention from higher headquarters. Heads rolled and commanders were relieved if the unit failed to meet the high standards and requirements of the system. One did not joke nor take a cavalier attitude toward nuclear weapons. XVIII Corps had never, repeat never, had a nuclear release program and we knew nothing about it. So guess who got responsibility for setting up and administering our nuclear release cell? You got it, the Current Operations Section of G3 and LTC Redmond. The good news was that the Corps Commander somehow managed to have assigned a highly qualified major from the Pentagon. He knew this business inside and out and was assigned to my office. He may have written the Army Regulation on nuclear release procedures. He really knew his stuff and although it was a pain, and he could be a bit haughty, when we finally deployed to the exercise in Germany we were ready. Thanks to him the Corps did well on Able Archer.

We had one special event, worthy of recounting, that I was involved with before the big exercise in Germany. It seemed that Forces Command (FORSCOM) out of Fort MacPherson, Georgia wanted to do a no notice operational test of the Ranger Battalion. The Rangers had only recently been created as separate battalion size units. This little test was touted as a check out of one of the Ranger Battalion's readiness for contingency operations. Corps got involved providing support assets and evaluators for the exercise. It was to take place at Camp Mackall, a little used WWII base, about twenty-five miles from Fort Bragg proper. The Special Forces School used the camp as a training area but most of the old cantonment area was gone. There was a functional airfield there but no facilities. To land an aircraft you had to bring in Air Force combat controllers and the stuff needed for safety (crash trucks, ambulances, et cetera). I would become very familiar with Camp Mackall over the next two years. The Test/Exercise Director was none other than BG Guy S. Meloy, now the deputy operations officer at FORSCOM. The Current Operations Element of G3 was directed to set up a simulated flying command post at Camp Mackall that would monitor the operation and provide reports to the exercise director.

We tasked for all the necessary communications assets, tents, and other support needed. I was present when the exercise went down. The Rangers did not do well at all. But as I sat around and listened to some of the evaluators talk I was stunned to hear things that led me to believe that the test and evaluation could have been deliberately structured for failure. The Rangers did have problems, of that there was no doubt. But I had the distinct feeling that the results of the test may have been preordained. The battalion commander was relieved. Many in the Army hierarchy saw the Ranger Battalion concept as a threat and a concept that would draw good men away from the Airborne. There was truth to that belief in that the best of the paratrooper noncommissioned officers gravitated to the Rangers. Whatever really happened during the test the First Ranger Battalion got a sort of a black eye and a new commander. The Ranger troops were always good and if there was a failing with them in the beginning it rested with the officers who thought their s**t did not stink. That of course is my opinion only.

Shortly before we deployed to Germany on Exercise Able Archer I was called to the G3 office and told that I was being given a new job and would take over the Corps Emergency Deployment Readiness Exercise Branch (EDRE, pronounced EEEE-DREEE). This was a real plum assignment and a fun job. Our mission was to design and plan "no notice exercises" for the Corps units, testing their ability to be called out unannounced and deploy on an exercise in eighteen hours; establish the unit in the field, sometimes at Bragg and other times flying away to other posts; and operating effectively per their mission requirements.

To accomplish this role I had two captains and three NCOs to plan and execute the EDREs. They were all good people. One of the captains was a West Pointer, brilliant analytical mind and super planner who had irritated someone and had a blemish on his record that caused him to be passed over for promotion twice. I tried my best with good reports and letters from colonels and even the Corps Deputy Commander but could not get him promoted. I can only say he never let me down; well maybe once and that was a key failure for me, or so it turned out.

In actual conduct of exercises we were augmented as needed by personnel who were experts in the operational aspects of the units we were testing. This worked very well as it meant that only a few select folks knew who was going to be tested next. We worked on the top floor of Corps HQ in a secure part of the building. To the best of my knowledge no unit we ever tested had any idea that it was their turn in the barrel until the notice hit at 0400, sometimes on a Saturday or Sunday. We were somewhat feared, needless to say, and it was amazing how folks kept asking questions over a beer at the Club seeking some indication of where the axe would fall next. Even Mary was approached and questioned at Officer's Wives Club affairs, at the "O Club" and amazingly the Post Exchange while she shopped. Frankly she had no idea what we were planning next. I kept her in the dark also. She did not even know where I was going when I said I was off on an exercise and kissed she and the children goodbye.

We planned and executed EDREs for a number of Corps units running the gamut from a medical battalion that we deployed to Shaw AFB, South Carolina, by both air and ground convoy; a transportation battalion that we exercised from Fort Bragg to Camp Mackall, twenty-five miles west of Fort Bragg; to an SF battalion from the 5th Special Forces Group that we deployed to North Field, South Carolina on a very difficult mission that they performed in typical superb SF fashion. To satisfy an urge of the Corps commander, we also "no noticed" the Corps Advance Tactical Operations Center and flew them to Fort Campbell air dropping on Yamota Drop Zone.

Other than one of the 35th Signal Group's radio vans streamering in from 1,000 feet and burying itself about four feet in the ground all went well. We deployed two companies from a battalion of the 82nd Airborne to Camp McCoy, Wisconsin, and crossed the Mississippi River in rubber boats in a blinding snow storm in late April. We also did a number of other exercises of reduced scope before we were tasked to do some very special exercises. Before I get into those special events I think a few of the initial EDREs we conducted deserve a little more explanation. Additionally I will provide some comments on Exercise Able Archer.

The first EDRE I was responsible for planning and conducting was for a medical battalion, a part of First Corps Support Command or First COSCOM. At the N Plus 2 hour briefing (N Hour was announcement/notification of the EDRE and N Plus 2 came two hours later) in addition to the unit battalion commander, COL Elmer Pendleton, a past Corps G3, and the current COSCOM commander was present. Colonel Pendleton was known to eat LTCs and any other rank for breakfast, lunch and dinner. He was notorious for interrupting, flustering and humiliating briefers. As our briefer started laying out the tasks and missions and the overall exercise scenario Elmer interrupted the lad several times. I take the liberty of calling the Colonel "Elmer" for reasons that will become clear shortly. After the second interruption I stood up and calmly said, "Sir, if you will just let my briefer finish I believe he will answer all your questions: specifically I know he will address your last comment shortly." Colonel Pendleton glared at me but nodded and let the briefer continue. When the briefing was over I looked directly at him and asked, "Sir, do you have any questions?" He stood, smiled and walked out of the room without a word. Obviously he was satisfied. The med battalion performed beautifully on both the road and air deployment and in going through the set up and operation of their hospital once they arrived at Shaw AFB. The debriefing gave them the highest of marks and COL Pendleton thanked my whole team for an excellent training and shake out opportunity for his troops. Later the G3 told me that COL Pendleton had called and thanked him for a great exercise and for the professionalism of the EDRE team.

One other EDRE specifically worthy of mention was a call out of one of the battalions of the 5th Special Forces Group. I forget the exact scenario, rescue of hostages or recovery of a nuclear tipped missile, I am not sure. The battalion commander was a super guy and an acquaintance. The alert went fine, the planning went well but then the weather turned "delta sierra" (that's dog s**t in civilian parlance). The scenario required a parachute operation with about 100 troops in the assault force jumping into North Field, South Carolina to accomplish the mission. I was serving as the Senior Evaluator on this one since I was SF qualified and my judgment was accepted by the Green Berets. A rainstorm dropped down much further south than had been predicted and the jump was about to be cancelled. We were marshaled at Pope Air Force Base next to Fort Bragg. The troops were "chuted up" and the planes standing by but the weather was a NO GO. Showers and heavy winds were about to force an end to the EDRE. The battalion commander and I were standing in base operations when the weather officer for the base walked in and calmly announced; "Well gentlemen, looks like you have a 'sucker hole' between 2300 and 0100. The weather over North Field will clear for two hours then close in again; heavy rain after 0100." The air mission commander, an Air Force colonel said to me, "It's your call, we are ready." I responded, "Let's do it," or something like that. Like Ike directing D-Day, I didn't like it but it had to be a go.

The planes were loaded and took off headed to North Field. It was a very bumpy ride and as we approached the drop zone, which paralleled the runway, it was approaching 2330 and all I could see were clouds. Standing in the door of a shaking C-130 being buffeted by heavy gusts of wind is an experience one does not easily forget.

Not being able to see the ground or lights, or anything but clouds, is a bit unnerving. Suddenly through the haze some lights began to appear and the ground could be glimpsed from time to time. I looked up from my position in the jump door, saw the jump light turn from RED to GREEN and I was gone. Pavlov's dog like airborne training at work again. After the opening shock I felt my chute deploy and I found myself swaying beneath the canopy. I looked around; saw the ground, other jumpers in the air and lights on the horizon. It struck me that the lights looked a little close and maybe I should drop my rucksack and radio and get ready to land. As I released the ruck it started to drop and I heard a distinct thud within two seconds of release. It registered quickly: I thought, "Oh my God that's concrete, the runway!" just as I did my first and only ever standing landing. Standing landings are a no-no in the best of situations. Standing landings in the dark, on a concrete runway, and basically unexpected are a disaster waiting to happen. My disaster had just happened. (NOTE: We were dropped a little low, like maybe 500 feet instead of 800. North Field was located at an altitude of about 300 feet and it appeared the Air Force had failed to put the actual elevation of the terrain in their altimeter computer. It was quite a jolt for me although there were no serious injuries among the assault force.)

I stood there literally shaking and quivering from my toes to the top of my scalp. Perhaps it was two minutes maybe five; I am not sure, before I was able to get my body parts moving. I hurt all over. I managed to get out of my chute, roll it up and stuff it in the kit bag. Normally you carried your chute to a central turn in point but we had planned to leave the chutes in kit bags where we landed for recovery by a support element in the morning. For me at 2400 hours, or whatever time it was, at that point it was a life saver for me to leave that chute on the runway. I managed to link up with the Special Forces command group and hobbled along until the operation was over. The Green Beret troopers did a super job and accomplished the mission in sterling fashion. They passed with flying colors. The rains did start again promptly at 0100 as the AF weather officer had predicted they would. All I remember beyond that is that when I finally got home and took off my boots my feet and shins were both black and blue almost up to my knees. Every bone in my legs and back ached. It took me about three days to stop hurting, and I am surprised my back survived the event at all. After my injury on the Golan Heights back in early 1974 this event was not what my spine needed.

The NATO Able Archer Exercise arrived, and although now the Chief of EDRE I went along as a CORPS G3 Tactical Operations Center (TOC) duty officer. I think the G3 wanted me along as I was the guy who had worked with our nuclear release expert as we set up and organized the nuclear release program mentioned earlier. We deployed to the British Sector of defense in northern West Germany. It was cold as the dickens. This was my first ever visit to Germany. We set up in a lovely white, snow covered, pine forest At least it was lovely and white when we got there, before turning to a bloody, brown sea of mud. We lived in unheated British squad tents and slept on Brit cots that were about six inches off the ground. Working in the TOC where there was heat was a blessing. When off shift our sleeping bags worked well enough to sleep comfortably but those tents were darned cold.

I had been working the night shift in the TOC when one morning the tent flap flew up and a figure loomed in the entry way. Who stood there but COL Elmer Pendleton. He said to me, "Redmond, get dressed, we're going to the village for a schnitzel." He had a jeep and the idea of a real German schnitzel sounded great to me. We drove down to the local village and ate in a quaint, typical German *Gasthaus* country restaurant. The schnitzel was fantastic; the beer even better. Colonel Pendleton and I must have bonded during that EDRE of the medical battalion as he was very open with me. His reputation of being feared and a tough guy to get along with was legend around Fort Bragg. It appeared to me that he needed someone to chat with who did not work for him. In the course of a couple of good beers I boldly asked him why he had not made general; most folks thought he deserved that rank. He smiled and said, "In two words, General DePuy." He went on to say, "When General DePuy retires I will be on the next list for Brigadier." Do you know that happened, just as he predicted. Elmer retired as a major general from Readiness Command a few years later. He was a good soldier. I used to see him at AUSA conferences when I worked for General Dynamics after retiring from the Army. He always stopped and talked. In spite of a gruff demeanor and reputation for being hard he was a great officer and at least for me easy to get along with.

The exercise went off well and XVIII Corps looked great and I will tell you that happened in no small way as a result of a certain major nuclear release expert. Without him I am not sure we would have looked so good.

(NOTE: A small tidbit of Cold War History for what it is worth. I typed these lines about Exercise Able Archer and Nuclear Release training in late 2012. I add this information in January 2014. Am I ever a slow writer! I recently read a book given me by a buddy, former Navy submarine skipper, entitled *Blind Man's Bluff, The Untold Story of American Submarine Espionage*. On page 265 of that book appeared a vignette about Operation RYAN the Soviet code name for a nuclear missile attack and Exercise Able Archer. A defector from the Soviet KGB (Secret Police/Intelligence), Colonel Oleg Gordievsky, made some interesting comments during debriefings by the British and U.S.

With Operation RYAN running wild and nearly unchecked Gordievsky says there was a real danger of a catastrophic mistake. That was never more true, he says, than during November NATO exercises coded named "Able Archer." From November 2 to November 11, the NATO forces were practicing release procedures for tactical nuclear weapons, moving through

*all of the alert stages from readiness to general alert. Because
the Soviets own contingency plans called for real preparations
to be shrouded under similar exercises, alarmists within the
KGB came to believe that the NATO forces had been placed on
an actual alert.*

So much for secrecy and operations security which we practiced,
or thought we practiced, to a high degree. They were aware of the
exercise purpose as it was going on! While we were learning and
training in a new technique our Soviet adversaries were seriously
worried that we might be readying to start World War III. Nothing
could have been further from the truth, I think.)

When the Exercise ended we had about five or six days before
we started redeploying to the States. With the G3's permission I
decided to hitch a ride down to Bavaria on a chopper to see Mary's
brother, Major Eddie Devlin. Eddie had just been transferred from
Okinawa back to Germany, and was assigned to Wurzburg. This
would give us a rare chance to visit. When I called and set up the
visit, Eddie's wife Marga said that they were staying in the village
of Langfeld near where she was born, and that they would put me
up there, vice Wurzburg. They were still living out of suitcases.
Typical of the Army in those days; we all moved too frequently.

The helicopter ride down was an experience, cloudy, foggy and
rain, with the ceiling being about 200 feet all the way there. I saw
some of Germany up close and personal on that flight. Langfeld was
a classic German village. It was like going back to the early 1900s
with manure piles outside every farm house for fertilizing the fields
and cobblestone or dirt streets the norm. There could not have been
sixty homes/farms in the whole town. We had a nice visit, most of
which I do not remember except that Eddie and I went to the Post
Exchange Class VI in Wurzburg and I bought a bottle of *Afrika
Korps* Brandy for $2.00. It had been bottled in Africa in 1942 by
Field Marshal Erwin Rommel's troops. That bottle remains in the

bar at home, now seventy-three years old, and it is probably vinegar; assuming brandy changes from booze to vinegar with time.

On Saturday I went with *Oma*, Marga's mother, to the village cemetery where she dutifully washed her husband's gravestone. She did this most Saturdays, rain or shine. As she scrubbed the stone, a flat granite piece the size of a coffin with a headstone at the top, I wandered around the cemetery looking at gravestones. After about three minutes I stopped short, looked back at the graves I had past and had a startling thought. I had walked past twenty graves, out of no more than seventy in the whole cemetery. Of those, at least fifteen had pictures of the person they represented and all of them were in Nazi military uniform. The startling fact was that of those graves most had the inscription, *"Vermisst in Russland-194?"* (Missing in Russia-194?). The whole cemetery must have held memorials to twenty Nazi soldiers, at least fifteen of them missing in Russia. These were not graves in the true sense but "memorials" to missing in action! There were only four or five graves of soldiers who died fighting us in France or who perished with the *Afrika Korps* and whose remains came back to Germany. Being a soldier, at that moment in history, and possibly facing the Soviet hordes, this was not a pleasant bit of information. I doubt the people of the United States could have handled casualty reports of that magnitude. Vietnam was bad enough.

The return flight to the British Zone in Northern Germany was quite nice with lots of sunshine, for a change, and a chance to really see the German countryside. Redeployment to Fort Bragg was uneventful. Things were about to take a different tack, however, for the EDRE Branch, and get very exciting.

33

MY BIG MOUTH:
DOING THE RIGHT THING

S hortly after returning to Fort Bragg I was called into the G3's
office, along with the Deputy G3, and told I had been selected
to be the senior evaluator on a very close hold (classified) test
of the 2nd Ranger Battalion. The test had been directed by BG Meloy
as Deputy Operations Officer for FORSCOM. It proved to be an
interesting exercise to say the least. The XVIII Corps Commander
would be the Exercise Director and in overall charge, hence EDRE's
role in setting up and executing the project. As a training option
for Readiness Command (REDCOM) at MacDill AFB, Florida that
Headquarters would provide the Joint Task Force (JTF) control
element for the USAF and Army Ranger elements. REDCOM had
an in place JTF, named JTF 7, which did not get used often. The
exercise would shake them out also. Seemed a little complicated
to this mere LTC of Infantry, but whatever. I was a small cog
in a big wheel.

The Deputy G3, an old Vietnam 101st Airborne troop and a very
good soldier accompanied me to FORCES COMMAND to get a
briefing from BG Meloy. This did not go well for Redmond. BG
Meloy gave us some guidance that caused the hair on the back of
my neck to stand up. The Exercise was to be conducted at White
Sands Missile Range and Fort Bliss, Texas. As a start that was not
bad. Things got interesting as the general continued talking. First
he wanted to cross the T with two serials of USAF C-130s. Now

crossing the T, having one serial of aircraft fly N to S while another comes in from the E to W about sixty seconds apart to drop the Rangers is tricky in the extreme. To add to this complex effort the C-130s were to fly totally blacked out, not one light visible. I did not like the sounds of this one.

The troops were to be airlifted out of Fort Lewis two hours, I say again, two hours after being alerted. The norm was that you always had eighteen hours for wheels up (aircraft take off) to launch an assault. That was chiseled in stone like the Ten Commandments; but not for this exercise. When I expressed surprise and challenged this one I was told to "do it." The Deputy G3 cast a jaundiced eye my way and I shut up. The Rangers would be flown to Fort Bliss, wheels up after a mere two hours, and stage and plan the assault there. Flight time was a little over two hours so the Rangers would arrive at Bliss about four plus hours into a normal eighteen hour "go to war" sequence. They would then launch exactly eighteen hours after initial alert and fly for over an hour to secure a nuclear tipped missile that had been stolen by terrorists. The terrorists, true to form, were threatening to launch the missile against one of our allies.

As we discussed the overall scenario and how the exercise should unfold it became clear that we had a problem. After the attack the Rangers had to be transported from White Sands to Bliss Army Airfield to be extracted. It was suggested that we would just position X number of 2 1/2 ton trucks in the desert to move them. The trucks would be from local indigenous sources. Well, I made some kind of comment that such a scenario was the dumbest thing I had heard lately and totally blew the realism for the Rangers. At that point the Deputy G3 said we should take a break and I was sort of led out to the woodshed. After a severe counseling that I could not talk to the General like that we reconvened. By the way the colonel went on to retire as a two star general. He was a good soldier but sure did not want to cross sabers with BG Meloy. As I recall the final decision was that once the missile had been secured and the mission accomplished we would go administrative and end the exercise. That made more sense than having eighteen trucks under friendly control waiting in the desert in the middle of bad guy country.

To further set the stage for what followed let me explain that the 2nd Ranger Battalion commander was a recently promoted full COL, Jerry Bethke. Jerry was completing a successful command tour leading the 2nd Ranger Battalion and was two weeks away from changing command and being reassigned. When the alert for this exercise hit Fort Lewis Jerry Bethke was one shocked Ranger commander. No way had he even an inkling this zinger was about to descend on his unit.

After the planning guidance session at FORSCOM we returned to Fort Bragg, briefed the Corps Commander, LTG Volney Warner, and planning for the EDRE went into full swing. I sent my young captain down to Fort Bliss to arrange all the necessary logistics, headquarters sites, terrorist opposing force and the actual missile. Things were perking along. JTF 7 was to be alerted early. REDCOM was not quite as "forward leaning in the foxhole" as a Ranger Battalion and no way could they be wheels up two hours after alert. As it turned out I went directly to Fort Bliss, linking with COL Bethke and his Rangers there. The Air Force piece of the action had come together nicely and everyone felt comfortable things were ready. I still didn't like crossing the T and flying with total blackout of all aircraft lights.

Redmond's Rule #17 - Murphy is alive and well out there --
If it can go wrong it will.

The EDRE Team flew out early and established our own operations center, received Joint Task Force 7 from MacDill AFB, Florida and waited on our Rangers to arrive. Somewhere along the way BG Meloy and LTG Warner flew in to oversee the entire operation. The alert went off on time; the Rangers were wheels up at N + 2 (N standing for notification hour) and arrived at Fort Bliss about N + 4:30. They were briefed by the JTF Staff on the mission and told that they had roughly twelve hours to plan and had to be wheels up at N + 18. The Rangers were sort of taken aback by that but sucked it up and drove on. I was introduced to COL Bethke as the senior evaluator and each of the company evaluators were married up with their respective company commanders. We all sort of over watched the planning phase that was pretty frantic but handled well by COL Bethke and his S3 Operations Officer. At this point I had been up well over twenty-four hours and was feeling pretty tired. The Rangers were operating on guts and adrenaline. It was their way.

Everything was on time and on the spot. The two aircraft serials commenced launching exactly at N + 18 Hours and the EDRE assault phase was happening. As we flew toward crossing that damned "T" I fell asleep in my seat, hard to do with a parachute and a forty pound ruck with radio in it, but I was tired. I actually woke up standing up and hooked up. I do not remember going through the jump commands. The green light came on and my stick shuffled to and out the door. It had to be the blackest night I can ever remember. It was like jumping into the inside of a cow; not one sliver of moon or ambient light. When I landed and rolled up my chute I looked around and saw and heard nothing. I thought, "Oh, fantastic you idiot. You will never link up with the Ranger command element." It truly was black as pitch. I was feeling just a little more than uneasy when I felt a hand grip my shoulder and a whispered voice said, "Are you the evaluator? Come with me." Sweeter words I had not heard lately.

I linked up with COL Bethke and the Rangers continued their mission. This was when things came apart for them. They had thirty minutes after jumping to find the missile before the terrorists could launch it. It took them until well after dawn, about an hour and half, before they found the missile. The exercise terminated, went administrative and the Rangers pulled out.

I wandered back toward the missile site where my young captain and a jeep were waiting to take me the twenty miles back to Fort Bliss. When I got to the missile the lieutenant from Fort Bliss asked if I wanted a cup of "joe." Hell yes, those were sweet words also. I was really beat and hot coffee sounded good. For Colonel Bethke this offer of coffee turned out to be a lifesaver. I sat down and began talking with the young lieutenant. The missile and all the ancillary equipment to support it had been placed in a deep hole. It was not readily visible from the surrounding desert. As we talked a thought hit me. I asked the LT if they had heard the aircraft pass overhead; answer, "Well we thought so but didn't see them, and then we heard thuds as paratroopers landed all around us in the desert. They were all over us (pointing up to the rim of the hole we were sitting in) but never found us until well after dawn. Pretty slick huh?" I then asked him what his crew would have had to do to fire the missile. His comeback shocked and stunned me. "Well, sir, we would have fired up that thirty kilowatt generator there (pointing) and started the thirty minute firing sequence." I then asked him if they had fired up the generator would the searching Rangers have heard it. "Sir, no way they couldn't have heard it, that's why I didn't fire it up." Uh oh, bad news for EDRE and our detailed planning for which we were reputedly the best.

Jumping in the jeep we raced back to Fort Bliss and I charged into the CG's temporary office just as BG Meloy was finishing explaining how the Rangers had failed in the mission. I frankly interrupted, not the smartest move I ever made. I explained what I had just learned in the desert and stated categorically that we had failed the Rangers, not vice versa. We had to pass them. Brigadier General Meloy did not seem to like that but LTG Warner and the REDCOM JTF Team Chief agreed. Second Battalion passed with flying colors. Colonel Bethke went on to retire as a two star general. To this day, to the best of my knowledge, he knows nothing of this happening. I was to hear about it again as you will read further on.

34

THE DAY OF THE BLUE LIGHT

ort Bragg seemed normal enough after Able Archer and the Ranger Exercise and we returned to our EDRE planning. Over a beer or two at the Club I kept hearing rumors of some special activities ramping up. After a couple of weeks I learned, via the old SF grapevine, that COL Charlie Beckwith was forming a special counter terror (CT) unit and it was being "stood up" in the old Post Stockade. It had nothing to do with me/us at EDRE and so I ignored it. Then rumors started flying about another special unit, code named Blue Light that had been activated within the 5th Special Forces Group. It was all pretty confusing and close hold. All the rumors of course only compounded the confusion. No one really knew what was going on, what was real or imagined, in terms of new units being activated or what their mission might be.

One morning about two weeks later I was called, along with the G3, to the Corps Commander's Office. When I got there he told us that there had recently been a test run in Hawaii of a special "interim" counter terror force called Blue Light. The test had not gone well. The Corps Commander had been directed by Department of the Army to set up another test and that effort would be run by EDRE. At this point I was getting confused and had no real idea what a CT Test consisted of. Calling the team together I briefed them on the new slant and my SF NCO planner said, "Give me some time and I will see what I can find out."

The info brought back from the Green Beret Parachute Club on Smoke Bomb Hill (home to the Special Forces) was that a battalion of the 5th SF had been designated the CT force until Beckwith could bring his new Delta Force to an operational status. The word was that LTC Joe Cincotti, who happened to be a neighbor and friend, was the Blue Light Commander. I had been in the dark as to Joe's role as commander of Blue Light-some close hold activities at Fort Bragg really were close hold. Apparently they had botched the exercise in Hawaii so bad that the terrorists had killed all the hostages on the target aircraft (simulated of course). It quickly became clear that hostage barricade situations where the training element in vogue using aircraft and buildings as the vehicle to test the counter terror troops' ability to rescue hostages. We began looking into different scenarios and locations to conduct tests.

As with most secrets on Smoke Bomb Hill, and Fort Bragg in general, the new role for the Corps EDRE Team as a test and evaluation element for CT actions leaked out. After several days I had a call at home from Joe Cincotti asking me to come over for a drink. I felt I could learn something from him so I agreed and we spent several hours chatting in his den. Joe pumped me hard for information on what we were planning but I think I got the most and better slice of intelligence from him. I learned that Joe's battalion, backed by COL Bob Mountel (commander of the 5th SF Group) quite an SF troop in his own right, had created their counter terror training camp out at Mott Lake. It was called the Stevens and Kramer (S&K) Range, named for the two SF NCOs who designed and built it. It was unique to say the least. They had all sorts of good stuff built to bring them up to speed. The principal training aid being a live fire shooting house built entirely from old tires for training on entering and clearing buildings and rooms. The old tire buildings allowed live fire shooting at targets representing terrorists interspersed among targets representing hostages. Joe invited me out to see what they were doing and I readily accepted. I then asked him what had happened in Hawaii. He explained that the target was a hijacked civilian airliner with terrorists and hostages on board the plane. Seems the reason that exercise was such a failure, at least in his eyes, was that the terrorist role players knew the exact time of the CT team attack. Also the hostages knew and were just waiting for the first sign of rescue. Knowing when the hit was coming allowed them to be aware of any outside sound or movement of the aircraft caused by troops stepping on the wing or fuselage, or placing a ladder against the aircraft. I made a mental note of that and decided we needed to overcome that advantage and ensure that the playing field was level in our tests.

Next day I asked my team to come up with some ideas on how we could get this problem licked. The guys brainstormed for an afternoon and recommended a number of fixes. First, we would tell the terrorist role players to anticipate being on the plane a minimum of three days. We also told them that they would have to interface with a hostage rescue negotiator starting about twelve hours into the exercise and to be prepared for that. We alerted them to the fact that possibly by day two the latrines could be filling up and that they would have to negotiate for a pumper. We also told them that food (C rations or MREs a newer type individual ration) and water would be available if requested. We went to great lengths to make them believe it would be a several day exercise but we always intended for the hit to come on night one. We also told them that they could not be overly abusive to the hostages. However their degree of friendliness toward the hostages could be tied to the hostage's level of cooperation over the period of the exercise.

The hostage role players were from various units on Smoke Bomb Hill and the 82nd Airborne Division. Many of the hostages were recruited from the Psychological Operations Group. A few of the hostages came from the 82nd Airborne Intelligence Battalion. They were asked if they would be willing to participate in a classified, extended duration exercise and that they would have to sign a waiver accepting the possibility that they could be physically touched and possibly abused physically and verbally. Their role as passengers on a hijacked aircraft was explained to them only after they had signed the waiver. We never had anyone back out, male or female after being briefed; or complain after an exercise. We also salted at least three SF troops, sworn to secrecy as evaluators among the hostages. These troops knew within thirty minutes the time of the take down and hence were keyed up and ready for any sound or movement of the aircraft before the hit. On more than one exercise we had these evaluators create a problem or distraction for the terrorists to keep them on their toes; but never in the direct time window of the pending hit. The evaluators were always ready to react to and evaluate the assault and takedown from the inside. These fixes solved the problem of the terrorist role players being ready and waiting for the assault team. They also proved to give us a great and excellent evaluation system. Debriefing of both the terrorist and hostage role players, along with the report of the evaluators, squirreled away among the hostages, gave us all the information needed to judge success or failure of the rescue effort.

Also getting a civilian plane to serve as the target appeared to be a possible problem. The Corps G3 solved that issue in short order working with the USAF. This effort had plenty of priority and a target airplane was the least of our problems.

I again visited the Mott Lake Counter Terror (CT) training site/ ranges along with several EDRE SF planners and we were all most impressed. With help from COL Mountel, the troops had, on a true shoestring with no help from XVIII Corps or Department of the Army, created a highly effective series of training facilities. Once again the ingenuity and resourcefulness of SF noncommissioned officers had come to the fore. Blue Light was gaining skills in CT operations that were amazing given any lack of previous experience in this field. LTC Cincotti was justly proud of his men and what they had accomplished. Colonel Mountel did however bemoan his lack of support in fulfilling the interim CT mission while COL Beckwith and Delta had an unending source of funds and access to every imaginable Army asset. We were shortly to see the difference between these two elements close up and not always so friendly.

We ran several aircraft take down exercises for Blue Light, one in Indian Springs, Nevada that was significant. I can say with no hesitation that Blue Light did very well and had come a long way from the debacle out in Hawaii. We had worked very hard to make the Indian Springs operation as smooth and well planned as possible. The Readiness Command Commander, GEN Hennessey, was present. He must have been impressed as I was awarded an on the spot impact Army Commendation Medal for this exercise. The hit was executed flawlessly and the Blue Light and Army Ranger Company that provided security were extracted without incident. I remember that the Ranger Battalion commander, LTC Wayne Downing, was on the ground with his element. Standing on the airstrip, as his troops loaded up for return to base, we exchanged a few words and comments about old times. We had been students together in the Infantry Officer Basic Course, Airborne and Ranger School back at Benning in 1962. Wayne later went on to wear four stars and command U.S. Special Operations Command at MacDill AFB, FL.

After the extraction of the assault forces I went to bed and so did most of the exercise support team (planners, terrorist/hostage role players and evaluators). A small group of our SF planners and role players produced several bottles of Jim Beam and proceeded to party hard and play poker most of the night. Our extraction was not scheduled till mid-morning the next day, so I cared not, but was too tired to join in the fun.

About 0700 I was awakened by one of my captains and introduced to an Air Force Major who stated the Base Commander wanted to see me immediately. Upon arriving at the base headquarters I was ushered into the commander's office where I received the "reaming out" of my life. It was not unjustified. It seems that Wayne Downing's Rangers had been a little more than aggressive and enthusiastic in their actions the night before. They had booby trapped a number of doors leading into various buildings and at least one hangar. Several of these nonlethal booby traps had gone off frightening to no small degree the airmen who triggered them. In one instance the booby trap, a smoke grenade, not dangerous from the stand point of an explosion, had broken free from its location around the door jam and rolled under a HUEY helicopter parked in the hangar. The colonel stated that the HUEY had an oil leak and the potential for a fire and major explosion had existed. Fortunately that did not happen, but I was told to get my team "The <u>hell</u> off my base" right now. Needless to say we quickly folded up what remained to be made ready to go and waited in a very low profile for the C-130 to take us back to Fort Bragg. Blue Light had done well but this was the second time in my career a sister service senior officer had shown me the door off his base. We all laughed about it later and to my knowledge no word of this incident ever got to LTG Warner, the Corps Commander, or GEN Hennessy, the REDCOM Commander. I never mentioned this incident to Wayne Downing although he and I were to spend a good deal of time together in the weeks to follow. Booby trapping the buildings was an unprofessional and dangerous thing to do and did not reflect well on the Rangers.

At one point about this timeframe COL Art Stang, a former Ranger battalion commander and a heck of a soldier, arrived at Bragg pending assumption of brigade command in the 82nd Airborne Division. Colonel Stang was a graduate of Pennsylvania Military College and quite a jock. He was given space on the top floor of Corps Headquarters in the EDRE offices. Not sure what his duties were but his presence gave us some time to get to know each other. He was very smart and somewhat quiet. At least it seemed that was his style at first. He usually had a pipe in this mouth and considered his every answer before speaking. Several folks commented that his seeming hesitation and pipe smoking would not survive in the frenetic pace of the All Americans. They could not have been further from the reality I would be part of in a few short months.

Shortly after our return from the Indian Springs Exercise I had a visit from COL Bob Mountel. He pumped me for any and all comments I might have concerning Blue Light. I frankly told him I thought they did very well and showed marked improvement since the poor showing in Hawaii. He wanted to hear more but I played my cards close to the vest. He got what he wanted from our talk I believe. Shortly after this discussion I heard from the G3 that Bob had started lobbying to have Blue Light become the CT permanent force and that Department of the Army stand down any further effort to bring Delta Force on line. Why waste time and money?

There were several schools of thought on that subject. A lot of folks in the SF community did not like COL Beckwith. "Chargin" Charlie had not gotten his nickname by being Mr. Nice Guy and he could ruffle feathers on many chickens at once. And woe to the troop who disagreed or resisted what he wanted to do. In the community you either loved him or hated him. At this point I was aware that COL Beckwith was having trouble recruiting some of the folks he wanted from the Special Operations community and that he had turned to looking for his people for Delta in the at large Army. He had even hired some civilians which was actually a good move. Colonel Beckwith's godfather was MG "Barbed Wire" Bob Kingston (more about him later). General Kingston had championed Beckwith, as I now understand it at the highest levels of the Army and Beckwith was a known quantity in the Pentagon. It was an interesting time to be on the outside looking in at this power struggle waged behind the scenes between Mountel and Beckwith. Mountel did not realize it but the hand had been dealt and Beckwith had all the aces. Colonel Mountel assumed the role as front man for Blue Light at about this time and LTC Cincotti took a less visible role.

35

A COUNTER TERROR DEMONSTRATION FOR THE VICE PRESIDENT

gain the fickle finger of fate fell on the EDRE Team when U.S. REDCOM decided that a demonstration of an aircraft takedown would be held for Vice President Mondale, the directors of the CIA and FBI and a myriad of other senior civilians and Pentagon folks to include the Chief of Staff of the Army. As I recall this was our first experience with Delta for an exercise. It was definitely not a Blue Light show. I base that statement on the fact that we were not involved in the operational side and we were not allowed to have any say in the hostage situation nor in the scenario pertaining to the takedown itself. I can't remember who did that piece of the action but it had to have been REDCOM. The Counter Terror Task Force was headed up by MG James Vought who at that time was commander of the 24th Infantry Division at Fort Stewart, Georgia. Major General Morris Brady, the REDCOM J3 Director of Operations, was in overall charge and the gentleman we were to support. Keeping him happy proved to be a full time job.

EDRE was tasked to set up the site and handle all the logistics associated with the event. The happening was to take place at the old Camp Mackall Airfield about twenty-five miles west of Fort Bragg. We first had to determine that a modern jet aircraft could safely land and take off from Camp Mackall. With the help of the Air Force folks at Pope AFB we checked that block as a YES. In my now semi-senile mind I believe it was "Air Force Two" that was the target aircraft. But for sure it was one of the presidential stable of planes. Whatever the number, that plane brought the vice president and several dozen D.C. big shots that landed at the much safer Pope AFB before the bird repositioned to Camp Mackall.

The problems associated with a demonstration of this nature, with so many VIPs in attendance, were mind boggling. As I recall Delta was not told who would be observing and we had to figure out a way to get the VIPs to the viewing area without tipping off the terrorists, hostages or the hit team; that was a major hurdle. It turned out that the only way to get them there in a clandestine manner was to walk through a swamp. Nope, could not walk the VP and other VIPs through the muck and "wait a minute vines" in that swamp. With the support of the Corps chief of staff we obtained help from the 20th Engineer Brigade who built a perforated steel planking (PSP) catwalk out through the swamp. Adjacent to the catwalk, and hidden from view in the dark, we erected a set of bleachers for the VIPs. Each observer would have a night vision device to observe the action.

Additionally, across the runway and slightly west of where the hijacked aircraft was to be parked, near the old airfield tower, the engineers constructed an arrival terminal of two by fours and target cloth all painted and decked out with the necessary airport accouterments and vehicles to look like a functioning terminal. Behind this phony façade were tents for the CT Task Force and tons of communications gear to support the entire activity and hostage negotiations et cetera. that would be going on for about twelve hours before the hit took place. From 500 yards away, to the untrained eye the Potemkin (phony) terminal looked real enough. We also set up and prepared the pre-exercise briefing area where all the VIPs would be read in on the who, what, where and why of what they would be viewing. For the briefing area we chose a Special Forces training classroom at Camp Mackall proper. It was adequate but we did do some hefty sprucing up and set up of audio visual gear to support the pre-exercise briefings.

One last major hurdle had to be overcome. Mackall was a large facility basically unused except by the SF School and an occasional 82nd Airborne unit jumping in and running a tactical exercise. It also was an open facility with perhaps six major roads and countless dirt roads and trails that allowed local North Carolinians to visit. It was a great place for teenagers and lovers for nighttime visits. Therein lay the problem. To close the base and ensure no unexpected visitors in broken down pickup trucks rolled up during the exercise I tasked the Military Police (MP) Brigade for a battalion of MPs. That action again got me called on the carpet and a very pointed tongue lashing from the Corps commander. I explained why the need for so many MPs and the requirement to ensure no one impacted the demonstration. General Warner was a great gentleman, a super soldier and he knew what was going on. He would be out there as the local host for the demo. But at this point he threw me out of his office. About thirty minutes later, as I mulled over what to do next, his aide called and said, "Sir, the general told me to tell you that you get what you want. Do you know what this is all about?" I thanked him and told him yes, I did know what it was all about. Camp Mackall was effectively sealed for the demonstration.

General Brady arrived several hours early from Tampa and was horrified to learn that we intended to walk the vice president and the other VIPs through a swamp on a PSP walkway. I informed him that there was a rope handhold on both sides and the way would be lit with green chemical lights and guides would be available to assist the VIPs. We went down and inspected the site and PSP walkway. That somewhat appeased him but only temporarily. He reminded me of a volcano and you never knew when he would go off. When he visited the briefing area, well spruced up and now outfitted with plush leather chairs expropriated from Fort Bragg proper for the half dozen key VIPs, he asked where the coffee tables and side tables were. He went on, "These folks can't be expected to hold coffee cups on their laps throughout the briefing and discussions." My senior

NCO, an old Green Beret, interrupted him and said, "Sir they are on the way." General Brady grunted and left to visit MG Vought over at the simulated terminal area where the CT Task Force had just landed. The target hijacked aircraft had landed earlier, was in place by then and the hostages were in the tender clutches of the terrorist role players. The scenario was playing out. I turned to my NCO and sort of calmly asked, "Where in blazes are you getting coffee tables and side tables? There isn't time to drive to Bragg and get back?" He told me to relax, give him an hour. An hour later there were the neatest coffee tables and side tables made from C Ration cases, borrowed from the SF school; all neatly covered with target cloth and tucked tightly in place. China cups and condiments were also arranged invitingly for the VIPs. Another major screw up averted by the quick thinking of an SF noncommissioned officer. General Brady was satisfied, and so was I.

I remember little about the actual exercise and the hit itself but I sure remember the briefing. The classroom was jammed with VIPs and general officers from all the services along with Vice President Mondale, and several cabinet officers. The briefer for the evenings show was from Readiness Command. I stood in the back of the room surveying the happenings. General Mackmull, Commander of First Special Operations Command caught my eye and motioned for me to sit down, and I assume relax. I chose an end seat near the back, one of the few open seats. After a minute or so I sensed a motion to my right front. I looked over and there was General Bernie Rogers, Chief of Staff of the whole U.S. Army, repeatedly jerking his hand and thumb up in the air, over and over. I gathered by that action that a mere LTC should not be sitting in this august group so I stood. Before I could turn to walk away he pointed toward the seat and I saw that I had unceremoniously sat on his field jacket. General Mackmull was watching this little tableau unfold, smiled and gestured for me to sit next to him. After the briefing as the VIPs were being led out to waiting buses to move them to the PSP catwalk and the bleachers,

General Rogers walked by and said to me, "I'm leaving after the demonstration for Europe and that is the only field jacket I have with me. I did not want it all wrinkled," or words to that effect. Not often that a lowly lieutenant colonel gets one on one counseling from the Chief of Staff of the Army.

Fortunately the PSP walk through the swamp went without incident; the hit went down and reportedly was flawlessly accomplished. The VIPs were whisked away back to Fort Bragg and Pope AFB for return to Washington. Those of us in the trenches breathed a sigh of relief and prepared for the cleanup and whatever awaited us next. Oh yes, General Brady thanked us for the superb support and asked that I specifically thank the NCO who solved the issue of the coffee and side tables.

Just after returning to Fort Bragg I was informed that I had been selected for Infantry Battalion Command and that command was to be the 1-505 Airborne Infantry, the H-Minus/Black Panther Battalion in the 82nd Airborne Division. It could not have been better, the 82nd Airborne was where I wanted to go and the family would not have to move again. It was perfect. Needless to say the kids were happy and Mary was very happy too. We were not going to have another move, at least not at this point. My assumption of command was still ten months away but I was informed by the Division personnel officer that they were looking for a job for me in the Division to help with the transition to life with the All American Division.

36

EXERCISE ONSET TRUST:
THE VALIDATION OF DELTA FORCE

I t appeared that the powers to be were very pleased by what they saw at the demonstration for the vice president. They had determined that Delta needed to be on line and operationally ready by the 1st of July. To make sure they were ready there was to be a full test/examination of their status and capabilities. Department of the Army (Specifically the Deputy Chief of Staff for Operations—DCSOPS) tasked, through REDCOM and FORSCOM, to have XVIII Airborne Corps and First SOCOM (Special Operations Command) do the evaluation. I was called to LTG Warner's office and informed that I and LTC Ron Ray from First SOCOM, a friend and holder of the Medal of Honor, were to be the planners and part of the "evaluation team." We would be assisted in the evaluation by COL G.G. Thomas who was a past Corps G3 and now assigned to FORSCOM DCSOPS. Colonel Thomas played little role in the planning but a key part in the evaluation. It was to be an experience I will never forget.

Major General Jack Mackmull took Ron Ray and me down to the old Post Stockade to inform COL Beckwith of this "great news." The four of us met in the conference room. The atmosphere was electric. I wondered if Charlie had a heads up as to the reason for our visit. General Mackmull explained to "Chargin" Charlie what had been directed by Department of the Army, specifically by LTG "Shy" Myer, the DCSOPS. LTG Myer was the prime mover on the

Army Staff providing full support to the fledgling Delta Force. Colonel Beckwith went ballistic; no way could this be happening. Delta evaluated themselves! They were ready! Then he looked at me and stammered, "I, I, I know that guy Redmond, I know him. He's a goddamn midget." General Mackmull then handed him the written directive from General Myer that spelled out by name (I was later told) that Ray and Redmond would be the planners for the validation and also evaluators during the overall assessment as to Delta's readiness to go fully operational. Beckwith was livid and stated that he would appeal this decision to General Myer. After much discussion the colonel stated that whatever we planned would be acceptable if it were briefed to representatives of the British Special Air Service (SAS) and German GSG 9 (both well-established counter terror units) and they agreed that the validation was meaningful. I was stunned and frankly wondered how in blazes we could do that. I should have realized that this effort had such priority that this requirement was about the size of a small mouse turd.

Ron and I put together our planning team built around the Corps EDRE Branch and started planning. We were given a budget of $500,000. Before we were done we had spent most of that. We were to evaluate and assess the readiness of all facets of the new Counter Terror unit. This ran the gamut from personnel recruiting techniques, to close in shooting, long range sniping, hand-to-hand-combat, internal security, nuclear weapons detection and neutralization, demolition and breaching techniques, covert entry, clandestine surveillance and photography, physical conditioning, operational planning and, well the list went on and on. The capstone of the evaluation was to be a hostage barricade simultaneous takedown of an aircraft and a building about a mile apart. Once more Camp Mackall was the selected site for the tactical field phase. Obviously we had to have outside help and assistance in many areas and this was forthcoming in no short order with blanket support from across the Army. We slowly built a team of evaluators from many elements around the country. Basically whomever we needed we got. Delta would get a complete and fair evaluation; at least that was Ron's and my opinion.

Colonel Beckwith was not terribly happy with what we were developing and said so several times. But his objections were moot when Ron and I flew to Atlanta and, in a downtown hotel room, briefed two majors from the British SAS on the full scope of the evaluation. Following the briefing we asked for their opinion as to the validity of the planned assessment. One of the majors, speaking for both, flatly stated something to the effect that, "Yes, it is bloody well difficult but not impossible. Spot on, but even we would have trouble passing with flying colors." A week later we briefed the COL commanding GSG 9 at the SF Headquarters on Smoke Bomb Hill. He was visiting for a series of meetings. His response was similar to the SAS major's, but he sprinkled additional holy water on our effort and COL Beckwith bit the bullet. No more was heard about the validity of our approach. Chargin' Charlie did add one more wrinkle in that he insisted the takedown evaluators were to be LTC Wayne Downing for the aircraft and Major Sherm Williford (GEN Myers' executive officer) for the building. That neatly cut Ron and I out of the planning and evaluation of those portions of the test. Colonel Beckwith was sly as a fox.

Prior to finalizing the complete concept Ron and I were briefed on some aspects of Delta's approach to operational planning. What they revealed to us was basically pabulum. There was no real substance or techniques for taking out a terrorist target, but it was the most that we were going to get. Ron and I both knew they were holding back much of their detailed in depth planning techniques.

Surprisingly I was invited to attend parts of a Fort Bragg Delta self-administered planning test. It was held in the old WWII barracks area where the ROTC cadets trained during the summer. There I finally met COL (now retired) Bull Simons who had been hired as a civilian consultant on terror operations. Colonel Simons had, since I last crossed his path in the 8th SF Group, become quite famous for his leading of the Son Tay Raid into North Vietnam in 1970. Sadly that effort found no prisoners in the camp. But the raid was a great boost to the spirits of the POWs still held and resulted finally in better treatment for them by their captors. After retiring he successfully extracted from Iran some of Ross Perot's employees during the height of the Iranian Revolution. Bull sat in the corner, after our introduction by COL Beckwith, eyed me suspiciously and said nothing while I was there. I had come all the way from the 8th SF Group at Fort Gulick, circa 1965, to a WWII building at Fort Bragg to meet this Special Forces legend.

Also there, as a full time employee of Delta, was Major (RET) Dick Meadows whom I had soldiered with in the mid '60s in Panama at the 8th Special Forces Group when he was a master sergeant. He had made a tremendous name for himself in Vietnam working special operations that resulted in his receiving a direct commission as a captain. He had been promoted to captain by none other than COL Bull Simons who this night was sitting just a few feet away. Dick was his usual super soldier self and it was refreshing to see him in this role with Delta. He performed yeoman service for Delta in the lead up to and execution of the failed Iran Hostage rescue. Major Dick Meadows was one hell of a patriot and special operations operator. He was in my mind, the brightest light in the spectrum of Delta planners. I remember very little about what was going down in this exercise and was not permitted to attend any of the detailed planning sessions. It was another overall dose of pabulum.

COL Beckwith was absolutely paranoid when it came to operational security (OPSEC). I agree fully with that position. Keeping techniques and tactics of Counter Terror operations close hold was, and remains today, important, but he truly carried it to the extreme. As you may recall, Desert One was the portion of the Iran Hostage Rescue operation that ended in disaster. In the analysis of what went wrong following the Desert One failure I felt that his obsession with OPSEC and the lack of a full up joint rehearsal contributed to that failure. But in total fairness the distances involved, the weather and especially the dust were major obstacles. Additionally, the totally unexpected arrival of a bus and fuel truck at the Desert One site in the middle of the night could never have been replicated, nor anticipated, in any number of rehearsals. That's just my midget opinion many years later.

The testing kicked off over a period of about a week in June 1978. Things went pretty darned well except that two hours into the hand-to-hand combat testing our super star, reputedly the best in the Army, hand-to-hand expert, had his shoulder dislocated. We did finally find a satisfactory replacement instructor and that phase of the testing continued. Chalk up one for the Delta door kickers. Other testing and evaluation went on all around Fort Bragg. As the reports flowed in we were daily analyzing the results; all were excellent and pointed to nothing that would preclude a finding that Delta was ready. Then we conducted a planning exercise, strictly a test of the S2, Intelligence, and S3, Operations, staff under the guidance of the commander to write an operations order (OPORD) for a hostage rescue. The OPORD provided back to us was a complete regurgitation of the pabulum briefing, almost word for word, that Ron Ray and I had received a month before. There were no specifics of the "how" of the hostage rescue scenario we had tasked them to plan for. Ron and I were flabbergasted and went home that night very concerned. What should we do about this? I could not sleep that evening and about 0300 in the morning I went down to our dining room and started writing. I finished my comments about 0500, showered, shaved and returned to the test headquarters. After telling Ron what I had done and showing him what I had written I delivered my comments, not very complimentary to the Delta planners, to COL Thomas and went about my business.

The next day the Fort Bragg portion of the validation concluded and the focus of activity shifted to the Aberdeen SF facility at the far western end of Fort Bragg and not far from Camp Mackall. Delta was given the scenario to plan for the simultaneous take down of a hijacked aircraft and a cabin we rented from Base Morale, Welfare and Recreation. At this point the key evaluators became LTC Downing and Major Williford. Ron and I turned our attention to making sure the aircraft, hostages, terrorists, and all the other support elements were in place. Sometime in the late afternoon of the first day of planning for the hostage rescue, Charger threw us a curve ball. We had anticipated the Delta troops would want to infiltrate by helicopter or parachute. Aircraft assets for either contingency were standing by at Simmons Army Airfield and Pope Air Base, just adjacent to Fort Bragg. In addition to helicopters the CT Team wanted trucks, civilian trucks, military vehicles would not do. I sent one of my sergeants with my credit card to Raeford, NC, the nearest large town. He found and rented the trucks. I got the bill, for which I was eventually reimbursed, and Charlie got his trucks.

The take down of the aircraft and the building went off well. None of us, COL Thomas, Ron Ray or I saw any of the action, but the reports were good. I was personally pleased but still had doubts that they were totally ready based on the exercise planning that had produced the pabulum OPORD back at Bragg. Following the extraction of the Delta Teams and the hostages we all assembled back at the Aberdeen SF facility. I won't comment on other specific evaluators' opinions but there were two schools of thought in the room that night. Lieutenant General Myer sat in the middle of a big room at Aberdeen SF Training Facility and listened to all the reports to include the really overall good news from the Fort Bragg portion of the testing. We each gave our opinion as to a Ready-Not Ready rating. When everyone had their say General Myer calmly declared Delta Force was certified and would be deemed operational as of that time. I was fit to be tied and stormed out of the building. Major General Mackmull and BG Meloy, who had also been present for most of the testing, followed me out. General Mackmull grabbed me by the shoulder and told me that we had done a great job under tough circumstances and to go down to the 82nd and command my battalion! I told him, "Sir, they just aren't quite ready. The individual troops and their skills are fantastic, untouchable. But their planning and staff skills need to be refined. Another six months is really called for." He looked at me and said "Larry, General Rogers told the president they would be ready by 1 July and that is tomorrow." I won't tell you what I said next.

Shortly after getting back to work at EDRE Branch I was informed my transfer to the 82nd Airborne Division for duty as the executive officer in the 3rd Brigade was approved. The 1-505 H-Minus Battalion that I was to command was a part of the 3rd Brigade. It sounded great and I was ready to be part of the All Americans.

I had assumed that the certification of Delta was history and behind me; but not quite. Before I left Corps Headquarters Onset Trust raised its head again, twice. The first time was when the civilian, XVIII Corps engineer came to my office and asked what the story was. "We built almost $100 thousand dollars' worth of walls, doors, buildings and obstacles, as you idiots had directed; and now they are all destroyed. What the hell is going on?" I told him he had his fund site to pay for the effort and if he needed more information he had to talk with the corps commander. He stormed out of my office, not terribly satisfied. I don't know if he went to see LTG Warner or not. Then in the mail at home I received a bill from the Morale Welfare and Recreation Branch for a little over $6,000 in damages to the Camp Mackall cabin. Delta had "done in" a few doors and windows and even interior lights and furniture during the rescue of the hostages. I took the bill to the G3, COL Cooke, who laughed heartily and told me to forget it. That was the final hurrah for Onset Trust. I marched off to the 82nd Airborne and new adventures.

(NOTE: Perhaps not quite the last hurrah for Onset Trust. If you happened to read GEN Carl Stiner's monumental book *History of Special Forces*, coauthored with Tom Clancy, you may remember GEN Stiner stated that <u>he</u> conducted a validation exercise for Delta Force. The time frame seemed to be several months after June 1978. General Stiner was not present during Onset Trust; or if he was there in any capacity he was not part of the evaluation team. So one can only deduce that a second validation exercise was ordered. Perhaps the questions raised at the Aberdeen Special Forces Operations Base had been listened to after all. I doubt we will ever know what prompted this second evaluation. Suffice it to say Delta passed this evaluation with flying colors. Surprisingly, Delta Force would come up on my radar screen again three years later.)

37

CATCHING THE "ALL AMERICAN" TRAIN, 1978

ife in the 82nd Airborne, the "All American" Division, is characterized as many things but never slow or boring. As the truly first unit to deploy in a serious crisis, it is the foremost "ready to go" element in the military. The U.S. Marines might want to argue that point, but they would lose. Unless the Marines happen to be lying off shore in U.S. Navy bottoms (aka ships) when a crisis occurs it takes time to get to the scene of the action. Only the "All Americans" can parachute into a crisis area on short notice, fight and hold terrain until the heavy stuff can arrive. The Army's paratroopers have been good at it since the invasion of France in WWII.

When I joined the 82nd the Division Commander was Major General Roscoe Robinson. He was a super soldier, a true gentleman and great leader who went on to be a four star general and commander of NATO.

Most who have served more than a day or two on Ardennes Street and Gruber Road at Fort Bragg deem life in the 82nd something akin to trying to paint a moving train. It's tough just to get on "the train" let alone paint it. In early July 1978 I hit the ground running. Three years later I would leave the Division, and I had never really painted or even slowed that damned train down. It was a monster that could not be tamed.

The day I arrived at the 3rd Brigade (aka the Golden Brigade) Headquarters they had a major event in that one battalion was deploying off post to Fort Chaffee, Arkansas. That day started as I expected. The brigade commander was COL Charlie Getz. A great leader, destined for stars. West Point and hard as woodpecker lips, he was a heck of a commander. (In doing research for this epistle I learned that COL Getz was the 11th highest decorated soldier, not counting the Medal of Honor, in the history of the U.S. Army. He never mentioned this distinction to me nor was it a well-known fact in the Division. I only recently learned of this through an article in the *VFW Magazine*.) He was finishing his command tour and would be replaced in two weeks by COL Art Stang whom I had gotten to know at Corps EDRE. Colonel Getz did have one fault if you can call it a fault. He was a tremendous jock and loved to run, and loved to run others into the ground. I was never what I called a jock and was not a runner but a plodder ever since the sucking chest wound in Vietnam. Upon checking in that morning he said, "Let's go for a private run, not with the troops." I told him, "OK, sir, but let me tell you before we go you can run me into the ground." He then did just that.

Before noon word started coming in that was not good concerning the off post happening. The 1-505, the unit I was to assume command of in about ten months, had deployed to Fort Chaffee that morning. The jump had not gone well. There were strong, unexpected winds after jumpers were in the air, and many were pushed off the drop zone into adjacent rough, rock strewn terrain. As I recall about eighteen troopers had to be hospitalized and quite a few limping and slightly injured stayed in the ranks for training. This operational happening certainly gave me a good look at the staff I was to direct as the unit XO. It also gave Mary an opening shock, so to speak, as she worked with Sue Devries, the wife of battalion commander Paul Devries, to handle all the issues with the wives and families back at Fort Bragg. I was quite impressed with both the brigade staff and the ladies of the battalion. Colonel Getz had hired only top notch folks and this fact would make my next few months as XO much easier.

The staff I inherited was superb. The S1, personnel job was held by CPT Bill Dickens a fantastic and recruiting poster soldier. The S2, Intelligence position was held by CPT Nelson "Chico" Nazario maybe the best intelligence type I had worked with up to that point in my career. The S3, operations officer was a lad named Major Bill Garrison. Bill, tall and lanky hailed from Texas. He was a bachelor, divorcee, totally devoted to his work, but not afraid to dance with the ladies when the opportunity arose; which was in his case often. I saw in Bill unlimited potential for further rank. He was to prove me correct in that assessment going on to be a major general. He had previously served with Project Phoenix in Vietnam and I always wondered if he had totally broken his ties to the Special Operations black side. The S4, logistics officer was Orest Kaczmarskyj and one of the best logisticians I had ever encountered. I never asked him how he solved problems but the "hard tack and powder" always arrived at the right time and place. Initially our signal officer, S6, was Major Cliff Engle and another expert in his field and later the J6 communications chief at Special Operations Command at MacDill AFB, Florida. He was replaced shortly by Major Pete Cotting an equally talented tactical communicator.

We also had a legal clerk, Sergeant First Class John Files who was not only a good legal beagle but a great hunter and woodsman. John had served in the 2-327 in Nam the same time I did. He was a great friend to young Larry and taught him how to hunt. My son would sleep with a pillow and a poncho liner right by the front door so that when John came to pick him up at 0400 to hunt we would not all be awakened. Together they were a heck of a team and far above average when it came to bringing home Bambi's father.

The change of command from COL Getz to COL Stang came just after the dust settled from the 1-505 return from Fort Chaffee. Things changed little, for me it was all so new that I just kept learning. Colonel Stang was a fair but hard task master and brooked no foul ups or slouches. He thought like and required that we all at least try to think like Rangers. He was a former Ranger battalion commander and the Ranger psyche was burned in his mind. In the field it was heavy camouflage paint on one's face; helmet (steel pot) on and chin strap fastened-always! The quickest way to get a solid counseling from COL Stang was to be shy of heavy camouflage or to remove your steel and or not have that chin strap fastened. Lots of folks complained to me about the chin strap issue. I agreed with them but never said so openly. One night in the field the COL and I were drinking coffee with our canteen cups resting on the hood of his jeep. I brought up the question of why not cut some slack on the chin straps. His response was, "No way, it's an indicator of strong discipline. I will not change from that rule." I could sense in his tone and manner that this issue was closed. After that talk I never brought up chin straps to him again.

The job of XO was multifaceted and whatever else COL Stang directed. He was also a runner but not at quite the speed of his predecessor. He liked to take the entire brigade on seven mile conditioning runs about every other month. I was always designated tail end Charlie and the straggler collector. My presence at the rear precluded folks from dropping out who just wanted to flake out and not go through the torture of such a grueling run. Yes even paratroopers will sometimes flake out. It also put a senior officer at the rear should someone have a serious problem. The medics always had an ambulance following the troops just in case. I will admit that I did not like these little forays into pain but bringing up the rear and bringing on the slow pokes fit my running speed. We never finished more than a minute or two behind the main body and we always sprinted the last couple hundred yards.

Things were in a constant state of turmoil and change on Ardennes Street; deliberately planned to be that way it seemed. Every unit, and specifically each Infantry brigade, three in the Division, cycled through three phases of training and operations every three months. These phases, or cycles, were Division Ready

Brigade (first to deploy in a real world crisis), Post Support Cycle and Unit Training Cycle. Each phase lasted three months and each was totally different providing new and exciting challenges daily.

During DRF 1 all unit vehicles, with a very few exceptions, were prepared for immediate dispatch to the rigging area to be palletized and prepped for airdrop in the case of a deployment. These vehicles were loaded with all the necessary gear and equipment to go to war. They were secured and guarded 24/7 and every day the drivers and leaders marched to the marshaling area to pull motor stables (maintaining the vehicles). Securing the area given the vast amount of equipment loaded on the vehicles was a never ending challenge; and a headache for the brigade executive officer. No matter how much security one put on the area where the vehicles were parked things just tended to disappear. Actually most missing gear had simply moved from one company's vehicles to another that was short something that was readily available on another vehicle.

During Post Support Cycle the brigade was required to provide personnel, vehicles and every imaginable sort of equipment support to other post units and activities. Woe be unto the company or battalion that missed a post support tasking, especially support to Airborne operations or ROTC Summer Camp support.

The *crème de la crème* for soldiers was the Unit Training Cycle. It was here that the troops really got down to mastering the basics of soldiering. Across the board this was the time the soldiers savored most. No more providing support, no more sitting around waiting for the balloon to go up. This was getting down to learning their trade out in the field or off post at some new training area. The 82nd Airborne was serious as a heart attack during Unit Training. There might be company size parachute drops in any of the cycles but in this cycle the Golden Brigade did battalion size, 500 jumper, mass tactical drops followed up by days of live fire and blank fire exercises of all sorts. And, oh yes, we marched, and with full rucksacks. Oh boy, did we march.

When I first assumed the duties as XO I made a decision impacting the family. We would all go to both Catholic and Protestant services in the brigade chapel every Sunday. The kids as I recall liked the Protestant chaplain's sermons as well as the Catholic priest's talks. There was truly little complaining from the children, I give them great credit for sucking it up like good paratroopers. If there had been a Jewish service at the chapel on Saturday we would have been there too. I did this not to flaunt my religious beliefs but to point up that soldiers living in the barracks needed to relate to God and I tried to set an example. This presence at both services raised some eyebrows and questions. Folks wondered what religion the Redmond's really subscribed to. More than one troop approached and asked me that question. I never gave a straight answer only alluding to the fact that men poised to go to war with eighteen hours notice needed to keep a good relationship with their creator. Both chaplains knew the truth but kept silent. In reality this gimmick worked to at least focus some soldiers' minds on God and religion. I was and remain firmly convinced that the battalion chaplain can be a great asset to any commander and for sure to the soldiers.

The battalions assigned to the brigade were the 1-505, 2-505 and the 1-508. The first of the "05" was led by a super field soldier, LTC Paul Devries. Paul and I had encountered each other before at Fort Benning and were pretty close friends. The second of the "05" was led by LTC Jay McDevitt and the "08" was commanded by LTC Bob Glass. All three were good solid soldiers and I liked them. We got along well. That would change when LTC McDevitt gave up his command.

Sometime shortly after assuming my duties the brigade was tasked to provide an element to represent the Division in the REFORGER (Return of Forces to Germany) Exercise for that year. I was selected to take a forty man staff with a communication team to Greece to play the part of the 82nd Airborne Division in a Command Post Exercise (CPX) a part of the overall happening. The bulk of the exercise was taking place up in Germany and we were all office and desk action, no field work. I must say Greece is a pretty country and Athens a great city. We were busy most of the time but did get in a little visiting at various historic sites around the capitol. We were billeted in a very nice hotel about fifteen miles from Athens. To say it was a far cry from the field duty we normally enjoyed at Fort Bragg would be an understatement. The Greek Army was very professional and treated us like kings. We all learned early in our thirty-five day stay that there is no love lost between the Greeks and the Turks. Several hundred years of Turkish and Muslim rule over the Christian Greeks left a lot of scars that may never heal. We also learned that winters in Greece were darned cold. Heck I thought the Mediterranean area was warm? The Exercise/CPX was nothing very challenging but our days were very busy.

Our Greek counterparts took us all out to a very nice restaurant for our parting dinner at the end of the exercise. It was quite an enjoyable evening and the food and belly dancing was excellent. Yes, I did say belly dancing. At the dinner we were introduced to a local wine called Retsina. Unless you like pine tar and turpentine I do not recommend it. My glass emptied several times that night to the delight of our hosts. (I strongly suspect that within two days the lovely potted plant behind my seat was dead.)

Shortly after we returned to Fort Bragg LTC McDevitt departed the 2-505 for duty at the Pentagon. His replacement was a soldier whom I will call Terrible Ted. He did not want to be at Fort Bragg in the 82nd as a commander and openly declared he had hoped to command in the 101st Airborne "Air Assault" Division. He always seemed to have a chip on his shoulder and proved to be a pain both for me as the XO and later when we both commanded our battalions. He was uncooperative, argumentative and a general irritant. Some of us began to think his problem was that he did not like to jump out of perfectly good airplanes. He only seemed to jump when it was absolutely required. (Paratroopers must jump at least once every ninety days to continue receiving jump pay.) He also resisted COL Stang in some of his brigade initiatives. The sad thing was he had a lovely wife and family who were liked by all.

My first saber crossing with Ted came when he walked into my office with charges against one of his lieutenants and requested a Special Court Martial for missing a PT formation. I thought that was a bit much and told him so. "Why not just a Field Grade Article 15 or even a Summary Court Martial from COL Stang?" I asked. He insisted on a Special Court Martial (CM). He was adamant on that point. I discussed it with COL Stang and he directed that I conduct the Article 32 Investigation to determine if a court martial was called for. Ted would get his way.

Sergeant Files and I started interviewing all those involved. The LT had some excuse that seemed a little flaky for why he had missed the formation but there were no flagrant violations that could be determined, at least not initially. But the whole thing seemed to be not so cut and dried; each interview led to another name. We started following names and issues, can't remember just what all they were. We interviewed witnesses A-Z and had started back on exhibit AA. I recall that we may have been about half way through the second run of the alphabet when a lady's name came up from our last interviewee. When John and I interviewed her the whole house of cards for the LT fell apart. He had spent the night with her and overslept. His whole flimsy excuse for missing formation fell apart. The Article 32 concluded that a Special CM was merited, not for missing formation but for lying and conduct unbecoming an officer in perpetuating the lie. Colonel Stang agreed. The CM convened and convicted the lieutenant. The young officer was off to the prison at Fort Leavenworth for a handful of years. Ted got more than his ounce of justice. I have no idea whatever became of the young man. Thanks to Terrible Ted's insistence on a court-martial and Sergeant Files and my persistence in following up each lead this sorry excuse for an officer was expunged from the ranks.

One night we were attending a masquerade ball at the Officers Club. I think it was around Halloween. I was there as W. C. Fields, the 1930's movie star, and looked pretty dapper in my father's old straw boater hat and tux rescued from the Salvation Army thrift store. You probably don't know what a "straw boater/skimmer" is. They are not seen around much anymore but it was a type of hat the comedian and actor W.C. Fields always wore. Heck, today most men don't own a hat except for a dozen or so baseball hats. That straw boater is still on my closet shelf. The only other costume I can remember anyone wearing that night was the Corps G3 who was dressed as the Easter Bunny. The event came to a screeching halt as it was announced there was a real world alert; and we were all ordered to report to our places of duty. At that time the 3rd Brigade was Division Ready Force One, locked and loaded to go to war. We all scurried home, and after putting on fatigues, and kissing the gals goodbye at the door, we rushed to the Brigade Headquarters.

Seems there was a real problem in the Congo and a number of Americans and Europeans had been taken hostage by one of the feuding tribes. As Division Ready Force we were tasked to go rescue them. The Joint Chiefs of Staff offered some reasonable number of C-141 airframes for the operation, maybe twelve. Major Garrison and Colonel Stang built a plan that required about seven or eight planes as I recall. We sort of relaxed after the plan was sent up the chain. We were however pretty *"gung ho"* over the thought that we might go into action, and do it by parachute assault. Sadly I was not going to be going on the operation. Bill Garrison and I were sitting in my office, I was at my desk and he was sprawled out on my couch. It was about dawn and we were drinking coffee. He was also chewing on his ever present cigar – seldom lit but almost always present. I made the following observation to him; "Bill, if I stay in the Army long enough I will work for you. You're going to be a general." He scoffed at that comment but it did happen, except I was retired when he made general so I never worked directly for him. I made that comment based on six months observation of the young major and on having watched him develop the brigade plan through the night. He was good: very, very good.

Fortunately or unfortunately by mid-morning the mission had been passed from the U.S. military to the French. Seems during the night everyone in the Corps wanted a piece of the action and the final package that went forward to the Pentagon called for over thirty C-141 aircraft. JCS told XVIII Corps to pound sand. The French did the job with a total of ten USAF C-130 planes. A couple of companies of Foreign Legion Paras, with minimal support, jumped in and successfully rescued the hostages. *Se La Guerre*, if I may use that trite phrase.

I enjoyed my time as XO of the brigade and it was a real learning experience. It truly helped me prepare for my command. I was able to observe all the problems, all the warts and watched a lot of different leadership styles in the ten months I was there. One small problem did arise with one of the battalion commanders (other than Terrible Ted). During a mass tactical parachute operation the battalion came up short four parachutes when the chute turn-in was over. Now in a parachute unit an extra parachute was worth its weight in gold as trading material. The brigade S4 and his NCOIC started an investigation to determine what had happened. The battalion commander was irate that anyone would challenge his unit on this issue. But a Report of Survey was a black mark on the brigade and Colonel Stang wanted the chutes found. After much weeping and gnashing of teeth the missing parachutes turned up but it did leave a bad taste in some folks' mouths. The unit S4 got a good counseling as it seems he was behind the missing chutes but that could not be absolutely substantiated. This incident almost cost me a friendship with a fellow lieutenant colonel but our relationship survived and our friendship continues today.

At some point while serving as XO I was sent TDY to Fort Benning and then on to Fort Leavenworth for the Pre-Command

Course. The Fort Benning phase lasted two weeks and I believe the Fort Leavenworth phase was also two weeks. This grooming for command was affectionately known as "Charm School." The Benning training was designed to bring folks who had been away from the Infantry up to speed with weapons and tactics associated with the commands they were to take over. Having been close to the Infantry for years, and a tactics instructor there at Benning earlier in my career, I did not learn much new.

The Fort Leavenworth phase was to prepare us all for brigade and Division level actions and operations. One stand out instructor is still fresh in my memory today. A retired colonel, Dandridge Mike Malone, taught us leadership and dealing with seniors and subordinates. His historical perspective and tales of successful commanders from WWII and Korea were classics. Later I even tried to emulate some of the leaders he described; one in particular being LT COL Edson Carlson from Carlson's First Marine Raider Battalion. They were the lads who hit Makin Island for the first counter punch operation against the Japanese following Pearl Harbor. He had some techniques for dealing with subordinates that included making sure everyone knew what was happening and disseminating information to the lowliest private. It was not beneath him to listen to any gyrene, of any rank, who had an idea he wanted to share. I copied his formula for creating a high performance system in his Raider Battalion. Little things like being willing to stop and talk to any private and listen if they had a good idea were among his trademarks and I followed suit. Being the man who makes the decisions and says yea or nay is the capstone of command. Where the idea comes from is secondary. I always made it a point to recognize good ideas and give credit where it was deserved. Dandridge Mike Malone helped many of us be better commanders. The Army was smart to have hired him and use his talents. He was quite a soldier. The pre-command training was overall very good.

One night at a cocktail party at a neighbor's home a young captain from the 17th Cavalry Squadron came up to me and said, "Hey, sir, my name is Captain Mowery and I am going to come to your battalion and I want to be your Operations Officer (S3). We will make a great team." Yes, this was Colonel Mowery's son, the Colonel Mowery from the 101st and Fort Benning BBOD. His son had a good reputation and I mentioned his comment to the cavalry squadron commander, LTC Lou Hennies. Captain Mowery was something else; never saw anyone who leaned so far forward in the foxhole or who was so intense doing his job. When I took command Lou released Jim to come to the battalion and I made him my S3 Operations Officer. To say Jim was good, and made me look good, would be an understatement. Jim had been correct, we made a good team, but he was certainly a tough guy to keep a rein on. Dynamic was his middle name. Jim had been an enlisted troop in the 82d Airborne Division from 1964-1966. He then went to West Point Prep School and on to West Point to get his education and commission. He only had one speed—FAST.

To tell a tale about Jim out of sequence you can best understand him if I relate a jump story that took place on a night mass tactical parachute assault many months later. Jim and I were positioned in the middle of our stick jumping on Sicily DZ (a stick being all the troops exiting from the same jump door). Being in the middle of our "stick" of jumpers would hopefully place us closer to our assembly point on the DZ. As we started shuffling to the door his rucksack came unfastened from his parachute harness and fell to the floor. Jim calmly reached down, picked it up in his hands and exited the aircraft just ahead of me. On the DZ he had his rucksack having held on to it when he jumped out into the aircraft 120 knot slip stream. This guy was quite the stud.

Just before I was to assume command of the 1-505 Colonel Stang decided he wanted to hold a "Prop Blast." Now for any NAP (remember non-Airborne Person) reading this the Prop (Propeller)

Blast tradition goes back to WWII and the old hard drinking, bar room brawling paratroopers of that era. It was a rite of passage for any Airborne officer. Colonel Stang was horrified when he learned that I was also to be a blastee! He could not believe that I had so many years in the Airborne but had never gone through a prop blast. Normally this tradition was quite an affair with physical training (read harassment), hard drinking (lots of it), and multiple exits from a mock aircraft door from which one had to simulate an exit from a plane in flight. Exiting the mock jump door was not a problem in that there was an electric shock device rigged to it. When the shock was administered you jumped! We had a problem in planning this one as a support brigade down the troop line had recently conducted a "blast" and a female officer complained to the Corps Commander about some form of abuse. After much discussion at higher echelons we were cleared to have our Golden Brigade Blast and it came off OK. I only had to jump twice from the mock door as I did it in the correct manner. Some of the blastees did it over and over and the more inebriated they got the sillier they looked. If you were not a popular officer, occasionally a little physical abuse did creep into the activities. I must admit being the oldest blastee, and a LTC, may have cut me some slack. I felt good when I got my card saying I was now officially a Prop Blast survivor and member of the Airborne fraternity. I stayed sober at this event by the way.

38

COMMANDING THE 1ST BATTALION
505TH INFANTRY

Shortly after the Prop Blast, on 6 July 1979, Paul Devries and I had our change of command and I took over the 1-505 Airborne Battalion, motto H-Minus, also known as the Black Panthers. Yes they were the Black Panthers. In those days those words were not politically incorrect nor did they carry a racial overtone. Our unit crest included a black panther with wings and the words H-Minus. The words having been awarded to the battalion by Army Heraldry since the unit jumped before H Hour (the designated hour for the Airborne operation to begin) on D-Day the 6th of June 1944. The panther represented the ferocity of the paratroopers leaping out into Hitler's occupied Europe.

Paul had left me a good unit, well trained and with an off post training deployment schedule that was somewhat daunting to include trips to Fort A.P. Hill in Virginia, Panama for Jungle Training, Alaska for Arctic Cold Weather Training, and a joint readiness training exercise in Florida. Most other battalion commanders were envious. In the next two years we would expand that deployment list to include a month at Fort Bliss Texas and five weeks at Fort Indian Town Gap, Pennsylvania controlling rioting Cuban Mariel Boat Lift refugees. The battalion was deployed almost as much as it was at Fort Bragg. Those almost two years in command (originally programmed to be only eighteen months) flew by and I had fun. I think the family had fun too. I hope I was missed, even just a little during those many off post exercises.

Paul had picked, and I inherited a super staff, with the exception of one officer who shortly left the battalion. At this point, by then Major Jim Mowery came on board as the battalion S3. The S1 was Captain Lonnie Vona and one of the best personnel officers on the troop line, bar none. Initially we did not have an S2 intelligence officer, that position being filled by a super senior NCO. Shortly after assuming command I assigned LT Walt Plummer to be the S2. The S4 logistics officer was good, but today, for the life of me, I can't remember his name. The Signal Officer was LT Leo Ledoux whose father was a Navy Admiral. All the company commanders were excellent but also had been in command awhile and shortly, as they departed, I would begin replacing them with men of my choosing. One commander, CPT Tom McNerney, Mary had known at Aberdeen Proving Grounds where their fathers had been assigned. Tom was on orders when I took over and departed shortly thereafter. The sergeant major was Jimmy Chandler, a former Special Forces trooper, ramrod straight and about 6'4" of intimidation. The troops respected him and walked a fine line; none dared challenge or disobey him. Even Mary thought him intimidating. My executive officer initially was Major Greg Sharpe. Greg was smart as a whip and great with administration and budget. He kept me out of trouble and the battalion almost always inspector general inspection ready. I relied on Greg and the sergeant major for good counsel and I always got it.

On my first full day in command I boarded a C-130 along with most of A Company and jumped into Fort A.P. Hill in central Virginia. John Dibert was the company commander and a good soldier, all 82nd through and through. It was a great way to start an Airborne command. There was one ironic event that day that is emblazoned in my memory. The jump went well but Corporal York landed in a mud hole almost up to his waist in brown muck on an otherwise perfectly dry drop zone. The troops got quite a laugh out of that one. I flew home on one of the birds that took us up and had landed at the post airfield, and then waited to take a number of us back to Pope AFB adjacent to Fort Bragg. After this it was at least one and maybe two jumps per month for me. I truly got to the point where I enjoyed it. The C-130 was and remains today a great aircraft. Lockheed Martin did well by the Air Force and the Airborne community with that bird.

While I was now commanding a top notch lash up, the battalion did have some areas that needed improvement. Although great in the field the barracks had gotten a bit ragged and throughout the Division there was a pot, and possibly a small crack cocaine problem. The sergeant major discussed these points with me over a cup of coffee. He concurred that the barracks could use a spruce up and the troops deserved to live better. We could fix that, and over time did so. He also recommended a sweep of the barracks with MP drug sniffing dogs. That was a good idea. We struck at 0300 on my third night in command. A few bags of marijuana surfaced and the owners were promptly disciplined. Each of the culprits was given the maximum punishment under Article 15 Non-Judicial Punishment that I was allowed to dispense. Then we called the whole battalion to the nearby theatre where I laid down the law. We leaders all recognized that there was a drug culture out there in Fayetteville and what the troops did off post we couldn't control. But bring it into our barracks, your barracks, and get caught, and there would be no mercy. I stuck by that rule my entire period of command and our drug problem never got beyond a mouse turd, at least not that we knew about.

I made it a point to visit every company and every special platoon as well as the motor pool several times a week. If I couldn't be there the executive officer did the honors. It kept the troops and leaders on their toes. The motor pool came in for special attention. We had a great Motor Officer in Chief Warrant Officer Harrell and Motor

Sergeant Joe Allen. Joe went on to be the XVIII Corps sergeant major, an honor normally reserved for combat arms troopers. They ran a tight ship and kept a bunch of old vehicles in top notch shape. My frequent visits were to encourage the company drivers who maintained their own vehicles on a daily basis. This was boring and dirty business but if I showed up for Motor Stables so did the company commanders and their lieutenants. The troops stayed motivated and so did the mechanics. It was a win-win for all. Later in my command we were hit by the Corps Maintenance Evaluation Team (COMET) and received the highest scores ever awarded an Infantry Battalion; great work by Mr. Harrell, Sergeant Allen and some dedicated soldiers.

I took runs alone wearing my rucksack. It was a good gimmick and most of the troops initially scoffed at it and thought that the ruck must be full of waded up paper. One day after I had finished a run I stopped by the Charge of Quarters (CQ)/Battalion Runner desk in the HQ. I left my ruck there while I went down the hall to get a cup of coffee. On my way back from the coffee mess I saw the CQ lifting the ruck and a true look of astonishment when he felt the roughly fifty to sixty pounds that I normally ran with. The word spread that the old man's ruck isn't filled with paper. Given the back problems I live with today, this gimmick was probably a bad decision on my part.

Also as a matter of course whenever we jumped I jumped a PRC 77 radio in my rucksack (about another twenty-five lbs.). It was not worth being caught on a drop zone with no radio. Sometimes radio telephone operators (RTOs) were slow to assemble or got hurt and for a time the commander could be without a radio. I will readily admit that I got the radio back to the Commo Platoon as quick as I could. Given the experience I had at An Phu in 1968, and losing commo with one of my platoons, I was death on having the RTOs respond immediately when a call came through. It took quite a few tail chewings and explanations about losing commo and men dying, but eventually we got a crew of RTOs who understood and were very responsive. I have recently been told that battalion commanders jumping their own radios was Division policy but I do not remember that at all and did it based on my experience in Vietnam

With the support of the sergeant major and the company commanders we initiated a policy of no cots in the field. If the troops were on the ground so were we officers and senior noncoms. Another gimmick that worked was my directive, tough on the Headquarters Company Commander, that when we were in the field the battalion policy said we locate the Command Post and Tactical Operations Center where we can hear the water running. Most likely this was a swamp and heavily wooded area. Our CP never got captured or attacked during any training exercise; the OPFOR couldn't find us. Sometimes the Headquarters Company Commander hid it so well that I couldn't find the TOC after dark, and had to be picked up by an escort and led into the site.

The sergeant major was most impressed with my jump boots instep being spit shined. He relished seeing the look on troopers' faces when they came in for counseling or punishment and saw my feet up on my desk with the instep staring at them. Yes, it was a gimmick and deliberate intimidation but it worked. The first time a trooper came in for an Article 15 (Non-Judicial Punishment) and saw my boots with the spit shined instep quite obvious staring at him the look on his face was one of amazement. After dispensing justice the trooper returned to the barracks and the word spread like wildfire, "The old man spit shines the bottom of his boots!" That is a paraphrase based on what the sergeant major heard through the NCO grapevine.

Sergeant Major Chandler also recognized that I had quite an Irish temper and sometimes tended to go overboard during staff meetings. I was not abusive but I could get hot quickly. He came to my office one day and counseled me (well deserved by the way) on my handling of a situation that should have been dealt with in a much calmer manner. He told me, "Hey, sir, you are doing great but we need to control your temper in staff meetings. Tell you what, when I sense you are leaning too far forward in the foxhole I will bring you a cup of coffee. That will be our code for you to relax and back off. OK?" I readily agreed, and was as trainable as Pavlov's dog. Jimmy was a great asset and made my job a lot easier. This would not be the last time he counseled me, and I always paid attention. We were a good team and it helped the troops to make life on Ardennes Street more bearable.

About halfway through my command SGT MAJ Chandler was replaced by SGT MAJ Bruce Pross from the 1st Ranger Battalion. It was another great happening both for the battalion and me. Like his predecessor, Bruce and I got along well and he was a super counselor for me and helped keep me out of a lot of potential trouble. After about six months in command we also had assigned a young West Point captain, Johnny Brooks. Initially I made him my S4 Logistics Officer. Like Major Mowery this trooper was stellar and helped make my job simple as far as equipment, maintenance and supply issues were concerned. Later I made him my headquarters company commander and he was the rascal who managed to hide my command post from me on more than one occasion. Johnny went on to serve as the 82nd chief of staff and retire a full colonel. Like any number of the lads who worked for me in the Panthers he could well have worn stars.

When I assumed command the Division commander was Major General Guy S. Meloy who has appeared several times in this tale already and with whom I previously had some interesting experiences. General Meloy was a great paratrooper and soldier-sensitive leader who believed solidly in meaningful and realistic training. He required a "brief back" from each battalion commander just before the start of the Unit Training Cycle. He wanted to know exactly how our training time would be used down to the minute and what each soldier would be learning.

These brief backs were not always pleasant experiences. The first brigade to undergo this exercise in detailed preparation of a training plan got clobbered. I heard through the leader grapevine that it was a blood bath. The general ate them alive for not having training planned for every troop all the time. Soldiers waiting to shoot at a rifle range were not sitting waiting but were being schooled in some other aspect of soldiering; patrolling, radio procedures, emplacing mines, first aid or marksmanship. The truck drivers who took them there were not sitting, they were being trained in something else or pulling maintenance checks on their trucks. There was no time when the troops were not training. Woe be unto the commander who did not have something planned for all his troops, all the time, and was not able to articulate that to General Meloy. The general could be intimidating to say the least, but the troops got trained like never before.

The word got to us as to what the old man was looking for and we prepared accordingly. Colonel Stang saw to that. Major Mowery planned it all down to the smallest item and he then schooled me till training was running like blood in my veins. Then came the day the Golden Brigade was in the barrel with the general. I was first up and came off like a champ; no questions were thrown at me that I could not answer. Tap dancing and talking at the same time was a skill I had honed to a fine art while working at Infantry Branch. The General was pleased and so was Colonel Stang. Lieutenant Colonel Glass had a few problems but survived and did well overall. Terrible Ted fell on his saber and the general did not treat him kindly at all. He had been warned as to what to expect but marched to his own drum. In this case, with the CG, the drum was darned quiet. When we were on training cycle we trained. We spent most of the time in the field only returning on Fridays to let the troops have some time off and particularly, if they were married, have some family time.

39

TAKING THE HIGH GROUND
AROUND THE GLOBE

As mentioned we had a number of off-post deployments in our training schedule. I will address them all now, with one exception, although these training events were spread out over the period of my two years in command. Each was unique and rewarding in its own right. Just getting away from Fort Bragg was a fantastic morale boost for the troops.

The first off-post deployment we had was to Camp AP Hill that started on the day I assumed command. It was only a company sized operation but served A Company well. I never figured out how LTC Devries had set up an off post for just one company but it happened. I described that operation earlier so won't go through it again.

READINESS COMMAND EXERCISE BOLD EAGLE IN FLORIDA

The next operation was a Readiness Command exercise called Bold Eagle that took place at Eglin AFB, Florida and throughout the Yellow River swamps and Ranger training areas. Jim Mowery and I planned things down to the "gnat's tail" and thought we had everything covered. It was not a long exercise, maybe eight to ten days. Frankly about the only thing I can remember was the beginning and end. For the parachute assault I was on one aircraft while Jim and the battalion XO were on another. This was one of the few off post exercises the XO deployed on. He normally stayed behind minding the battalion rear activities. My aircraft got a weather abort and we air landed at an Eglin Auxiliary Field and I was ignominiously trucked to the operational area linking up with the rest of the battalion there. For some reason, known only to the USAF, my plane was the only one from the battalion that was diverted from the jump. Thank heavens, although the winds were high, there were no jump injuries on the operation. And there I was, arriving by truck, a real bummer. This didn't speak too highly for all that detailed planning for the Airborne insertion.

Redmond's Rule #18 - No plan is <u>certain</u> once you cross the line of departure; you <u>can</u> be <u>certain</u> it will change.

The only other standout aspect of the operation was the final event. The 1-505 and a battalion from the First Brigade, the 1-504, were to attack the Command Post (CP) of the 197th Infantry Brigade out of Fort Benning, a part of the opposing force (OPFOR). Their CP was located alongside an auxiliary airfield on Eglin Air Base proper. We got the order for the attack just at dusk and H-Hour (time of attack) was 0500. This would not have been such a major problem except that we were fifteen kilometers from the objective CP and had to wend our way through several battalions of the 197th to get there. Major Mowery and I huddled under a poncho plotting a line of march through the least likely occupied areas (read swamp) to our probable line of deployment for the assault just across the runway from the CP. Oh yes, another typical Airborne operation, not a bit of pressure. We moved out in a column of twos, about 350 to 400 troops. Soon, as we left the trail we had initially used, we were forced into a Ranger file one man behind the other strung out through the pine forests, occasional streams and lots of swamps. I remember it was pitch black, not a bit of light. It reminded me of the Ranger EDRE at White Sands Missile Range. We passed close by several OPFOR units but were never engaged or challenged. At one point we walked right past a tank whose crew must have been asleep. No way did we expect this.

As the hour for the attack crept closer both Jim and I were getting antsy. We kept pushing the lead element to move faster. Finally Jim went to the point and started breaking trail himself. At 0502 we were able to deploy one platoon, about 35 men, on line and ready to go. On the far side of the airfield and in the early light Jim could just make out tents of the CP across the runway. Still back in the column I told him via radio to attack. That was just what he wanted to hear. Not wanting to miss our H-Hour and certainly not wanting to be beat to the punch by a sister battalion from another brigade I felt I had no choice. We continued to feed troops forward and across the runway until we had at least a reinforced company in the middle of the 197th CP. We had caught them with their guard down, asleep and not expecting to find any "enemy" in their midst with the exercise scheduled to end later that morning. As far as they knew the nearest 82nd troops were over fifteen kilometers away. I crossed the runway and almost immediately ran into COL Mike Spiglemire, the brigade commander, and at that point my prisoner. I had met COL Spiglemire before and he and I sat on some C ration boxes and drank coffee until the Exercise ended. The battalion from the First Brigade, by the way, never did reach their attack positions. We had captured our objective and had attacked in a Ranger file (aka single file) with less than a battalion. Couldn't make this up, it happened.

RETURN TO PANAMA AND THE JUNGLE OPERATIONS TRAINING CENTER

We had one deployment that I was truly looking forward to; that was the thirty day training exercise to Panama and the Jungle Operations Training Center (JOTC) at Fort Sherman. Having worked the jungle there when assigned to the 8th SF Group and served as an instructor and lane grader at the school I was really looking forward to this deployment. In my mind it would be a totally different experience for the troops and one they would enjoy. That is exactly what it turned out to be.

We jumped in on Gatun Drop Zone and then road marched about seven miles to Fort Sherman. On this off post deployment I had asked for and been provided an SF Team and a Psychological Warfare Loudspeaker Team. We made it a point to always try to bring along attachments that we might employ in a real world operation. I think we also had a squad of 82nd Engineers attached. It was a nice package of about 900 troopers. When we arrived at our barracks at Fort Sherman there was a note written on the blackboard in the headquarters office from one of Major Mowery's West Point classmates. The note was from the S3 of the battalion that had preceded us at the JOTC. I can't repeat what the note said as it was more than slightly vulgar and showed a distinct knowledge of my Operations Officer. The entire S3 Section, except Jim, thought it was a hoot. The training from the school cadre was excellent and the time in the jungle outstanding for the companies. Basically training was done at company level. The battalion staff and I just monitored and checked on the operations. They all learned a great deal about operating and living in the jungle. The school was everything I remembered it to have been and more. The jungle was, however, still the jungle.

I visited Colon in the Republic to get a haircut one day and was disappointed in what I saw. Not quite as clean or nice as when we had been assigned next door at Fort Gulick fifteen years earlier. The barber expressed deep regret that President Carter had announced our turn over to the Panamanians of the canal and total withdrawal from the Canal Zone. I suspect shortly after the U.S. finally left that he was making a decent living cutting the hair of the Chinese who replaced us post haste after we departed.

(NOTE: Along with two other couples, all of whom had been together in the 8th Special Forces Group in the mid-1960s, we cruised to Panama in 2010. Colon, the city proper, was for the most part, a total disaster except for the Free Zone and Port. Even the cruise ship purser advised staying out of the city. We took a tour of the canal that required landing at the Coco Solo Yacht Club, which still looked pretty nice. As we departed the Yacht Club we passed a new development that appeared very expensive and quite modern but was surrounded by a twelve foot high wall that had broken glass embedded in the top. For me this was a sign of the have's living pretty high on the hog and being desirous of keeping out the other folks.

In traveling by bus to pick up the boat to go through the canal, and several of the locks, I was horrified at the trash along the Pan Isthmian Highway. The Republic was never immaculate like the Zone had been back in the 1960s, but now the trash was incredible. Garbage and litter was everywhere and in many cases piled just outside the houses directly under the windows. We asked the guide what had happened since when we were there nothing like this was anywhere to be seen. He told us that two years earlier the Government had ceased "free" trash pickup and given a contract to collect garbage to a Columbian company. The average Panamanian could hardly afford to feed and house their family let alone pay to have the garbage removed. Holy Toledo, Batman, it was a mess.

Panama City on the other hand was a bustling and booming place, or so it seemed. It was much cleaner and modern overall with high rise apartments and tall buildings of all types. It appears whatever profits were being reaped from running the canal after Jimmy Carter gave it back were staying near the capital and not reaching the majority of Panamanians. The old Canal Zone for all its faults and Ugly American facade helped the average Panamanian more than their own government was doing. That is just my senile opinion, but there it is.)

Now back to our jungle training experience. I remember one particular day during this deployment that was marked in my memory as the "day from hell," or Black Monday, 17 September 1979. We had moved a small Tactical CP into the jungle down near Fort San Lorenzo to monitor training and just check out our S3 operations and Standing Operating Procedures. This was a Major Mowery initiative again, making sure his folks had their act together and ensuring that everyone was getting trained. Turned out it was a good thing we did have our stuff together. We received a report mid-morning of a weapon that was lost crossing a pretty wide stream that was running hard from recent rains. The company launched a full scale "rescue the M16" operation. Before that issue could be resolved another report came of a trooper bitten by a snake that had gotten away. No one at the scene could determine if the snake was poisonous or not. The company was nowhere near a helicopter pick up zone. We scoured the maps and picked the closest area we thought would allow a helicopter to land and directed that the trooper be carried there as quickly as possible. The rain was coming down in buckets at that point and it took about four hours to get to the extraction site. By that time the rain had let up and the trooper was safely transported to Coco Solo hospital. He lived, so to this day we all assume the snake was not of the poisonous variety; or perhaps paratroopers were just immune to snake bite. Sometime just after the extraction of the snake bitten trooper we got a report that the missing rifle had been plucked from the water and all then seemed back on track and OK. At least that was what we thought.

What else could possible go wrong? Little did we know. Suddenly the radio crackled that one platoon of B Company had walked through a nest of scorpions and two troops had been stung. Although painful, scorpions are not deadly but their sting can be darned uncomfortable. The troops were treated by the unit medics and training continued.

Then the *coup de grace* fell on us. One of the Special Forces team troops went berserk, over something that never did become clear. He just went bonkers and ran off into the jungle. Well you could chalk that up to fate and so what, but the rascal had taken his weapon with him! Not good at all. We organized a search party of troops from back at Fort Sherman augmented with JOTC cadre. The situation resolved itself when the next day the lad walked out of the jungle, safe and sound with his rifle. To say I had a few minutes of extreme angst over that missing lad is an understatement. The sergeant major was giving me coffee every few minutes. The coffee only helped a little. I can't recall if I ever got a full explanation of what sent this Green Beret over the edge. There was no confrontation with the soldier as the sergeant major wisely kept him away from me. Maybe I was just glad to have him and his weapon back safely. While this incident didn't please me at all I continued asking for and taking an SF Team whenever we deployed off Fort Bragg. We all breathed a sigh of relief when Black Monday was over.

We had one other JOTC training accident that bears telling. We received a report that one of our men had done a commando rappel down the ninety foot climbing/rappel tower but had not braked himself and sort of streamered into the ground at max velocity. Normal rappelling technique is for the butt to go first but the commando variant puts one going face first down the tower. He had been medivaced to Coco Solo Hospital. The sergeant major and I dropped whatever we were engaged in, jumped into a jeep and rushed the eighteen to twenty miles to the hospital. Specialist Wyatt was lying in the emergency room being treated. The doc told us nothing was broken but that he had a lot of scrapes and bruises. When we walked over to his bed he looked up and said, "Sorry, sir. I sure didn't do that rappel the right way. But I am going to go back and do it right as soon as they let me out of here." Two days later he did just that.

Other than the initial jump into the Canal Zone, I don't recall if we ran any parachute operations on this deployment. Gatun DZ was only seven miles away and if we had I am sure I would have remembered. The JOTC deployment was a big training success for the men and the battalion looked good in Division's eyes. We jumped back into Fort Bragg at Sicily DZ with the families of our troops in the grandstands watching and applauding. It had been a great experience.

NORTH TO ALASKA AND SOME VERY COLD WEATHER.

The Alaska deployment was to Fort Wainwright near Fairbanks. Again we took a task force of about 1,200 paratroopers including an engineer platoon, a section of air defense guns; a section of 105MM artillery from our artillery support battalion and an SF detachment; and a psychological warfare team. There may have been some other attachments but I can't remember for sure. Major Mowery and CSM Chandler were still with the battalion but a number of the company commanders were new as were several of the first sergeants. Captain Johnny Brooks was with us by this time and was serving as our S4 logistics officer. Major Sharp, the XO, as usual remained behind to watch the store so to speak. We prepped and were issued some winter clothing at Fort Bragg. The deployment was to be for thirty-two days and we were going in February. As I recall we were transported by five or six civilian charter aircraft and received great treatment from the flight crews. When we departed Fort Bragg the temperature there was 39 degrees, cool but tolerable. We landed at an Air Force base near Fort Wainwright and I was the first person off my plane. Within about two seconds the tops of both my ears were pinging and stinging like crazy and I was totally struck by the coldest weather I had ever experienced. I immediately pulled down the nice ear flaps on the cold weather cap I had been provided and should have had down when I first left the plane. I passed the word back into the aircraft for everyone to do the same. I had expected cold but this was far beyond my wildest reckoning. For the next thirty days it only got a little better.

We moved rapidly to waiting buses and the trip to Fort Wainwright. My God but it was cold. I really thought, "Boy, Colonel, what have you gotten into?" Needless to say the battalion arrived as planned and we were billeted in very nice barracks; for sure they were warm. I was informed by a Fort Wainwright operations officer who was helping get us settled that the temperature that night had fallen to 70 below zero. Yes, that was 70 below, not a misprint. That first night was quite hectic as we got settled and drew the necessary gear to survive even a few minutes outside in the stark cold.

The morning after arriving, as things were still sorting out from the planes that arrived after mine, I had a visitor. The door to my office flew open, literally flew open, banging the wall, and a two star general stalked in. After I popped to attention he said, "Colonel, I am Major General Jenes and I am the commander of all Army forces in Alaska. That includes your outfit. I don't care if you never leave these barracks for the next thirty days you will have no frost bite. Is that completely clear, no frost bite, got it?" I was somewhat taken aback but nodded an affirmative. He spun and left the office His sergeant major stepped into the doorway and said something like, "Sir, excuse the general but last night we had our best battalion, the Airborne Battalion, get separated from its equipment, tents and heaters and we had over sixty cases of frost bite. This was a bad time to arrive for training. I recommend you have all the arctic boots you are issued checked closely for serviceability." He then turned and followed the general down the hall. That was quite a wakeup call and my first and only meeting with the main Army mug in Alaska.

Our normal staff and commanders meeting was set for 0900 and it proved interesting. Before I got there the word on the very low temps from the day and night before, and the frost bite injuries to the Alaska Airborne Battalion, had spread through the troop barracks. I remember only too well telling the staff and company commanders that we needed to pray for warmer weather so that we could get in some good training. I also directed that all of our vapor barrier arctic boots (aka Mickey Mouse boots because they were white and very bulky) get a recheck for serviceability. The S3 told me that we were going to hit a warm spell for the next six to eight days. The temps were predicted to hover only about minus 20 to minus 30 degrees Fahrenheit. Great, a real heat wave but it was training weather by Alaska training standards. As I recall training stopped at minus 35 degrees and you set up tents and heaters and just survived. Before the meeting broke up my battalion physician's assistant, Warrant Officer Carter Stevens, spoke up and said, "Colonel, you go ahead and train. We may have a lot of chilblains but there won't be a single case of frost bite in this unit". Carter was a two-time Vietnam SF NCO medic who had gone on to become a physician's assistant and warrant officer. He was as close to a real doc as I ever saw among the Physician Assistants that I encountered. He was as good as his word. We had no frostbite casualties and only a couple of chilblains reported.

Redmond's Rule #19 - Never fool around with Mother Nature, she wins every time.

For the first week we were in the barracks area and getting class room instruction on Arctic operations. All facets were being covered from *akio* (a sled pulled by men, no dogs) loading and movement, to setting up tents, to wearing skis and snowshoes, to how to set up and tend the arctic stoves that heated the tents. Not properly watched and tended those life giving, warmth producing stoves could be killers. It helped us all to go through this training in a barracks environment before putting hands on the gear at minus 30.

There was also a second battalion, from the 9th Infantry Division, in nearby barracks going through initial orientation training along with us. The fifth night there the sergeant major woke me around 0300 and told me, "Sir, we had a little problem down at the NCO Club last night. But it is all taken care of. Everybody is happy, especially the club officer." As I rubbed the sleep from my eyes I had the good sense to ask what "a little trouble" amounted to. His response knocked me for a loop. "Sir, it was our guys against the legs from Fort Lewis. We won and the club officer has $15,000 for repairs. He will be getting a lot of new furniture." I thanked Jimmy for the update, rolled over and slept soundly.

The next morning as I sat at my desk doing some administrative paperwork my door again flew open without so much as a gentle knock and in strode the LTC battalion commander from the 9th Division. He was quite nattily attired with a camouflage cravat, well pressed heavy winter shirt and pants, a swagger stick and gloves. He did not give me his name but immediately launched into, "Well colonel, I have given Article 15s to all my brawlers, what are you doing to your troops?" I looked him over once more, leaned back in my chair and said, "Colonel, I don't know what the U.S. government pays the 9th Infantry to do but they pay the 82nd Airborne to fight. I am not doing anything to my men. Now get out of my office." I have no idea what prompted me to say what I did about the 82nd and fighting. It just came out of my mouth on the spur of the moment. He was taken aback by my response and turned and left. I never saw him again for the remainder of our time in Alaska.

(NOTE: I did, however, see him on TV following the first Desert War. A recently retired war vet, female, gay, colonel, Medical Corps "came out" on TV and told her story as a basis for opening the Army fully to homosexuals. To bolster her tale she then trotted out an Infantry full colonel, retired, who had served twenty plus years honorably and successfully. You guessed it, no kidding, it was the same gent.)

The battalion completed its instruction in those nice warm barracks and began taking to the cold. We had runs every morning in sweat suits and balaclavas (woolen face masks that covered the whole head and face, minus the eyes) and everyone ended those runs with chunks of ice on the woolen portion that covered the mouth. By the time we transitioned to the outdoor phase of training we were somewhat acclimated to the severe cold. The troops took to the ski slopes, the cross country snow shoeing and cross country ski walking and every other facet of the outdoors in Alaska in the dead of winter and loved it.

We also managed to do a lot of parachute jumping from CH-47 helicopters on a nearby DZ called Husky DZ. You haven't jumped until you jump at minus ten to minus 20 wearing all the clothes needed to preclude frost bite on the way down. It was fun and exciting. It was particularly exciting for Specialist Fourth Class Canfield who became a towed jumper on one of these jumps. Somehow his static line got tangled and his chute did not deploy leaving him dangling just off the helicopter ramp. The jump master and chopper crew chief brought him almost inside the helicopter before it landed. I met them at the airfield. Canfield told me, "Hey, Colonel, stuff happens, I want to jump again." I followed him out of a CH-47 the next morning. By the way, he led the stick, no hesitation on his part, a great young soldier.

It wasn't all training and field work. Fairbanks was not far off and every evening that we weren't in the field the troops trekked into town, cold be darned. I remember being told about CWO Harrell, our maintenance technician and several of my troopers who had been frequenting one of the local Fairbanks hot spots. I confronted the chief and asked if he was wearing all his cold weather gear when he went downtown. Sheepishly he grinned and said something like, "Yes, sir, when I am going from gin joint to gin joint. But, sir, you can't boogey with your VB boots on." You definitely had to remove those vapor barrier boots (aka Mickey Mouse boots) to boogey. I also remember Specialist Fifth Class Lopez who was arrested in Fairbanks one evening for drunk and disorderly conduct. Lopez was one of our cooks and a super trooper. The next morning he was arraigned, found innocent of all charges and released. That afternoon I had the pleasure of promoting Specialist Fifth Class Lopez to the rank of staff sergeant. That almost smacked of the "old" Regular Army I had joined in 1962.

The companies all spent considerable time in the woods living in tents and training in the cold. It was a new experience and one hard to forget. If the troops were sleeping out, so was the staff. I can remember having to get up at night to relieve myself. Now let me tell you that getting out of a warm sleeping bag, even into a heated tent and then stepping out of doors at minus 30 took a lot of courage. Putting on your boots and parka was a major event and not something you really wanted to do. But one had no choice. Have you ever heard a call of nature turn to ice before it hit the snow? I have.

About three weeks into the deployment the sergeant major came to me with the keys to a Jeep Cherokee and a .45 caliber pistol with live ammo. He told me that I had been talking about the Black River Rapids Glacier Training Site so much that I really ought to go visit the place to complete my experience of Alaskan training. Well, Black River was not just up the road, I think it was more like 100 miles over far from the world's greatest highway. But Jimmy was right. After hearing about it from some of the local Fort Wainwright officers I had talked about the training site and I did look forward to the journey, seeing the glacier and just getting away. I think maybe the staff needed a break from me also. Arrangements had been made and the cadre at the site were expecting me. They would billet me for the night. Like the trip in Bolivia there was a .45 caliber pistol, loaded with ball ammunition, on the front seat. I was not sure why the pistol. About half way to Black River I came to understand. I had stopped by the side of the road to answer Mother Nature's call when I happened to glance down. There in the snow were fairly fresh tracks of what could only be a big bear, a very big bear, maybe even bigger than a .45 caliber could handle. Needless to say I finished my business, got back in the vehicle quickly and continued on to Black River Rapids. There were no further stops en route.

I remember that if you could find a more isolated and out of the way place to put a military training facility it would have to be near the North Pole. The training camp itself was quite small, but from a hunter or naturalist's standpoint it was heaven on earth. Not my cup of tea however. It was just too isolated and very cold most of the year. The briefing they gave me relating to their mission was outstanding. The camp facilities were adequate but quite austere. The cadre was dedicated; they would have to be to handle duty there. Training on the glacier, which was what the place was all about, was done in small groups. My orientation tour was well done and they even introduced me to the Mayor of Black River Rapids, an elderly lady, who was visiting the camp for some purpose never explained. The scenery was truly spectacular. I am not sure if the facility is still there today or gone the way of the Passenger Pigeon. If it is still there it would be a great site to train our troops prior to hitting the mountains of Afghanistan.

I slept well and got an early start back, bidding my hosts farewell and securing that .45 pistol from the arms room. On the way up I had noticed a roadside inn, quite rustic, near Black River Rapids, the town, or what passed for a town. This would be a great place to have breakfast. Pulling into the parking area I saw that the inn itself was almost buried on three sides by snow. The front of the log edifice and part of the gravel parking area was clear of snow but they were obviously having a tough winter. Perhaps it was for them a normal winter. As I entered the inn proper through a covered walkway intended to keep the entrance somewhat clear of that white stuff, I was immediately struck by the blackness that hung over the entire interior.

It was dark and dreary, smoke hung in the air and the whole impression, to me, was of a frontier 1870s saloon from maybe Wyoming in the dead of winter. There were tables and a bar and a lunch counter. A very large fireplace was off to the right and a crackling wood fire was blazing away. That accounted for the smoke. While the burning logs had a great aroma the smoke was truly thick and enveloped everything. I sat at the counter and ordered bacon, eggs and coffee. I was surprised to see that the waitress was a Latino or perhaps a mulatto as her skin was quite dark. After she took my order and walked away, based on her accent, I realized that she was neither Latino nor a mulatto. She was simply dirty. The weather was not conducive to taking baths and she worked, and I assumed lived, in the inn which was filled with smoke. Such was life in 1980 around Black River Rapids in the winter.

The trip back to Fort Wainwright was uneventful. Upon return we were scheduled to start full up field training and spend eight straight days maneuvering and surviving in the wilds. By the way several of the staff told me they were glad I was back but did not provide further elaboration. Perhaps Major Mowery had been leaning too far forward in the foxhole again.

Once we moved out to the woods the temperature ranged from minus 10 to minus 30. In those temps with the gear we had been issued we had no real trouble training. There were no frostbite cases, thanks to WO Stephens; for real, no frostbite. The companies operated on their own for a couple of days and then we conducted a battalion movement to contact and attacked to the Tanana River. Quite an impressive river perhaps 150 to 200 yards across at the point we reached. The river was frozen solid and presented an almost totally flat, unbroken sheet of ice from our tree line to the opposite bank which was an impact area for all caliber of weapons.

We dug in; rather we built ice and snow fortifications above the ground, and prepared for a live fire defense of the river line. Every asset we brought along for training participated in the shoot. It proved to be a most impressive sight especially when we conducted a "mad minute" with all weapons firing at max rate of fire to include our mortars and all our small arms. The air defense 20mm guns were very impressive. Our machine guns laid down a stream of fire interlaced with red tracers that let every soldier on the line see what interlocking MG fire streaming across a flat surface between two and three feet above the ice really looked like. Our unit mortars and the section of artillery fired in support and the far bank of the river took a pretty good pounding. Major Mowery and the staff had done a great job planning and coordinating this one. The leaders and troops all learned from it. That event made living and operating in the cold almost enjoyable. The men were impressed with their own capability in coping with and soldiering in such extreme cold.

With this live fire exercise our Alaska training experience ended and we prepared to fly back home to Fort Bragg. Going home was a mixed delight. Some of the troops were really going to miss Alaska, the naturalists and hunters for sure. But most troopers were ready to get back to the relative warmth of North Carolina in March. It had been a great experience that none would soon forget.

40
LIFE ON ARDENNES STREET

Commanding in the 82nd had many facets and challenges for leaders at all levels. That is a true statement for every Army unit and remains so today. Mentoring subordinates was a task approached differently by each commander. But, the good leaders always went the extra step to train and instruct their officers and sergeants in the various aspects of soldiering. In doing so the leaders were better prepared to support their men. That was a major part of what the Army is all about: "mission and men." Now of course I would have to say men and women.

I had the opportunity, as brigade XO, to observe other commanders up and down Ardennes Street working on developing leaders and producing a high performance system in their units. Some were very successful while others achieved either moderate success or failed to various degrees. With lots of observation from my time as XO to help guide me, we, the battalion leadership team, undertook many programs aimed at officer and noncommissioned officer development. We prepared, published the written word, and conducted bimonthly classes (unless we were deployed) aimed at improving leadership within the ranks of our junior leaders.

Among the officers and NCOs I stressed the importance of the medieval concept of *"Noblesse Oblige,"* Nobility Obliges. As leaders, better paid and sporting the rank, they needed to put the troops ahead of any personal consideration. They owed that to the men as the "knights and pages" of the 20th Century. Believe it or not, most of the folks understood and took the idea to heart. We also prepared and distributed reading and movie viewing lists, and then had round table talks about the books and flicks recommended. While I cannot say that everyone read or watched all that we recommended there were always a few who could relate to a given book or movie and the training value or concept those conveyed. Some movies, such as *Zulu, She Wore a Yellow Ribbon,* and *Cross of Iron,* were particularly well received by the troops. The last movie mentioned will come up again during one of our real world deployments to a little place called Fort Indiantown Gap in Pennsylvania.

General Meloy gave responsibility to each brigade to be the lead in some aspect of tactical operations affecting the whole Division. The one Achilles Heel of the Airborne ground pounding infantry facing the Soviet hordes (our enemy at that time) was dealing with an armored force. This is not an easy nut to crack for a light infantry paratroop outfit. Our battalion was assigned the responsibility of codifying and developing how the Division would fight tanks and armored elements. The concept, which General Meloy had come up with, was called the Airborne Anti-Armor Defense. While it was not a be all and end all, nor a sure fire armored attack stopper, it had merit for the light Airborne force. I think it is fair to say that with the help of my three operations officers (Jim Mowery, Tom Lippy, and John French) we were fairly successful in evolving the idea. We stressed the concept in our field exercises, and held seminars for leaders from the other brigades explaining the concept that had been developed and blessed by the general. Basically it involved a fluid defense in depth utilizing all our available anti-armor weapons; Tube launched, Optically-tracked, Wire Guided (TOW) anti-tank missile systems, Dragon Missiles, and in a counter attack mode, when the enemy had been slowed and attrited, the Sheridan, a light parachute droppable mini tank, as our stop gap. We also assumed that some Air Force tank busting capability like the A-10 Warthog (which is still a fantastic tank killer and close air support platform today) would be available to throw into the fray. It was the best we could do at the time. Today's much more lethal artillery and aircraft munitions with a distinct anti-armor capability would add a whole new dimension to the concept. Regardless, I am glad we never had to test it for real.

One afternoon as I sat at my desk the duty sergeant came to the door and stated that my wife was on the phone and needed to talk to me. Mary only called me if there was a real problem, normally a family emergency with one of the children. When I picked up the phone she asked me if I had my little TV in the office turned on, and had I heard the news? She went on to explain that there had been a hostage rescue attempt by Delta Force in Iran and that it had failed. After sort of thanking her for the call and turning on the TV I sat and listened to the bad news about Desert One. My mind was drawn back to a night at Aberdeen Special Forces Base almost two years earlier. I almost cried as I listened to what had unfolded in the Iranian desert.

As part of leader development efforts the operations guys and I developed several other papers that we publicized and spread around. It appeared to us that our training was not challenging enough. Not enough realistic situations were planned for and executed. Too often troops attacked hills and objectives where there were no bad guys and nothing that resembled what they would encounter in a real battle. It was boring, end of that story. We wanted to fix that. So the S3 Operations gang, with guidance of course, put together a little briefing for all the officers and NCOs that stressed getting realism into our training. When our troops attacked an objective there would be bad guys there. We took the sick, lame and lazy who could not hump the boonies and positioned them on the objectives. Not during live fire exercises certainly, HA. That's an attempt at Redmond humor, an area my children would tell you where I am sadly lacking. We put them in OPFOR uniforms, added some ketchup representing bloody wounds and salted them and the area with maps, papers and other items of intelligence value for the troops to find and process. It spiced up the operations and added a much needed degree of realism to field training.

Among the other papers we developed, briefed and trained to was "How the Squad Fights Through" an objective. This document got right down to the nitty-gritty of what each member of the fire teams in the squad did as the element advanced by bounds with each fire team providing covering fire to the other. We also prepared a paper on how to conduct and safely manage "Noncombatant Evacuation Operations." The Iranian hostage situation was still a matter of concern and evacuation of U.S. nationals from foreign nations was a hot topic. This, "how to get the job done," paper was passed by Division to all brigades for their consideration.

General Meloy required that every company conduct live fire attacks with all our assigned and supporting weapons employed to support the attack. The lifting and shifting of fires was critical as the troops approached their objective. We never really had a problem except when one company started angling toward an adjacent hill scheduled for a heavy artillery barrage. From the hilltop where we were observing it was obvious to us that they were drifting off their assigned line of attack and into a danger area. The necessary orders to sort that one out were rapidly sent. We had several of these events, one for each rifle company. This phase of training culminated with a battalion coordinated attack with all guns blazing. We trained with live ammo as often as we could. I only recall one issue when several hand grenades were momentarily not accounted for on a grenade range. After several recounts the errant grenades appeared. I always wondered if some nefarious plot were afoot.

Live fire of the TOW and Dragon weapons was not easily done. The ammo was just too expensive. But the Army had some great and effective training devices (simulators) that allowed gunners to maintain their proficiency. The best gunners in the training simulators were selected to fire the few live rounds we got each year. Competition among gunners and among battalions was strong. Everyone took the requirements and techniques of the Airborne Anti-Armor Defense to heart. The Russian threat demanded it. The Black Panthers were always among the top three infantry battalions in the Division when it came to anti-armor capability and we prided ourselves on that.

There are some things that are emblazoned in one's memory, like your first date with a hot chick or the first time you get shot at in combat. Such events can never be erased. This next happening is one such event. It was a Friday night, probably in December and quite cold by North Carolina norms and going well below freezing before morning. I was at home about to sit down to dinner when the phone rang. We were in a training cycle and had been conducting company and platoon field training all week, but stood down for the weekend. The Duty NCO was calling to tell me that the reconnaissance platoon had reported one trooper was missing and could not be accounted for. The platoon had been out all week training and apparently tried to cap the week with a land navigation activity through a beaver swamp. One man was missing, Private Williams for purposes of this tale. All efforts by the recon platoon to find him had thus far failed and it was now dark.

I directed that the staff be immediately notified to return to the headquarters, and that the companies execute the alert chain and bring in all the troops. I then called Johnny Brooks who was the S4 at that time. I directed him to get Division to provide us ten, 2 ½ ton trucks as soon as possible. In reality, on a Friday night, Captain Brooks could not get ten, 2 ½ ton trucks but managed to dragoon several eighty-passenger bus like vehicles, some 5 ton and a few 2 ½ ton trucks. I never asked the good captain where he got the transport and probably don't want to know.

In the short time it took me to get back to the Headquarters the S3 had prepared a search plan and trucks were pulling up outside in the street. The medical platoon and two ambulances were also lined up waiting. The mess steward was alerted to be prepared to serve hot soup in the field all night if necessary. Soldiers were returning from all over post and Fayetteville and getting ready for a long night. To say the troops were a bit unhappy at this turn of events would be a true understatement. We briefed the company commanders on their respective search areas and loaded up and departed. Sergeant Major Chandler and I, along with the key staff and medics, set up an open air command post just off Longstreet Road not far from the swamp in question. By 2100 we had several hundred troopers knee to waist deep in cold water looking for our errant private. The temperature continued to plummet as the night progressed. We felt certain Private Williams would not freeze if he kept moving but if he stopped, and hypothermia set in, given the cold and wet he could easily die. Throughout the night the cooks provided hot soup and coffee at various locations along the perimeter of the swamp as the search continued with no sign of the missing soldier. It was a long, worrisome night. Just after 0700 the S3 got a report that the lad had been found. He was walking along a firebreak adjacent to the swamp. He had wandered off post and spent the night in a farm house, warm, well fed and dry. We called off the search and redeployed the troops back to main post to start a delayed weekend off.

Shortly after returning the sergeant major came into my office and calmly told me something like, "Sir, Private Williams is a dead man. He won't see the light of day Sunday. The troops want his scalp." Jimmy and I were both exhausted but it was obvious something had to be done and done right now if Williams wasn't going to have some real problems. I directed that the whole battalion be assembled in the brigade theatre just down the street. This order created no small amount of grumbling but it was accomplished fairly quickly in true paratrooper "suck it up" fashion. Once the troops were in their seats I pulled a "mini Patton" (no flag behind me) walking to the middle of the stage and facing the troops. At that point I began reciting Rudyard Kipling's poem, *Gunga Din*. Yes, I knew that poem by heart, each and every verse.

> *You may talk of gin and beer when you're quartered safe out here*
> *And sent to penny fights and Aldershot it,*
> *but when it comes to slaughter*
> *You'll do your work on water and kiss the bloomin boots*
> *of him that's got it.*
> *Now in Injia's sunny clime, where I used to spend my time,*
> *A servin' of Her Majesty the Queen.........*

Ending with

> *Though I've belted you and flayed you*
> *By the living God that made you*
> *You're a better man than I am Gunga Din!*

At that point I am sure there was more than one lad sitting there wondering where in blazes the old man was going with this talk. Kipling? I then stated, "Men, last night you went and searched for one of your fellow troopers. It wasn't fun. I want you to know that should we go to war tomorrow, anywhere in the world, and if you become separated from your buddies, that we will come find you. We won't abandon you. Paratroopers never leave a buddy behind, not the water boy or the machine gunner, the cook, the reconnaissance scout or the truck driver. We take care of our own… clear enough?" I then turned and walked off the stage. Later the sergeant major came to my office and said something to the effect that the troops understood and Private Williams would survive. And he did.

To succeed in those days in command one needed more than a few gimmicks. The boots with the spit shined instep being one decent gimmick that worked. The sergeant major and I also had a little spiel that we gave all the new troops assigned to the battalion. It was not so much a gimmick as historical fact. Normally every Friday we would get anywhere from four to ten new troopers fresh from basic training and jump school. We would assemble them in the conference room of the headquarters and I would talk them through the significance of our unit crest and a hefty portion of paratrooper history. Our unit insignia consisted of a silver shield with a winged black panther descending from the sky with three lightning bolts reflecting the regiments' three World War II combat parachute assaults. The significance of each depiction was explained; as well as the fact that our unit had jumped early on D-Day, <u>ahead</u> of H-Hour when the airborne assault for the other Airborne elements began. Hence, we had been awarded the motto H-Minus for our unit. As I hit them with history, the sergeant major pinned unit crests on each new man. It may not have been perfect but it did instill a sense of being special to the men. I also discussed Panther Rock, a very large boulder with a black panther on top, coiled to spring which stood just outside the headquarters entrance. I stressed that while we paratroopers would move on, that rock would always be there representing our history and the valor of those who served before us. It was a very motivational affair and meaningful welcome to the Panthers for the new troops.

Now that rock was interesting in itself; and there is a story that goes with it. It had been around a long time and I can't tell you where it first came from. The sculpting of the panther left a little to be desired and it was the target of many a raid by other unit troopers. They got great satisfaction painting that rascal pink in the dark of the night. Our Charge of Quarters had a can of black paint and directions to make it black again before reveille should some dastardly renegade paratrooper slip in and turn our panther pink. We had a young troop, one of McNamara's "100,000" (named for Robert McNamara, Secretary of Defense) from the late 1970s, who served as our Repair and Utility (R&U) chief fixing things for the companies and troops throughout the battalion. For purposes of this telling his name will be Zacharia.

Now, by way of explanation, McNamara's "100,000" were men who volunteered for the Army but were below the mental requirements, or for some quirk could not pass the tests, for acceptance under current Army standards. Most of them proved to be good soldiers and hard workers. There were a few who were different in some respects and our R&U lad was one of them. While his test scores were below standards for admittance to our Army he had a photographic memory. Don't ask me to explain this but it was the case. He memorized the name, date of action and heroics of every Medal of Honor recipient in the history of the Division (for starters) and went before the Brigade Soldier of the Quarter Board looking like the greatest troop who ever donned jump boots. With his sharp mind and depth of recall he wowed the Board and won. He just couldn't pass the tests to get in the Army without some help from the McNamara "100,000" program. And so what does that have to do with Panther Rock?

One evening, Sergeant Major Chandler came in and told me that Specialist Zacharia wanted to speak to me about Panther Rock. When he came in he said; " Sir, I don't mean to be out of order but our Panther really looks sort of pathetic, more like a lizard with a much too long snout and no real muscle showing. It's just wimpy looking." He told me that he would like to re-sculpt the Panther and make it really ferocious looking. The sergeant major, standing behind him kept nodding his head yes. We all walked out front and stared at the rock. Specialist Zacharia was right; our panther looked much too much like a lizard. I asked him what he needed to do the job and he told us, "Not to worry, sir, got all I need in the R&U Shop." For three weeks he worked every day after hours and on the weekends, covering his efforts with a tarp so they were not visible. After the second week I began to have some anxiety about what might be going on but kept my fears to myself. Finally Zacharia announced that Panther Rock was ready to be unveiled. We had a little ceremony, the tarp was pulled back and by golly we had a first class black panther lying poised to spring, freshly painted and newly sculpted on that very large white rock. The job was fantastic and the difference in appearance and ferocity of that sculpting was unchallenged. When the 505th Regiment again became reality, with three battalions bearing the designation 505 in the 1990s, our rock left the First Battalion and was moved to the Regimental Headquarters where it remains today.

Another interesting tale that smacks of McNamara's "100,000" comes to mind. I had one trooper who was married to a soldier in First Corps Support Command; both of them were McNamara "100,000" quality but overall good troops. His wife had gotten pretty involved with the "distaff side" of battalion activities. With the battalion deployed on training exercises as frequently as it was the ladies had become a pretty tight knit group. I have avoided discussion of the distaff activities since they are another story in themselves and I didn't live those tales, only witnessed them from a respectable and safe distance. At any rate one Saturday the doorbell to our quarters rang and lo and behold my trooper and his lady were standing there. Well, not being much on ceremony I invited them in along with the critter in the cage they were carrying. It only took a minute for the reason for the visit to surface. They were going on leave in a day or two and wondered if we could babysit their pet ferret while they were away. Yep, a pet ferret declawed as I recall and who had the run of their quarters. I was taken aback by the request but Mary, quicker than I on the uptake, explained calmly that we simply couldn't babysit the ferret. The reason was our killer, attack dog; "Muffin" (a miniature poodle and a fact not known to the couple) would not tolerate another animal on her turf. They were crestfallen but said they understood and left quietly. When I had closed the door Mary and I both stood there for perhaps sixty seconds, and then broke out laughing. We had dodged a small bullet there. I don't think Muffin would have lasted ten minutes with that ferret in the house, declawed or not. Muffin was a wimp, but a wonderful wimp.

Some commanders on Ardennes Street worked long hours. If the commander was there then the staff and company commanders and senior noncoms hung around on the chance that the boss might need something. Having watched that phenomenon as the brigade XO I told my folks when it was quitting time, if they had nothing to do, "go home." No matter how often I told them this, or beat them up for not following my guidance, some insisted on waiting till I departed. I started going home for dinner at about 1700 and then, after a family gathering and coffee with Mary, I would return to the office. If I needed someone I always knew how to reach them. It truly bothered me that so much time for these great young soldiers and leaders would be wasted waiting on me.

Not long, perhaps three months, after assuming command I noticed a problem with the efficiency reports on some of our junior non-commissioned officers. The initial submissions from several of our lieutenants had errors and were poorly written. This caused a delay in submission of the reports and in some cases caused troops to miss promotion boards. No amount of talking to the company commanders seemed to help. So I started correcting, in red pen, mistakes and what I thought were omissions concerning the duty performance of some of our non-coms. I would then call the writer of the report to my office, hand it to him and state, "If you would like, I will ensure that your efficiency report looks like this before it is forwarded." I did that about three times and the word spread; the problem went away.

As I alluded to early on in this writing there are always natural leaders in the ranks (Corporal Charlie Norman from C Company 1-506 at Fort Campbell in 1963 was an example). These soldiers made up an informal chain of command among the troops. They were respected and listened to and men who could help make things happen. The Panthers had several of these lads but the one whom I remember clearly was Specialist Thomas Laskey our truck master. Tom was certainly a key player in the informal chain of command.

He knew every facet of what was going on and when vehicles had to be where. If there was a mistake in tasking, or the wrong time for an action was announced, Tom could be counted on to fix the mistake and save some officer or noncoms bacon. The battalion was deployed a lot and the when and where of our return was always of great interest to the ladies. My wife would get the word from the headquarters, usually the XO or S1, as to when we would be jumping back in and which drop zone and what time. She would dutifully implement the family notification telephonic alert chain and the word would get out. Normally within several hours she would get a call from Specialist Laskey correcting the word from the staff on what time the drop would be and in some cases even what drop zone we would be jumping on. He was never wrong.

He was a bit of a hell raiser though and imbibed to excess at times. One Christmas Eve he and four other troops rolled up to our quarters about five sheets to the wind in one of our jeeps. A large American flag flying in the cold December wind as they sang Christmas carols at the top of their lungs. Everyone on Watts Court where we lived learned who Laskey was that night. One day Tom told me that he wanted to be a pathfinder. I sent him to Pathfinder School and on return he left us for the Division Pathfinder Team. He left the Army as a staff sergeant and worked for years at the Ford Motor Company just outside Detroit. Knowing the informal chain of command and using it to help the unit look good, was a technique that bears adopting today.

41

A WATERLOO EVENT AND
BAD NEWS ON ARDENNES STREET

E very battalion was required to go through a major unit evaluation called the Army Training Evaluation Program (ARTEP) and ours/mine came I think about ten months into my command. Exactly what we would be evaluated on in the way of activities was a closely held secret. Being Airborne obviously we would conduct an Airborne assault on one of Fort Bragg's many drop zones, that was a given. After that the scope and exact activities we would be tested on was up to Colonel Stang. He was, as I have commented, a tough task master, but fair.

The week long exercise kicked off with a parachute assault that came off great. There were no serious injuries and the assembly of all units was near perfect. We were then ordered to conduct an approach march and attack and seize a series of hills. That also came off well. Then we were informed that the enemy had counter attacked and we were now cut off and had to conduct a break out from encirclement; not an easy task. We accomplished this in fine fashion also, but then as we were moving to linkup with friendly forces I got the word that we had a lost weapon. This was not a part of the ARTEP but a real happening. That's a "no-no" for sure. When a weapon went missing everyone paid attention. We continued to move and search for the missing rifle at the same time. Luckily the weapon was found and we continued to move into a defensive position and wait for our next mission. Unknown to us at the time we were now several hours ahead of where the ARTEP schedule said we should be. Our success would prove to be our undoing.

Word came down that we were to next conduct a night attack. I selected B Company to do this mission. The commander, Mike Grady, was good, a former NCO who knew his stuff. Major Mowery did the high level planning and we issued the order. Night attacks require detailed planning and pre assault preparation and the establishment of attack positions and release points for the company, platoons and squads and a final line of deployment from which the assault is launched. Not an easy operation and one requiring that all aspects are properly handled. Captain Grady reported that the platoon and squad release points were all recon'd and established and he was ready to go. Major Mowery and I went along to observe. After about an hour of very quiet movement we came to a halt. We waited, and waited and waited. Nothing happened. I sent Jim forward to find CPT Grady and see what the holdup was. It seems they could not find the final line of deployment for the attack. This position had been marked on our side of the trees with chemical lights all along the final line of deployment. But now the lights were not visible and no amount of searching revealed them. In the dark it was impossible to see the line of deployment let alone the objective which was little more than a pimple, not a hill that was easily recognizable. There was no panic or pressure to launch an ill prepared attack. We allowed CPT Grady to sort through the problems and get it right. Finally just before dawn, almost two hours late the assault went in on the correct objective. We set the conditions to achieve victory and we did so. To have pushed B Company to attack blindly would have been a disaster and in a real war would have resulted in heavy casualties and could well have ended up in an assault on the wrong objective. But we had failed this part of the test by missing our time of attack by nearly two hours. This was a real bummer for us all after having done so well up to this point. The rest of the ARTEP was a blur but overall we passed every test in true Airborne fashion.

Colonel Stang was not happy over the failure of the night attack and while we passed the ARTEP it was made conditional on the proviso that we practiced night attacks and took a retest and passed that. We spent a lot of time in the field and night attack practice became the name of the game. The retest was perfect. Later two things came to light that frankly disappointed me terribly.

First, it seems that we had done so well initially that we were twelve hours ahead of the ARTEP schedule set by the brigade S3 operations officer. Colonel Stang decided to fill that time with this simple company night attack. He hated to see troops and the battalion staff get a twelve hour break rather than press on hard. That was typical Ranger thinking. The brigade S3 had trouble finding a suitable objective for this assault; one that could be easily recognized in the dark. Normally that is a required condition for a night attack; an identifiable objective. He selected a slight bump in the ground along a small trail. Not the best objective to evaluate a unit's ability to go through the many facets of a night attack. I got this info directly from the brigade S3 who had done the planning and selected the nearly unrecognizable objective.

Second, I learned from the battalion commander who provided the opposing force for the ARTEP that, unknown to him, the reconnaissance element that established the final line of deployment was observed putting out the chemical lights. Two of his troops went down and removed them. Hence the reason we could not properly deploy and get on with the attack. This was an error on our part as we should have left observers there to watch the final line of deployment. In a real world situation the recon party would have been blown away when they were first observed or the enemy would have planned massive fires around the area and waited to ambush us. At any rate the damage had been done. Major Mowery's and my Irish luck had run out. It hurt to learn these things after the fact. I never mentioned the "unscheduled night attack" issue to Colonel Stang; his Ranger persona would never have allowed us any down time. It turned out not to matter. The efficiency report he gave me later was outstanding. But still it was close to my Waterloo and, of more importance, hurt the battalion image.

One morning a sister battalion commander from the First Brigade came to see me. He asked if he could share something with me in confidence since I was "in good" with the Division commander (Commanding General or CG). I told him sure but the fact that I survived the training briefing torture sessions, with some success, did not mean that I was in tight with the two star CG. He began by handing over his efficiency report. It was a good one from his brigade commander and the assistant Division commander and the CG's comments were OK, but he had middle blocked him for potential. In those days the potential scale had five blocks ranging from top block #1, <u>outstanding</u>, to #5, <u>no potential</u>. Having worked at Infantry Branch I believed that the middle #3 block was the kiss of death. I did not, however, share that thought with my buddy. We talked a long time and my guidance to him was to go talk to the CG and see what he said.

Several weeks later another battalion commander from the Second Brigade came to see me. The issue was the same, a good efficiency report in the words from all raters but a middle #3 block for potential from the CG. It appeared that there was a pattern here. Again, the only guidance I could give him was to try to discuss it with the CG. Neither officer came back to tell me the results of their efforts.

Not long after this my own report card arrived; great and glowing words from Colonel Stang and BG Scholtes our Division Assistant Commander for Operations. The CG's comments were also outstanding. But I, like my two sister battalion commanders, was given a middle (#3) block for potential. As I said, I viewed this as a kiss of death. After mulling it over I decided to go discuss it with BG Scholtes. He told me that he had talked to the CG three times about my report and that he was adamant that he would not change it. General Scholtes cleared me to go talk directly with the boss.

I went in and the conversation went something like this: and I will paraphrase the entire meeting. "Sir, I want to tell you that I got the message, I will retire and start a second career. But it appears that you are ruining the careers of a whole generation of paratroop commanders with your #3 block for potential ratings. Some of those guys, in my opinion, have general officer potential." I went on to explain that two other battalion commanders had come to see me about their efficiency reports so I was making that comment about hurting a generation based on more than just my report.

The General responded, "Heck Larry, you're going to be a full colonel, go the war college and you will command a brigade. That was a great report."

I again told him that I was a big boy and could handle retiring as an LTC, about two grades higher than I ever expected to be, but that he was hurting more than just me. I went on to say I did not know what he had against me, but whatever, so be it.

He then leaned back in his chair and said, "Well, you talk too much."

I agreed with him that talking too much was a fault I had, but I always spoke what I thought was the truth.

He continued saying, "You remember that night in the desert when you corrected me in front of Lieutenant General Warner? You just talk too much."

I responded that what I had done that night was correct, we had failed the Rangers. They had not failed that EDRE, and if I had it to do over again I would again say what I had said. If I had embarrassed him in any way that was not my intent, just ensuring that the right thing was done was my goal.

The General again told me that I would be a full colonel, attend the war college and command a brigade. I responded that I doubted any of that would happen but that I was glad we had cleared the air between us. We shook hands and I returned to the battalion. Not sure if I ever shared that event with any of the battalion staff at the time but certainly have over the years. Of course I did tell Mary who said that we could just start a civilian career somewhere.

About two months later I had been out on one of my rucksack runs and upon returning to the headquarters the runner handed me a note telling me to call the Commanding General as soon as possible at his private number.

When I called he answered and again I am paraphrasing the conversation. "Larry, the War College List is out." (Silence)

"Yes, sir"

A moment of silence, then; "Well, I wanted you to know, and hear it from me." (Silence)

"Yes, sir"

"Well I wanted you to hear it from me." (Silence) "You aren't on the list." (Silence)

"Yes, sir."

"There are people on that list who aren't worthy of tying your boot laces." (Silence)

"Yes, sir, thank you"

"Well I wanted you to hear it from me." (Dial tone)

Needless to say I was disappointed with the news. But I also felt vindicated in my standing up to the boss over his magnanimous award of so many three blocks. I was not the only LTC commanding on Ardennes Street that year that missed that list. As I remember only one Infantry battalion commander made it, and he was a minority. His selection was well deserved; he was a good soldier well known and liked by all.

42
BEING LUCKY ON
ARDENNES STREET

everal months later my phone rang and it was Major "Wild Bill" William Garrison, by this time assigned to Saudi Arabia as an advisor to the Saudi Arabian National Guard. We chatted for a few minutes and I finally said, "Bill you didn't call me from Saudi to discuss training or the weather over there, what's the issue?" He said, "Well, sir I wanted you to know that I am going to be early select for LTC, and deep select for battalion command and I am coming back to command the 1-505 cause you have the best battalion in the 82nd Airborne!" I told him, "Bill you have more bullshit than a Texas barn yard." We talked at some length and then he hung up. I thought that was quite a strange call but frankly had bigger gators to wrestle and promptly forgot about it. There was no way all that could happen; no one in the trenches had that kind of insight on what Army Selection Boards would do. As you will read, all that and more came to pass.

Every battalion was supposed to get an IG inspection once a year. Sometimes this event slipped a month or two but like death and taxes it was always coming. Ours came about the time it was expected. Now the IG team, they were like a plague of locusts, inspected every facet of battalion functions from the Personnel Actions Center, to motor maintenance, weapons maintenance, equipment accountability, medical and mess hall operations, to barracks cleanliness to a full blown in ranks Class A uniform inspection. You name it those locusts inspected and checked it. Like the IRS they were there to help you. For the most part that was true, and we did pass with pretty glowing reports except for two small actions that were beyond the pale.

First one company was caught with a footlocker full of spare weapons parts. This was a real "no-no" as it defeated the whole purpose of the logistics requisitioning process and distorted everything in the parts demand system. This came to light when the company armorer casually announced that the "footlocker of spare parts really let him keep the weapons in tip top shape" or some such words and he stated that he seldom had to report a weapon on deadline for lack of a part. The really bad part was the locusts tracked the footlocker down at a lieutenant's quarters. Both the lieutenant and the company commander initially denied having such a footlocker both to the IG, Major Emory Mace, and to me. After the smoke cleared, and it was clear they had lied, I was faced with what to do. The lieutenant got an Article 15 and I relieved the company commander. Being a commander sometimes means making the truly tough calls. I had just ruined that captain's career.

Redmond's Rule #20 - "When in doubt tell the truth" Mark Twain.

The second problem was in our combat support company where six night vision devices could not be accounted for. Somehow there must have been some sleight of hand, or whatever, when the last change of command inventory had been done. There was no way around it, the company commander was stuck missing six expensive night vision devices. He was later found liable to the tune of about $8,000 in a report of survey. This ruling was later deemed excessive by the Division Logistics Officer, G4, and the $8,000 charge was dropped.

Overall, in the full scope of things, the battalion came through the IG inspection with flying colors. The troop inspection, motor pool operations and the Battalion Personnel Action Center all got outstanding ratings. The 1-505 Panthers were riding pretty high.

One morning while running with the battalion on Ardennes Street, General Meloy passed me going the other way. As he drew abreast he yelled over, "Congratulations, Larry, you have been extended in command a couple of months." I was flabbergasted. Seldom did anyone ever get extended in command. It just didn't happen. Command tours were eighteen months and another LTC was waiting to take over. Again, I didn't think too much about it and certainly never put the extension in command together with the call from Major Bill Garrison in Saudi Arabia.

By this time most of the original battalion staff and company commanders had moved on and I had a new team. The executive officer was still Major Greg Sharp (due to leave shortly) and the sergeant major was still Jimmy Chandler. The staff was, I think, made up of S1 LT Day (a pseudonym), S2 LT Kevin Jackson, LT Bill Cain as his assistant, S3 Major Tom Lippy, S4 Captain Johnny Brooks and Signal Officer Leo Ledoux. Chief Warrant Officer Harrell was still my maintenance chief; Captain "Father" Jack Prendergast was the battalion chaplain and one heck of counselor and friend. Father Jack had been an Air Force air policeman in Vietnam and was great with the troops—they could and did relate to him. The company commanders included captains John Walus, Mike Grady, John Innis, Scott Mooney and Kim Jacobs. These guys were all good. I could not have asked for a better support team. They made my job easy and they made me look good. I owe them all, along with hundreds of troops whose names are lost in haze, more than I can ever repay.

One day the CG, General Meloy, called me to his office and told me, "Larry, we have been getting some pretty questionable captains assigned to the Division by Infantry Branch. I want you to go down to Benning and interview captains in the next two graduating Advanced Courses and recruit some good talent. You pick them; I'll get them assigned here." I followed orders and dutifully traveled to

Fort Benning and did some recruiting. While I was at it I picked two really sterling infantry captains to come to the H-Minus Battalion. Unfortunately both the lads I recruited got ripped off by other brigade commanders and neither of them made it to the 1-505.

We were designated to be the Army Training Evaluation Program (ARTEP) support battalion for our sister brigade unit the 1-508. Lieutenant Colonel Bob Glass had a good lash up and we looked forward to putting them through their test under the guidance of COL Stang. I was determined that their test would be fair and that there would be no shenanigans such as befell us on our ARTEP.

We were about three days into the scheduled seven day ARTEP when I got a radio call saying the exercise was over and the sergeant major and I were to report to Division Headquarters immediately. I checked with COL Stang not believing that they had stopped the ARTEP half way through. Things like that just did not happen, especially with Art Stang. He confirmed the order. He then went on to explain that the sergeant major and I were being flown up to Fort Indiantown Gap for a reconnaissance prior to replacing the 1-504 Airborne Infantry currently there. That battalion had been sent up a month earlier to control rioting Cuban refugees from the Mariel Boat Lift. At that point (I have recently been reminded of this but don't remember doing it.) I turned to Major Lippy and told him to get the battalion to the rear and do whatever it takes to get the troops up to Fort Indiantown Gap. Captain Brooks was standing there and I turned to him and told him to put together a convoy of five jeeps and trailers and bring them to "the Gap" also. We might well need them up there. I have since learned that Johnny Brooks had a very interesting trip north with that little convoy and that all the riding and bouncing gave him a serious case of hemorrhoids. The trip up there dictated that they spend the night somewhere between Fort Bragg and Fort Indiantown Gap. Fort Belvoir in VA filled that role but being totally unexpected guests Brooks and his troops had to spend the night in the Belvoir stockade (jail).

Sergeant Major Chandler and I rushed to Division HQ and were briefed that a plane was standing by to take us to Fort Indiantown Gap and that the battalion XO would take over getting the troops on the road to us in the morning by bus. Neither Jimmy nor I ever got a good understanding of why we were being hurriedly moved north to replace the 1-504 who had been doing a great job. I didn't get it then and still don't.

43
DEALING WITH THE
MARIEL BOAT LIFT PEOPLE

The 1-504 from the 82nd First Brigade had been providing security support to a Joint Military-Civilian Task Force at Fort Indiantown Gap, Pennsylvania for almost a month. The Task Force at the Gap included all sorts of Federal and civilian agencies; U.S. Border Patrol, Federal Police, State Department folks, Federal Marshals, the Red Cross, Catholic Charities, and many other nongovernment agencies. Additionally there was a contingent of Spanish speaking Special Forces and Psychological Operations specialists from Fort Bragg assisting the civilians. This Task Force had been receiving and processing refugees from Senor Castro's Cuban workers' paradise. Mr. Castro was flushing some of the worst dregs from his prisons out of the Port of Mariel, Cuba along with some very good Cubans who were thankful to be out of the Cuban workers' paradise. The U.S. military had become a key player after the bad guys among the refugees started acting up. They were truly creating problems for the good Cubans in the camps where they were being processed. The Indiantown Gap Camp had been particularly bad in this respect with numerous injuries to some good folks. The 82nd had rushed a battalion of paratroopers, the 1-504, up there to add muscle to the Task Force.

At Fort Indiantown Gap the sergeant major and I were briefed by LTC Rock Hudson and his staff as to what was going on and the day to day routine of keeping peace in the massive camp. He explained that we were basically "strong arm backup" and that the civilian agencies ran day to day activities in the camp. Rock took me to meet the camp commander, a Brigadier General Grail Brookshire. An armor officer, before making general, he was a good leader. For the next thirty five days I would meet with him every morning, along with the senior representatives from all the Government and Nongovernment Organizations (NGOs) working there. At this point there were about 10,000 Cuban refugees warehoused at Fort Indiantown Gap. (Eventually around 19,000 would process through that site.) These folks ran the gamut from every day "good folks" who were fleeing Castro's Cuban wonderland to hardened criminals of every stripe including the worst of the worst; yes even murderers and rapists. Screening these refugees to identify the good from the bad was not an easy job in all cases. That was a task done by Federal Agents and NGO Agencies. Once a good refugee or refugee family was clearly identified a U.S. sponsor family would be linked up with them and the refugees would be released to a life in the U.S. Those found to be criminals, who had been released from Castro's jails to flood the U.S., were either processed for deportation back to Cuba or sent to U.S. prisons. These bad folks, both male and female, had been the instigators of problems at the base. At some point before the 82nd became involved many of those identified as being trouble makers had been placed in several barracks off by themselves to protect the other refugees from harassment. This would prove to be a mistake in the weeks ahead.

After the arrival of the 1-504 the rioting and beatings of fellow refugees had almost ceased. The "04" had done a good job of calming things after their arrival almost a month earlier. Under Rock's leadership the battalion kept one company on immediate alert to respond to any dangerous activity. Every morning the battalion ran the five miles around the compound without a sound except that every time the left foot of around 600 paratroopers hit the ground they stomped their boot. It was an intimidating and effective technique that we immediately adopted. The folks in the compound, secured by two, repeat two, coils of barbed wire, really not much of an inhibitor, could hear the soldiers coming a long way off. While we did not go into the compound some of the Special Forces and Border Patrol agents and other government agencies did. When the 1-504 had arrived at the Gap the SF soldiers had told the Cubans that the paratroopers from Fort Bragg were bad folks. Now they told them that the hard core "baby killers" were coming to replace the paratroopers already there. For whatever reason they painted a picture of the H-Minus Battalion/Black Panthers as the grim reapers of the U.S. Army. It worked, at least initially. The battalion arrived by bus from Fort Bragg and the 1-504 departed that night on the same busses. The turnover of responsibility occurred smoothly and we assumed the duty of Cuban control and observation.

The first three weeks we were there things were very quiet. Our S3, Major Tom Lippy, put together a great training program and the troops kept quite busy and were enjoying the overall change of venue from life at Fort Bragg. Major General Meloy, with a cast on his foot from a jump injury and navigating with the help of a cane, visited and was very impressed with all aspects of the training especially the basic soldier skills we were stressing. All the briefings were done by our NCOs and it pleased the CG that the officers were taking a back seat. That's the way it was supposed to be. Soldier skills were meant to be taught by the NCOs. The General congratulated the sergeant major and me for the training and the job we were doing in keeping the lid on the refugees. After a private session with the camp commander, General Meloy departed with no comment. I took that as a sure sign of his satisfaction with what he had seen and heard. If he was leaving unhappy I would have been the first to know.

One afternoon I was summoned to the Commanding General's Office for an unscheduled meeting. Present were the top Border Patrol, Federal Marshal, Federal Police, Military Police, the Special Forces Team Chief and myself. It seemed some of the Special

Forces NCOs had been hearing rumors about guns in the camp. Yes, real bullet launchers. We had already determined that the bad guys had made spears, swords and knives from bunk bed metal slats and anything else they could get their hands on. After much discussion General Brookshire decided we would have to go into the camp and do a detailed search. We were being asked to provide the muscle to seal the perimeter; back up and support the Border Patrol, Special Forces (language fluent) and other Police elements that would do the actual search of the barracks. We did get the dirty job of crawling under selected "known bad guy barracks" and clearing the area there of any weapons or hidden contraband.

The plan called for us to move quietly into position, surrounding the barbed wire with troops just before dawn. We were to place soldiers every 5 meters in riot gear carrying three foot long billy clubs and wearing face shields and body armor. That equipment could be intimidating to any good refugee for sure. We also provided squad size reaction teams every half mile around the camp just in case any of the bad guys tried to break out. It was further decided to divide the camp in the middle into two segments with two designated search parties. One search team would move north from this midpoint while the other moved south. There was a road near the center of the camp that provided a perfect break point. Should real bullets start flying the role of countering that situation fell to the Border Patrol, Federal Marshals and Federal Police. Those elements were armed, loaded and locked. The Black Panthers were strictly muscle.

My only problem was people. There were not enough infantrymen to cover the perimeter and split the camp into the two sections. I called the staff and company commanders together for the briefing on the operation. When we finished I said to all that while our plan sounded good we had a small problem in that there weren't enough infantry troops to make it work. Before I could say another word Captain Brooks, the S4 Logistics Officer, said something like: "Sir you can have all the cooks and maintenance personnel." Before it was done, a few sick and lame along with most of the medics, signal platoon troops and the administrative types from the headquarters had all been "volunteered." Anyone who could walk and stand position in the cordon was going to be there. This could last all day I told them. Captain Brooks was quick to respond, which was his normal approach to soldiering; "Sir, they can handle it." And that next day the legend of the "505 combat cookies" was born. Seems the mess sergeant was none too happy with the tasking but the cooks were thrilled and did a sterling job on the perimeter. The American soldier is an amazing being.

Starting about 0400 we began positioning troops and splitting the barbed wire and breaking the camp into two sections. As near as we could determine this action was totally unobserved by any of the refugees. For sure the bad guys and gals were quite surprised when the sun came up. The search came off without incident and some forty-plus weapons and a few dirty pieces of ammo turned up under barracks, but no guns. Everyone breathed a sigh of relief. This whole operation lasted over twelve hours and to say the troops performed in super fashion is an understatement. As I toured the cordon line throughout the day with the sergeant major we never heard a gripe or complaint. We did have to change out a couple of troops who we probably should not have put on the line in the first place but overall it was a moment of glory for the soldiers. They subsisted for about fifteen hours on water and C-ration chocolate bars affectionately referred to as "John Wayne" bars. Good Cubans came down to the wire and thanked our soldiers for helping to make the camp safer for them. They recognized what was going on. The whole affair ended by 1700 that day and a sigh of relief came up from the entire Task Force. Not only had they removed many weapons but the exercise had allowed them to identify more of the bad guy and bad gal ring leaders. There were some truly nasty females in that camp as well as men.

But in total fairness there were a great many good and accomplished Cubans there also. They were looking for a chance at a better life. I remember one morning on the run someone pointed out an older gentleman sitting in a second story barracks window holding a sign saying, "I am a good Cuban, Please Help Me!"

44

THE OLD MAN GETS AN R&R
AND A STARTLING REQUEST

After the visit by the General and this cordon and search operation the sergeant major came to me and told me, "Sir, you need a break. You're leaning too far forward in the foxhole. Go see Gettysburg." He then handed me the keys to a Government station wagon and a relatively long range hand held radio. "We can reach you if needed via this radio. Call in twice a day to the operations center and we will update you; nothing is happening here. Go unwind. Take a few days off." Frankly he was correct, I was wound pretty tight. I took the keys and radio, packed a small overnight bag and after clearing my absence, but stressing my ease of recall with General Brookshire, departed into deepest, darkest south central Pennsylvania. I enjoyed the time away, Gettysburg and some very quaint Amish towns like Bird in Hand, Intercourse and many others provided a great and needed change of venue. I stayed at inexpensive motels in the Amish country that were immaculate and well kept.

On day two after visiting Gettysburg for six hours (I had been there before.) I took a remote, but paved, road cross country and stumbled upon Michter's Whiskey Distillery. The main building had been built in the 1760s and it sat next to a stream with a large and still working water wheel that crushed the grain into pulp for mash. I stopped and took the tour. It was quite interesting and informative. As I moved through the plant I got one of Redmond's fantastic mental fire storms. I bought two quarts of Michter's finest, pretty pricey for a shanty Irish lad even on a lieutenant colonel's pay but I did it. I will return to the substance of the brain storm in a few pages. The sergeant major was almost about to regret sending me off but I am sure the likes of Lippy and Brooks and some of the company commanders had put him up to it. I laugh about that to this day.

On day three check-in I learned some very sad news. Colonel Stang had passed away suddenly. He had recently changed command with Colonel Jim Johnson and moved on to be the Chief of Staff of the Division. That morning he led a two mile unit run, a walk in the park for him, and finished in fine fettle. The colonel stepped to the podium at Pike Field to address the unit troops before they conducted a change of command. He suddenly collapsed, dying from a ruptured aorta before he hit the riser. Mrs. Stang had requested Major Lippy be the survivor assistance officer. Tom was one cool and savvy soldier and I cleared his immediate return and told them I was on my way back at that moment. It took me about two hours to get back to "the Gap" and Tom had already been picked up by U-21 aircraft and was en route back to Fort Bragg. I liked Colonel Stang immensely and it hurt me that I could not attend his funeral but it was simply not possible. Knowing that Tom Lippy was there to make everything happen for Mrs. Stang was great consolation. Art Stang was a heck of a soldier. Had he lived there is little doubt in my mind that he would have worn stars.

Upon return to the Gap things settled into the day to day activities of running, attending staff meetings, intimidating our Cuban detainees and training in soldier skills. Things had been so quiet that we were allowed to send one company at a time into the field areas for unit training. That was super and we rotated all companies off to the woods by themselves for short two to three day training excursions. The company commanders thought it was great and so did I. The troops also appreciated training on new terrain. At some point the battalion S1, LT Day, visited on some pretext of getting important papers signed. It never struck me that this overnight stay qualified for a Humanitarian Service Medal Award. I learned later that after returning to Fort Bragg he had promptly put himself in for that award. His service in the battalion would shortly end under bad circumstances.

We were billeted in World War II barracks that were exactly as the "Greatest Generation" had trained and lived in during the early 1940s. I relate that point to set the stage for one of the strangest encounters with junior enlisted troops I ever had. If the reader at this point is a current serving soldier he will doubt the veracity of this yarn. I assure you, it happened as I am about to relate, well pretty close for sure. With my senile memory now, perhaps I am forgetting some aspects of the conversation; but I think not.

One morning, while I was reading through some papers, after our usual staff meetings, the sergeant major came to the office and said, "Sir, I have five troops outside who want to talk to you and you aren't going to believe it. They represent two different companies." I immediately thought, "Oh great, some grievance." Maybe the fact that there is a club here and I had forbidden drinking given the imminence of a mission down with the Mariel lads and lasses. At any rate five very sharp young troops came into the office, saluted and the spokesman began to talk. The more he talked the more amazed I became. The sergeant major just stood there grinning. The gist of the comments went something like; "Sir, we have a question for you. Why can't we live and train like this at Fort Bragg? We are all living together in those platoon bays with our NCOs. We are getting to know each other as never before. We like this approach to being a team and training together. This is great. Why can't Fort Bragg be like this?"

That is a rather simplified relating of their tale. I was taken aback. Several other troops chimed in that this was not just their feeling but that most of their buddies in other companies also agreed. Nods from the other troops signaled their concurrence. I was stunned and for a moment at a loss for words. I then started talking about WWII, life in the Army in the early '60s and the fact that the barracks they now lived in back at Bragg, with two man semiprivate rooms, came in with the all-volunteer Army. Before that those barracks had been platoon bay set ups similar but more modern than the barracks here at Fort Indiantown Gap. They had no idea this had been the case. I made it clear that while I personally agreed with them, the All-Volunteer Army had ended "platoon and squad bay" living forever. Changing that was far beyond my ability. We talked a long time. The troopers left satisfied that we had what we had at Indiantown Gap and enjoy it while they could.

U.S. Augmentees to United Nations Truce Supervisory Organization-
Palestine. Major Redmond, second row, center. Israel, 1973.

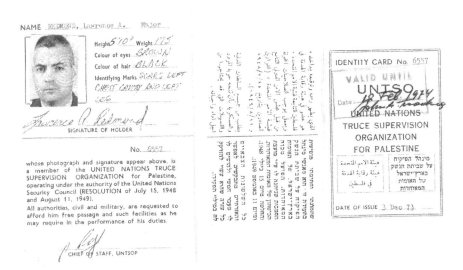

United Nations Truce Supervisory Organization-Palestine
(UNTSO-P) identification card, front and back. 1973.

Formal dinner with
the "short, fat major"
tactics instructor and
his lady. Fort Benning,
GA, 1975.

(BELOW)
Joint Casualty
Resolution Center
Staff, Major Redmond,
center second row
from top. Sameson,
Thailand, 1975.

Change of Command, 1-505 Airborne, Redmond family seated lower left front row. Fort Bragg, NC, July 6, 1979.

(ABOVE) Memorial graves, Village of Langfeld, Germany. All engraved *"Vermisst in Russland."*

Panther Rock, 1-505 Airborne, H-Minus Battalion, 82d Airborne Division.

A little command "guidance" being imparted while deployed to the Jungle Operations Training Center, Panama, 1979.

FT SHERMAN CANAL ZONE   1979

(BELOW) Lieutenant Cain's (Mr. Bill) guerrilla kidnappers before the abduction of Panther 6.

CAIN'S GUERRILA BAND 1-505 (ABN) 1981

H-Minus Battalion passing in review, Fort Bragg, 1980.

Celebrating promotion to colonel with past and present commanders of H-Minus. *Left to right:* COL Jerry Scott, COL Mike Plummer, COL Paul Devries, COL Larry Redmond, LTC Bill Garrison.

(ABOVE) Air Commodore Mickey Witherow (*right*) and COL Redmond at Seaford House, 1983.

In Normandy they still name streets to honor their liberators. St. Mere Eglise, France, 1983.

Royal College of Defence
Studies ID card that
"could not get a room at
the Portsmouth, UK, Royal
Navy Base for my son and I."

(RIGHT) RCDS Mid East Tour in
Jordan with the Dead Sea in the
distance, just before crossing
into Israel.

(BELOW) Lady Pillar, wife of
Admiral Sir William Pillar,
College Commandant, and Mary
solving world problems. Royal
College formal dinner, 1983.

(ABOVE) "The Cricket Match," Chelsea Barracks, London. *Center, left to right*: Redmond displaying "Airborne Death From Above" shirt; Geoff Bentley, Australian Diplomatic Corps; COL Dick Cowling, Canadian Army; CAPT Larry Andrews, USN.

The family, U.S. Central Command, 1985.

General Jim Lindsay (*left*) doing the retirement honors in the BLUE ROOM at U.S. Special Operations Command

The RCDS Reunion in Florida, 2003. John Morgan, President Bush impersonator, flanked by pseudo Secret Service Agents Mac McCarty (*left*) and Butch Cicatko (*right*).

45

THE MICHTER'S MOMENT AND THE FECES FESTIVAL

A s related earlier I had returned from my short R&R refreshed but saddened by the news of Colonel Stang's passing and also carrying two quarts of Michter's Whiskey. The mental fire storm that had struck me while out flushing my dead brain cells was that maybe the officers could have a Dining In (A male only dinner as opposed to a Dining Out where ladies were in attendance.). I called Jimmy into my office, told him my idea and asked him; "Sergeant Major, would the NCOs and troops be upset if the officers were to have a Dining In and get a small sample of real, early American booze?" He said he felt we had earned it and with some twenty-five plus officers and a mere two quarts of liquor no one was going to get anything like soused. The troops would not mind this one time violation of my no drinking policy. We discussed the NCOs taking all the leadership roles for one night. He agreed and the Dining In became reality. I ran this plan by Brigadier General Brookshire and he also concurred.

I did have a second, hidden agenda. My A Company Commander was CPT John Walus. He was an imposing, big, and very effective soldier/leader. Like me he was a "war flick" nut. We had been having a running gun battle about the last line in Sam Peckinpah's World War II film *Cross of Iron*. This is one of the best movies ever made about war on the Eastern Front as the Russian juggernaut began rolling west pushing the Germans out of Mother Russia. It is quite realistic and frankly not for the squeamish or faint of heart. It had an all-star cast consisting of James Coburn as the hero, Corporal Steiner; James Mason, as *Oberst* (Colonel) Brandt; and Maximillian Schell as the Prussian aristocrat Nazi officer, Captain Stransky, who left his cushy job in Paris, on sabbatical basically, to get his Iron Cross for valor. At any rate, Captain Walus had his mind made up that the story ended one way and I was convinced that I really knew the correct ending. I called in our battalion chaplain, Father Jack Prendergast, gave him the keys to the rental station wagon we had been provided and sent him off to Washington. He was to come back only after he had a projector and the film to show at our "Dining In." He was back in two days and the Dining In was about to happen. In the spirit of good paratrooper fun I would prove my young captain wrong in his understanding of that last line in that movie.

The cooks did a great job of prepping the battlefield for our dinner. I turned control of the battalion over to the sergeant major and first sergeants about 1400 and then took a nap. We assembled at the designated Dining In site at 1700 and just chilled out. The mess hall personnel had set up a large U-shaped table with the screen for watching *Cross of Iron* at the open end of the U. Father Jack, who had gotten training on the projector and running the movie, set it all up. The tables were decorated appropriately and place settings neatly arranged and every seat had an empty C-ration can with open lid sitting by it; reason for same not stated. I don't remember for sure but I think the dinner started off with the usual toasts done with water, tea and soft drinks…whatever. I had a few comments about the evening and thanked all for their fantastic efforts in a certainly different mission. The meal itself I am not sure about but I think the mess sergeant, SFC McKinley Bunch, served us C-rations and then followed up with steak, baked potatoes and all the trimmings. It was great.

Then came the movie. Most of the officers had not seen it before and sat semi-mesmerized as the Russians overwhelmed the Nazis with a whole bunch of Sam Peckinpah blood and gore. Just before the end I called a halt. I stood and then broke out the Michter's, which was passed from hand to hand with a healthy portion going into each C-ration can. I dispensed the officers from the no drinking rule for the next hour. Then we proceeded to the grand finale of the flick. When Corporal Steiner turns to Captain Stransky and says, "Come, Captain, I will take you where the Iron Crosses grow," just as the Russian tanks are overwhelming them; the place went ballistic. A somewhat crestfallen Captain Walus swallowed his pride and admitted I had been right. It was a great night and ended about 2100. Oh yes, the Michter's was all consumed. We officers did not assume control of the battalion again until reveille the next morning.

As a second thought, when I tasked Father Prendergast to come back with *Cross of Iron*, I challenged him to see if he could also round up the relatively new film, *A Bridge Too Far.* The good Padre had also accomplished this mission. A few nights later the troops were privileged to see this WWII Airborne tale at an outdoor theatre. It was a little chilly this late in September but the flick held the lads' attention. Sadly they did not have any Michter's to sweeten or warm the viewing.

Frankly life at Fort Indiantown Gap was really pretty good. The mission was real, the threat immediately visible and the training time was superb. We were about to be visited by the new brigade commander, COL Jim Johnson, who would go on to command the Division during Desert Shield/Desert Storm and retire as a three star general. Jim and Edna, his wife, were a class act and super people. The brigade was getting top notch soldiers to lead it. The day COL Johnson arrived started off like any other. He received the usual rounds of briefings and visited training around the camp. He then visited with the CG and got an orientation on what had been happening and how things were going. The battalion actions during the cordon and search were praised by General Brookshire. Jim then asked if he could visit the company we had about five miles away training on a real hill unlike the pimples at Fort Bragg. We traveled out to the site and were in the process of getting briefed by the company commander when my jeep radio crackled with a short cryptic message saying there was trouble in the compound and that I should return immediately. Colonel Johnson said something like, "Go now, I will get back when I am done here." He never made an effort to interfere or oversee what I was about to get into. That was his style.

On the way back to the camp the Tactical Operations Center updated me that there was major rioting underway in several of the bad guy-bad girl barracks and that at least one barracks was on fire. The CG had already requested that the alert company be deployed to the site to assist the police elements trying to control and contain the riot. I directed that the entire battalion be put on ready status and that the company in the field be recalled to garrison. It was not hard to find the problem in the camp as the smoke was visible from the time I came out of the woods. Captain Mike Grady was the alert, immediate reaction, company commander and had moved promptly with about 130 paratroopers in full riot gear to the street immediately in front of the rioting Cubans. To see 130 "baby killers," as our SF friends had dubbed us, standing there in full riot gear with three foot long hickory batons was somewhat intimidating to all but the meanest, "baddest" of the rioters. Mike had positioned the troops not more than fifty yards from the three buildings involved with concurrence of the Border Patrol (BP) leader who was trying to negotiate an end to this fun and games. All the key leaders were present to include BG Brookshire. The actual negotiations to end this activity had devolved on the chief of the BP element.

Apparently this incident had started around noon over some minor issue and then escalated. To say it was a sight I won't forget is an understatement. The police elements were attempting to contain the area of the rioting while the fire department stood by unable to get to the point of the fire, inhibited by the bad guys. There were bad Cubans all over the roofs and many of them were nude to include the ladies. They were defecating on the roof and throwing it down at the Border Patrol, Marshals, Pennsylvania State Police and federal police. It was a sight not to be forgotten. The fire continued unabated and no one was sure what was happening in the barracks. Finally the chief of the Border Patrol element got into a cherry picker and was hoisted up close to the roof of the building that was burning with ominous clouds of smoke roiling up. The BP chief was a Latino from Texas so language was not a big problem, although Tex-Mex is not exactly colloquial Cuban. After about thirty minutes and a lot of animated conversation and pointing and gesturing down toward Mike Grady's awesome troops, some level of sanity returned to the scene. We watched as the ring leaders decided to call it a day. We would only learn a little later what the BP chief told the ringleaders that had prompted this decision.

In the meantime three large black, tinted window buses with iron bars on all but the front windshield slowly worked their way down to the entrance to the three barracks where the bad folks were doing their thing. The side of the buses proudly proclaimed "United States Federal Prison, Philadelphia, Pennsylvania." The firefighters were escorted by the BP agents into the burning building and a second barracks that was smoking but in which no flames were visible. Slowly the fire was brought under control. Suddenly the rioters were being led out one at a time. Those that still had clothes on were stripped naked. No questions asked and no apologies given. This was quickly followed by an all cavity body search in view of everyone present. Yes, I did say a public equal opportunity all body cavity search. Once totally screened, the rioters, both male and female were led onto the buses by several burly prison guards. While this was taking place I asked if I could look inside one of the buses. I was escorted into the bus by another rather intimidating guard and what I saw made me smile with glee. The bus was stark to the extreme. Metal seats with no backs; an iron bar in front of each seat was present and the rioters were chained to the bar. The temperature inside was perhaps just below 40 degrees; more than chilly enough. I looked at the driver who shrugged his shoulders and made a comment to the effect, "Yeh, cold, they will be quite docile till we get them to Philly." Now this was punishment for a crime that I related to. No molly coddling or Club Gitmo mentality here.

Upon leaving the bus I ran into the chief of the BP who had gone up in the cherry picker. I asked him what he had told the ringleaders that convinced them to give up their little feces infested holiday. He responded that he told them that if they thought Castro's goon enforcers were bad news they had better wake up because he was about to order the paratroopers to move in. If that happened bodies would be flying out windows and off the roofs. The SF propaganda campaign concerning how bad we paratroopers truly were had paid off. Slowly the compound was cleared, body searches conducted and some very chilled Cuban bad folks started a slow trip to Philly. As things broke up, General Brookshire went over and thanked Captain Grady and his troops for their support and demeanor throughout the operation.

I turned to walk away and saw COL Johnson also standing over near the B Company troops chatting away. He had apparently witnessed most of the activity but never came over to speak, interfere or see what I was doing. I was impressed with his leadership style and remain so today.

After this event things turned back to training and running and just enjoying some time away from the Fort Bragg flagpole. Our sojourn at Fort Indiantown Gap was about to end. We were replaced by a battalion from the Second Brigade, the 1-325 Infantry, but their stay at "the Gap" was not quite as exciting as ours had been. The bust-up of the bad guys and gals at the "feces festival" had defused most signs of martial intentions on the part of the remaining Cubans; most of whom were fine folks. The majority of them went on to become good and productive citizens of the USA.

46

THE DESERT RATS OF
DONA ANA RANGE CAMP

Upon return to Fort Bragg we settled into normal activities for an Infantry battalion chasing the 82nd Airborne Division "train."

Following our sojourn at Fort Indiantown Gap, Sergeant Major Chandler was reassigned and I had a new sergeant major, Bruce Pross, who came to us from the First Ranger Battalion. He was another hard charger. Like Jimmy before him we made a good team. Bruce would become a confidant and friend over many years. He was famous for his quaint comment response, "That there" to almost any statement or situation that presented itself. He was one savvy NCO in spite of that small quirk. Major Greg Sharp my original XO had moved on and been replaced by another super administrator in Major Bowman "Bo" Olds. He proved to be another genius with the battalion budget and we never wanted for anything. In fact Bo had a knack for finding money that other battalions did not use as the fiscal year end approached and some hefty additions found their way to our balance sheet. Additionally, about this time the battalion was fortunate to receive a hard charging young captain named Gary Harrell. He was destined to go on to wear two stars. Much to his chagrin I posted him to the job of S4 freeing Captain Brooks to become my Headquarters and Headquarters Company Commander. Gary later commanded C Company and did so in a truly outstanding manner.

Then on 1 November 1980 the battalion suffered a shocking and tremendous loss. It was a Saturday afternoon and I was working on our car in the driveway of our quarters when I got a call that shattered me. Warrant Officer Carter Stephens, my battalion physicians' assistant, had been injured in a car wreck out near Camp Mackall. He was being airlifted to the closest civilian hospital at that very moment. I changed clothes and drove with Mary directly to the hospital. Carter was on life support and the surgeons were frantically working to determine his overall status. We comforted his wife Joyce, as much as we could, and all prayed that the test results would be negative as to brain damage. Captain Father Prendergast, our battalion chaplain, was there and provided great counsel and comfort. After about twenty-four hours the word was not good. Carter was effectively brain dead. His family was faced with the decision to leave him on life support and continue a hopeless effort. After long talks with Father Prendergast and her pastor the decision was made by Joyce to remove Carter from life support. He died shortly thereafter. His loss was mourned throughout the Division and also at XVIII Airborne Corps.

As his battalion commander it was my sad duty at the funeral to give a Commander's Testament about Carter. I sat up most of the night before the funeral working on it. I remembered so much and what a great man he was and how he went out of his way to help troopers and their families. No issue was to small and no illness too common for him to provide his curing support. He was always available to the lowest private or officer at any hour. Like an old time doc he made house calls rain or shine. Oh, but woe be unto the troop slacker who tried to get the doc to help him skate out of some operation or activity. He had been a fantastic help to me and I surely appreciated his help up in Alaska with the chilblains. I really mulled over what to say. I was still at it just before dawn and think I got about two hours sleep. At the service the Third Brigade chapel was packed, not a seat to be had. A former Corps commander, Lieutenant

General Hank Emerson, now retired, was seated in the front pew along with Major General Meloy. The service was solemn and meaningful. The chaplain's comments were excellent. Then I got up to give my Testament.

Commander's Testament

> *Chief Warrant Officer Carter Dwyer Stephens was born on September 11, 1944 in Birmingham Alabama. Born into an Army family, the son of Master Sergeant Fred and Ann Stephens.....*

> *Sometimes in this life we are privileged to meet and know people specially blessed by God with extra talents. Carter Stephens was such a man. His life was one of duty and devotion. Life for Carter was full; full of challenge, opportunity, bravery, achievement and a close and deep relationship with his wife Joyce and his family. Life for Carter was the Army, the Airborne, Special Forces and the soldiers for whom and with whom he worked. Those of us close to him know the true and unbounded enthusiasm and compassion of a healer who especially loved the children he cared for in the clinic. Excellence and selflessness were his trademarks. Nights, weekends, at the expense of his own family, be it soldier, wife or child, if there was a need, Carter was there. He touched the lives of countless thousands of us by his performance of duty and by the example of professionalism that he set. We are all better people for his having passed this way.....Chief Warrant Officer Carter Stephens-a professional soldier."*

His replacement, while a good man, was not his equal in any way. Thanksgiving, Christmas and New Year's came up in short order. It was tradition on Ardennes Street that families ate in the unit mess hall with the troops on those holidays. In those days maybe twenty percent of the troops were married, unlike today where I think that number is closer to seventy-five percent. Battalion commanders and officers attended these meals in their dress blue uniform. The Black Panthers followed that tradition. The mess sergeant and cooks truly outdid themselves for the troops and families. The decorations were super, the food tremendous and our battalion even capped the events with ice sculptures. I can't remember a meal that was not spectacular. My children would spend hours visiting, laughing and talking with the other kids and with the troops. I never heard a grumble from them. It was a thrill to visit and hang around the dining facility which was then and always will be in my mind a "mess hall." The old regular Army is ingrained in my psyche.

Then over the Christmas holiday I was again informed that my command tour had been extended several more months. What the dickens was going on? I was to have a twenty four month command instead of the normal eighteen.

Early in January 1980 we began serious planning for our last off post deployment that would take us to Fort Bliss, Texas. This was a previously unscheduled deployment that the S3, Major Lippy, and I had managed to convince the Division G3 that the battalion needed. We had acquired sufficient aircraft to deploy the battalion with a number of attachments. We would insert in a battalion mass tactical parachute assault on Old Coe DZ at Bliss and play Lawrence of Arabia in the dust and sand for about thirty days. The troops had been to the swamps of Florida, the jungles of Panama, the frozen tundra of Alaska and the relatively docile land of eastern Pennsylvania so why not experience a little of the desert. I was looking forward to it and stressed that the training should focus on company and platoon level operations once the initial battalion parachute drop was completed. It was to be a true learning experience with at least one twist based on the time of year. I remember that the S2, LT Jackson, briefed us that the chance of precipitation at Fort Bliss in January was one percent. Boy did he get that wrong.

We deployed in late January after much detailed planning. Division had just received some new en route communication systems that allowed up-to-the minute intelligence to be passed from advance reconnaissance parties on the ground to the task force winging its way to battle. Via this system a commander had truly current info on what awaited him on the ground. We sent a Special Forces recon team in by C-130 Combat Talon (a very sophisticated Special Operations aircraft) two days in advance and they had our drop zone under surveillance for us. The S3, Major Lippy, was on the radio talking to the SF Team leader as we in-flight rigged for the drop and learned that there were several opposing force (OPFOR) armored vehicles and a few enemy troops in the area. A bunch of light infantry paratroopers jumping into a desert area with armored vehicles waiting. Not the best thing. We had arranged for a small OPFOR element to play the role of the bad guys against us so this was not terribly unexpected. Also we were jumping with lots of light anti-tank weapons (nonlethal training devices of course) and our organic anti-armor Dragon Weapon Systems. If this hadn't been training, and we had arranged for the OPFOR the very thought of armor would have caused what little hair I had in those "white wall haircut" days to stand tall. The real surprise was that the SF reported rain near the DZ and all across the surrounding desert.

The drop itself went well and we were able to overcome the limited resistance put up by a couple of OPFOR armored personnel carriers (APC) and perhaps fifteen bad guys. Not a real match for 500 plus paratroopers but a learning experience. Our situation would have been quite different had there been twenty or thirty APCs surrounding that drop zone. It began raining harder just after we landed and kept it up intermittently for two days; so much for the intelligence briefing and a one percent chance of rain in January. After the jump and assembly we then conducted a battalion "movement to contact" across perhaps twenty kilometers of desert. Why I allowed that and actually contributed in the planning I am at a loss to say. By that I mean the desert is not necessarily your friend, particularly for large bodies of troops all moving in one direction. I knew that from five months on the Golan Heights in 1973-1974 but let the fun and games of training over take my common sense. Light infantry moving in large formations across open desert cannot hide from a sophisticated enemy. On our objective for that first day the OPFOR had several ground surveillance radars and they tracked us all the way to the objective. Against a sophisticated bad guy we would have been toast. Lesson relearned by the old Ranger.

Following the approach march and successful attack, well it seemed successful to us, we settled into barracks at a place called Dona Ana Range Camp (actually located in New Mexico not Texas). The camp was adequate for our needs to be sure as most of our time would be out in the desert in small unit training. The troops enjoyed the change but quickly became disenchanted with the boonie rat troops of Dona Ana. They really were sort of a grungy lot at that time.

Our stay at Fort Bliss flew by and I remember very little of our activities. Somehow arrangements were made and I was given the opportunity to fly in the front seat of a Cobra gunship and flit around the desert while the pilot got in some training. That helicopter was quite the agile bird and impressive hovering back up in the hills in little hide sites waiting for a target to appear. The thrust of our unit training was at platoon and company level with the battalion staff and myself coordinating and observing. Overall for the troops it was a good training opportunity and a new experience. Captain Brooks was the Headquarters Company commander and dual hatted as the S1 Adjutant "forward" on this deployment. I remember clearly he helped keep me out of a lot of trouble.

As we were preparing to redeploy, the aircraft taking us back to Bragg were delayed by a major winter storm that dropped down much further south than expected. We had about six to eight inches of snow and an underlying coating of ice at the Fort Bliss airfield. Everything was at a standstill while they cleared the runway. We were staged in two large hangars beside the runway waiting on our transportation home. Father Jack had a great guitar service for the troops. He was one hard charging chaplain. Food became an issue and Captain Brooks had to order something like sixty pizzas to feed an unruly group of hungry paratroopers. The pizzas arrived late when most of the men were fast asleep. The pizza did get consumed and Brooks somehow got his money. I do remember getting up on an aircraft boarding ladder and addressing the men. Can't tell you what I said but folks seemed to appreciate it. The troops were all on their feet cheering when I finished. We were supposed to in-flight rig (put on our parachutes en route) and jump in at Fort Bragg. The snow delay changed that and we air landed back at Pope AFB. The flight back went off without a hitch and our last off post deployment was behind us.

47

THE RETURN OF WILD BILL GARRISON
& AN EAGLE LANDS

Shortly after return to what passed as normal activity in the 82nd Airborne Division, the G1 called to tell me that my replacement had been named. It was Major "Promotable" William F. Garrison coming from Saudi Arabia. No way, Jose; but yes it was true. Bill has never told me how he pulled that off. But the phone call from Saudi, his early promotion and deep select for command, and his becoming my successor did all happen. I wonder to this day, could it have just been luck? Believe it; this did happen just as I have related it.

The last couple of months in command are a blur but several events are worth relating. Mary and I were talking about my retiring and starting a second career. Infantry Branch was calling me about an assignment to the Pentagon in the Deputy Chief of Staff for Operations Directorate; certainly the last thing I wanted. Retirement was looking pretty good. I was convinced there is life after the Army. Then one morning the full colonel's promotion list was released and lo and behold my name was there. Well it was about thirty names from the bottom but sure enough I was going to wear an eagle. That is if I stayed in I would wear an eagle. Major General Meloy had been right that day in his office when he told me I would be a full colonel. Unfortunately, as I mentioned above, the Colonels Branch flesh peddlers were after me to come to the Pentagon. I was not interested and the possibility of retiring was looming large.

One day I got the bright idea to do an internal Battalion Emergency Deployment Readiness Exercise for one of our companies. We would alert them, fly them away to Camp Mackall and jump them in with the mission to rescue American hostages held by some bad guys. At this time I had a particularly sharp, hard charging young first lieutenant, Vance Richmond, in the assistant operations officer position. Together we worked out the plan, obtained the necessary aircraft from a sister battalion so that the airplanes were not on our airlift schedule. No one could deduce something was up. We even kept the S3 in the dark as to what we might be planning. Then I managed to con the 82nd Aviation Battalion to fly the company out after they had secured the hostages. The aviation lads had just gotten the new Blackhawk helicopter and they were anxious to fly a night extraction.

The scenario was simple enough. Jump into a Latin American country with no name; move overland and link up with a CIA agent named Raoul (aka LT Vance Richmond) who would lead them to the rebel camp where the hostages were held. Rescue the hostages; then move a couple of kilometers to an extraction zone where the Blackhawks would pick them up and fly them to a nearby friendly country where they would be extracted by Air Force planes. A bit corny I admit but it was what we came up with. The alert, planning and fly away and all the rest came together just as we had laid it out. B Company, Captain Mike Grady, was the lucky unit that had the honors. They did well. The rescue was truly professionally done. The bad guys were taken completely by surprise. The single thing that most strikes me about the operation was the look of surprise on his face when Captain Grady stepped out of the woods and found Raoul, neatly disguised with beard and campesino attire, was actually Vance Richmond. It was a fun exercise and good training and no one got hurt. Oh yes, I am pretty aware of how things unfolded since I went along as the chief evaluator.

Commanding in the 82nd was always challenging and for those of us focused on mission and men it was normally fun. There were times however that were not fun, nor happy, such as the death of Chief Warrant Officer Carter Stephens described earlier in these pages. I recall two other incidents that pointed up the problems and dangers of parachuting and serving with the All Americans.

The first of these events was at Camp Mackall on Luzon Drop Zone. A jumper just standing back from the door of a C-130 accidentally activated his reserve parachute and the partially deployed chute was sucked out the door. The trooper was jerked out with the chute and as he was pulled out of the plane he was decapitated on the jump door's trailing edge. We were doing DZ support coverage that day and I happened to be there on the DZ at the time. After an exhaustive search the troopers head was recovered. Not a pleasant episode. I hope this doesn't shock the more sensitive reader. Jumping out of airplanes is dangerous.

The second occurrence was even more startling, if startling is the correct word. A captain from Brigade Headquarters was killed when his chute failed to open and he streamered in on Sicily Drop Zone. This one I did not witness. Why it sticks in my memory is the fact that when they checked his chute to determine the cause of the streamer they discovered his static line had been cut nearly thru with a sharp knife. All jumping was halted while the entire stock of Division parachutes was inspected. They found four additional chutes (as I recall) with cut static lines; all had been packed by the same rigger. The Army Rigger Creed is pretty strict and an incident like this was almost unheard of. All our lives rested in the hands of the troopers who packed our chutes. The rigger in question was arrested, admitted his actions and tried for murder and sent to the disciplinary barracks at Fort Leavenworth. He may well still be there. Paratroopers get extra pay because it is dangerous but this incident went far beyond anything I had experienced or heard of in almost twenty years of jumping. For the next few weeks we all paid close attention to our static lines when we took part in a jump.

Then came one of my bigger goofs as battalion commander. I let my personal feelings overcome my better judgment. I received a call from the commander of the Airborne Test Board that he had a really sharp captain who needed company command time to be competitive for promotion to major. I told the colonel who called to send him up for an interview. In walked a decidedly recruiting poster quality black officer; very well spoken and quite impressive. I forget now what rationale he gave for not having been with troops and getting his command already but it worked. I should have smelled a rat but he was also a graduate of Providence College; and that sort of sealed the deal. I hired him to take over Combat Support Company (CSC) as the current commander, Captain Kim Jacobs, was resigning and going into the civilian world.

Initially all seemed OK with the new commander; then came a somewhat disappointing happening during company field training. I visited CSC out in the boonies and found the leaders sleeping on cots, a "no-no" while I commanded. This was the first violation of that policy that I was aware of in almost two years in command. I counseled the lad severely and he insisted he was not aware of the policy. A little later, as I was leaving, First Sergeant Cady met me outside the tent and shook his head, shrugged his shoulders and rolled his eyes. I should have gotten the message. About eight months later Bill Garrison, deployed on a highly sensitive nationally important mission relieved the rascal for a series of actions to include bad checks, wife abuse, failure to support his family, gambling with his troops, drunkenness, and I don't know what else; so much for Providence College, gentlemen.

My phone rang one morning about a month before the scheduled change of command and the XVIII Corps deputy chief of contingency plans, an old friend, asked me if I would be interested in his job. Well, hello, now we were talking turkey. I discussed it with the family and we were in agreement that staying at Fort Bragg for family stability and allowing me to remain on jump status with troops was not a bad deal. It would allow our son to finish high school without going through the turmoil of changing schools in his senior year. I began working the issue of staying at Bragg and moving back to XVIII Corps.

My last mass tactical jump as battalion commander came about two weeks before I changed command. Major General Meloy had been reassigned, and our new CG was another fantastic paratrooper, MG James Lindsay. General Lindsay decided to tag on with us on a night "mass tactical" jump. I think we had about six C-130 aircraft in trail and we were heading for Sicily DZ. Everything went well initially and the wind and weather were perfect. The ten minute warning came while we flew over NC farmland as always; then the six minute warning. We stood up, hooked up, checked static lines, checked equipment, sounded off for equipment check and stood by. The jump doors were opened and the crescendo of noise from the four engines rolled into and through the plane. I was first man in the stick of jumpers out the right door and General Lindsay was directly behind me. The AF crew chief came up to me and shouted over the noise that there was no contact with the Drop Zone Safety Officer (DZSO) on the DZ and we would have to make a race track turn and come back again. Without contact with the DZSO and confirmation of the winds and safety of the DZ there would be no jump. We waited, and waited and waited. The lead aircraft with five more birds in trail made a wide circle and headed back to Sicily DZ. We did this twice and I can tell you that General Lindsey was not a happy camper. And that dear reader may be the understatement of this whole tome. Finally the DZSO arrived, late, but now in position. The drop came off beautifully and as I floated down I thought, "You're going to miss this." I am sure that episode, with the new CG witnessing an occurrence that seldom happened, a DZSO not being in position on time, led to some serious counseling of the

Post Support Brigade commander. I was very glad we were not the designated Post Support unit.

Almost the last memorable event in my command tour, and totally different happening, was driven by a personality quirk. The battalion had the good fortune to have a particularly gifted and ingenious young second lieutenant, Military Intelligence Corps, assigned as my assistant S2 Intelligence officer. His name was Bill Cain and we called him Mr. Bill. He was several cuts above the norm, a graduate of North Georgia Military College, and one heck of a good man. The battalion had a succession of less than great S1 personnel officers after my first Cracker Jack S1, Captain Lonnie Vona, had been reassigned. Well several months before I was to change command we had a real problem develop. Lieutenant Day, the S1 who had managed to qualify for his Humanitarian Service Medal with his overnight stay at Fort Indiantown Gap, got himself in deep trouble with the law down in Fayetteville. The issue included drunkenness, destruction of property and a weapon was also involved. I fired him and sent him packing leaving justice to the Fayetteville authorities. The S1 shop needed help and needed it badly. Major Olds and I talked at length and decided that Mr. Bill's talents were much more needed in our S1 shop than in a peace time assistant S2 Intelligence job. Bill became the personnel officer and did a fantastic job. But, he had this little quirk; he liked to come up with surprises. He was sure going to surprise me.

About two weeks before the change of command as I was returning to the Battalion Headquarters from a meeting I noticed a large sedan, it could have been a Mercury Marquis or some equivalent vehicle, parked by the curb. Just as I neared Panther Rock, six burly kidnappers in desert fatigues, wearing gorilla masks and carrying weapons seemed to emerge from every direction. They grabbed me and manhandled me, placed a gunny sack over my head and threw me in the back of the car and sped away. They sat on me, sort of, as I recall and we drove for about ten minutes. I had no idea where we were headed. Resistance was futile I assure you. I was convinced during the ride that I was in no real danger but truly did not know exactly what was happening. It had to be a joke, on me. The car came to a halt and I was taken out and the gunny sack removed. We were at a small family restaurant out on Bragg Boulevard. I was led inside where the battalion officers were awaiting my arrival and sort of "formal roast." And did I ever get roasted. Turned out the whole plot had been hatched in the young mind of my personnel officer, "Mr. Bill." Obviously every officer in the battalion knew what was going on but I sure did not. It was a raucous affair with no holds barred and a lot of roasting of the old man and his many idiosyncrasies. Lieutenant Cain (now a retired colonel) insists to this day that Major Olds gave me a heads up on what was to happen; such was not the case. I was one surprised trooper; kudos to Mr. Bill.

Three days before the change of command the sergeant major asked me to accompany him to a meeting. Turned out the meeting was in the theatre down the street where most of the battalion had been assembled without my knowledge. Bruce took me up on the stage and waxed forth eloquently about how I was going to be missed and "that there." Then he handed me a brand new Browning 12-gauge pump shotgun and wished me good hunting from all the Black Panthers. I was almost in tears.

Several days later Bill Garrison and I stood together on the reviewing stand with the battalion in formation on the Division Museum Parade Field. The Battalion Colors were brought forward and the two of us along with the sergeant major moved to the front of the reviewing stand for the ritual passing of the Colors. Once the Colors had been passed we returned to the reviewing stand; each of us to address the troops. My change of command speech was different. In the five years that I had been at Fort Bragg, Mary and I must have listened to over fifty change of command speeches. Most of them lasted fifteen to twenty minutes, a few upwards of thirty minutes. I told Mary that I would not inflict something like that on the troops.

Mine would be short. It was exactly two minutes and forty seconds and it was aimed at the soldiers standing in ranks to my front. I began:

> *General Lindsay, General Klein, past commanders of the Black Panthers Colonel Plummer, Colonel Scott, ladies and gentlemen, friends and men of the 1st Battalion 505th Airborne Infantry.*

> *Today is a day of immense pride, a day I will never forget. I begin by thanking my leaders and commanders over the past five years for allowing me to serve and especially to command, and I thank those who served with me and worked for me, supporting me and putting up with my many idiosyncrasies.*

> *For the last twenty-three months I was afforded the privilege of leading United States paratroopers, prepared and ready if called upon to defend our nation's freedom. Those twenty-three months were marked by countless activities and operations— and as those of us in the beaten zone know, "It ain't all fun." But I leave with memories, some happy, some sad that no one can ever take from me...*

I then went on to describe with short declarative statements much of what you previously read above, and more, and finished with:

> *I remember Raoul, Laskey, Nelson, Harrell, Meaghar, Persnakis, Lefkowitz, Hoobots and a thousand others known only to those of us who sweat clammy beads of sweat in Panama, froze in Alaska or felt a tingle when the aliens surged toward the barricades at Indiantown Gap; soldiers who jumped, marched, laughed, cried, drank and prayed or just goofed off with us.*

I will miss you all: the camaraderie, the challenge, the real Airborne mystique. I salute you all, for who you are, what you did and what you stand for and the service you are giving our country. I will miss you. I will never forget you. And, in the words of an old Irish Blessing—May you all be in heaven half an hour before the devil knows you're dead.

Airborne...All the Way

And with that, the curtain was down. I went home and had drinks with a few close friends. When the festivities finally ended I sat with Mary and told her I missed it already. She took my hand and said something like, "You don't realize it but you're tired." In retrospect she was right.

48

BACK TO XVIII AIRBORNE CORPS: THE PLANNING BUSINESS

I may have been tired but there was not to be a big break. A couple of days' relaxing with the family and then it was off to XVIII Corps Plans for me. As the Deputy Chief of Plans my duties were focused on the major war plan then being prepared to support the newly formed Rapid Deployment Joint Task Force (RDJTF). XVIII Airborne Corps had been designated the Army element of the RDJTF, and given the additional name of "Third U. S. Army" pending the actual reestablishment of the real Third U.S. Army. After being briefed and oriented by the G3, Colonel Jerry Scott, I reported to the Chief of Plans, Colonel Corless Mitchell, up on the third floor of Corps Headquarters. He told me that I was taking over a "pretty hot shot team" of planners but that he had some misgivings about some aspects of the major plan, then being developed. He did not elaborate further but told me to draw my own conclusion once I had been briefed and had time to assess what was happening. Without further specifics as to what he didn't like I walked down the hall to the compartmented plans work area.

After meeting my planning team I was impressed, a good group for sure and folks who knew the planning business. The previous Deputy Chief of Plans, an old friend by the way, had gotten some truly good troops to come to work for him. I was not prepared however, for the plan that lay hidden behind a curtain. When they pulled back the curtain and began briefing me it was clear what Colonel Mitchell had seen that led him to have misgivings. It was "a town too far" and Dien Bien Phu for the USA in the Middle East. (The "town too far" comment relates to the British Airborne disaster during Operation Market Garden in Holland in 1944. Dien Bien Phu of course relates to the French debacle in Indo China in 1954.) I let the briefing go to its conclusion. When they had finished, about two hours, it was clear that the team had done the best they could with the commander's guidance they had been given. But it was still "a town way too far." The guidance that led to this effort had come from the recently departed Corps Commander. Still, it did not look like something we could live with; it appeared that some major modifications were in order. I thanked the group and after some questioning of each of the briefers returned to talk with Colonel Mitchell.

When I gave him my candid assessment he concurred smiling and said we were in complete agreement. I asked what had led to the plan that we both saw flaws in and he told me guidance from on high, meaning somewhere possibly above the now departed Corps Commander. I asked him for permission to talk with the new Commander, LTG Jack Mackmull, with whom I had worked closely on the Blue Light and Delta evaluations three years earlier. I then cleared this approach with Colonel Scott who gave me the green light with a sort of a smile that said, "Good move." General Mackmull, a real gentleman by the way, listened to my concerns and when I was finished he told me to; "Do what makes sense, pull in our horns; when you have a new concept, get back to me." Once the planners had different guidance it did not take them long to come up with a slightly less ambitious plan and one with a lot better chance of success. This plan was being developed following the Soviet invasion of Afghanistan as a U.S. counter move against possible Soviet incursions at other sites in the Mid-East. To say that this was a daunting task may be a bit of an understatement but there it was.

As an aside, one of the planners in the planning cell was a very sharp, female intelligence NCO who was also quite attractive. She was truly smart about the Mid-East and Soviet capabilities. She also was a national celebrity. I do not remember all the circumstances, no need to know, but she and her husband had become embroiled in a CIA operation (he was an Agency man) that had a problem. There had been no disasters but it was national news stuff and all the mainstream media interviewed her. She had also been put in for a commission as an Intelligence Warrant Officer. That promotion came through and she was reassigned. I don't know what happened relative to the CIA issue but she later divorced her husband and married a full colonel. Like I said, she was one smart lady. We missed her uncanny ability to divine the truth through the toughest question on terrain, enemy, airfield capability, whatever. However I did not miss her during morning physical training as she could outrun me the best day I ever ran.

Now for a soldier who had just put in three years at the dusty boot level thinking battalion operations, the adjustment to a major war plan of national significance was somewhat challenging. This mission opened some new vistas I had never considered and had only a minimum knowledge about. The biggest thing I had to come to grips with was Time Phased Force Deployment Data (TPFDD) Planning. The rudiments of TPFDD development had been explained at the Navy Command and General Staff College at Newport some twelve years earlier; but it was a very basic orientation to say the least. Fortunately I had some good lads who knew what they were doing. Trying to get a major force half way around the world with the units flowing in a manner that allowed them to arrive with the right mix of combat power and support units to fight using minimal and constrained Air Force and Navy assets was not easy. Not only did I have a good team that understood TPFDDs but the Air Force component of the RDJTF, from Shaw AFB, South Carolina, had the greatest TPFDD expert in the world, Colonel Wally Wallace. At least I thought he was the greatest and between us we tap danced through more tough briefings than I care to remember. He always dazzled the Generals with his TPFDD info. Bottom line, there was a lot to learn in my new job.

I will never forget Colonel Wallace was having dinner at our home one night. He and young Larry were talking about what it took to be a fighter pilot. At that point Larry, a cadet at the Citadel (the Military College of South Carolina), was considering trying to make the Air Force a career. Now, whether my son was serious or not, or just jerking my chain, I don't know. The two of them were discussing training and being in a fast mover fighter in a G suit and with oxygen mask, et cetera. The issue of bodily functions came up and Wally described how those could be handled. Then young Larry asked what did one do if you got sick? As Wally shoveled in another bite of whatever Mary had served up he looked at my son and calmly said, "Swallow it." That ended young Larry's infatuation with the U.S. Air Force.

49
THE STOCKADE AGAIN AND
A SECOND ROUND WITH DELTA

O ut of the blue Colonel Scott called me to his office, one afternoon, and said that the Corps Commander had been informed that a Letter Order from the Chief of Staff of the Army was on its way directing me, by name, to conduct several additional evaluations of Delta Force. I was shocked. Why me? The boys at the stockade had hardly spoken to me since Onset Trust and it was clear I was not popular with them. Colonel Scott was pretty canny about this sort of thing and he said, "Larry, they opened their kimono before to you and they would prefer to not let anyone else see anything. Better the devil they know." He was correct in that assessment.

The purpose of this evaluation was to establish if the Delta "door kickers" could shoot. Apparently allegations had surfaced following Desert One that they had trouble launching bullets. Being able to shoot had nothing to do with what took place at Desert One in the Iranian desert. I found this one hard to believe but had my marching orders. Colonel Beckwith had moved on to the new Joint Special Operations Command formed as a result of the Desert One failure. The new Commander of Delta was Colonel Rod Pascal. I had known him previously when he commanded the 4th Psychological Operations Group. Rod was a totally different personality than Charger. He read my Letter Order, having been advised in advance that I was coming by direction of the Chief of Staff of the Army, and was most cooperative.

While I had some assistance from the G3 this was basically a one man operation, me. The Delta troops provided me great support and several of them assisted me at every evaluation and test set up. First we conducted a detailed analysis and evaluation of the Squadron shooters ability in close quarters combat shooting and ability to instantly identify friend from foe. I can assure you the lads were superb. I stood in the back of a darkened room in the shooting house along with a Delta operator wearing night vision goggles while teams of door kickers from the squadrons burst in and methodically "double tapped" (two rounds per target) the silhouettes of the bad guys and never put a round in a friendly target. I was impressed. Oh yes, just to keep them honest, after we entered the shooting room, and before they burst in, we observers repositioned the targets. All the teams went through this routine and the results were uniformly superb.

One morning, about 0600, I was sitting in the stockade mess when the S3 wandered in. As he walked by I asked if he would like to join me for coffee. He shrugged as if to say well why not you don't have leprosy. We talked for a few minutes about the ongoing evaluation and the results to that point. I then asked him why the folks were so cool toward me. His response floored me. He said, "Well you talked to people about the evaluation (Onset Trust). You shouldn't have done that." I told him that I had not talked with anyone who did not have a need to know and that they were all general officers who did need to know. He responded, "No, you signed the 'black book', you can't talk to anyone." I then told him that I had never signed any black book and didn't have a clue what he was talking about. He told me he would prove it and left to get the book. He returned with a large black three ring binder filled with lots of papers. The book was set up alphabetically and he tore through the Rs only to find no page with Redmond's name or signature on it. He then went through the whole book, A to Z. We both had another cup of coffee. When he was satisfied that I had never signed any oath not to talk about Delta to anyone he looked at me and said, "We owe you an apology." To this day I have never signed their black book. I can also say that I have never divulged any tactic, technique or counter terror specific fact about Delta Force.

It could have been one or two days later as I was about to check out the snipers with their long guns (sniper rifles) and I needed to see the S3 about something. Asking one of the NCOs where I could find him I was told that he was down the hall, second door on the right. I wandered down, knocked on the door and hearing nothing I opened it and stepped into a brightly lit room. It was the wrong room. There before me, in a fairly large mockup, was a potential target. It didn't take a rocket scientist to recognize it for what it was. My heart was in my throat as I comprehended what I was looking at. I calmly stepped back, closed the door and went to the next room where I found the S3. I never mentioned my error to him. Since my retirement several books have been written by former Delta troops and both allude to a possible mission that never was approved. It had to be the mockup I stumbled upon. Since this possible mission has come out in open source books written by several Delta operators I feel comfortable in relating this tale.

The long range sniper evaluation was, like the close quarter hand gun shooting, fantastic. We started at 800 yards as I recall and the shooters were dead on. No pun intended. At 1000 yards I suspected they might have some problems especially since we were throwing in a mix of moving friendly and terrorist targets passing by several windows. I bet one NCO that he could not make a successful shot that I knew was going to be made more difficult by the appearance of both terrorists and friendly hostages. My portion of the wager was a cold case of Budweiser back at the stockade when they returned. I lost. After a quick call to the rear the beer, iced down, was awaiting them upon return. Talk about dumb, I made the same wager the next day with a different shooter and it cost me another case of Bud. What do they say about doing the same dumb thing twice? At any rate my report basically said someone had wasted time and effort with false allegations. Delta snipers and door kickers could shoot. I believe they have maintained and over the years enhanced those skills. They can come save my rear end anytime.

50
RETURNING TO THE MUNDANE
ACTIVITY OF PLANNING

In addition to the major war plan our cell was also responsible for over two dozen other war plans in support of Atlantic Command at Norfolk, Virginia, Readiness Command at MacDill AFB, Florida as well as FORSCOM at Fort MacPherson, Georgia. XVIII Corps answered to many masters as the Army element in those Headquarters. Many of those plans involved Noncombatant Evacuation Operations (NEO Plans) throughout the Caribbean and Central America. A second set of planners worked these plans and did a great job. Several of them felt slighted that they were not involved with the "real" war plan. They did yeoman's work with little thanks.

Redmond's Rule #21 - "They also serve who only stand and wait."
John Milton

The fledgling Rapid Deployment Joint Task Force had some real issues. How in blazes do you move half way around the world to stop the Soviet hordes and do it from a standing start? Well one of the first things you do is you get Arab States to support you and you get equipment and supplies out there ahead of the troops so that you don't have so much to move. Great idea in concept but getting the Arabs to let the U.S. even put a can of C-rations on the ground was a nonstarter, at least initially. They didn't trust us.

Remember Vietnam where we pulled out; they did, plus we were infidels. One ploy we did use was the Maritime Pre–Positioned Ships option. We, the USA, put five ships afloat in the Indian Ocean prepared to steam with their cargo to wherever needed. Neat plan and it was well broadcast for the Soviets to internalize. The only problem was that the gear afloat initially was mostly Meals Ready to Eat (MREs or "meals rejected by everyone"—including Ethiopians), sand bags, lumber, toilet paper and body bags. I jest not, maybe a few vehicles and some artillery but no armor. It was a great gambit and it worked. At least the Soviets never went beyond Afghanistan. They had their hands full there at the time. Over a period of perhaps eighteen months those Maritime Pre-Positioned ships did become laden with lots of very sophisticated and lethal war fighting equipment. They may still be out there today in some form or other.

The Navy was perhaps our biggest challenge when it came to getting the equipment moved efficiently to our area of operations (AO). The sailing time on many ships was going to be so long that upon arrival in the AO vehicles and equipment would have mechanical problems. Basically batteries would be dead, oil leaks and other issues would most likely mean that when the equipment was off-loaded the gear would need a major maintenance effort. For certain it would not be immediately available to move to defensive positions or to fight. We came up with a scheme to put a maintenance team of twelve to fifteen personnel aboard each civilian contract cargo ship. Well, you should have heard the Navy howl! No way would they permit that. The seaman's union would object. There were no bunks for the troops to sleep on; solution, sleep on air mattresses in the passageways. No way could the ships mess handle that many more mouths; solution, we would send along lots of meals ready to eat and only ask for coffee, tea, et cetera, and maybe a bowl of soup every day. No way could we do this there was no doctor on board. When I heard that one I told one very excitable Navy captain that we were sending these lads possibly to die for their country and that we felt the inconvenience of shipboard life could be handled. And, I reminded him, "Oh by the way, there is no doctor for the crew itself." This was no easy fight but we did finally arrive at an acceptable solution. In defense of the Navy they were facing lots of rules and regulations that applied to the civilian ships that would be moving most of the gear to the area of operations. Except for the doctor question I think all the problems were overcome. As close to a doc as we could get was to put a medic with each maintenance team. By the time of Desert Shield/Desert Storm most of the vehicles and equipment were being moved on Roll On-Roll Off ships of much more modern design. I have been told maintenance of equipment and vehicles on those ships, while still difficult, was much more easily handled.

One day about six months after arriving at G3 Plans I was called to the G3's office and told, "Congratulations, you just came out on the War College List." I was stunned. General Meloy's second prediction about my future career had come true. I was very pleased to say the least. Then Colonels Branch called me and asked me where I wanted to go to school. Huh, you have to be kidding, where do I want to go? I was to get a choice? The old Infantry Branch mafia was still out there. I could pick the Army War College, the Air War College, the National War College or, the French or British War College (The Royal College of Defence Studies in London-RCDS). I went home and talked it out with Mary. The French War College was out. I couldn't speak more than two words of French. I had attended the Navy Command and Staff College so the Navy War College was not an option they even offered. The National War College was in D.C., a town I hated. After much thought, I decided to ask for the RCDS in London. I needed a change and since Mary and I were both of Irish ancestry I felt it would be good for the children to get a look at their ancestral homeland. We both felt certain that a year in the UK would give us the opportunity to cross the Irish Sea.

Several days later I had a surprise visitor in my office, then Brigadier General Charlie Getz from my first days in the 82nd Third Brigade almost four years earlier. General Getz congratulated me on my selection for the War College and said, "You are going to the National War College because that's where the generals are made." I told him it was a little late, that I had already informed my assignment officer that I wanted to go to the RCDS. I explained why. He gently told me I was making a mistake and that he could help change that. I in turn "gently" told him, "Thanks, sir, it's my mistake." I was crossing my Rubicon. We parted friends and I admire the general still today. He was quite a caring soldier.

51
THE MOLE HOLE:
MEETING BARBED WIRE BOB KINGSTON

The Planning Team and I traveled to Tampa, MacDill AFB probably twice a month to interface with our Rapid Deployment Joint Task Force (RDJTF) counterparts. As I recall the Chief of Staff was BG Carl Stiner later Commander of Special Operations Command and a heck of a soldier. The RDJTF Commander initially was LT GEN P. X. Kelly, USMC, and another fantastic leader and all around good guy. We were making good progress except for one facet of the plan that involved the Rangers that I will discuss shortly. On one trip to Tampa we were informed that General Kelly was to be replaced by Lieutenant General Robert Kingston, U.S. Army, coming from command of the 2nd Infantry Division in Korea. We were told to be ready to brief him on the major war plan on short notice.

The notice came on a Tuesday or Wednesday and the briefing was to go down on Saturday at MacDill at the RDJTF Headquarters in an old Strategic Air Command B-52 Alert Facility known as the "Mole Hole." Now LTG Kingston was an old Special Forces type and a heck of a commander. He was nicknamed, and not affectionately, Barbed Wire Bob, due to a pretty irascible streak. He was known to devour briefers like so much confetti. At Bragg it was decided that I would give the briefing myself, much to the relief of some of my troops who had heard of the general's tendency to hammer briefers who did not measure up to his standards. Three of the key planners would come with me to back me up. There were several briefings on the RDJTF status that preceded us. They went off pretty well, no real bloodletting. Then it was my turn. As I started briefing the Army role, and plan, the general leaned forward quite attentively. After about three minutes he stopped me and asked a question that I answered promptly and to his satisfaction. I continued on for a few more minutes. Then he again stopped me with a question that I again answered. I did ask for one of my troops to provide additional elaboration. He seemed to like that and I sensed the team effort pleased him. About two minutes later he again interrupted me with a question. At that point I stepped from behind the podium and standing squarely in front of him said, "Sir, if you will permit me to continue the briefing I believe I will answer all your questions, and if not my team and I will then answer any issue that you still have." Barbed Wire Bob smiled, nodded and simply said, "OK go on." At the end of the briefing the general stood, thanked us for our work and said to press on. He left the room with no further questions for us. I and the 3rd U.S. Army (aka XVIII Corps) planners had survived a crucible of fire. It would be my pleasure to work for General Kingston later when he commanded the U.S. Central Command that followed the RDJTF. If you had your stuff pretty much together he was almost a Teddy Bear, not Barbed Wire.

The issue referred to three paragraphs above concerning the Rangers part of our major plan was an item that bothered all of us. In the original concept for the plan the two Ranger battalions had been spread out over a large area. Our concept and new mission brought them together in a combined force that had a much better chance of success. When the idea had been evolved we visualized that the two battalions would act jointly with one battalion providing a Task Force Headquarters to command and control the activities of both. A date to receive their plan came and went; no plan. We sent a message to both battalions reminding them of the need for a written plan. A week passed and no plan. They just blew us off.

Shortly thereafter both battalion commanders were present at Fort Bragg for a conference. We sent word asking them both to report to the plans shop. Once in my office I told them that we needed their plan now. It was obvious the two commanders were at odds and had not come to a reasonable solution as to who would be in charge. Lieutenant Colonel Terry Scott was senior by a few months to the other commander, LTC Emory Mace, who had been the IG in the 82nd just two years before.

I told them both in very clear terms that if we didn't have their plan by a given date, about ten days, that we would assign a Task Force (TF) Headquarters (HQ) to control and lead them and do the planning for them. That TF HQ could be from XVIII Airborne Corps or Readiness Command. It was to be their call which way things went. They could lead themselves and keep it a Ranger show, or they would end up under another TF HQ. Ten days later we had their plan. Lieutenant Colonel Terry Scott would be the Ranger ground force commander. The plan was a good one by the way. Scott went on to be a LTG and Mace went on to become a BG. Such was the fate of most Ranger battalion commanders in those early years; they were anointed.

One day in late 1982 while still assigned to Corps Plans I had a chance meeting with COL Beckwith at Headquarters First SOCOM on Smoke Bomb Hill. We crossed paths in the Hall of Heroes where all the SF Medal of Honor winners' pictures and stories were on display. At that point, following Desert One, Charlie had moved on from Delta Force to be the Deputy Commander of the new Joint Special Operations Command. That organization had been created to hopefully preclude another Desert One happening. I had not seen Charlie since the validation exercise. When he came up to me he threw his arms around me and gave me a great big bear hug. I was shocked but not too embarrassed as there was no one else around to observe this. He then said; "Redmond.... Redmond you and I did not always see eye to eye but you're a damned good soldier, damned good and I respect you." He then told me that he was going to retire and become a contractor. His eyes glossed over and he added, "You know, after you got hit back at Hue in '68, I lost a lot of boys out in the A Shau (the A Shau Valley west of Hue). Then there were the troops at Desert One…Lost a lot of boys." He looked down at the floor then looked me in the eye, nodded, shook hands and he strode off. He was hard to figure but he had served his country as best he knew how and whatever you may have thought of him he was a patriot. He did mention me in his book as the LTC who planned the Delta validation exercise, but he misspelled my name. That was not a biggie in my mind. I respected him also.

Young Larry departed for the Citadel in August 1982 and the family continued getting ready for the move to England and a year at the Royal College of Defence Studies. As a precursor I was allowed to go over to the UK, Permissive Temporary Duty, to find a place to live and check out the College. After coordinating with the Embassy and the Army Attaché I took a medivac flight to a C-130 base in Arkansas and launched from there to England. I think we had one stop over in Newfoundland for gas. After wheels up from the base in Arkansas they invited me up to the cockpit and then offered me a bed in the rear of the cabin where I could sleep or watch the ground and ocean flit by at 33,000 plus feet. I slept. This kind gesture they told me was in deference to the fact that I was on the promotion list to colonel. I am not sure how they knew that except the flight and trip had been arranged and greased for me by the Embassy in London.

I think we landed at Lakenheath or High Wycombe Royal Air Force Base where I was met by an NCO from the Army Attaché's Office. I would be under the Attaché's care for the duration of the tour although officially "seconded" (assigned) to Her Majesty's Forces. London was quite impressive I must say, and at that time a beautiful and very "proper" British city. I was taken to the College at 33 Belgrave Square and was overwhelmed. It was a minor palace known as Seaford House. To say it was beautiful and beyond my wildest dreams would have been an understatement. I could not quite believe that one family had lived in such a great house. Since that time I have watched all the episodes of *Downton Abbey* on TV and realize that in its grandness Seaford House was still a minor palace.

Several days into my visit I received a note from Major "Promotable" Buck Kernan who was at that time the exchange officer with the Parachute Regiment. (Later, Major Johnny Brooks from the 1-505 Black Panthers would take Buck's place with the regiment.) Buck invited me down to Aldershot for an overnight visit and sightseeing. He had been one of my students when I taught Offensive Operations at the Infantry School and I had been his faculty advisor. He had learned that I was coming to the UK to attend the Royal College and just wanted to get together. I readily accepted the offer and with help from the Army attaché slipped away for an afternoon and evening with the Kernans. Buck showed me around Aldershot, very historical going back to the early 1800s and the time of my favorite author, Rudyard Kipling. His stories and poems relating to the British Army in India had always fascinated me and I was an avid reader of those tales. After dinner Buck and I sat in his living room drinking gin and tonic. It was a new drink to me and frankly I was drinking and liking it too much. In the course of the evening, as we imbibed of that demon drink, we both proceeded to get blotto. His next assignment as commander of the 1st Ranger Battalion came up. I told him that he was golden and destined to be a general. He looked at me and said, "Oh, sir, no way. Look, I am too old, gray hair and an OCS grad. That will never happen." Well it did happen and Buck went on to wear four stars and command U.S. Special Operations Command at MacDill AFB, Florida.

The real significant part of the evening is that both of us by this time were quite inebriated. Notice this is my third bad bout with inebriation in my Army career. The first was the promotion party in Panama. The second was in VN when I was on my way to see the USARV G1 and now a casual evening with an old buddy in the

UK. I was pretty good about not getting inebriated in the USA. But the real capstone to this evening is that Buck and I, at least in the morning at breakfast, could not remember going to bed. There was a reason for that; we were both totally drunk and passed out in the living room. Somehow Mary Ann Kernan got us upstairs and put us to bed. She is the only woman other than my mother and my wife who ever did that.

The American students studying at the RCDS that year were all very anxious to tell me about their experiences and the "course" as it was referred to. The USMC representative told me his home in a small village called Eastcote near Heathrow Airport had not yet been rented. He said the house, a duplex, was quite adequate and close to the London underground train system. The other half of the duplex had already been rented to the USAF student who was to attend with the Class of 1983. I ended up renting the Marines' quarters. It was a pretty nice house, by British standards at the time. One did have to excuse the fact that you had to break the ice in the downstairs bathroom in the morning during winter (no heat in the downstairs loo, aka toilet); and that the curtains sort of stood out into the center of the room when the wind hit twenty mph (poor insulation) and that the fridge and stove were both tiny by U.S. standards. But it had some nice advantages; four bedrooms, two and a half baths, a garage and the house was partially furnished and very clean. Life, albeit different, was going to be good. I returned home, again compliments of the USAF, via another C-130 with pictures and information as to what we were getting into. The family all felt good about it. Well not quite the entire family. Our two daughters were a little apprehensive and not fully committed to leaving their friends and Fort Bragg. Mary and I on the other hand were ready for a slower lifestyle after seven years of the Fort Bragg 100 mile an hour pace!

Just after returning to Fort Bragg my promotion to full colonel took place. The corps commander did the honors with Mary pinning on one of my eagles. We capped the day with a party at our quarters attended by quite a group to include four past commanders of the 1-505 (Mike Plummer, former Division chief of staff; Jerry Scott, the corps G3 chief of operations; Paul Devries assigned then to the Pentagon, myself; and the new commander, Wild Bill himself). It was quite a party.

One afternoon the phone on my office desk rang with another unexpected turn of events that would impact the H-Minus Battalion. It was LTC Joe Argentieri from the Joint Staff Special Operations Directorate calling. He had been an observer with the team that went over in 1973 to Israel supporting the UN. He was the lad, then a captain, who taught me how to disarm hand grenades that day up on the Golan Heights. He said we needed to talk secure and to call him right back on a red phone at his office. He gave me the number.

When I called him back he told me that the political decision had just been made by the Israelis and Egyptians to form an organization to be named the "Multinational Force and Observers." The unit's mission would be to oversee the Peace Treaty those two nations had agreed to. Thirteen countries were to provide forces to this organization. The U.S. was selected to send an infantry battalion as part of our role in this force. XVIII Airborne Corps was to provide the battalion and Joe was coming down the next day to brief the corps commander. Over coffee in my office before his brief to the general he asked me who should get the mission. I told him the 82nd Airborne and the 1-505. Joe smiled and made a comment about my being somewhat parochial in my outlook. He knew of course that I had just turned over command of that unit five months earlier. I am not sure what horse trading may have gone on behind the scenes but Joe influenced making it happen. In early spring 1982 I was there at Pope Air Force Base to see the H-Minus/Black Panther Battalion and Bill Garrison, Johnny Brooks, Bill Cain and a lot of my old troopers depart for the Sinai. They did a sterling job on a tough mission for our country.

Planning on our major War Plan continued and the plan was really taking shape. Every week it became more viable and the TPFDD planning improved markedly. We all felt that we were making progress and doing something meaningful for the country. The announcement was made in November 1982 that Third U.S. Army would be stood up at Fort MacPherson, Georgia and our role as the major planning headquarters would shortly pass to them. With the holidays rapidly approaching, and with them our departure for England, this did not bother me in the least. My days at Fort Bragg, after almost seven years, were about to end.

52

THE ROYAL COLLEGE AND SOME TRULY AMAZING MOMENTS

We flew over to England just after Christmas 1982, steerage, back of the aircraft, and ate rubber chicken. We were close to First Class and the girls kept smelling steak. Alas, not for them. But overall it was not a bad experience. We were met at Heathrow Airport by the same NCO who had met me when I went over on the reconnaissance. He had brought an Embassy van that proved adequate for the bags but not all of us. The ladies had not packed light. As a result our first trip in England was in a classic Brit taxi. I think the children both sat on the little jump seats on the back of the front seats, facing back, and watched their Mother and I and the scenery as we proceeded to downtown London.

The Embassy had put us up at a nice, clean but older hotel called the London Elizabeth just down from Marble Arch and across from Hyde Park. Not the Ritz but quite adequate. If you ever saw the TV series "Fawlty Towers" then you know what the London Elizabeth was like; from the owner down to the waiters in the Chez Joseph restaurant it was "Fawlty Towers." The girls had a wonderful time. Another American student for the Class of 1983 was also billeted with his family at the London Elizabeth. Captain Larry Andrews, USN, had taken quarters in another part of town not out near Eastcote. He and his wife Carol had a young daughter, and the kids hit it off and had a great time harassing the staff at the hotel. It is fair to say the staff was befuddled by such requests as peanut butter and jelly sandwiches for breakfast.

I think it was on the first night in the hotel my girls saw what they claimed was a murder in the hotel across the street; I believe it was the Dorchester. It was possible to see into the rooms directly across from ours. Amazing what kids can come up with. I checked the papers the next morning but there were no reported killings at that hotel.

We had to wait about ten days to move into our quarters in Eastcote so there was plenty of time to see some of the sights of the big city. I was in-processing through the Embassy and also at the Royal College which was basically just across Hyde Park from our hotel. The walk to the College was pleasant and I started a regimen of running daily in Hyde Park that would continue for the year in London. History was around every corner and I loved it. We went to Buckingham Palace and watched the changing of the guard. The ladies went more than once to the palace and met a very nice old former soldier named Cyril who delighted in telling the girls all that was happening and a little history to boot. Not sure how close to the truth the history was but my daughters were quite impressed. We visited Clarence House where the Queen Mum lived, watched the Beefeaters at the Tower of London and toured that great old castle. The historical displays and armaments were fascinating for a historian like me. I was particularly impressed with Henry the VIII's suit of armor; more so than the viewing of the Crown Jewels. I won't go into the "why" of that but leave it to you to visit and see for yourself. The reason will be immediately obvious and it isn't just the size of the king's chest or his height.

Downtown London was a shoppers' heaven, but most things were very pricey. We took the time to get oriented on how to use the bus system and the London underground (aka the tube). Nothing was exactly like the USA. The Brits had their own quaint little mannerisms. The beer was warm but great. And I will tell you in those days people knew the protocol for queuing up to ride the tube, the bus or just buy things in the store. No one pushed or tried to cut in front of you in 1983. Everything was quite proper; not like my experience in Israel. The biggest problem we had was the language. We all spoke English but British English is not American English, and it does take some adjustment and thought to get things done. We managed to muddle through with a stiff upper lip.

My in-processing and orientation at the Royal College was pretty uneventful and handled in proper Brit fashion. I met many of my classmates, with few exceptions they were all Brigadiers or Air Commodores or of appropriate flag rank from various countries from the old Empire and around the globe. It was quite an eyeful to see the Pakistanis standing talking to the Indians, the Egyptian and Jordanian talking politely with the Israeli, et cetera. The only sensing of animosity was between the Israeli and the Saudi and I must say the source of that hostility seemed to stem from the Saudi side. That is my opinion only of course. Our Israeli brigadier, while not an outgoing type or a big joiner, did meet and greet any and all of his classmates with that one exception. The Saudi brigadier kept pretty much to himself and during the year seldom stayed after lectures or seminars and just seemed to disappear into London. We had a Nigerian admiral on the course who was quite an interesting study. I think a book could be written about him. He was pretty high up in the pecking order back in his home country. Our Jordanian brigadier, Salem Al Turk, was superb and I believed a friend of the U.S. Our Egyptian brigadier, Hossam Al Zatar, will reappear in this tome later when I was Chief of Plans at U.S. CENTCOM. The same is true for Hossam as it relates to his being a friend of the U.S.

I was assigned a sponsor, Brigadier John Alexander, Royal Signals Regiment, who assisted me in adjusting to the College and helped out in a myriad of ways. He and his wife Mary were truly concerned that our arrival and transition to life in the UK and at Seaford House was smooth and enjoyable. Shortly after the course started we spent a great weekend at the Alexander's home, Barton House. You haven't enjoyed England till you sleep in a giant feather bed in a "thatched cottage," that must have had over twenty-five rooms. Only a dozen or so of those rooms were normally used. The cottage had been built in the 1450s. The Alexanders, in deference to their Yank visitors, had heated more rooms than normal, a costly but superb gesture to their guests. This effort however raised the temperature enough that it energized the thatch beetles. Lying in that giant bed at night hearing those beetles chewing away on the thatch just overhead was a happening none of us had expected. Both our girls were a little taken aback by that experience but loved staying in such an historic residence. That certainly was a learning experience for them.

The first gathering at the college was an icebreaker with a cocktail party where we met our classmates, all in national uniform, and their spouses. I think at this first cocktail hour we were standing in the very large, beautifully paneled, thirty foot high ceilinged lecture hall (previously the dining room) where our lectures would be held. There were nearly 200 of us counting our wives, plus most of the college staff—to give you an idea of the size of this monstrous place, or palace, if you prefer. Mary turned to me and whispered, "I feel like we are in a 1930s British movie, just listen to the accents." She was right. We were standing with our about-to-be next door neighbor, COL Nick Lacey, USAF. He and his wife Patricia both agreed with Mary's observation. The accents were very reminiscent of 1930s movies and Cary Grant in his youth.

Several nights later we all assembled again for cocktails and then watched a movie in the main lecture hall. This was followed by another cocktail gathering and film the following week. The films both related to the old Empire. The first was *Breaker Morant*, an Australian flick based on a true incident from the Boer War. It was very well done with a great cast. I was unaware of the incident but have since read a lot about it. While the movie was very complimentary of Australia it did not reflect well on the Empire. The second movie was *Gallipoli*, another Australian movie starring Mel Gibson. I believe it was one of his first films. Once again it did not put the Empire in a good light. The Australians have never forgotten, or forgiven, the Brits for their staggering troop losses during the ill-fated invasion to capture the Turkish Dardanelle Straights at Gallipoli in 1915. Our British hosts were not trying to cover up any wrongs from the past.

The school itself was challenging, but not graded, so there was little in the way of threat that one might fail. Class started at 1000 each morning when we were in London and there was not a holiday. The Brits have a lot of holidays. Nick Lacey, my next door neighbor, and I normally departed for the tube station at 0700 so as to arrive at the college in time to work out and get in a run in Hyde Park. Then we would clean up before having coffee with our other classmates and discuss ongoing world events, the College and life in general. The morning class was a lecture by some distinguished civilian, politician, civil servant, professor or senior military personage followed by a question and answer period. We focused for several months at a time on economics, grand strategy, the business world, societal aspects affecting national priorities, the Cold War and the West versus the Soviet monolith. There was little or nothing to do with war fighting directly. In the afternoon, two and sometimes three days a week, we would meet in seminars to discuss some aspect of that morning's lecture and the thrust of our study at that time. When there was no seminar we were basically free following the morning lecture.

I normally stayed for lunch in the very nice but very British restaurant in the basement of Seaford House. Following that I would walk. I walked all over downtown London; main streets, backstreets and streets I probably should not have been on in a suit with a vest and tie. But I learned a lot about London doing that. Some afternoons Nick and I would ride home together on the tube and try to solve the world's problems. Sad to say, as you can realize, we failed in that endeavor.

Sometime in late winter one of my classmates, Brigadier James Templar, invited us to his home for the weekend. James and I had become close in the first two months of the Course and our ladies enjoyed each other's company. James lived near Salisbury and the Royal Artillery training areas. The girls came with us but they were not initially overjoyed with the trip in that the Templars had no children at home. They said they would be totally bored; that proved not to be the case. James's home was another interesting experience. He lived in half of an "old" Church of England parsonage; it consisted of eighteen rooms! Yes the entire parsonage had been thirty-six rooms. James said the pastor had a large family when it was built in the late 1800s. Obviously the parson lived well and the Church of England had great influence. It was quite nice and the parlor was huge with a grand piano at one end of the room that appeared about a football field away. Well maybe that is an exaggeration but it was a very big room. It was a great weekend but unlike the Alexander's thatched cottage the Templars only heated the kitchen and parlor. The hot water bottle in bed was fantastic. The bath experience was another matter. In spite of initial hesitation the girls actually loved the weekend. They were most impressed with the huge swimming pool (closed for the winter) in the back garden and the grand piano in the parlor.

53
HOW THE IRA MADE IT INTO
THE ROYAL COLLEGE

The one threatening aspect of the course was that you had to produce a paper on some topic approved by the College Directing Staff. My staff monitor was a retired Army general and a really good soldier, Major General D. M. Woodford. In talking with several of my British classmates who had served in Northern Ireland (NI), it struck me that this was an area that probably did not get a lot of attention. Northern Ireland at that time was truly an unhappy spot. It was not something the Brits wanted to talk about. They just wished "the troubles" would go away. My colleagues were unanimous in their opinion that the sooner England gave the six Northern Counties to the Republic and got out of NI the better. Politically that was not acceptable or feasible without, at that time at least, a Protestant–Catholic civil war. I decided to investigate and write about "The Irish Republican Army (IRA) and the American Connection." When I proposed this to General Woodford I could tell that he was somewhat taken aback; a paper on the IRA? But he did clear that topic for me and even gave me the good counsel to start at the Republic of Ireland Embassy which was about two blocks from the college.

During the twelve months we were there, the paper referenced here was an integral part of the course from the beginning until I turned it in during the tenth month. I will cover it now before discussing other happenings during the course.

Doing the research on the U.S. and the IRA was a fun exercise for me. I started digging through books, papers and reports on Northern Ireland in the college library only to find a real paucity of information relating to America and the IRA. The librarian had a number of papers loaned to Seaford House for my use from other sources around London. They were to prove invaluable. One name however kept popping out whenever the U.S. did make print. That name was an organization called Northern Ireland Aid (NORAID). It appeared NORAID, based in New York City, was a major funnel for money to the IRA and the folks stoking the fires of trouble in the six counties of Northern Ireland. That organization became a major focus of my effort.

I finally decided that the trip to the Irish Embassy might be in order. I went there in three piece suit sporting my RCDS tie. In Great Britain school, regiment, guild and other organizations all have distinctive ties that quickly identify you as a member or graduate of that group or school. After being admitted to the embassy lobby, heavy with security, I asked to see the resident intelligence officer. The look I got would have stopped an eight day clock. I was told, "We have no intelligence officer working here." I identified myself as an American Army colonel serving with Her Majesty's Forces and presented both sets of credentials. For the second time I asked to see their resident spook. Again I was told that they had no intelligence officer, but that I should wait.

After a few minutes a gentleman appeared and introduced himself as the Second Secretary in the Economic Section of the embassy. I told him who I was, and what I was doing, and that I needed information on the IRA and NORAID. He smiled and said something to the effect that, "You Americans, you're all alike. You don't have a clue what the IRA is all about. You still think of them like the boys back in 1921. Nostalgia is your and our worst enemy when it comes to Irish Americans. Well I can tell you that the IRA are a bunch of bloody Communists who want to take over

Ireland and make it a Communist/Socialist country. They could care less about the six counties in the north; they want the whole bloody country. We hate them almost as much as the Brits do." I am paraphrasing here but that is close to what he told me. He went on to say, "You want to get to the IRA, which I don't think you will (emphasis added). I suggest you call Jane Denmark (a pseudo name) in Dublin. She's a writer for the *Economist Magazine* and has close ties to the boys. She may just talk with you. Her number in Dublin is...." Yes, he was from the Economic Section for sure, uh huh.

I did call Ms. Denmark, and she did talk to me, but she would not put me in touch with any member or even "fellow traveler" (a sympathizer of a cause) supporter of the IRA. She did know about NORAID and was open about the fact that they did provide money to the lads keeping the troubles alive. Most of that cash came from America and most of it, she insinuated, went to buy weapons, ammunition and explosives. Aid to the poor "downtrodden Catholic Northern Irish" was not high up on their to-do list. She was quite evasive as someone with links to a major terrorist organization would have to be. The basic thread of my thesis was coming together and there was now emerging significantly more information.

As I continued researching I thought of my wife's uncle, George Devlin, in Boston and that perhaps he, good Irishman that he was, might have some insight on NORAID. I wrote George and asked about NORAID and if he had any information about what might be happening with the Irish community in the Boston-New England area. He promptly replied that he knew nothing about NORAID and that he had not heard of any IRA activity or fund raising support for Northern Ireland going on around Boston; so much for that avenue of information, or so I thought.

About two weeks later I got another letter apologizing for his initial response. It seems George did not move in the right circles nor attend the correct Catholic Churches. Through other friends he had learned that NORAID representatives, dressed in black fedora hats, tan trench coats and Sam Brown belts stood on the steps of many an Irish parish shaking their cans and collecting for NORAID after every Sunday Mass. The black hat, tan trench coat and Sam Brown belt was the classic IRA uniform from the war to oust the Brits and later the Irish Civil War of the 1920s. Intelligence can have a funny way of emerging from areas and places one least expects.

I also had a strange happening that gave me further insight on American Irish support to NORAID and the IRA itself. I was offered the opportunity to visit a U.S. Army Special Forces–Special Air Service (Brit SF) Exercise being held at Sculthorpe Royal Air Force base. Colonel Dick Potter who had been Charlie Beckwith's Deputy Commander at Delta when we were doing the Delta evaluations and tests invited me to come up. The reason for the invitation will become clearer when I relate a visit I had at the college from Brigadier General Joe Lutz, the Commander of Special Operations Command at Fort Bragg. Well the college cleared me to be gone for two days and Dick sent a helicopter to West Ryslip RAF Base to pick me up. I don't remember much about the exercise proper but Dick was a quite good host and we enjoyed telling war stories. When he learned what topic I had chosen for my paper he commented, "We have a Reserve SF colonel with us who is from Boston; maybe he would have some insights that might help. We will have breakfast together tomorrow."

I can't remember the colonel's name but he was a nice guy, of Irish heritage and he knew about NORAID. He also told me a story that I definitely included in my paper. It seems that NORAID had sponsored Miss Bernadette Devlin, a real leftist radical supporter of the IRA, on a fund raising trip to the United States. Miss Devlin (no relation that we know of to my wife) was an infamous trouble maker in the six counties. One of her first stops was Boston Garden. Over 20,000 rabid Irish-American supporters jammed the place. When she began to talk she had the folks in the Garden mesmerized. But after about five minutes the only sound you could hear in the arena was her voice and 20,000 wallets slamming shut. She was preaching Communist/Socialist tripe to hard working, blue collar Irish-Americans. Their eyes were opened, their wallets were closing and they were not buying it. He went on to tell me, "I was there, I witnessed it. She was a complete turn off. NORAID cut short her tour of the U.S. and she returned to Ireland." The tale was just too good not to include in my paper. By the way, Miss Devlin later was elected to the British Parliament representing Northern Ireland.

My research uncovered a lot of points about America, Britain and the "ould sod" (Ireland) that I had not known. For example the first Saint Patrick's Day Parade in New York took place in the mid-1750s. A British regiment paraded, bands playing, flags fluttering, seeking local Irish volunteers to fill their ranks. In my mind that was an amazing factoid. I also learned of the elusive "Clan na Gael" that may or may not have actually existed in the late 1800s and early 1900s. They were American Irish whose goal was to kick the British out of Ireland, a rather farfetched aim to be sure from the shores of America. The Fenians, Irish revolutionaries from the period after our Civil War, were another little known piece of American history but one that I had certainly heard of. In the late 1860s they had undertaken an abortive invasion of Canada led by Union Army Irish veterans. The invasion was a dismal failure. The Clan Na Gael was the interesting piece that if I had the time I would try to run to ground. At any rate the paper was ultimately completed and turned in; and the IRA made it to the RCDS. I did not win any awards for it nor was it "mentioned in dispatches," to use the Brit term for getting special recognition for a great soldierly act. Whether this was because the effort was that sorry or the topic discouraged further exposure I am not sure. Fortunately, in the years since 1983 things in Northern Ireland have gotten a little better; not great, but a little better.

54
THE ROYAL COLLEGE
LEARNING EXPERIENCE

The Royal College was an eye opener as to grand strategy, society, economics, industrial issues, the world at large and the political spectrum. The British view was that it is a very large world and to appreciate it one had to be exposed to as much as possible and to differing views. Hence the eclectic class makeup, with officers and civilians from countries around the world, and the selection of lecturers from every facet of politics, business, education, and the military made this a truly unique experience. Overall it was a continuation of the National Security Management Course I took by correspondence in 1975 from the U.S. Industrial College of the Armed Forces, but on a world stage. It was without a doubt a fantastic learning experience. I will not bore you with more details on the daily aspects of class work or lectures. Suffice it to say I enjoyed both immensely. There were, however, a number of activities that are well worth relating that did not deal directly with Seaford House learning.

As an integral part of the course we were exposed to a myriad of fantastic experiences. Our entire class took a trip to the "Midlands" to visit numerous large and small businesses during the economic and industrial phase of our studies. We traveled north by British Rail which I found quite comfortable and very punctual. At that time Brit Rail was a popular mode of travel and remains so today. This trip was quite an eye opener for me having spent, up to that point in my career, all my time as basically a simple Infantrym?

I was exposed to many facets of industry from the mundane and arcane to the most modern hi tech computer driven manufacturing techniques. The Brits did not try to hide shortfalls in their economic and industrial base but were quite open with the good and the bad. Overall I was impressed with what I saw.

One day my seminar group (about eighteen students) went to Royal Dutch Shell (RDS) in downtown London for a briefing on oil and the international implications of oil. I would point out and stress this was mid-1983. The RDS building was, I believe, the tallest building in London with seven stories. There was, at that time, some government regulation that no building could be so high that it could look down into the grounds of Buckingham Palace. We were ushered into a very plush, seventh floor mahogany paneled conference room and greeted by one of RDS's vice presidents (VP). What we heard from this gentleman stunned us all.

In the course of the briefing, which had been basic information up to this point, the VP calmly announced, "Of course there is more oil in the western United States than in all the Middle East." You could have heard a pin drop. One of the Brits challenged this statement and the VP went on to assure us that the oil was there, in shale, whatever that meant; none of us having ever heard of shale oil at that time. He added that they had been working on a system to get it out of the ground successfully at a reasonable cost. When asked how the research and development of this new technology was going the VP responded to the effect: "We have stopped research and development on that." A Brit brigadier sitting next to me leaned over and said something like, "Yes, bloody hell they stopped. They have the secret locked up in a safe waiting for the right time to use it." Remember this was mid-1983 and I had just been told of the BAKKEN oil deposits, although that name was never mentioned. Today, recovery of oil from shale deposits is common place and potentially the source of $2.00 a gallon gas, if the environmentalists can be put in their proper place. That oil is there and can be extracted safely, or if they have an environmental disaster the big oil companies can pay to have the problem fixed. This can and should be done until the day we truly develop meaningful non-fossil fuel alternatives.

As part of our studies of government and municipal activities, each of us on the course was to spend a minimum of six hours at night with a Metropolitan Police "Panda" Car Team. These were black and white patrol cars, hence the name Panda. Now one of my best friends at the college was Commander Maurice Taylor, the Deputy Commander of the Metropolitan London Police (aka Scotland Yard). He and I hit it off well from day one at Seaford House and passed many hours talking about life, the world, the USA, Great Britain and the status of the Brit Bobbie. Thanks to Maurice I knew something about the Bobbies; their average age, attitude and the rules under which they operated. Maurice had told me how, when he was a child, the Bobbies would stand and watch the parade, or the Queen pass by, with their backs to the crowd. By the 1980s they were facing the crowd (emphasis added). Brit society was changing and not all for the better. Nothing we discussed prepared me for the six hours I was to spend riding through Brixton; you might compare that area with Watts in Los Angeles. Not a place one chooses to be at night.

Captain Robin Shiffner, Royal Navy, and I were teamed and joined up with two Bobbies; one aged nineteen and the other twenty-one. We two old military rascals could have been their fathers! We both marveled at their youth. These lads were terribly correct and proper. Smart, good looking, articulate and properly turned out; they made both Robin and I proud of the Metropolitan Police. Now, you may or may not be totally aware but guns are practically nonexistent in the UK except some hunting pieces, antiques and a few special permit cases. The police in Britain are for the most part unarmed except for a night stick and some form of pepper spray; at least that was the case in 1983. Many Panda cars do have weapons secured in their trunks. Why, you might ask? Because since law abiding Brits don't have weapons the only folks who do are the bad guys. The Pandas in Brixton, at least at that time, had weapons secured in the trunk for that unexpected encounter with the armed criminal element. To this day I am not sure what good the weapon in the trunk would be in the case of a true unexpected encounter with an armed bad guy.

We started our orientation tour and exposure to some of London's seedier side just about dusk. As they drove the area we got a running commentary on life on the streets from our two young policemen who probably wished we were not there. They responded to one call for backup from another Panda, chased a couple of ladies of the night off the street and in general did their thing to keep the peace. Responding to one call about a family disturbance they asked that we remain in the car as the presence of two non-Metropolitan Police employees might provoke more antagonism than help them; or enlighten us. Later they pulled up in front of a bar and invited us to join them in what was for them a nightly ritual. As we entered the joint, and it was a joint, the smoke hung so thick in the air you could cut it with a knife. The pungent odor of marijuana and heaven only knows what else wafted up to us instantly. As I looked around it was immediately obvious that we four were the only white faces in the place. We also were the only folks not sporting dreadlocks and a ferocious "what are you doing here whitey" look on our faces. Frankly I was glad when we walked out of the place and my respect for the London Metropolitan Police knew no bounds. Those young Bobbies had big *cajones*. My hat went off to them. All in all I think we went into three similar establishments, none of which I would desire to return to without a Thompson submachine gun and a squad of armed paratroopers. It was an interesting night. I told Maurice about our experiences the next day and he just smiled and nodded. All in a nights' work for the Metropolitan Police.

There were social and cultural aspects and exchanges that took place at various times throughout the year. For example, we attended the races at Ascot and had the Queen Mum and many of the Royals walk past us as they proceeded to the paddock to view the horses. Later we enjoyed a fantastic lunch just before the big race. The cream of Brit society was in attendance along with some of us common folks.

The foreign students were challenged by our Brit colleagues to a cricket match. Now playing cricket to me was like watching the grass grow. It was the closest sport to boring I ever participated in. We traveled in central London to an Army barracks in Chelsea all attired in traditional white outfits to be soundly trounced by the Brit team. Had it not been for our Pakistan and Indian classmates, who knew the game well, it would have been much worse. While we "played," or if you prefer stood and watched the grass grow, the ladies and children all sat in their finery and ate strawberries and cream while being serenaded by the Guards Band in full dress uniform. It was one of those not-to-be-forgotten moments.

Not to be outdone, on the Fourth of July we Americans hosted our classmates at the Lacey and Redmond "estate" for our traditional hot dog, beans and potato salad celebration of our break with the crown. There was plenty of beer and conversation and I believe it is safe to say that a good time was had by all.

One afternoon I received a message from the Army attaché telling me that Brigadier General Joe Lutz, Commanding General, Army Special Operations Command at Fort Bragg, was in London and wanted to come to lunch at the college the next day. I was told his sergeant major and his aide would be with him and that he had something to discuss with me. Arrangements for a four person table were made. The general had been in my SF Officer Course in 1964 as a senior major. I had not seen him since that time. We had a cordial meal telling war stories and then he suddenly asked me if I would like to come to Bragg as his G3 Operations Officer. I was taken aback, flattered with the offer and immediately told him that I would be honored and thanked him for such confidence in me. After some further small talk he stated that he needed to get on to an exercise then underway at RAF Sculthorpe (which was discussed earlier when treating of my paper on the IRA) and we got up and walked to the college entrance.

As the party was leaving the sergeant major grabbed me by the arm, pulled me aside, and said, and I am paraphrasing, "Sir, you know why the general needs you? The Army is changing. Special Operations is emerging as a major player now, not just some wild guys in Green Berets the country sends out to do their dirty work. You are one of the few who have been successful on both the conventional side and the snake eating side. He needs someone who can talk with the folks at Mother Army." Whatever the reason, I was flattered, humbled and terribly pleased. But, was this assignment really in the cards?

55

RETURNING TO MY ROOTS AND A VISIT TO NORMANDY

Every August is a time of relaxation and holiday throughout Europe, and the UK is no exception. Everyone it seemed saved all year for their annual holiday somewhere. Folks throughout the region travel to Spain, Majorca, Austria, the USA, Malta, Russia, Greece, wherever; anywhere except where they live and work. So for the RCDS it was a stand down month. Well surprise of surprises, even as a colonel with a cost of living allowance we weren't flying to Spain, let alone the USA. The purse simply wouldn't permit too much extravagance. Then again maybe we could have gone to France or Spain, but the lure of Ireland, the "ould sod," was in my blood.

Young Larry was in the UK for his summer away from the Citadel so we had a full house. We were amazed to hear that the kids didn't want something exotic, like Portugal; they all wanted to go to the beach at Brighton! To be honest, Mary and I were not very excited about that. We both wanted to go to Ireland. Her family came from a farm in Donegal near Ishkaheen Mountain, the village of Muff, just outside Derry (aka Londonderry). My family came from County Wexford. Taking the children to see the country both our families came from seemed like a perfect holiday. Frankly, the battle of Gettysburg saw less fireworks than raged in the Redmond household for about two weeks. Finally a truce was arranged and an itinerary developed. Patricia suggested that we go to Scotland and to Loch Ness to see "Nessie" first! Then a visit to Ireland would be OK.

Young Larry was fine with that and Miss Katherine readily accepted the idea. Planning commenced in early July for our trip. With the help of a classmate, Brigadier Keith Prosser, who had served in Londonderry, arrangements were made by the Church of Ireland Bishop of Londonderry for our initial stop in Ireland, the village of Muff.

We journeyed in our Mazda 626 up through central England to Scotland; it was a little crowded but there was really minimal complaining from the kids in the back seat. We stopped and checked out the usual tourist sites, Hadrian's Wall and the walled city of York, plus a few other historical sites along the way. From there it was on to north central Scotland and Loch Ness. We had a great B&B in the village of Drumnadrochit looking directly down into Loch Ness the home of the famed, elusive monster. Patricia looked hard but the monster never materialized. We drove further north to Inverness and the battlefield at Bannockburn where Robert the Bruce defeated the English King Edward II in a smashing victory. Returning to Inverness we had the best fish and chips wrapped in the local newspaper while gazing up at Inverness Castle. I was impressed with the castle. The girls liked the chips. Young Larry liked the beer, and admittedly so did I. The return trip to Drumnadrochit took us through a magnificent forest with huge stately trees. It was a most impressive drive, even the children enjoyed it. I will now make a comment that may cause my sainted Irish grandfather to spin in his grave. Northern Scotland is, in my mind, the prettiest part of the British Isles.

From Drumnadrochit we proceeded to the coast at Stranrar near Glascow to catch a ferry to Northern Ireland. On the way we traversed some truly beautiful mountains. The roads were narrow and quite twisty. At one point Patricia announced calmly, "Dad, I'm getting sick, slow down." Well, being the big bad Airborne Ranger I ignored her entreaty. We then passed about an hour on the side of the road cleaning the car and changing Patricia's clothes. Larry and Kathy begged me to listen to their sibling in the future. Lesson learned. We spent the night in a rather rustic but scrupulously clean B&B with adjoining farm yard; all of us in one large room. Now my son won't appreciate this but his tennis shoes gave off an aroma in those days that was quite pungent. To ensure some degree of air quality we had him place them on the outside of the window ledge. When we awoke all the cows in the lovely little muddy pen outside the window were lying down causing his sisters to exclaim, "Mom, Dad look! Larry's shoes have killed the cows!" Fortunately such was not the case.

The trip across the Irish Sea was uneventful and quite nice. I stood by the rail of the ferry and thought about all the history I was about to encounter and the fact that the roots of the Redmond and Devlin families lay ahead. We landed in Northern Ireland at the height of the "Troubles" at a town just north of Belfast called Larne. I personally had not given a thought to the "Troubles" or that there could be complications. That was not very smart on my part. The security was tight and the screening getting out of the port quite slow. My Royal College ID and my U.S. Army ID got us no slack and after some serious questioning about where we were going a burly Royal Irish Constabulary Sergeant asked me to open the trunk. When I popped the trunk he was confronted with the aroma of Trish's eruption on that Scottish mountain road. The trunk was immediately slammed shut and we were cleared to proceed. I might have had a couple of machine guns and an 81 millimeter mortar back there. Patricia could have been the IRA's secret weapon.

As we drove into and through Belfast the girls actually scrunched down in the back and hid. Larry took in all the sights and sounds. The British Army was everywhere. Sandbagged positions, armored cars on corners, foot patrols moving down the sidewalk with all around security. It was all there and evident. Things in Northern Ireland (NI) were on a knife's edge. Mary appeared a little apprehensive and I began to wonder myself if this was such a good idea. Maybe we should have entered Ireland down in the Republic near Dublin. At that point it was too late to wonder. The ice breaker came as we moved through Belfast and hunger pangs struck the girls. They began to look around and suddenly spied a Blimpies hamburger joint. Hunger overcame fear and we stopped for lunch.

On the way out of town I pulled into a petrol station for gas. As I looked at the building just ahead, maybe fifty yards distant, I noticed that the side facing us was covered with Orange (Protestant) propaganda and comments like "Papists out of Northern Ireland." This was definitely not a hospitable start to our visit. I nodded to Larry to look ahead at the building. He returned the nod and as soon as the gas tank was filled we got the blazes out of there. After this experience Larry and I both paid close attention to the political persuasion of the villages and neighborhoods where we stopped.

The trip through NI to Derry was actually very enjoyable. The kids were all up and having not been shot at yet, were taking in all the scenery. They fought to see who could pick up the next patrol of British soldiers walking the hills and fields to left and right. The troops were everywhere. Sandbagged security positions dotted the roadside manned by very serious looking British soldiers. As I recall we did not pass any formal checkpoints until we got to the outskirts of Derry. We were rapidly passed through by British troops when I presented my RCDS Identification. Driving through Derry we observed a few burned out houses and stores as well as the ever present sandbagged positions and armored cars. As we drove, the graffiti favoring one side or the other was all around us and when the wording changed from "Up the IRA" to "Papists out" we knew the political and religious ideology of that neighborhood had just changed. We crossed into the Republic without incident and drove through Muff; three bars, ten or so homes and little else to recommend it except our B&B.

I mentioned earlier that Brigadier Keith Prosser, through the Church of Ireland's Bishop of Londonderry, Bishop Peacock, had made our B&B reservation. Well Mrs. O'Rourke was proper in meeting us at her lovely ranch style home but appeared a little aloof. Not that she was unfriendly, just a tad more reserved than I would have expected when being visited by a Yank family. She had afternoon snacks for us but we did not get to talk till the next morning at breakfast. She set a fine table and we all enjoyed the food. In the course of small talk Mrs. O'Rourke asked us how we might "....be knowing Bishop Peacock?" I told her we didn't know him but that a classmate of mine was a friend of his and had arranged for our stay via the Bishop. We were to have tea with the clergyman and his wife that afternoon. I told her we didn't know what to expect as we were Catholics and had never met a Church of Ireland bishop. Well good heavens did things change when she heard we were Papists and that Mary's family came from Ishkaheen Mountain just about five kilometers from where we sat. Mrs. O'Rourke could then not do enough for us. She volunteered to do the laundry for Mary while we were out and about. Mary warned her that she really did not want to do that and related the incident with Patricia and what the bag in the trunk smelled like. Mrs. O'Rourke could not be deterred and she did the laundry while we visited with the Bishop. Being Papists at that point definitely had its advantages.

Our return to Derry through the border crossing point went smoothly with the lads on the British side now checking the trunk without being assaulted by the sickening odor. The visit with Bishop Peacock and his lady was quite nice but sheer agony for the kids who sat there all prim and proper in their best vacation clothes. This was not their idea of a good time. I cannot tell you a thing that was said during the visit but we had closed the loop and thanked the Bishop for his help in securing such nice accommodations for us. Re-crossing into the Republic was uneventful although such was not always the case as we would hear the next afternoon.

The following day we left Muff and headed up the coast stopping to visit the ancestral home of Field Marshall Viscount Bernard

Montgomery, Patton's nemesis. The home was now a hotel and we had a nice leisurely lunch. Then we proceeded north in Donegal till we were further north in Southern Ireland than any point in Northern Ireland. Confusing isn't it. When we ran out of road, literally looking out at the Atlantic Ocean there was a stone farmhouse with a stone barn, both quite old and weathered. The barn now served its owner's as an antique shop. I have no idea where the customers came from because we were the only car we had seen in the last fifteen or so miles. A young woman, quite attractive, appeared from the farm house as we all browsed and looked at the antiques in the barn. Mary bought a very old iron that worked on the principle of adding hot coals to the body of same and when it got hot enough you could press clothes. Not very 20th Century but it worked in its day. For years it served as a door stop in the Redmond household. As we drove away the girls both exclaimed, "Did you see, did you see; that lady had no shoes on!" Fair observation, and frankly it was darned cold up there on the coast. We had reached the extreme northern point in Southern Ireland, and it was "shanty Irish" poor.

On the way back to Muff we stopped in Buncranna for a snack and to just look around. We visited a pub where Irish fiddle music abounded. I think Larry and I had more than one beer. The town was nice and in some ways a tad above the other Republic of Ireland villages we had driven through that day. I must observe that in 1983 the transition from Northern Ireland to the Republic was like turning out the lights. NI was much cleaner, nicer and more modern even given the troubles and all that went along with them. The Republic looked like it did in the 1930s; much poorer and less well maintained than NI. (NOTE: All that had changed when we returned to Ireland in 1993. The European Union had jump-started the Republic's economy far beyond anything I could have imagined during that first visit.)

While having pastries and tea late that afternoon with Mrs. O'Rourke, we mentioned that we had stopped in Buncranna. The good lady went ballistic. "Oh glory be to God, you didn't? That place is a hot bed of the IRA. Do you know the bastards have shot at me twice while waiting to cross from the Republic into NI to shop? The worst of it is my husband is a bloody member of that bunch (IRA). We lived in Birmingham for a number of years before returning to Muff. I am after my husband to move back to Birmingham, but he won't do it. I liked the UK a lot more than living here." Mrs. O'Rourke, once she opened up, was a font of information.

We then visited Ishkaheen Mountain looking for the old Devlin homestead. Mary's uncle had visited the farm a few years before, found it and provided pretty good directions. We were looking for both a farm house and a place Uncle George called the "cottage in the cut." The Devlin ancestors had brewed and moved poteen, Irish moonshine, over the mountain and down to Derry via that cottage. We got to the general area and had no trouble finding the farm house, a very nice Georgian home from the late 1800s. At some point, before they left Ireland, the Devlin family had money. We kept looking for the cottage Uncle George had told us about. Larry and I thought we had found the right little trail and walked down the path breaking through some brambles. Suddenly the area opened up and there was a very old stone cottage with most of the roof gone and the door hanging half off the hinges. When we entered the place we glanced around and taking in the aura decided it really was not the place we were looking for, nor wanted to be. There were signs of frequent camp fires and possible sleeping places. Was this an IRA way point? Very possibly we both thought. It was close to Derry and remote enough for a degree of safety. Returning to the girls we told them it was best that we went back to the farm house pronto. We did that and met the current owners, the Flynn's, who remembered the visit by Uncle George and were quite happy to show us around. Mary had at least found her family homestead and the children also experienced a piece of their roots.

We departed Muff and Mrs. O'Rourke and proceeded to do the tourist thing, heading south through the Republic leisurely enjoying the thatched cottages, old castles and scenery of Ireland. Now this summer had been the driest in twenty years and the countryside was a little on the brown side. Kathy, who had been keen on the Brighton option for our holiday, was truly on a roll complaining about the "...supposed Emerald Isle that wasn't green but brown!" Her mother solved that one buying her some very cheap sun glasses with green lenses that produced a somewhat Emerald Isle. We all chuckled and Kathy even enjoyed the joke. She also stopped complaining.

We had all wanted to see the Ring of Kerry, a world famous tourist stop. So we drove south to Killarney and spent several days there. The kids got to ride in an Irish jaunting cart pulled by a cute pony and loved it. They also got to swim in the Atlantic not far from Killarney. Everyone, me included, rapidly decided that the water off the coast of Ireland was a lot colder than they cared to swim in. Suddenly the original Brighton Beach option was no longer in favor. There were no more swim suit outings this trip. We drove the Ring of Kerry proper and I must admit the ride was beautiful and well worth our time. We stopped at several tourist sites, gorgeous glens with huge old trees and shady spots that truly took you back to quieter more relaxed times. Before we departed Killarney our B&B host was shocked when we reported that we owed her six Irish Punts for twelve showers at fifty pence per shower, roughly six dollars. "Glory be to God, you Americans take a lot of showers," she exclaimed. And yes people in Ireland talked like that, at least in those days. She did not hesitate to take the money I might add.

From Killarney we drove east and north into central Ireland doing the normal tourist things to include stopping at the fabled Blarney Castle. The ritual kissing of the Blarney Stone took place and we then proceeded on to Dublin. Dublin was a great city and I got to see the famous Post Office where the 1916 Rebellion began and ended rather ingloriously but which ultimately led to Irish Independence just six years later. We visited all the requisite pubs and eateries and also both the Catholic and Church of Ireland Cathedrals. The Church of Ireland Cathedral, St. Patrick's, was quite nice and we found some very interesting handmade needlepoint kneelers, some of which went back many years; World War I military unit crest kneelers were among the striking finds. It was a fascinating place. From Dublin we took the ferry back to the UK and Wales. Now compared to Scotland, Wales has been denuded almost completely of trees if there were ever any there. The mountains were sharp and stark but majestic in their own right. I am sure a Welshman would tell me I was off my rocker and that there are lots of trees in Wales. That may well be so but we saw darned few of them.

We returned to Eastcote just in time for young Larry and me to prepare for and depart on our own little sojourn to France. We both wanted to see Normandy and the World War II battlefields there. The ladies could have cared less especially since we men had decided we would rough it with backpacks and travel by hitching rides around the French countryside. Having commanded the 1-505 Black Panthers, H-Minus, I was particularly interested in visiting Sainte-Mère-Église where that unit had jumped in and fought on D-Day, 6 June 1944.

We took the train to Portsmouth on the south coast and a ferry over to Cherbourg. The weather was balmy and the two of us started hiking up toward Sainte-Mère-Église and the other D-Day sites and beaches. Well frankly we bit off a lot with that walk. It was eighteen plus miles to Sainte-Mère-Église and the first two miles, from the port up to the Cotentin Peninsula proper, was via a windy, twisting narrow road; and it was almost straight up. We covered the first ten or twelve miles in fine fashion and the weather was great. We hardly broke a sweat, but night was approaching and so we decided to bed down in a small hay barn in a cattle field by the side of the road. We ate a cold dinner from our packs and passed the night undisturbed by man or beast. We felt like a couple of Boy Scouts and slept like lambs.

The next day we continued our hike, shanks mare (by foot for the younger reader) to Omaha Beach. There was much to see along the way; monuments, memorials and cemeteries, were everywhere. The beach itself was fascinating. Enough remnants of the great German "West Wall" were visible to satisfy the most ardent historian. We bought wine, cheese and super French bread at a small shop, re-crossed the strand and sat on the beach eating our lunch where Americans and Germans had bled and died on 6 June 1944. After satisfying our curiosity about D-Day and Omaha Beach we decided to find another field and spend the night. The next morning we started on toward Sainte-Mère-Église. After a couple of miles we both agreed that getting there via wheels would beat walking and began to seek transport. Almost the first car we signaled the need for a ride stopped to pick us up. A very nice French lady who didn't speak a word of English, but understood Sainte-Mere, and kept saying *"qui, qui,"* gave us a lift. The car was a classic old French auto with no modernity about it. Modernity? Well it was more of a dilapidated wreck but it did get us to our day's destination without more walking.

Sainte-Mère-Église seemed little changed from WWII except that there was a museum on one side of the town square. The old church, where a 1-505 paratrooper hung for hours when his chute became entangled with the steeple while the battle raged below him, was still there. It looked just like it appeared in the movie *The Longest Day*. The museum was fascinating, very well done and had both a C-46 jump aircraft and WACO glider in the main hall. It was heady stuff for a guy who had commanded the Black Panthers, albeit not during the war.

After two and a half days of roughing it Larry and I both decided a bed and shower sounded good. We found a decent looking hotel just off the square and took a room for the night. The place was adequate but frankly looked like it had been ridden hard and put up wet. The room and bed had both seen better days; I judge those days came before WWII. However there were clean sheets and no hay. The shower was down the hall and tiny but the water was hot. There was a bar and restaurant and with our U.S. and British Para shirts we could not buy a beer. No one really spoke English but they knew Allied unit insignia. We did pay for what passed as a steak dinner. In spite of shortcomings it beat the previous two nights fare. I even found 1-505 Street and had my picture taken sitting on a wall directly under the sign. All in all I enjoyed the day and night in Sainte-Mère-Église.

We made our way the following day to Carentan another French village, of WWII fame, this one associated with the 101st Screaming Eagles. Once again there were a number of memorials and cemeteries along the way and we just took our time and enjoyed it all. The citizens of Normandy for the most part truly remember the Liberation and gave us a most hearty welcome wherever we roamed. They recognized the symbols on our shirts and ball caps. The story of the French not liking foreigners may be true for France proper but that was not the case in Normandy at least not in 1983. From Carentan we took a very modern French Rail train back down to Cherbourg and caught the ferry back to Portsmouth.

In Portsmouth we missed the last train to London for that night by about ten minutes. There we were sort of stranded until after 0600 the next morning thanks to the punctuality of British Rail. What to do? Well old Dad had the solution. We would just go to Portsmouth Royal Naval Base and get VIP quarters. Piece of cake solution; well not exactly. At the gate, with fog and a light rain coming down, four Brit "Rent a Cops" looked at my RCDS identification, our rather scruffy dress and possible odor and politely told us we could not enter. One of the guards said, "The Queen Victoria Sailors Rest is one block down the street." Rather than make a fuss we decided to find this reputed Sailors Rest.

Well the "Rest" was there, easily found. I venture to say in its day it was magnificent; if the façade was to be believed. It was opened by Her Majesty Queen Victoria in the mid-1880s. It had been grand in its day but was now well past its prime. The lobby was impressive but somewhat shabby. The petty officer clerk behind the desk stared at the two of us and my RCDS and U.S. Identification cards with a good deal of incredulity. But he did give us keys to two rooms. I asked him for a wakeup call at 0530 so we could catch the train to London. We were informed that there were no phones in the rooms but that he would make certain we were awakened at 0530. With that Larry and I made it up to the second floor and our rooms. Now to call these rooms is a bit of an exaggeration. A monk's cell had more class. There was a bed, a very beat up dresser, one chair, hardly room to turn around and one nautical ship picture hanging on the wall somewhat askew. The loo was down the hall. But the sheets were clean and it beat the fog and rain.

Sometime after I lay down I heard an awful banging and assumed it was the norm for the Sailors Rest in the middle of the night. It stopped and moments later the banging arrived at my door with a fervor that nearly took the door down. I jumped up and somewhat cautiously opened the door. I was greeted by a quite tall and burly Royal Navy Chief Petty Officer in white uniform with an SP (Shore Patrol) arm brassard, a sidearm and a rather intimidating billy club. Behind him stood four impressive, nattily attired, and also intimidating, shore police. They looked like an 18th Century Royal Navy press gang come to shanghai us into the Royal Navy. Off to the side in the middle of the hall I could see young Larry in his T shirt and boxer shorts. It had been from his room that I had heard the initial banging. The chief asked if he could see some identification. Now at this time of night, confronted by this possible press gang, I was not about to argue. I produced both my picture ID cards quickly and he verified the pictures were of the rascal standing in front of him. He glanced down at my T shirt which I had put on to sleep in, the last clean one in my pack, and asked; "I say, Colonel, you aren't one of those Green Berets are you?" Well if you could read English you might deduce that fact since the words and beret were screaming out from my chest. Before I could answer he turned to his mates and said, "Lads that explains it all. He's one of the Yank Special Forces, you know our SAS guys." Turning back to me he went on, "Do apologize, sir, for the inconvenience but we don't get many officers of rank staying here. The desk clerk wondered, and with the IRA boys so active, we needed to check you out. Apologize, get some rest." With that the press gang departed and we were not about to become non-volunteer members of the Royal Navy as we might have two hundred years earlier. We slept soundly till 0530 when just like clockwork we were woken by a knock on our doors. The train ride back to London was uneventful and my son and I felt good about our sojourn in Normandy. Quite a father–son experience for sure.

I assumed that trip was behind me and returned two days later to the college and normal class work. The holidays were over, but not quite this last incident. After the morning lecture the college president, Admiral Sir William Pillar (a true, proper British gentleman and one heck of a brilliant mind), arose. He did his usual thanks to our guest speaker for a memorable and "splendid forenoon." Then he turned, and looking directly at me said, "I also want to welcome back Colonel Redmond and his son from Portsmouth. The admiral commanding the Royal Naval Base asked me to inquire if you enjoyed your stay at the Sailors Rest? You seem none the worse for the event, Larry. And I am told you are the first RCDS student ever to stay there." And I strongly suspect I was the last. Before I got downstairs to the restaurant all my Army and RAF buddies had been informed by our Navy chums exactly what the Sailors Rest was like. It sure was a peg or two down the ladder from Seaford House. I took a good bit of gentle ribbing from my classmates over that event.

The real shocker came about two days later when I found a note in my message box to come to the embassy that afternoon to see the Army attaché. When I got to his office he asked me if I had gone to Northern Ireland and was I sponsored there by the British Army. I explained Brigadier Prosser's helping with a B&B and that it was a holiday trip for the family to see our family roots. The attaché went on to tell me that the ambassador was furious. Somehow he had learned that a serving, American Army colonel had traveled to NI; that I was a student at the RCDS; was a Special Forces officer and that I was a Catholic. The attaché knew some pieces of my background and that I had been involved tangentially with our counter terror units. Putting it all together he told me that I wasn't thinking. In so many words he said something like, "If anything had happened while you were there you could have created one heck of an incident. The IRA could have claimed you were there helping the Brits (who needed no help from me) or the Brits could have claimed you were an IRA Catholic sympathizer" (not likely). At any rate he added that the ambassador had decided that no American officer serving with the Brits in any capacity would, as long as he was ambassador, go to Northern Ireland on holiday. I had managed to create another almost incident just trying to see the "ould sod." One could almost deduce that I was a sort of loose cannon. I never did figure out how my vacation travel through Northern Ireland had come to the attention of the ambassador. Cocktail party talk perhaps, but talk by whom? In my mind the whole thing was a tempest in a tea pot, typical State Department over reaction, but maybe not.

56
HOW I BECAME A BRIT PARA

There were three foreign paratroopers on the course: COL Dick Cowling, Canadian Army and former commander of the Canadian Parachute Regiment; COL Antonio Milani, Italian Folgore Parachute Regiment and myself. We chummed pretty much together and had great tales to tell. We had a learning experience of a different nature that was an exception from our studies at Seaford House, and for the most part quite enjoyable.

To set the stage let me explain that also on the course was a British Brigadier, former commander of the Special Air Service (SAS) Regiment and a soldier destined for far greater things. That gentleman was Brigadier Peter de la C de la Billiere who would go on to be Sir Peter and a full general who led the British forces in Operation Desert Storm. Peter and I gravitated to one another since I was SF. One day he asked me if I knew COL Charlie Beckwith. I told him that I knew him only too well. Without revealing anything classified I told him of my experiences with Chargin' Charlie Beckwith from the 2-327 in Vietnam, with Delta Force and also some of my Blue Light counter terror testing activity. That sort of sealed a bond and trust between us. I can say categorically that Peter was pretty closed mouth about his experiences especially in Northern Ireland and how he led, as commander of the SAS Regiment, the successful attack to take back, from terrorists, the Iranian Embassy in London. Terrorism was always a keen topic between us to include from time to time talks about the IRA in Northern Ireland. He had no insights about the IRA and NORAID; at least none he shared with me.

One day Peter asked if we three Airborne soldiers would like to get our British Jump Wings; become Brit Paratroopers, aka "Paras." Well, Dick and I jumped at the opportunity and Antonio followed suit. We were excused from class for this extracurricular activity and went to an SAS site not far from London for training. Although we were all qualified paratroopers, such was not the case in the minds of our British hosts even though the overture to jump was sponsored by Brigadier de la Billiere. We were assigned an SAS sergeant major, young troop, who was one of the lead parachute instructors. He was our personal instructor and evaluator as to our ability to exit an RAF C-130 in-flight. Good man but I must tell you that short of long runs and hundreds of pushups we were required to demonstrate proficiency on all the para training devices. He took nothing for granted. Maybe he had been told to make sure these crazy allies were really able to jump, but more importantly, land safely.

We did a rather lengthy stint of parachute landing falls and enjoyed a number of other training apparatus before being allowed to jump from a balloon, to demonstrate our readiness to exit a real airplane in flight. Now if the reader is a paratrooper and has never jumped from a balloon, floating and gently rocking at 1,000 feet, I can tell you categorically that you have missed out on a great experience. The balloon, shaped like a small dirigible, has a basket, perhaps fifteen feet wide and twenty-five feet long suspended beneath it. The "dispatcher," as the Brits term the jump master, stands to the left of a small gate and dispatches the jumpers to exit the basket. Everything is just like jumping from an airplane, except there is no engine noise, no aircraft slipstream and no shuffling to the door. Nothing, just silence initially. When you jump and assume a body position, there is no prop blast and you fall straight down.

You can then hear the parachute lines pulling free from the rubber bands holding the lines in the pack tray; a distinct SNAP, SNAP, SNAP, SNAP and then suddenly an opening shock as the chute deploys. It was exhilarating, unique and surely a different way of training paras.

As I recall we made three jumps from a C-130 following which we were awarded our British Jump Wings. I was made an Honorary Member of the 3rd Para Battalion. Following this little exercise Peter de La C de la Billiere asked us if we would like to become free fall qualified. We all said yes and back we went to the SAS base at Hereford for more training. Our instructor was the same SGT MAJ who put us through our initial jump training. It all went pretty smoothly and we jumped, from 10,000 feet. Let me tell you that if it had not been for a free fall trainer noncommissioned officer who jumped right after me and flew directly in front of me I might not have survived. I could not obtain and maintain any semblance of a stable body position. The training had been quite adequate because Dick and Antonio had no trouble in maintaining a stable body position--I was the only one out of synch. Twice that NCO moved in and held me to help maintain stability. At 4,000 feet I pulled my rip cord and went under canopy. The ride down was super, the experience exhilarating and I landed within a couple of feet of the X, it was miraculous and I was amazed. Believe me that was pure beginners luck but I was very close to landing directly on the target X. We went back up for a second jump and I had the same experience except this time a major jumped with me and flew right in front of me helping me keep a stable body position. Again, at 4,000 feet I pulled the rip cord and had a great ride down; was looking at British countryside for miles in all directions. I again landed close to the X, this time maybe fifteen feet away. I was impressed with my ability to get close to a target and guide that chute. I was frankly not impressed with my ability to obtain and hold a stable body position. I determined that free fall parachuting was not my bag. I would not do it again. In fact, I believe that was the last free fall, at least in England, for my two compatriots as well.

Now this may be hard to believe but on four or five occasions the college Head Porter, a retired color sergeant major, would find us after lunch, come into our seminar group and whisper, "Suh, the balloon is up at Greenham Common. Would you care to go jump?" Well the three of us maintained a set of fatigues and boots in the basement locker room and off we would go. Balloon jumping was quick, easy and beat sitting in a seminar trying to solve world problems far beyond our meager abilities to influence in the least.

The last jump I made in England was a thriller for sure. On this occasion only my Canadian buddy, Dick Cowling, and I went to try the balloon. When we got to Greenham Common the dispatcher that day was our initial SGT MAJ trainer. We had a number of good tales to relate to him and then we popped up in the balloon and did a jump. It was great. As we were turning in our chutes the SGT MAJ hollered over, "Suh, would you care to do a second?" Well Dick and I exchanged glances and nodded, sort of implying to each other that we really couldn't say no. The second jump was equally good. As we were again turning in our chutes, that voice offered another jump if we were willing. We again exchanged glances and it was obvious we two colonels couldn't seem like wimps. Up we went. Now in the UK the weather patterns are constantly changing and what had been a nice, quiet, sunny afternoon began to look threatening. As we were being raised to 1,000 feet suddenly the basket shifted ahead and our anchor line cable tightened up as a front with strong winds arrived. I looked at Dick and we both said at almost the same moment, "This one won't go." That was a bad assumption on our part. We were told to stand by, then, *Go!*, and like Pavlov's dog we jumped. I fought to face into the wind and hold that position as I descended hoping to slow down the landing as much as possible. The winds were not quite howling but I was sure flying across the drop zone at a much faster pace than I would have liked.

I landed like a ton of bricks and had a terrible pain in my right shoulder and a sensation that something was out of place. It was; my shoulder was dislocated. I had not a clue what to do. In almost panic mode, not wanting the Brits to know that I was hurt, I rolled over a little and slammed my left arm and hand into my right shoulder. I immediately felt the pressure release and sensed that maybe the shoulder had gone back in its socket; fortunately it had. I struggled to my feet, managed to roll up my chute and join Dick who was finishing packing up his chute. I whispered to him, "Dick, get me the hell out of here and stop at the first pub you see. I think I dislocated my shoulder. Don't say anything, let's just go and get me something to deaden the pain." Dick, good troop that he is, got me sort of sloshed, and then took me home.

Next day I went to the Medical Clinic at U.S. Navy Headquarters Europe across from the U.S. Embassy at Grosvenor Square, not far from the college. An X-Ray of my very sore shoulder was taken and the doctor told me that the best thing that happened was that I had forced the shoulder back into the socket so quickly. He said it had not been out of place long enough to do any real long term damage. That proved to be true but for about seven days I wore a sling and took a lot of ribbing from my classmates. Thus ended my days as a Brit para; it had been fun.

57
BACK TO GERMANY AND
ANOTHER VISIT TO THE MID-EAST

As part of the course we did several "grand" tours; one to the British Army of the Rhine in Germany and one to a specific part of the world. Let me address each in turn.

The entire Class of "83" flew to Europe and the visit with the British residual troops in Germany. I say residual since they had been slowly reducing their forward deployed troops since 1945. I don't remember a lot about this trip except some excellent briefings on the current NATO/UK posture vis-a-vis the Soviets. We visited a number of Brit units in the field conducting exercises. I distinctly remember crawling in the back of a truck along with several classmates to discuss their new logistics computer system. It was all magic to me having never personally used a computer. The young corporal working the computer was quite enthused about the system and all that it could do. He waxed forth eloquently and at some length. You could tell he had either been pimped to say what he did or he was truly a believer. One of the brigadiers with me asked, "Do you keep paper copies of all the data just in case the system goes down?" The look on the young man's face told us instinctively that they did not. I am sure that shortcoming was rectified immediately after the first "crash" of that early stage, and very susceptible to crash, computer logistics system.

We flew on an RAF C-130 to Berlin. That was quite interesting. By 1983 West Berlin, even given the horrendous pounding Berlin took in the last year of the war, was a beautiful, modern and inviting city. We visited Check Point Charlie, at the Wall, and were permitted to take a drive through East Berlin. Once through the check point the difference was not just stark, it was horrifying when compared to what the West Berliner's had accomplished. There were still piles of rubble, bombed out buildings and all sorts of signs that recovery was not just slow, it was almost nonexistent. The new buildings that were there were concrete edifices with no redeeming architectural qualities. They were just large grey boxes. The value of western materialism was readily evident when we re-crossed the border at Check Point Charlie. That pretty much wrapped up the trip to the British Army of the Rhine.

Redmond's Rule #22 – Believe it, Communism is a disaster for the common man.

Next came the part of the course where we were broken down into groups of twelve to fourteen students along with a Senior Directing Staff Member (SDSM) and taken on a tour of a specified portion of the world. The tours all included some sightseeing but mostly focused on military, economic and social aspects of the nations visited with briefings and meetings hosted by national officials. The areas offered were Northern Europe, Central Europe, the Far East, the Middle East, Africa, North America and South America. Each student group would tour up to five countries in the part of the world they were designated to visit. We were all allowed to submit our first and second choice for area to tour. Having been in Israel, Jordan and Syria during my stint as a UN Observer I asked for and was designated to take the Mid-East tour. Some of what I am going to relate may seem unbelievable but it did happen. Our tour was scheduled to visit Cyprus, Jordan, Israel and Egypt in that order. Our SDSM was Air Vice Marshall Phipps, a classic Brit gentleman. He helped make the trip quite enjoyable.

Our first stop was Cypress and a site called Akrotiri Royal Air Force Base in the Sovereign Base Area. The Brits had a long history on Cyprus and were privileged to have a Sovereign Base where British Law held sway. I am not sure how we traveled but we landed at that RAF facility so I am assuming it was by C-130. I do not remember a civilian airliner. Akrotiri is a site used frequently as a staging base for U.S. Special Operations forces focused on the Middle East. We stayed at a civilian hotel not far from the base and right on the coast. The first day there I went for a run along the beach and as I plodded along, after about 300 yards, something flashed through my mind; "My God, all the women are topless!" Well that was an eye opener for sure. We toured Cypress, ate at some great restaurants up in the hills and experienced life in the Mediterranean at its best. The Greek Cypriots were very nice folks and obviously liked the Brits.

We received a number of briefings on the history of Cypress and the fairly recent fighting between the Greeks (Orthodox Christians) and the Turks (Muslims) who had at one point after the Crusades ruled both Greece proper and Cyprus for hundreds of years. To say there was no love lost between the Cypriots and the Turks would be quite an understatement. Recent 20th Century fighting had pushed the Turks into an enclave in the northeast portion of the Island now separated by UN Peacekeeping forces along something called the Green Line. We visited the Green Line and saw firsthand the Cypriot and Turkish forces glaring at one another. Thirty years later I believe this is still the situation with United Nations Military Observers (UNMOs like I had been in Israel in 1973) sitting between the lines supposedly keeping the peace. The peace is really kept only because the two sides don't want to fight, with all the problems that entails, and face world opinion. This pointed up the problem between Christians and Muslims that the United States later saw in the Balkans. To me it solidified the fact that living with the Muslims is not fun, nor easy. Israel is not the only place in the world where confrontation and turmoil is rampant. Then, of course, we had our own 9/11 attack by radical Islamists, a portent of the future in the 21st Century. The visit to Cyprus was certainly an eye opener, in more ways than just running on the beach.

Our next stop was Amman, Jordan. By Mideast standards I found Amman to be a very nice, modern and relatively clean city. I was destined to return here a number of times while serving as the Chief of Plans at U.S. Central Command. The Jordanians were most open and hospitable and we were not subject to any anti-Israeli speeches. The Jordanian Army was quite professional and their Special Forces were very good. We received several briefings from the Jordanian SF commander, whose name now escapes me, but I remember being told that he was what they termed a "White Russian" Jordanian. I assume that had something to do with his family's ethnic background. He was a very smart soldier educated at Sandhurst in the UK, the British equivalent of West Point. It baffles me that the Jordanians continuously fared so poorly in their fighting with the Israelis. They had some first class military leaders and the Army appeared quite professional.

A large part of our stay in Jordan revolved around sightseeing. We visited an old Crusader castle west of Amman near a Royal Jordanian Air Force base. The castle itself was not very big but having stood there for 800 years it was rather impressive. The area around it was flat desert as far as the eye could see. The only reason the castle was there had to be, at one time, the presence of water within its walls. Then we headed south to see the ruins of Petra dating back to well before the time of Christ. Amazing place, Petra, and very well preserved. Most impressive how they had channeled water along the side of the very narrow walls of the canyon entrance and stored it in reservoirs inside the city proper. Petra had only one entrance, through that narrow canyon, and for centuries had defied many enemies' efforts at entry. The buildings and temples in the city proper were hewn into solid rock and were most impressive.

From Petra we continued to Aqaba on the Red Sea. Aqaba is interesting because it figured centrally in the World War I exploits of Lawrence of Arabia. He and the Arab army, such as it was, won a great victory over the Turks there in 1918. It has a sister city, Eilat, which is part of Israel, right next door. Both of these towns are major tourist sites for both countries. The two beach areas are divided, as I recall, by barbed wire. In 1983 there was no wall separating them at the beach unless my aged memory is truly failing me. I have no idea what is there today.

We were properly treated by our Jordanian hosts and put up in a first class tourist hotel. At dinner that night we were invited to go to Wadi Rum, to watch the sunset. This is the wadi where Lawrence formed the Arab army and launched their assault on the city during World War I. Sunset there was reputed to be a most striking event with the walls of the wadi changing color at various times as the sun slipped down over the Red Sea. Fortified with several jugs of gin and tonic and some snacks, escorted by a Jordanian major, four of us climbed into a van and took off for Wadi Rum. The rest of the gang chose to avail themselves of the sites in town. There was surely more booze there than we took with us to the wadi.

The ride out into the desert was unremarkable; when you have seen one desert you have sort of seen them all. But approaching the wadi was truly a beautiful sight. The walls rose up several hundred feet on both sides and one could perceive the narrowing of the wadi at a distance of some five to ten miles. Then the real surprise met our eyes. There in the middle of the wadi stood a true French Foreign Legion fort; shades of *Beau Geste*. It truly looked like a Hollywood studio set but it was for real. There were four young Jordanian conscripts fulfilling their responsibility to the nation manning the outpost. Two of them spoke very good English and were pleased to have visitors. This was not exactly like Grand Central Station and visitors were the exception not the rule. They augmented our provisions with fruits and nuts as we all sat and watched the sun set and the wadi change color as darkness slowly set in. It was a once in a lifetime experience and well worth the time and modest inconvenience of the ride. Several of the Jordanian soldiers expressed great interest in the USA and stated they intended to visit. This was a sentiment held by many Palestinians and Arabs that I had met back in 1973 and now again in 1983. How times have changed, at least among the radical Islamists.

We returned to Amman the next day and the following morning prepared to transition to Israel. En route we traveled to a site overlooking the Jordan Valley and the northern reaches of the Dead Sea. Here we were briefed on the history of the area and specifically Jordan's claim to the West Bank of the Jordan River. The briefings were professional and well done. Frankly no anti-Israeli invective was sensed in these talks; just facts as the Jordanians perceived them. We were shown lots of weapons and tanks were paraded, well not paraded but driven by. We were treated to a very nice lunch; nice except for the flies which were everywhere and quite anxious to visit our food and every uncovered portion of our anatomy. The Jordanians were very friendly and I took a liking to them, as I had Brigadier Salem Al Turk back at Seaford House. After lunch we were led down to the Dead Sea and a bridge over the Jordan River. There we left our Jordanian hosts and walked across into Israel and the waiting British Army attaché and a handful of Israeli military representatives (Israeli Defense Force-IDF).

From the Dead Sea crossing we were bussed up to Jerusalem. We stayed in a very nice, extremely clean hotel that dated back to the time of the British Mandate of Palestine (1920s -1940s). The first night we were feted by the IDF at a very nice cocktail party. In the course of the evening an attractive female IDF captain walked up to me and said that she wanted to welcome me back to Israel. Apparently one of the other members of the group had mentioned to her that I had been there in 1973 with the UN as an observer. Somehow we got into an exchange over the proper title of the UN Military Observer

Group and I insisted that it was UNTSO-Palestine, which was the proper name for the organization. Ascribing the name Palestine to it did not please the lady at all and after a couple of minutes she stormed off not to be seen the rest of the evening. In her mind the land was not Palestine, it was Israel. While technically she was correct, the name of UNTSO in 1973 was UNTSO-Palestine; that was non-negotiable.

The next day we were given a number of briefings and meetings that I remember little about with one exception to be addressed momentarily. I can tell you that construction around Jerusalem had gone gang-busters since I had been there ten years earlier; many more homes and apartments had sprung up all around the periphery of the city. The old city itself seemed unchanged overall. It was still like stepping back into Biblical times in many areas. As a group we visited the Wailing Wall, the Church of the Holy Sepulcher (still in need of repair) and the Dome of the Rock Mosque: nothing new there for me.

We moved on to Tel Aviv for more briefings and visits with high level Israeli officials. One specific briefing was given by the Minister of Defense (MOD). I cannot remember his name but he was born in the USA, spoke fluent English and was sharp as a tack. In the course of the briefing the issue of Syrian military support from the Russians came up. The MOD admitted readily that they estimated well over 5,000 Russian military advising and actually assisting to man and run some sophisticated systems; particularly the air defense command and control facilities. A Brit air commodore asked how they would handle this Russian presence should a war with Syria erupt. The MOD shrugged and said, "We would take them out; next question." The brigadier sitting next to me leaned over and quietly whispered, "He just announced World War III and didn't bat an eye." Such was the Israeli attitude toward survival in 1983.

From Tel Aviv we went by bus to an Israeli Air Force (IAF) base and were treated to some close up and very impressive scrambling of the latest Israeli fighters (originally American manufacture but modified to meet IAF requirements, I am sure). Sitting in bomb-proof shelters, the aircraft, pilots and ground crews could scramble and be rolling in no time at all after an alert was sounded. For our benefit they scrambled two fighters. It was a most impressive demonstration and showed clearly how serious the IAF took the threat from their neighbors. Flight time from Egypt and Syria was only a few minutes, especially in the case of Syria, and any delay could mean disaster for the nation. When the planes landed we were allowed to walk over and inspect them. A Brit air commodore looked at the air-to-air missiles hung under the wing and commented, "Well I'll be, U.S. Sparrow missiles with Israeli markings." One of our guides got a little hostile and insisted they were of Israeli design and manufacture. The RAF officer did not push the point, but I believed he was probably correct. The Sparrow was apparently top of the line air-to-air weaponry at that time. Personally I wouldn't know a Sparrow from a turkey. With this, our visit to Israel ended and it was on to Egypt and some real eye openers.

Egypt is an ancient place; Cairo a very dirty, crowded city, and some of what I describe may strike you as overly dramatic. I assure you it was far beyond the descriptions which follow.

We were met at the Cairo International Airport by the British attaché and a small team from the embassy. After paying the standard baksheesh (aka bribe) and being told our luggage would be taken care of (and in proper British fashion it was) we were whisked off into the almost nonmoving traffic of an ancient city then occupied by twenty plus million people; most of whom are poverty stricken fellahs (average citizens). It was amazing to watch the drivers cutting in and out and constantly honking at everyone and everything. One's first impression of Cairo is that the city could not get any dirtier, noisier, and more crowded or the drivers more rude. I was wrong in that impression, it would get worse.

They billeted us at a first class hotel and visited lots of tourist sites to include the Pyramids, the Sphinx, and were taken later to the Khan El Kalili to shop. I will return to the Khan in a few lines. The visit to Egypt was not all vacation and touristy stuff, either. Our itinerary included briefings at various government agencies, visits to military industrial complexes and a short side trip to the Suez Canal among other activities. I will tell you that while very important to world commerce the canal can't hold a candle to the engineering masterpiece the U.S. produced in Panama. I know I am comparing apples to oranges given the terrain differences but just wanted to bring that to the fore.

We were taken to the ministry that administered Egypt's oil reserves. The ministry was in an old British rule palace of sorts. In its day it was truly magnificent, once upon a time, maybe seventy years ago when the Brits kept order and added a degree of cleanliness to things. The building and grounds were somewhat run down and very dirty. Soap and water had never touched a wall in the place since the Brits pulled out. For a major government ministry building it was in my mind a disgrace. During a lengthy briefing several of us had to visit the men's room just down the hall from the minister's office. It was absolutely filthy. I won't say more except to mention that it almost made me sick. My Brit colleagues who visited the room agreed. It was appalling. I can't tell you what we heard at the ministry except that they wanted to find more oil. So does the whole world.

Our itinerary took us to several military industrial sites where tanks were rebuilt and those were quite impressive. Overall it appeared that maintenance and preventive maintenance to preclude breakdowns was not very good. But they were obviously making an effort to overcome a camel dung and wood society and come into the 20th Century and cope with steel and technology. If you looked at the cabs in Cairo as a guide then it is true that maintenance was not a top priority.

We took an evening dhow ride on the Nile and that was enjoyable. A dhow is a unique sail boat type vessel used for commerce and pleasure. I think this particular dhow was built around 1750, and reflected the accumulated dirt and paint of 230 plus years, but it did float and sail around, sort of. The drinks and chow, which we had brought, made the evening quite enjoyable and the sunset was spectacular. By the way, one had to be very careful and not drink the water or use any ice. The penalty for such a mistake was usually a very good case of Pharaoh's Revenge; not pleasant I assure you. None of us got sick but such was not to be my lot on one of my visits to Cairo when I served later at U.S. Central Command.

We also drove to and around the "city of the dead" in the middle of Cairo. This site is a real, and ancient, cemetery dating back many, many centuries. It has no water, no electricity and no sewer system. What it does have is a lot of people. In 1983 our Egyptian guide announced that somewhere around three million people lived, or more correctly existed, inside its boundaries. This was the 20th Century and yet there was this blight on the city of Cairo and the nation.

The Khan el Kalili is a covered street where tourists are privileged to support the Egyptian economy buying every kind of trinket and souvenir you can imagine. This street certainly dates back centuries and it shows. Gold was everywhere with shop keepers doing their best to entice tourists into their show rooms, such as they were. Brooches of Nefertiti, cartouches, scarabs and gold chains were plentiful and we all bought something. If it related to ancient Egypt, the Pharaohs or the pyramids it was reproduced and peddled to the tourists on the Khan. Brass bowls and trays of all kind were everywhere and well made. We visited several small plants just off the Khan where such items were produced. Each was done by hand in rooms that had not seen paint or cleaning in I have no idea how long. After leaving the Khan our Brit Royal Marine exclaimed, "Bloody hell, we certainly failed these people. We were here for 150 years and couldn't teach them about cleanliness, or repairing things. This whole place is so filthy it is a wonder it hasn't been devastated by the bubonic plague."

I could not argue with him on that point; the dust and dirt of centuries was everywhere.

We visited Alexandria up on the Mediterranean but I remember very little about that visit except the Nile ended there and we saw some truly nice remnants of ancient wonders of the world. Our next stop took us by plane from Cairo to Luxor and a visit to the Valley of the Kings. Luxor was tiny compared to Cairo, the streets wider and the traffic much reduced. We were put up in a quaint hotel that dated from the British time in Egypt around the late 1800s. It was exceptionally nice and well maintained. The corridors were quite wide, the ceilings high, the rooms large and clean. A *fellah*, usually quite old, sat on the floor in the corridor about every twenty yards waiting for a call from a guest for some service. These gents actually made decent money for their effort compared to the average *fellah* on the street. One morning when I was out for a run I noticed a woman in a burka walking about half a block ahead of me. She squatted right there on the sidewalk and as I approached from the rear, she stood and walked off leaving a steaming deposit of feces in her wake. The accepted societal norms in Egypt were certainly different than the UK or USA.

The Valley of the Kings was impressive. The trip out was most amazing in that the terrain and scenery was lacking any redeeming value. The area was desolate desert and it was hard to understand what brought the Pharaohs to be buried here. Maybe 3000 years ago it was forested, green and pretty, I can't say. However, when you have gone down into one tomb, no matter how ornate or well preserved you have once again seen them all. The people in those days certainly went out of their way to give their rulers a great send off to the nether world. Given that the labor was done for the most part by captive slaves maybe this should not be surprising. We visited three tombs and it was obvious that the Pharaohs had each competed to outdo their predecessors. The poor *fellah's* recruited, or enslaved, to build these tombs were never properly rewarded I am sure. Many thousands died in the process of construction; again, completely different societal norms. This about sums up my first trip to Egypt; it was not to be my last. We returned to the UK and life and learning at Seaford House.

58

WRAPPING UP A GREAT YEAR IN THE UNITED KINGDOM

We were into the last phase of the course and each Overseas Tour Group briefed the College on what we had seen and experienced. The briefings were enlightening but not surprising in the main. One point made by my Navy buddy Larry Andrews was that the only country in Africa they visited where you could flip a light switch or turn a water faucet and count on something happening was South Africa. The other countries they visited were lacking in infrastructure, quite backward and rife with corruption. It was about this time that we also turned in our papers for review. It was great to have that off my plate but I did enjoy researching and writing it. There were a number of interesting events I would like to relate that had nothing to do directly with the RCDS.

First we had a number of visitors come to the UK during our year there. Mary's Uncle George and her Aunt Pat were early arrivals and we had a great visit with them. Our old friends from the 101st Airborne at Fort Campbell and the 8th Special Forces, the Buyles came over and spent time with us. Then to cap it off, the Brooks, Johnny and Christine, came over. At that point Johnny had been promoted to major and was slated to become the Parachute Regiment Exchange Officer. There was one thread associated with all these visits in addition to visiting the hot tourist attractions. That thread was antique market shopping. Mary had become quite skilled at finding the good deals and bargaining with stall dealers. I think the stall owners at the Bermondsley Market saw her coming and retreated. She took all the ladies shopping and I can only say that they all went home with some new (read old) stuff. They had fun and Mary and Christine wound up one day at Seaford House with several large antiques that they needed help getting home. This was a sort of out of the norm happening at the stately and very proper Seaford House and the Head Porter had a good laugh over that one. Leave it to the Yanks to provide some levity within the College walls. All in all it was a super time for the ladies. Our visitors also helped drag us to other sites and areas reflecting the history of England and for that we were most appreciative.

I also made it a point of attending the major Auction Houses, especially Sotheby's. I had my heart set on acquiring a Martini Henry Rifle similar to those carried by the "Thin Red Line" (aka the British soldier) for many years. Guess I watched the movie *Zulu* too many times. Sotheby's was always having estate sales where weapons were available. I purchased several old, non-serviceable rifles from WWI, and finally successfully bid on a Martini Henry, single shot, lever action, .455 caliber cavalry carbine (carbine being a short rifle). It was in perfect shape and completely functional but only a fool would ever try to shoot it since no ammunition for it has been produced since the late 1800s. At any rate I had five weapons and a month before the Course ended I proceeded to the Embassy to have them shipped home. The Bureau of Alcohol, Tobacco and Firearms (BATF) representative there looked them over, said no problem: "These are nonfunctional relics, antique wall hangars, and I will be happy to ship them to you in the States." Now that was service and with a smile. But I had no orders at that point so I asked him to stand by and I would get him an address. We left it at that for the moment as I was expecting my orders to Fort Bragg to be the Special Operations Command G3 any day.

I also wanted to buy and ship home, in the worst way, an older, early 1950s, Jaguar. Well as I searched for something in my price range it became very obvious that if I shipped a car home it was not going to be a Jag. Finally I stumbled upon a 1967 Morris Minor, right-hand drive, garaged out near Heathrow and in mint condition. The price was right at 600 pounds (about $900) and along with it came a bunch of spare parts and two new fenders. I could not turn it down. It ran like a top and I loved it, right-hand drive and all. We then began worrying about shipping it back to the States. At that point we were three weeks from the end of the course and I still didn't have orders.

One day while at the college I got a call from Colonels Branch telling me that they were cutting orders sending me to the Pentagon to my old nemesis, the Deputy Chief of Staff for Operations (DCSOPS) Office. I asked the assignment officer if he held a "by name general officer request" for me to be the DCSOPS at SOCOM? He said something like, "Well you can call General Lutz and tell him you don't want to go there." I told him that I had given the general my word that I would be his G3 DCSOPS and I would not go back on that. I hung up.

About four days later I got a call from another assignment officer who said they were cutting the orders to the Pentagon. I asked very calmly, "Have you told BG Lutz that you aren't honoring his by name request for me?" His response was, "No, but _you_ can do that." I told him to pound sand, I wanted that job. He went on to say, "Look we aren't assigning you back to Bragg, you spent seven years there. You're a homesteader." I politely told him that Infantry Branch had left me there for seven years and that they had facilitated my assignmen.s and command there. Continuing, I told him, "I don't own a home there; I don't have a girlfriend there; you lads at the Office of Personnel Operations left me there; and I am not a homesteader." This time he hung up on me.

The next day I received a call from the head of Colonels Branch. The conversation was short and basically one sided and I will paraphrase: "This is Colonel Jones. I just got off the phone with BG

Lutz. He knows you aren't coming to be his G3. I just directed that orders be cut assigning you to U.S. Central Command in Tampa, FL, on jump status for duty as the Chief of Plans in the J5 Directorate." Then the line went dead.

I had just missed the Special Forces train that was about to take off like a rocket. I often wondered what my career would have looked like had I gotten that assignment or even if I had submitted and gone to the Pentagon. It matters not. I called the shots and don't look back with regret. Choosing to be with soldiers was what the Army was all about. I did that. Getting ahead in the Army is partly luck, partly availability, partly who you know and who knows you, and who you work for coupled with some degree of common sense and professional skill.

Now at least we knew where we were headed. We had orders in hand so we could get our household goods packed and shipped, the Morris Minor on a ship, the Mazda, also on a ship, on its way home compliments of the U.S. government. Lastly I could now get those antique, non-shootable guns in the mail. I stopped by the embassy, BATF office, and dropped off copies of my orders and was told, "Not to worry, I will get these guns in the mail shortly and all the paperwork for importing them taken care of. Have a great time in Tampa."

We shipped our Mazda 626 and it was waiting for us in Charleston when we arrived back in the States. I drove the Morris to the port at Portsmouth, filled out the shipping documents and paid another $600 to have it transported to Florida. We moved out of our house at Stevens Close and into an old but nice hotel in downtown Eastcote very close to the tube. Nick Lacey would stop by and pick me up as we continued our last few days trek to downtown London for class. Things at the college were rapidly winding down and learning was not the prime interest. It became more of a lengthy goodbye to buddies from around the globe we were not sure we would ever see again. It had been quite a broadening and unforgettable experience.

We flew back to the States arriving around the 18th of December ensuring a Christmas without roots, but we didn't mind because we would all be together. Initially we stayed at the MacDill Air Force Base guest quarters until the roaches drove the girls to insist on a change of location to a motel off base. Not an auspicious introduction to MacDill but it did get a lot better. I flew to Charleston and picked up the Mazda, and my son, releasing him from the clutches of the Citadel. He had become quite a man thanks to the system in vogue there for well over 150 years. Sadly, that "system" is changing and I fear not for the better.

Christmas was fun with all the family together again. Mary bought a scraggly bush of some ilk that we decorated with bows and other junk and called it our Charlie Brown Christmas tree. That tree stayed with us a long time before it ended up planted in a friend's back yard up in Spring Hill, Florida. I did visit CENTCOM over the holiday and saw my new office but there were very few folks around. We started looking for a new home to put down some roots. Between the holidays we stumbled on a rental right on the water with direct access to Tampa Bay. It was perfect for us and the transition to Florida was rapidly falling in place.

59

CENTCOM:
THE BEGINNING OF THE END

I was happy with my assignment to Central Command (CENTCOM) as you may deduce from what came before in this litany of happenings. I was satisfied not to be in the Pentagon. Not very career enhancing but it was my choice. I reported for duty mid-January 1984 to my new job and was quickly processed through the system. The U.S. CENTCOM had occupied a new building, close to the main gate of MacDill AFB, and far away from the original RDJTF location, an old B-52 "Alert Facility" known as the Mole Hole. I would be one of four Division Chiefs within the J5 Directorate working for Admiral, Lower Half–one star, Mac Gleim a former P3 aircraft driver (P3s were submarine hunters). He was sharp and a good guy but new to the joint arena and had not yet gotten into the swing of dealing with General Kingston (who by this time wore four stars). Kingston did not get his nickname of "Barbed Wire Bob" by being Mr. Nice Guy. Admiral Gleim was a geographic bachelor, his family was still in Jacksonville, and so he kept long hours.

When I finally got to the Plans section of J5 there were two rather interesting packages awaiting me.

One was a letter that I still hold, from COL Johnson, the Army Attaché in London, explaining that he had recently hosted GEN Kingston, Commander in Chief (CINC) CENTCOM for dinner. In the course of some heavy imbibing COL Johnson had told the general about me, my background, and how well I had gotten along with the Brits at the RCDS. General Kingston was married to a British lady and many years earlier in his storied career had been an exchange officer with one of the Brit Parachute Battalions. The general was now looking forward to my presence and services with the command. Oh wow, advance billing was not something I sought.

The second package was a rather large and long cardboard box in which I found the five rifles I had purchased at auctions in the UK. Shock of shocks, those relics had arrived at CENTCOM ahead of me. Another surprise would reach me in about four months relating to those antique firearms.

At any rate the Plans Shop had about twelve officers (representing all the services) and three enlisted administrative staff. At this point we had three word processors, nothing like today with one and in some cases two computers on every desk. There were three distinct elements in the Plans Division: Plans, Time Phased Force Deployment Data (TPFDD) and Compartmented Plans. Because of the sensitivity of the latter elements planning they were located in the Intelligence Directorate Special Compartmented Intelligence Facility (SCIF).

My initial office call with the CINC went well and I came out of his office feeling we would get along OK. I was wrong in that. We got along much better than OK. As long as you had your stuff in one bag and were willing to stand your ground when challenged, surviving Barbed Wire Bob was easy and could even be enjoyable. The deputy commander at that time was an Air Force two star, Bob Taylor, with whom I would interface on many an issue. He was a prince of a man and always gave me good counsel.

Much of what I did at CENTCOM Plans was highly classified, compartmented and for the most part nationally sensitive. Over the years, and thanks to open source books like Bob Woodward's, *VEIL, the Secret Wars of the CIA*, I now feel secure in relating some of those activities and incidents albeit in somewhat vague terms.

About two days after I reported to work, and long before I really knew much about my team, Admiral Gleim called me into his office to give me some guidance. He had been tasked by the CINC with a pretty tough assignment. The U.S. State Department and military had been negotiating for certain basing rights with a number of Middle Eastern nations for quite a while, with little success; at least no success that was being admitted. An opening for a dialogue with Oman had just been received. Problem was the Sultan of Oman's military was actually led by former British officers assigned to Oman by the UK Ministry of Defence. The Chief of the General Staff was a crusty old, hard-nosed four star Brit Army type, Sir Timothy Creasey. Sir Timothy was not a great lover of the U.S. meddling in Oman, or so Admiral Gleim had been led to understand.

My guidance was to get a team together, prepare strategies for our upcoming trip to Oman and brief Admiral Gleim on the proposed approaches. Working with several members of my new planning troops we put together several briefing packages that we thought might get our foot in the door. After a week of work, and long hours, we had several viable ideas. We ran them by the Admiral. They were not good enough; back to the drawing board. After another four days we were ready, and the admiral was happy with what we had done. I let each of the primary staff officers who had developed their talking points brief the boss. The troops seemed to like that and put even more effort into the project. I was impressed with the lads' work and acumen and felt we were ready. The admiral was still apprehensive about what to expect from our Brit/Omani counterparts and it showed. As for me, I must admit I was not looking forward to possibly crossing sabers with Sir Tim.

We flew to Oman, on a commercial plane, and arrived the day before talks were to begin. The country was pretty much desolate around the capitol, Muscat, with no trees, not even palms to speak of. And the temperature was somewhere around 110 in the shade, where there was any shade. But the capitol itself was clean by comparison to

Cairo and no traffic jams. As Mid-East countries go Oman wasn't all that bad. The hotel was very nice and after being met and welcomed by an Omani colonel we took some time to rest, let our body clocks adjust, and get ready for the next day's discussions. The following morning, dressed in suits and ties, in order to avoid questions concerning what American military folks were doing there, we were escorted to the Ministry of Defence. We were ushered into a nice, well air-conditioned conference room with a long rectangular table; the U.S. on one side and the Omani representatives on the other. At that point the senior Omani representative present was the head of the Omani AF, a UK RAF two or three star general. We imbibed of the necessary coffee and tea and stood around exchanging pleasantries awaiting General Creasey.

The general arrived promptly on time, introductions were made and he and the Admiral took their respective seats across from one another. Moments after sitting down Sir Timothy leaned forward and said, "Colonel, I must ask, is that an RCDS tie?" I had deliberately worn my school tie and immediately responded, "Yes, sir, I graduated last December." He immediately responded, "Well I think you and I need to adjourn for a little private talk; our respective teams can carry on here."

The admiral was flabbergasted as was I. I had hoped the tie might be an ice breaker but the thought of a private, without the admiral, meeting with Sir Tim never entered my mind. The general and I went to his office and talked RCDS and United Kingdom issues for perhaps two hours. I returned alone to the talks that had made more headway that morning than any previous meeting with any of our erstwhile Arab allies. At lunch the admiral asked me what we had talked about. For the life of me I could not remember what had transpired during that talk except in vague generalities. But, we left Oman with more in the way of support than we could have hoped for when we departed Tampa. The RCDS connection had helped us make inroads of great value to U.S. national security. The admiral and I got along famously after this little trip. General Kingston was amazed and quite pleased with the results of our visit and I think my bona fides were established firmly with him.

60
TELLING CENTCOM'S STORY
AND THE RCDS CONNECTION

Shortly after returning from Oman, General Kingston called me to his office along with Admiral Gleim. He told us he wanted me to go to Camberley, England and brief the British Command and Staff College on U.S. CENTCOM and what we were all about. He felt that my tour with the Brits would lend credibility to the information that the normal J3 briefing team might lack. The trip back to the UK was enjoyable and I was able to visit the RCDS while in London. The commandant at Camberley had been one of my classmates and we had a great time telling war stories about our year together. This was to be the first of several sojourns I took to various locales both in the U.S. and overseas selling our CENTCOM story. I got pretty good at it.

On one particular trip I briefed the Army War College at Carlisle Barracks, Pennsylvania. The briefing was well received but it was classified Top Secret and the Allied students could not attend. The Commandant of the College asked me if I could clean it up and give an unclassified version to the Allies. I spent the lunch hour purifying a version of the CENTCOM story and our capabilities and at 1300 I joined the Allied students and spouted our tale. The Commandant introduced me and provided a comment about my having served with the UN as part of UNTSO-Palestine during the 1973 War of Attrition. During the Question and Answer session one of the students asked me what the Russians were like during my 1973 experience. I pondered that for a second and responded that they were very much like us. Finally I said, "Some are tall, some short, some thin, some fat, all seeking a better life and a better life for their children"—or some other rather neutral words. Suddenly from the rear of the class room I heard, "Colonel, you are wrong. They are not nice people." I asked who was commenting and heard, "Brigadier Mustaffah Kamal Mohamed (a fictitious name), Turkish Army. We have lived next to the Russians for 500 years. They are not nice people nor are they like us." He promptly sat down, and I, at a loss for a proper response, promptly took the next question.

Our main thrust at CENTCOM was to deter the Russians from any more adventures beyond Afghanistan. Our planning focused on how we could get sufficient forces into the region quickly enough to counter any adventurism on the part of the Soviets. The crux of the issue was planes and ships to get us there and how the forces would flow to the area of responsibility. That ubiquitous Time Phased Force Deployment Document (TPFDD) that made or broke all the sexy planning and tactics one cared to strategize was the issue. Since my first encounter with TPFDD planning over three years earlier we had come a long way. Actually we had evolved to the point where our efforts were not pie in the sky but really executable war plans. Beyond that I will not comment but it is fair to say that Desert Storm in 1991 proved the validity of the efforts by so many planners in the early and mid-1980s.

Sometime in late spring, perhaps four months after leaving London, I received a letter from the Bureau of Alcohol, Tobacco and Firearms in Washington. It stated categorically that my request to import those five antique firearms had been turned down. I could not bring them into the U.S. Well, how about that; government bureaucracy at its best. And now they want to manage our health care.

In May 1984 there were some serious issues with a country in the Mid-East and it was of great concern to many western nations. We were informed that a team from the UK would be coming over for discussions on how this problem could be dealt with. It was to be headed by a former RCDS classmate, Air Commodore Eric Macey. I was tasked to take the lead along with several of my planners who focused on the subject nation and see what could be done. Eric and his team arrived and were billeted and introduced to my planners. He and I took off to my home to enjoy several gin and tonic, say hello to Mary and watch the sunset on Tampa Bay. Sitting on the back patio looking at Tampa Bay, we agreed between us that whatever happened in the next few days could not be any type of formal plan. Whatever was decided would remain close hold between our two nations.

In the end a "Conceptual Arrangement" was agreed to but not signed. It was a model of give and take by both parties and it did not, of course, exist. It took just four days to complete, all sixty pages of it. We briefed it to the admiral and CINC. Barbed Wire Bob gave it his blessing. Eric and his team returned to the UK with our arrangement. We had agreed that I should visit the UK for discussions with MOD representatives in about forty five days. The trip took place and all MOD staff seemed quite satisfied with what had been accomplished. Everything with the "Arrangement" appeared workable, was acceptable and it was on the shelf. At that point I was feeling pretty good and truly appreciated the value of the year I had spent at the RCDS. In my mind, Great Britain was, and remains to this day, a real and true friend of the United States.

About thirty days later we received a request from MOD that I return for more discussions. No further information was provided and both the CINC and Admiral Gleim were as puzzled as I was. Upon arriving at Eric's office in MOD he said, "Brace yourself, the Minister of Defence, Michael Heseltine, wants to see us." I could not imagine what the big chief wanted to say to me and I could only imagine the worst. Eric also seemed befuddled by this audience as we walked the hall to the meeting. I must comment that the minister's office was not quite what I expected, rather plain and not terribly impressive. That was far from my impression of Mr. Minister. He was quite sharp, to the point and impressive. After a few pleasantries and "attaboys" to Eric and me he said something like, "Maggie (Prime Minister Margaret Thatcher) is very pleased with this un document you two put together. She asks that you tell Ronnie (none other than our President Ronald Reagan) how pleased she is with what has transpired and how much she appreciates your efforts." That ended the meeting. Well, I was not just amazed, I was flabbergasted! How in hell was I supposed to tell this to the president? The UK operates totally differently than our bureaucracy. Access to the highest levels is not just a fluke over there, it is part of the system, or at least was in those days. Eric and I went out and had a couple of drinks and patted each other on the back. We had accomplished a lot and felt it was meaningful. Upon return to Tampa I went immediately to General Kingston and told him what had happened. He laughed and told me to relax. He would get the message from Maggie to Ronnie. I can only assume that somehow he did that.

MY FIRST AND ONLY ENCOUNTER IN THE "TANK"

In late 1984 the Compartmented Plans shop put together a very dicey plan directed by General Kingston but the guidance to create this baby could have come directly from the Pentagon. Admiral Gleim wasn't even read in on it. It called for a clandestine Special Forces operation in a semi friendly country. When the plan was finished and the CINC liked what he saw we, just the two of us, flew to D.C. in a U-21 aircraft, to brief it to the JCS and the Secretary of Defense (Sec Def) in the famous or infamous "tank." If you have ever heard of the "tank," but never seen it, I was somewhat disappointed. I had always envisioned some sort of Star Wars technologically advanced briefing room where the Joint Chiefs and other key leaders of our nation got the hot info. To my complete surprise it was not that, at least not in 1984. It was a simple conference room with rear view display and a podium off to one side. I had the Chief of Compartmented Plans prepare a short, precise but full explanation of what the plan called for. I was assuming that I would be the briefer; that was a bad assumption. No way was some upstart CENTCOM weenie going to brief the Secretary of Defense on Joint Staff turf. Our plan and my briefing slides were taken away by an Army colonel from the Joint Staff, and the general and I went to lunch.

In the afternoon we assembled in the tank with the general and me off to the side away from the main conference table and pretty close to the briefer. I assumed that would be to facilitate helping him answer questions about the plan. The Joint Chiefs and Caspar Weinberger entered the room, were seated and with no further ado the briefer started. "Cap" Weinberger was famous for apparently sleeping through briefings; eyes closed the entire time. That proved no different this day. Except that the Sec Def may have appeared asleep but I honestly think he was taking it all in. The problem with this briefing was that it bore almost no resemblance to what was in the plan or the briefing that I had provided them. The only thing that resembled our plan was the fact that the title was the correct name. I was shocked. I looked at General Kingston questioningly but he simply nodded and conveyed a sense of "just be patient." When the briefer finished there were several inane questions and equally irrelevant answers and then Cap stated softly that the plan was approved. I turned to the general and quietly whispered, "Sir, they don't have a clue what they just approved. That briefing was pabulum." He nodded but did not respond.

Late that afternoon, in some off-the-beaten-path room in the Pentagon, the CINC and I sat with two civilian reps from the State Department while he informally explained the plan to them. They seemed to understand but I truly can't say for sure. If head nods and a few grunts represented understanding then maybe they did understand. We returned to Tampa and the plan was put on the shelf and was never executed. Personally I was quite satisfied with that result. It was a questionable undertaking in the extreme and could have been an embarrassment to the U.S. not to mention possibly getting some good men killed. It has never bothered me that I did not return to the "tank" for another briefing, ever.

I am somewhat hesitant to relate this next story but feel it is important enough that it bears being told and merits a separate chapter. Somehow General Kingston, through an unknown source, had an in with a special organization up in Virginia that was quite clandestine and at that point known to only a select few. This element has been written about in a number of books that are open literature and has over the years gone by any number of cover names. At the time of this happening it was generally referred to as the "Secret Army of Northern Virginia" because it was located in that general area, i.e. the operational area of General Robert E. Lee's boys in gray.

In late summer 1985 General Kingston called me in and told me that we were to get some clandestine support from this organization. He further directed that I restrict tasking this agent to obtaining only information for our main Operations Plan for which we had no other source. One morning my Navy petty officer, administrative assistant, came to the door and told me that I had a visitor, in civilian clothes who was a little different. In walked a dapper, bearded gentleman in a three piece suit who I had known as a lieutenant in Vietnam in 1967. After telling Screaming Eagle Nam war stories we got down to the issue at hand. Frankly, I was hesitant to send a man out on the mission I had in mind, and I told him so. After listening to what was needed he commented to the effect that he felt he could handle that. We went to see the CINC, just the two of us, and after hearing the proposed mission he also asked our agent if it was possible. Again the troop responded, "Yes, I am comfortable getting you those answers." He departed saying that he might be gone several months.

One day in the fall of 1985 my admin assistant came to the door once again and announced, "Sir, the bearded one is back." He was the same dapper gent I had dispatched on a nearly "mission impossible" two plus months before and he was all in one piece. Along with General Kingston the three of us went to the Special Compartmented Intelligence Facility. Standing before a map of the country in question we got the answers we had requested. With one exception, as I recall, we got everything we had asked for. The CINC and I were impressed to say the least. And much needed planning data for a major OPLAN was in the bank, so to speak. My planners were quite inquisitive as to how we got the planning information that I passed on to them as gospel. I never revealed the source. We sent this soldier out one more time and again he returned with the goods. He will appear in this saga once more shortly having a new job.

(NOTE: Later, when I was a civilian contractor, I worked with and socialized with this gentleman, then a full colonel, at both the Joint Special Operations Command at Fort Bragg and United States Special Operations Command at MacDill AFB. He was the closest thing to James Bond in uniform that I ever met personally. He was a great soldier and an American patriot who died much too young. I must add that his death was of natural causes doing something that he loved doing.)

63

THE HANDWRITING ON THE WALL, 1986

n 1983 and 1984 I had been selected as an alternate on both the Infantry Brigade and Special Forces Group Command Lists. In neither year was I activated. There are so few Infantry brigade and SF group commands that unless you are a designated commander the chance of being activated is next to nil. Folks just don't turn down these commands as they are a necessary step if one hopes to have any chance at being a general officer.

One day General Kingston called me to his office. When I entered and reported he tapped a rather thick file on his desk and asked me, "Colonel, do you know what this is?"

I responded, "Sir, it looks like a personnel file."

"Yes it is, in fact it is yours," he stated. He went on to say that I had more of a picket fence file than he did; lots of ups and downs.

"You did some interesting career moves and I sense managed to irritate a few generals along the way," he said. "Guess you liked being with soldiers. I am doing my best to get you a brigade command. Now get out of here." It was that short and sweet. I thanked him and left the office but was not optimistic about ever commanding and being back with soldiers at the real dusty boot level.

Shortly after this, in 1985, a source called me and asked me if I could meet him at Fort MacPherson in Atlanta. I always had a reason to go to Fort Mac since our Army component, Third U.S. Army, was located there. After a morning of planning discussions with Third

Army planners this source met me for lunch at the PX snack bar. He told me that what he had to say was strictly off the record. He had been involved with the latest Colonels' Command Selection Board. He went on to say that he shouldn't be telling me this but I was about to be an alternate for both Infantry and Special Forces commands on the next list. He told me one particular general that we both had known at Fort Bragg, had done everything he could to get me a command that year. It just could not be done. From my days at Infantry Branch I knew the degree of horse trading that goes on at these boards and was not surprised by what he told me. I thanked my friend and two weeks later came out on the Colonel Command List again as an alternate for both SF and Infantry commands; another year with two shots at the brass ring.

In the interim I asked a buddy at Colonels Branch to do a file review and give me the real bottom line on my chances for command. What I got back was about what I expected with several somewhat surprising exceptions. I wrote down all that he had to say and still have those notes in my personal records. His comments included:

> You have ridden to the sound of the guns more than most to include the 1973 War in Israel. You have more than your share of overseas time. Your file shows probably too much light force time in the Airborne and Special Forces. The Board this year was not Airborne oriented. The swing right now is back to light forces. Your education could be looked upon as not very Army oriented with the Navy Command and Staff College and the Royal College of Defence Studies. Your real problem is General Meloy's 1973 report from Fort Benning and again his first report on you as a battalion commander in 1981. The three block for potential is a killer even though his second report puts you back in the top block and says you are his best battalion commander. We need to do a

better job of teaching our senior officers that when a new efficiency report system is started, "first year" reports do hurt. You look super for possible pick up next year for an SF command. You have a great reputation there. The Infantry command possibility is not as good. Just keep doing what you are doing and doing it well. You have a great lineup of raters; a Navy 1 star, a Marine 2 star and an Army 4 star. That can only help.

I asked him where I stood on the then active alternate list. He replied, "You are in the TOP third." The surprising parts to me were the comments about riding to the sound of the guns and more than my share of overseas time. I felt I had not gone often enough. The issue of Army schooling being a little thin did not surprise me. The last, only really Army school I "graduated from" was the Infantry Basic Course, having been taken out of the Advanced Course two months before graduation to go to Infantry Branch. In my early days going to Special Forces didn't really count as an Army school. Special Forces were the bastard stepchildren of Mother Army. I reflected on the info for a few days and then began seriously, really seriously for the first time, thinking about retiring.

One day an old friend stopped by to visit. He was at MacDill for a meeting at Readiness Command. In the course of our conversation he mentioned that he had run into Wayne Downing in Europe. At that time Wayne was a full colonel commanding a brigade in Germany. Apparently they were discussing old friends and my name had come up. My buddy told me that Wayne had made a comment to the effect that, "Yes, I know Larry, good guy. He and I disagreed one night over an issue; he was right and I was wrong." Apparently Wayne did not elaborate on that comment. I can only assume that he was referring to the night at Aberdeen SFOB at the end of the Delta evaluation. I would meet and visit with Wayne over the years many times but he never made such a comment directly to me. On the other hand there is no way my buddy made that story up. He had to have heard it directly from Wayne. My friend did not have even an inkling about Wayne and I being involved in the Delta testing.

64

A NEW CINC AND A
NEW CULTURE AT CENTCOM

General Kingston's retirement was announced for later in 1985. While some folks breathed easier I would miss him personally. His replacement was to be a USMC four star, George B. Crist. His reputation as a hard-nosed, hard to deal with, self-centered and unpleasant man marked his advance billing. He had made a reputation as a political general and confidant of Ronald Reagan. We were told he had been a sort of personal advisor and spy during the Grenada invasion reporting directly to the president. He had served as the Vice Director of the Joint Staff and also a short stint at Headquarters USMC, in some staff position. Those assignments had painted a picture that was less than flattering; just not a nice personality. Several of my Marine buddies were very upset to hear he was going to replace Barbed Wire Bob. They were quite ready to leave CENTCOM before he arrived. As I recall none of them escaped. I felt that surely he couldn't be that bad. He was to prove me wrong.

In the late summer of 1985 we conducted a major exercise in the Mojave Desert. I forget the name but it was significant for two major events. First, one of my old classmates from the RCDS, Major General James Templar, then a member of the UK Ministry of Defence Staff, was coming over as an observer. I was assigned to be his escort. James was a very "proper troop" and a gunner (read artillery man) and we had a super relationship. You may remember that our family spent a weekend at his home, an old Church of England parsonage, discussed earlier in this writing. We met out in California and traveled all over the exercise area seeing whatever he wanted to see. We witnessed a major parachute operation observing, a full brigade jump, from a hill about a mile away. It was a very impressive operation until a major disaster befell the 82nd Airborne troops that I cannot forget.

We had twelve troops killed, dragged to death on a drop zone (DZ) with no apparent wind. It later came to light that there was a wind shear coming down from a mountain pass that was producing winds of over fifty miles an hour in the middle of the DZ. At the leading edge of the DZ, where the DZ safety officer was located the wind machine recorded two to five knot winds. Not a safety issue; perfect jump winds. As an aside, General Kingston got in hot water when he told a reporter when questioned about this incident: "That's why they get $55 a month hazardous duty pay. Parachuting is dangerous." While the statement was irrefutably true, that comment was not well received in Washington. Nonetheless a dozen troopers from the 82nd lost their lives in this tragic accident.

The second happening was a bit of an embarrassment to me. At another jump, later in the exercise, the jumpers from the 2nd Ranger Battalion, were assembling after the drop. I had mentioned to General Templar that the troops would be dropping their parachutes along the road that ran the entire center of the DZ before they double timed off to their unit assembly points. I made the comment since it just made sense in the heat of the desert to get rid of those heavy chutes as quickly as possible. The road was there and it was the right call. That's the way I would have made it happen. James suddenly said, "I say Larry, those lads seem to be carrying their parachutes with them wherever they are headed." I borrowed his field glasses and sure enough the troops were carrying their chutes along with all their gear as they double timed off the DZ. In the desert heat this was, to me, almost criminal. Leaving the chutes along that center line road for pickup later by a work team made all the sense in the world. I told James I really wanted to go down and see what prompted this action. We hopped in the jeep and drove down to the valley floor. We found the battalion commander at the second stop. It turned out to be LTC Keith Nightingale who had been the D Company commander in the 1-502nd in Nam in 1971 when I was the battalion operations officer. (I believe my memory serves me correct in that.) I commenced to chew him out in rather colorful language for abusing his troops when he said, "Sir, I agree with you, this was not my idea. The regimental commander ordered that we double time with our gear and parachutes to the assembly area." I was dumbfounded by the response but at that point there was nothing I could do about it.

James enjoyed his stay and told me off line that CENTCOM certainly displayed the makings of a credible force if it ever had to be called on to fight. He had visited armor units, airmobile elements and straight infantry troops in addition to the Rangers and 82nd Airborne as well as watching USAF fighters and transport planes doing their thing over the Mojave. With the exception of the Navy element he had been exposed to the full gamut of forces available to the CINC. I sensed that he took back to the UK a good report on CENTCOM and its capabilities.

As General Kingston departed in mid-1985, so did Admiral Gleim, the J5. He was replaced by Navy Commodore (later Admiral) Hal Bernsen, another good man and pretty much another unflappable personality. Also about this time, Major General Bob Taylor, the DCINC, retired and was replaced by AF Major General Davis C. Rohr. General Rohr and I were to become traveling companions as I will relate. He had a totally different personality than General Taylor but we got along well. It was a sort of changing of the guard as General George Crist, USMC, became the new CINC.

There used to be a TV program called "The Naked City" that had a line in its introduction referring to "six million stories in the Naked City"— aka New York. Well there may not have been six million stories about General Crist but there were a lot. I will try to honestly relate some that I lived through.

General Crist was a cadaverous looking man who chain smoked constantly, one cigarette smoldering in the ash tray as he lit the next. He also, as I recall, drank more coffee than I did and that is saying a lot. Several days after he arrived at CENTCOM I was summoned to his office without Admiral Bernsen. That surprised me. When I entered he had his head down, cigarette in his mouth dangling loosely, his right hand on his coffee cup and his glasses very low on the bridge of his nose perched precariously as if about to fall. He appeared to be reviewing a document. I announced myself and stood there for about thirty seconds with no recognition of my presence on his part. He slowly looked up and greeted me with, "Colonel, you and General Kingston have got it all wrong. I have been privy to the real intelligence about the threat and what they intend to do. You have our forces oriented in the wrong direction." With that he gestured with his arm in the air indicating the direction the bad guys would attack from. I asked him how that was possible given the geography of the region. He told me that I didn't know what I was talking about. He had gotten the real intelligence from a certain three letter agency. I responded, "Begging your pardon, sir, but I believe General Kingston and I both got the same briefings." The general then told me to get them down here and we will settle it.

As I left his office I knew I was in trouble. It was obvious every time the new CINC looked at me he saw a big K emblazoned on my forehead. I was Bob Kingston's boy, not his. My Irish luck had once again abandoned me. I informed my boss about this meeting before inviting the Washington three letter agency to come give us a briefing.

The briefers from a certain agency came down to give us the D.C. gospel. The CINC and I, again just the two of us, went to the SCIF for the briefing. When it was over the CINC stood up, thanked the briefers and departed without a word to me. At the next planning session, with all concerned, including Admiral Bernsen, in attendance, the CINC commented to the effect, "Well now that we understand how the threat intends to attack and the direction he will take we just need to adjust things a little." There was no major readjusting of the current planning document. Just enough tweaking would be done to make it Crist's plan, not Kingston's. When the meeting ended I sat there justified but also fully cognizant that the CINC and I were going to have problems. General Crist was an interesting study. The days ahead were not going to be a pleasant time for Colonel Redmond.

Redmond's Rule #23 — Never argue with a 4 star; it's like wrestling with a pig, you lose and get dirty.

I remember one Saturday I was the Acting J5, the admiral being away on a trip to the Mid-East. Colonel Butch Neal, USMC, who was a fellow Division Chief, Political Military Division, came to the office door and said his son was participating in a wrestling match that morning and he hoped to go watch the match. But, he added he had an action paper up in the Command Group and hated to leave till the CINC sees it. I can't now recall the nation that the paper related to but I had signed off on the action as it came through the office. I told Butch I could handle any question that might come up. I told him to go to the match. Butch lived in Pinellas County, quite a distance from Tampa and MacDill AFB. About two hours later I had a call from the CINC's executive officer asking to have Colonel Neal report to the CINC. I went to the CINC's office and approached the old man. I told him I was the Acting J5, Colonel Neal was attending a sporting event with his son, and that I was knowledgeable of the action before the CINC now for approval. I asked what his question was. He responded, "You're not Colonel Neal, I want to see Colonel Neal." End of that discussion.

I returned to my office, then called Butch and explained what had just happened. Being a good Marine and a super officer he responded that he would be back as soon as possible. When he arrived we both went in to see the general. It was the usual head down, cigarette dangling from his lips, glasses perched on the bridge of his nose routine. We stood there awhile. He looked up and asked, "Colonel, is this your action?" Butch responded that it was. General Crist picked up his pen, initialed the approved block and handed it to Butch. We were both dumb struck. Not a question about the action, not a word, nothing. He then returned to reading whatever he had been reviewing when we walked in. As we got into the foyer outside the office I tried to apologize to Butch that I could not handle this without his presence. Butch said that it wasn't me, it was the CINC. I don't recall exactly what was said but it had something to do with the blatant abuse of power. He also said and I quote, "I am going to retire and go back to Hull, Massachusetts and tend lobster pots." Fortunately for the U.S. military, and our nation, that didn't happen. Butch went on to be a general officer, returned as the DCINC at CENTCOM and finally retired as the Assistant Commandant of the Marine Corps with four stars. He was a gentleman, a friend and a true patriot.

General Crist also had a habit of calling, out of the blue, and directing someone to accompany him on various short trips, sometimes overnight. We all got in the habit of keeping a small bag and a change of uniform in the office. Such a call came one day and I grabbed my gear and headed out to the flight line where there was to be an aircraft waiting. Sure enough a U-21 twin prop plane was standing by. Also waiting was a very curious Major General Davis Rohr. He asked me what was up and I replied I didn't have a clue. We were both in the dark as to our destination and the purpose of the trip.

The CINC arrived, joined us on the aircraft and without a word started working on papers. General Rohr and I both did not think to ask the pilots what our flight plan called for. So we were in the dark till we arrived at Andrews AFB in Maryland near D.C. Not a word passed between us till we landed and finished taxiing when the CINC said, "Ok, let's go." We drove to the Pentagon and established ourselves in one of the suites designated for Unified Command Commanders and other VIPs. A few minutes later the CINC came out of his office, stopped and looked at us both and, rubbing his chin, said, "I need a message for the chairman (Chairman of the Joint Chiefs) that says XXXX." He then disappeared out the door and down the hall. General Rohr and I labored over the draft for about thirty minutes before General Crist returned. He sat down, put on his glasses and went over our efforts to read his mind. He liked some of our words and ideas, other parts he rewrote. He handed it to one of the administrative assistants to be put in the proper form to be sent to the chairman. When it was done he signed it, stood up and said, "Ok, let's go." We returned to Andrews and flew back to Tampa. Little was said on the ride back but General Rohr did get some conversation going about a project that he and I had been designated to head up. Well, he headed it up, I was just his gopher; more on that to follow.

A few months after the change of command General Crist began firing people. Literally firing briefers and stating, "I don't want to see that officer again. Get him (in some cases her) out of this command." The J1 personnel officer, Air Force Colonel Gene Gardner, and a good guy, tried to explain that some of these officers had only been here a few months of what was programmed to be a three year assignment. They could not be reassigned. The CINC was adamant these folks were persona non grata and he had better never see them again. Unreasonable, yes, but true. They set up a holding area (nicknamed, by me, the "leper colony") out at the old Mole Hole where these lepers were held in purgatory. At one point I think there were nearly twenty officers of all services hidden away out there. I was told they basically did nothing but check in daily and read books. I strongly suspect they did work for their respective J Staff but never set foot back in the Headquarters nor put their names on an action paper. The Plans troops escaped this fate initially but finally one of my best planners, an Army LTC, smart, articulate and quick on his feet said something that fired up the CINC and off to the colony he went.

One night around 2300 I received a call telling me to be at the general's quarters at 0500, he had an action to be worked. I arrived on time not having a clue as to what was up. Today I only remember that his wife, a most gracious lady, was there and got us both coffee. At some point the general left the kitchen and his wife looked at me and asked, "How can you put up with him?" Well I had no choice, but I thought, "How can you put up with him?" but I kept that one to myself. It happened, and such was life with George B. Crist. As I said earlier he proved to be every bit as difficult as his pre-billing had said he was. I just did not believe it was possible

65

A SPECIAL PROJECT AND
OTHER EXOTIC THINGS

General Rohr and I were selected to support a series of compartmented programs (close hold special access to a limited few) with two countries in the CENTCOM area of responsibility (AOR). Every three months we led a planning team to each of the countries we were working with. I have flushed from my memory exactly when and what we did but the whole affair was truly remarkable for what we accomplished. A book was written about these activities, which took in a much broader area of the globe than just our AOR. We were a small part of a much bigger program. At the time of its publication the book created quite a stir but at that time I was unaware of any linkage to General Rohr's or my efforts. I was reminded of the existence of this book years later by a former team planner and told that perhaps I should read it. I acquired a copy after I had retired from the Army and was flabbergasted by what it contained. The three programs that I had worked were all explained there in detail. It was a bull's eye. They can put me on a polygraph, the info was not leaked by me.

General Rohr had the lead in this effort and my role was to prepare the team for each visit to the two countries in our AOR that we were working with. One country had two programs that related to it. The general and I traveled to D.C. and the Pentagon for briefings and guidance from the Joint Chiefs of Staff J5 before each trip. I must state categorically that the issues we worked were good, and to this day, I feel in our nation's and our allies' best interest. Due to the sensitive nature of these programs I will say no more.

Being an Air Force two star, General Rohr got some special perks when he flew USAF aircraft. We usually traveled to Europe, most comfortably, by C-5 and we both had private cabins. Yes a mini cabin with desk, chair and bed. This was the way to cross the Atlantic. Prior to these trips I did not realize that many C-5s had private executive cabins in the front on the upper floor. We would leave Dover AFB in Delaware, fly to Germany then take British Air or Lufthansa to the first country we were to visit. There we would meet the rest of the team. Although we were working with friendly nations on these projects we had to be very circumspect and careful. Those nations had their own agendas. We always assumed that our hotel rooms were bugged and conducted all our planning discussions in a secure room at the Embassy. On occasion the general and I would step out on the balcony of our hotel rooms with the cacophony of traffic in the national capitols drowning out our whispered talks. It was effective, and not too dangerous nor James Bondish. I never found a "bug" in my hotel room but then I am not a trained operative and would not know exactly what a planted listening device might look like. My time with SF had given me a rudimentary understanding of what to look for but I was and remain no expert. We all did use the hair in the briefcase and suitcase trick and never found any of them disturbed. You could not be too careful even with friends.

On several occasions I stopped in Cairo as part of other actions we had ongoing with the Egyptian military. I always made it a point to meet up with MG Hossam Al Zatar one of my classmates at the RCDS. He was at that time the Chief of the Cairo Air Defense Sector. I recall one night we went to dinner at the Cairo Hilton. Very nice hotel and we both were in our Class A uniforms, medals and all. During dinner Hossam suddenly jumped up and ran across the room to a short, grizzled, rotund older gentleman in a Brit para sweater that had several holes in it. If I had seen him on the street I could easily have assumed that he was a beggar. When Hossam and this gentleman got to the table I stood. I was very glad I did. Hossam said, "Field Marshal Abu Gazala I would like you to meet my dear friend Colonel Larry Redmond." Now for those who don't remember him, or never heard of him, Abu Gazala was "the" power in Egypt, commander of all the military in the mid-1980s and a real friend of the U.S. We chatted for several minutes and then the Field Marshal excused himself. Another amazing happening that flowed from my year in the UK and attendance at RCDS.

Hossam took me shopping on the Khan El Khalili several times. Most of the gifts I selected for Mary are still in her jewelry box or hanging on the walls at home. He and I would go to selected stores, pick out items that I liked and then leave. His aide would then go in and purchase the items in Hossam's name at perhaps half the price. Tourists were always ripped off, but the rip off was a onetime only good deal in the visitors mind, so it was a win-win for all. It sure helped the Egyptian economy, of that there is no doubt.

During one such Cairo stop over, early in the morning, I went out for a run along the banks of the Nile. This was a normal happening for me in those days. As I trudged along, I was never a fast runner, taking in the sights and smells of Cairo I sensed something was different, amiss, not quite right. I looked around for a car following me or another jogger or walker approaching. Nothing appeared out of the ordinary. No nefarious looking characters were lurking ahead. Then I glanced down on the sidewalk to my right and toward the river bank. There, running stride for stride with me was the biggest rat I had ever seen except the capybara that we had killed and eaten back in 1965 in Air Force Tropic Survival School in Panama. I was not sure whether to stop, bolt away into the street to the left or what. Before I could decide on a course of action Mr. Rat turned sharply to his right and disappeared into the grass along the river bank. That was the last time I jogged along the Nile.

On several trips General Rohr and I stopped in Saudi Arabia to brief selected folks on what was going on about which they had a need to know. I can tell you in those days Saudi Arabia was, for me at least, a strange and unpleasant place. The restrictions on women were truly frightening. Basically any woman on the street not in a burka was a foreign national and not a Muslim. Saudi women could not go out without an escort, drive a car, nor ride in an elevator alone with a strange man. And those restrictions were just the tip of the iceberg. Walking the streets of Riyadh was an experience. One could never be sure that the "religious police" approaching you were not going to look upon some action on your part as offensive to Islam and start beating you with their canes. They were the final arbiter of right and wrong under Sharia Law. It was not my cup of tea. I have no plans to return to Saudi Arabia.

The bearded one, now cleanly shaven, and working on the joint staff reentered the picture. He was involved with a very sensitive activity involving one of the countries in our area of operations. Several of us were read in on it so that we knew what was happening and could preclude any conflict with the project. General Crist was not happy that we weren't running this activity but quite frankly it was something we didn't need to be doing. Aware of it yes, for all the right reasons, but running it no. Enough said.

When I had first arrived at CENTCOM, Special Operation Command Central (SOCCENT) was headed up by Colonel George Marachek. Colonel Marachek was a well-known figure in SF circles. We got along OK but George was a strange duck and I had heard, from other SF buddies, some stories about his activities in Nam that gave me concern. George wangled an assignment as the Army attaché in Somalia and departed.

His replacement at SOCCENT was a super SF soldier, Colonel Jerry King. Jerry had quite a black side background in special operations and was a true clandestine operator. We worked together on a number of enhancements to our major war plan that greatly improved SF support to that effort. Jerry and I would become good friends and jointly endure life under General Crist. The general did not like Special Forces or Green Beret soldiers.

66
THE DECISION:
FIND THAT SECOND CAREER

In the summer of 1986 Colonels Branch called and opened a dialogue about my next move that was scheduled for winter. As always they were talking D.C. and the Army Staff. After discussing things with Mary, and having the family established in Tampa with two girls in school, I made the decision that it was time to step aside and let some younger troop have my eagle. At this point I had been a colonel almost six years and that was one quarter of my entire career. I did not want to end up as the base commander at some out of the way post, or a grizzled old colonel advisor to some National Guard or Reserve command somewhere. I told the assignment officer that I intended to transition to mufti (civilian clothes) and that I would retire before June 1987 if they would just allow me to stay at CENTCOM. They agreed. My intention was to seek a second career that brought in enough money, coupled with my retired pay that would allow me to send the girls to college and live decently.

Redmond's Rule #24 – Finding a job is a job.

I prepared my resume, studied all the appropriate books on transitioning and talked to anyone who might provide guidance. I began answering ads from the Sunday papers and talking to all the defense contractors in the Tampa area. With Readiness Command, the Joint Deployment Agency (JDA) and CENTCOM all located at

MacDill AFB there were lots of defense contracting opportunities; or so I thought. From summer through late fall I pushed hard looking for that second career. Nothing materialized although MITRE, SAIC and CSC all interviewed me more than once. I tried every avenue I could. I almost had a job as a trainer working for United Services Automobile Association (USAA) in Tampa. Colonel (RET) Joe House, who had been with me at XVIII Airborne Corps, was the southeast Region Manager for USAA. He wanted to hire me but could not get the money for the position put in his budget. After literally fifty or sixty interviews, from which nothing materialized, I was beginning to get frustrated. Surely I had something to offer someone.

Several interesting things did take place during these few months that are worthy of relating.

One day I was home at lunch, all alone in the house and looking at the morning paper job opportunities; feeling somewhat discouraged I might add. There was a small, one inch long, one column wide, ad stating: (nearby) County looking for Deputy Director of Corrections. I thought; wonder what this is all about? I called the number and spoke to a gentleman in the county personnel office. After hearing my background he asked if it would be possible to come for an interview. Well since it was not like, just next door, we set up an interview for later in the week.

I arrived for the interview and found three people waiting to meet me. One turned out to be originally from Columbus, Ohio and that seemed to help a little in terms of breaking the ice. The interview was sort of going in circles until the gent from the personnel office said, "Look, Colonel, let me be completely frank. We have a great Director of Corrections, very competent. He was a second string All American football player, has a master's degree in Penology, is a super public speaker and gets along with all the county commissioners. He handles the public a lot better than most. The problem is he is black and has trouble dealing with the red neck guards. We need someone who can kick ass and keep the guards in line. Do you mind carrying a gun as part of your duties?" I laughed, thanked him for his candor and told him that would not be a problem reference carrying a weapon. I received a call that night stating that I was one of the two finalists and the gent who called said, "I think you will get the job." The next morning I got a call saying the sheriff had selected the other candidate. He lived in the county, I did not. Politics had reared its head.

The second incident is also politically embroiled. Several months earlier, just after I started the job search I had interviewed with Mrs. Phyllis Busansky, Personnel Director of Hillsborough County. I interviewed with her for a position with the county but there were no jobs for someone with my talents open at that time. Phyllis was a great lady and running for county commissioner against a reputedly unsavory opponent. I decided to support her campaign and did so working very hard on her behalf.

One morning while the campaign was still on I came downstairs and Mary handed me a cup of coffee and said, "Congratulations, you made the front page of the Tampa Tribune." It had to be a joke was all I could think. Wrong. There was my name, Colonel Larry Redmond, a finalist for the job of Hillsborough County Administrator right on the front page. I had not applied for the job! I assumed Phyllis had a hand in that newspaper report. Nothing was to come of it and to this day I am not sure if that is fortunate or unfortunate.

(NOTE: She did win the election and she asked me to serve as one of her two representatives on the Hillsborough "Shadow County Commission." I accepted and met monthly with all the other Shadow Commissioners working various issues and papers on her behalf and providing recommendations to the whole commission. When Phyllis moved on to bigger and better things, her replacement, Ed Turanchik, asked me to stay on as one of his reps. I did this for seven years and was approached several times to run for commissioner myself. In each instance the pay reduction from the civilian job I then held was too great to even consider entering the political arena.)

The job search continued. I can't tell you how many interviews I went through but it was a lot. I kicked every can and turned over every rock I saw.

67
THE FINAL DAYS AT CENTCOM

Work continued at a fast pace in the office. We did have another change of J5 bosses with the departure of Admiral Bernsen. His replacement was another super leader in Admiral Laverne Severance, a submariner. But my days to work with him were drawing short. Our major War Plan had been through the last of its wickets and was just about done. No major plan is ever put away totally completed, there is always room for improvement as new forces come on line or new information is uncovered or things like Roll On–Roll Off ships are commissioned and the ability to move and deploy forces is improved. The art, and it is an art, of Time Phased Force Deployment Data development had come a long way and we had a plan that was executable and feasible if needed. I had two superb lads working TPFDD planning for us. One was a Marine LT COL, Cal Lloyd, and the second was LT COL Bill Robbins, USAF. Bill was also part of the team that worked many special projects for us and he went on to be a full colonel and retire in Tampa. I was never a big enthusiast for the deployment TPFDD work as done in punching in data to a computer day in and day out. These officers did fantastic things for me and I am appreciative to this day of their efforts. They both made me look good.

At one point in the late summer of 1986 we were directed to put together a special plan to curtail some issues in the waters around Saudi Arabia and Oman. It was to be a Navy and Air Force component operation. Planning went quickly with the CINC, the J3 and the J5 all involved daily along with several of my planners and members of the J3 Operations staff. It was a good plan, and basically short and sweet. In message format it was just over forty pages long. When it was ready it was sent to our AF and Navy component commands for their input. They had worked with us throughout plan development so comments were minimal. Once the CINC was satisfied, no easy task, the plan was forwarded to JCS for their approval. Such approval was forthcoming the next day.

All the key planners gathered in a small conference room between the CINC's and Deputy CINC's offices with all the principal J Staff present. The CINC seemed satisfied and said; "All right, now we just need to send out the plan to all the participants and tell them to initiate operations." Like a bloody fool I said, "Sir, we only need to send out a JCS Planning Message number XX [I have forgotten the actual number] saying to execute OPLAN XXX as written. Everyone has the plan already." You could have heard a pin drop. Well "that tore it," to paraphrase my hero John Wayne from a scene in the movie *The Searchers*. The CINC was hell bent on resending the entire forty page message again. I just sat there as Admiral Severance gave me a "belay" that talk look. It was to be my last confrontation with the old man. Several folks later said it wasn't worth trying to make the general look good by not sending out the entire plan a second time. In my mind, knowing the Joint Operations Planning System as I did, it made CENTCOM look like we didn't know the Joint System. At any rate, the entire plan went out over the ether once more.

The following week the CINC invited Colonel King and me to his office. At this point, the decision to form SOCOM using Readiness Command as a start point had just been announced. Readiness Command was located about five hundred yards from our headquarters and was at that point commanded by an old friend, General Jim Lindsay. He appeared earlier in this tale as the commander of the 82nd Airborne Division. Jerry King and I were to be General Crist's personal reps to the planning team designated to write the Terms of Reference (TOR) that would create U.S. SOCOM. He hoped to get some leavings from the carcass of the old Readiness Command. He had several relatively minor requests for concessions that frankly were pretty good and in the nation's and CENTCOM's best interest. Have to give him an attaboy for that one. Jerry and I were pleasantly surprised at this turn of events and went about the task with enthusiasm.

This effort at standing up the new U.S. Special Operations Command would last for over a month and would require that Jerry and I fly weekly to Washington to work in the bowels of the National Defense University at Fort McNair. It may be hard to fathom, given the number of disagreements the CINC and I had, that he would pick me for this mission or that he would call me to report to his quarters at 0500 in the morning; but both of those things did happen. He was good at using folks is the only explanation I have for this. I also have wondered why I was not fired and sent to the leper colony at the Mole Hole. In retrospect I don't think there were any full colonels consigned to that site.

Our work at Fort McNair was generally successful and when all the smoke cleared the General got most of what he had wanted. One point I must make about this exercise was the problem we had with the Navy in setting forth the Terms of Reference (TOR) that assigned forces to be part of the new command. The Navy representatives to the planning group were adamant that no, repeat no, Navy forces would be directly assigned. This meant no SEALS or Special Boat assets would be part of the command. It was like pulling teeth to get the Navy to give up any assets but in the end they were forced to provide the SEALS and some other assets to the new SOCOM. And today SEAL Team 6 is the darling of the military world. And that is a well-deserved status, let me add.

While we were at Fort McNair working the TOR for SOCOM, General Lindsay, CINC Readiness Command, and the designated first commander-to-be of SOCOM, along with his J3 Operations Officer, Major General Bill Klein, visited often. Of course they were concerned as to how the TOR were evolving. Jerry and I were minor players in this process and there was very little we could really share with them. It was good to see the two of them again having served with them at Fort Bragg. They were both good men and much admired in the Airborne community.

It is worth observing that forming U.S. SOCOM from the existing U.S. Readiness Command had, in my mind, two results. First, it allowed standing up of the new Special Operations oriented organization to happen quickly. There were lots of bodies there on site and ready to go. That was the good thing. The bad thing was that only perhaps ten percent of the staff could even spell Special Forces, SEAL, Ranger or Special Operations. That was not good. Thank heavens General Lindsay was a former Green Beret and a great leader.

When I finally transitioned to the defense contracting world I watched the command grow and become a fantastically successful organization. Under the leadership of men like Jim Lindsay, "Country" Carl Stiner, Wayne Downing, Hugh Shelton, Peter Schoomaker, Buck Kernan and Doug Brown, SOCOM evolved and became a high performance system. But initially the learning curve was straight up. One does not become a special operator or special operations expert overnight; that is just my minor league opinion but shared by many.

68
COLONELS BRANCH STRIKES AGAIN

The phone on my office desk rang one day in the early fall as the job search continued. It was Colonels Branch. The action officer stated that they knew I was considering retirement but had one more assignment they thought I might like to consider; Director of Strategy and Tactics at the Army War College. That job certainly complimented the road I had traveled the last twenty-four years. It was tempting but three years later I would be leaving the Army, if I chose to do so, at Carlisle Barracks, Pennsylvania. The family had no ties to the area and none of us were drawn to the winters up north. The impact of another move on the children in school helped me decide that I would turn down this assignment. The family was not unhappy. However, I was truly beginning to wonder where that job for me and a second career was hiding.

About two weeks later the phone rang again. This time the Colonels Branch action officer prefaced his remarks with, "We know you want to retire, and not leave Tampa, so we have another offer for you. Would you consider taking the job as Army Liaison Officer at the Air Force War College in Montgomery, Alabama? There is a USAF flight between Montgomery and MacDill every Thursday night returning on Monday in the morning. You would be home most weekends and the family would not have to leave Tampa." I thought long and hard about this one and was quite flattered that anyone cared. By now it was clear to me that I did not want to be just another used up old colonel and that it was time to retire. I thanked them but politely told them no to this offer also.

A week later that darned phone rang again. It was the head of Colonels Branch, no underling this time. The conversation went something like this: "Larry, we realize you want to retire but we have one last assignment we want you to consider. The Defense Intelligence Agency has concurred in this, the UK MOD has accepted you, and we would like you to accept the job as Army attaché in London. We also would put you on permissive parachute status without pay. What do you say?" What I told him was I needed to discuss this one with my family. It was very tempting. Along with the job came a beautiful townhouse in Mayfair near Hyde Park, a butler/chef and a car and driver, as needed, plus a very healthy yearly budget for entertaining VIPs. It was also an easy walk from the townhouse to the embassy. It was a real plum of a posting.

Mary and I talked through it, but decided we did not want to tell the girls because we felt they would want to go back in a heartbeat. They had enjoyed the UK so much we really believed they would chuck school, friends and Florida for a return to London. After much soul searching we jointly decided that while the offer was great, the idea of entertaining every visiting fireman, congressman, senator and staffer overnighting in London was not how we wanted to spend the next three years. Plus I was not certain I wanted to play the legal spy game. But what made this decision even harder was that I would have been working for my close friend and next door neighbor in Eastcote during the RCDS, Colonel Nick Lacey who was the attaché. Nick and I had already solved half the world's problems on our tube travel back and forth to school. I think we would have made a good team but it was time to change careers. Calling back the Chief of Colonels Branch I thanked him immensely for the offer but that I had decided to continue on to retirement. I told him for sure I would be out of the Army before 30 June 1987. We ended the conversation with him wishing me good luck in retirement. That was the last I heard from Colonels Branch. Overall during my twenty-four plus years in a green suit the Officer Personnel Directorate had taken pretty good care of me. If anything had truly been out of step it was on my end, not theirs.

69

HOW THE TPFDD BUSINESS FOUND MY SECOND CAREER

n late October, or early November, my home phone rang one Saturday afternoon. It was LT COL Mac McCartin (RET USAF) who had been one of my planners when I first got to CENTCOM. He had retired and taken a job with GTE Government Systems in Billerica, Massachusetts. He told me that they had a contract with the government to upgrade and develop a new Joint Operations Planning and Execution System (JOPES) for the Joint Deployment Agency (JDA) still located with Readiness Command (soon to be SOCOM). He asked me if I was considering retirement. I told him that retirement was more than possible and that I was actually pursuing a new line of work at that time. He thanked me and told me I might be hearing from the GTE Personnel Office.

Redmond's Rule #25 – There is life after the military, when the time is right, go for it.

Five or six days later I received a call from GTE and asked if I could come to Billerica for an interview. Flying to Boston the next week I managed to make it through that convoluted road network north and slightly west of "Bean Town" to Billerica. The interviews seemed to go well. I liked all the folks I met. The best part of the opportunity was that I would have an office in Tampa interfacing as a liaison with the Joint Deployment Agency (JDA), no move. Mac had apparently sold the GTE hierarchy on the idea that I was the smartest kid in sixth grade when it came to JOPES and TPFDD development. Perhaps that was a bit of an over statement but not too far off the mark. Not many colonels had the in depth planning and TPFDD experience at that point that I did. I flew home thinking maybe this was the opportunity I had been looking for.

Thanksgiving came and went and no call. My spirits were lower than whale dung, and last time I checked that stuff is on the bottom of the ocean. One day in early December Mac called to say that I would get a call with a job offer, "Congratulations." Several days later the personnel officer at Billerica called to say that they wanted to extend an offer and we then discussed money. The question of salary had not come up while I was in Billerica. When we finished talking he told me to stand by I would be getting a registered letter within a couple of days. Sure enough, three days later the letter arrived and the starting salary was several thousand more than I had asked for. My office was to be collocated with a GTE Telecommunications Group in downtown Tampa. Nice facility with a great view of Tampa and the bay. I called Billerica about the new salary offer and was told, "You don't know what you are worth." Guess I should have asked for more but the number was well above the threshold for surviving that Mary and I had agreed on. Army folks transitioning to the civilian side need to be aware of what they may be worth to a potential employer. Not always easy to find out one's real value to a given company but some digging can usually get you in the ball park. This was one area in which I had not done enough spade work

The die was cast, I would retire. I called the CENTCOM Army Personnel Office and asked the warrant officer who handled our records how soon he could process my retirement papers. He had my package on his desk; it had been there for about sixty days. His guidance to me was to get my retirement physical done before Christmas, and to be sure the bureaucracy had time to process the package properly. He recommended my date for transition to civilian life be set for 31 Jan 1987. I called GTE Government Systems and spoke to Mr. Irv Zaks, who would be my new boss. He was happy with a report date there of 2 February. I was on my way to a new career.

Walking the hall to see the J5 and give him the word there were truly mixed emotions going through my head. This was the right decision for sure but it still bothered me after twenty-four years to take off the uniform. The life I was leaving would be missed. Admiral Severance said he was sorry to see me leave and thanked me for my service to the nation. I did not go see or tell the CINC. The word would leak up to him. He could have cared less. In fact, I suspect strongly, he may have been happy to be rid of an officer he perceived as a trouble maker.

A week before I took off the uniform I exited a C-130 aircraft at 1,000 feet with most of my buddies who were on jump status in the command. We had started jumping on MacDill AFB proper about a year earlier. It was easier in terms of time than the normal drop zone up at Brooksville some fifty miles distant. But at MacDill one jumped on a grassy strip between two concrete runways. Remembering the jump at North Field where I landed on concrete once before during an EDRE I requested and got the Brooksville cow pasture for my last blast. The bus that took us back to MacDill stopped at a Veterans of Foreign Wars post near Brooksville and more than a few brews were downed and toasts drunk to the retiree. It was a nice close to a twenty-four-year Airborne career.

I was asked who I wanted to have conduct the actual retirement ceremony. After some serious thought I picked up the phone and called the newly established U.S. Special Operations Command and asked for General Lindsay. When he came on the line I told him I was retiring and would he be so good as to do the honors. He immediately responded yes. On 30 January 1987, with most of my planners and friends from CENTCOM, along with my family in attendance, I was retired by an Army paratrooper, four star general, in the Blue Room at Headquarters U.S. SOCOM. A fitting end, I felt, to twenty-four years of service in Uncle Sam's Army for a poor kid from Columbus, Ohio. It had been quite a journey. And I had done it my way.

EPILOGUE

When it finally happened, my transition to civilian life and a new career was not all that difficult. I also found that I was pretty much on my own to develop my new job as I saw fit. After about a year the JDA was relocated to Virginia and GTE elected to leave me in Tampa working with CENTCOM, SOCOM and the Joint Communications Support Element. Over the next fifteen years I worked with soldiers, blue suit Air Force lads and a lot of Marines in the role of an ombudsman for initially GTE Government Systems and later, after they were bought out by General Dynamics, for the latter company. I was working communication equipment, computer issues and sales to various units around the country. When I was on active duty, if my communications failed, I hollered for help from a good NCO. In my new life I would holler for a good engineer or technician. It worked.

If anyone had told me that I would be paid good money to be a representative for two major corporations with next to no responsibilities except to ensure the customer was happy I would have said they were smoking something. But it happened and I was happy doing it. Oh yes, I also marketed for my employer but it was a very subtle form of selling and it opened lots of doors for me and the folks I represented. The good news was I was still working with and supporting dusty boot troops from Fort Irwin, CA, to Fort Bragg, NC, to Camp Pendleton, CA, to Fort Campbell, KY, to Camp

Lejeune, NC, to the Joint Communications Support Element, U.S. SOCOM and U.S. CENTCOM—the last three units all at MacDill AFB. I would sit one day in a fancy conference room talking to senior officers in a suit and tie. The next day in the field dressed in jeans and sweatshirt in the mud or snow talking with and drinking field coffee with privates and sergeants. I crawled in and out of more communication vans than I care to recall. Some of my bosses might argue that I was too customer-oriented. They might be right in that. But most would also admit that I helped bring in a lot of business for those corporations. I was a darned good facilitator and welcomed by the customer wherever I went. I retired completely in 2002 and moved to our retirement home in a community called Solivita near Poinciana, Florida.

In closing I want to relate one major happening in 2003, two years after I had retired from my second career. It relates back to my green suit days and my experience with the Brits. Following graduation from RCDS, Air Commodore Mickey Witherow was instrumental in organizing class reunions both in the UK and around the world. In 2003, Colonel Nick Lacey and I volunteered to organize and host the reunion in the USA at Disney World, supported by our other American Class of 1983 students: Captain Larry Andrews, USN, and Mr. Jim Montgomery from the U.S. Department of State. We could not think of a place more American than Disney World and it was just twenty-five miles from my home. It all fell in place nicely. We decided to have a dinner in our community, Solivita, and our guests from all around the globe would be bused here from the Beach & Yacht Club at Disney where lodging had been arranged. A cocktail party was planned by the Laceys and Redmonds in our home before the dinner.

Then I came upon an interesting idea. I had heard a George Bush impersonator (our president at that time) on a local TV station. He was very good and looked more like the president than the rascals appearing on late night TV on the main stream media channels. He happened to live in Lake Mary, FL about sixty miles away. I thought, "What the heck, wouldn't it be neat if we could get him to come to Solivita for the cocktail hour we had planned at our home?" I called and explained what was in the works. His name was John Morgan and he was very cooperative and understanding of the whole idea. I then asked him how much he charged. He told me he normally was paid $10,000 for a two hour gig. I must have gulped because he then politely asked how much money we had. I told him about $300. There was a moment of silence. He then said, "Look, if I don't have another show scheduled I will be happy to come and entertain these folks. Their support to our nation is important and it is worth doing given our current war against terror." About seven days before the dinner John called and confirmed that he would be able to attend and put on a show. He asked me what I thought the president might say to this group. I gave him about half a dozen meaningful ideas and he said he was good to go. I called Nick and Patricia to let them know we had a special event over and above the norm. Nick was convinced this would be a happening that could not be topped.

I had arranged with two retired military friends, Butch Cicatko and Mac McCarty, both thin, lean mean types to play Secret Service agents in blue suits, ties, et cetera. We war gamed how they would bring the president in to greet the guests in a clandestine manner to maximize surprise. They had some great ideas to enhance the spoof that added to the realism of the event. I also arranged for a photographer, a good friend, Walter Fair, who lived just down the street to come in later and take pictures of all the couples with the "president."

I picked up the fifty plus attendees at the Beach & Yacht Club Hotel at Disney in a very nice contracted bus and brought them to Solivita for cocktails and dinner. As we came into the community they were much impressed with the many trees, lakes and homes. I explained that our community had been a hunting preserve and that we had more than our share of wildlife to include gators, deer, raccoons, armadillo, bobcats, turkeys and other Florida critters. Just at that moment a flock of approximately fifteen turkeys slowly crossed the street to our front causing the bus to stop. One of my Brit friends commented something to the effect that surely you could not have planned that. He was right, it just happened. I was as surprised as the guests were.

The cocktail hour began and all was going nicely. Folks from the UK, Canada, Germany, Sweden, Australia, New Zealand, the U.S. and several other countries were all talking, laughing and sharing experiences since our last gathering. The doorbell rang and two gentlemen in dark blue suits, white shirts and red ties asked to be allowed to enter. They commenced walking into every room and passing among the guests in the living room, family room and checking the lanai area where most of the attendees were gathered. The security role players kept up a chatter with each other talking into small hand held microphones with readily visible ear phones, none of which worked. Admiral Brian Brown or his wife commented, "Larry, you certainly have great security here." I replied they had told me they were from the Secret Service and I assumed they were asked to check on the guests with so many four stars and a Brit "Knight" present. The wife of our U.S. Navy captain, Carol Andrews, who was as much in the dark as everyone except Nick Lacey and our wives, asked me in all seriousness, "Larry, those guys look like CIA, what's going on?" At that moment one of the role players said something to the effect that the house was clear and, "It was OK to bring the 'man' in."

At that point one of the pseudo Secret Service agents announced, "Ladies and Gentlemen, the president of the United States." John Morgan, aka George Bush, entered, walked directly to the open lanai door and went into his act. And you would not believe the looks on the faces of the attendees. Incredulity, amazement, doubt, shock was on everyone's face. Several of the senior officers present had met the president prior to this. Even they were initially taken in by Mr.

Morgan. Nick, Patricia, Mary and I enjoyed watching the attendees' reactions and were hard pressed to keep a straight face. John Morgan was fantastic; he was George Bush. Mr. Morgan thanked the attendees for their support to our nation in the War on Terror and especially thanked the UK attendees for the special relationship that had existed between our two nations over the last century and expressed his sincere hope that they all had a great stay in the USA. About four minutes into his performance he began to take shots at himself. Slowly the light came on in folks minds that they had been had. Then they began to clap and applaud. Mr. Morgan proved to be one of the highlights of the reunion topping even the many events enjoyed by all at Disney World and EPCOT. Pictures of every couple were taken in our living room before an American flag borrowed from our Veterans Club. Our classmate, former commander of the Special Air Service, who had met the real George Bush, declined to stand for a photo: classic SAS covert operator. Over the years at other RCDS gatherings we learned that several couples had those pictures displayed on mantel pieces around the world. I found that a fitting salute to a fine day and a much maligned and underrated president of our country.

And so ends my tale of those fantastic and fun, well mostly fun, twenty-four years in Uncle Sam's Army. It was a great run for a lad from the wrong side of the tracks in Columbus, Ohio. In this country, determination, some smarts and a lot of hard work can take even the average person to new heights. I believe that as much today as I did when I was a young man.

God bless this great country and keep it strong.

Airborne, All the Way!

ACKNOWLEDGMENTS

An endeavor at retelling history (some of it fifty plus years old), that results in a tome of this length, could not be done without a lot of assistance. In this case the author owes much, to many, who encouraged and assisted me along the way over a period of three years. My children were the initiators of this book as explained in the Preface. Not just did they encourage my writing but they read drafts and cajoled me to "keep writing" when I would be discouraged or just lost focus. They were the catalysts from which came this effort. I would be remiss not to thank them also for tolerating my lifestyle and the nineteen moves and the jerking out of schools and away from friends that they endured; they are great troops. Mary, my wife of fifty plus years, was also a pusher, counselor, editor and proofreader who just would not let me stop or produce something that was not also correct in her mind. Much of my initial error and misstatement she caught and corrected.

Along the way I also received help from a number of military acquaintances and military authors concerning the writing and publication of this work. Among those deserving mention are Major (RET) Doug Bonnot, LTC (RET) John Taylor, LTC (RET) Ray Morris and COL (RET) Bill Cain, all published authors. Specific commentary on portions of the book was provided by various former soldiers who were there for the events on which they provided their insights. Among them LTC (RET) Tom McAndrews, LTC (RET)

Ken Buyle and COL (RET) Joe Peden for portions of my time with the 8th Special Forces; Major (RET) Jesse Myers and LTG (RET) John Miller for reviewing portions of the text concerning my first tour in Viet Nam; COL (RET) Bill Cain, COL (RET) Jim Mowery, COL (RET) Johnny Brooks for the period of command in the 82nd Airborne Division; COL (RET-USAF) Nick Lacey for the time in London at RCDS; COL (RET-USAF) Bill Robbins and Air Commodore (RET-RAF) Eric Macy for my time at U.S. CENTCOM. One last acknowledgement from the military side is in order. I ran some questions past MG (RET) Bill Garrison concerning the events we shared together in the pages you have read. Bill's response was he didn't need to read the words, "If you wrote them they are true." Thanks for that comment Bill.

Several civilian acquaintances were also of great assistance to me. Mr. Walter Fair, my computer guru, provided technical help with the photos along with much needed guidance on copy organization. Mr. John Kevgas, one of my bridge buddies, also ensured that I stayed on track. He listened to more war stories than he surely thought he would ever hear; all the while insisting that he was getting a free autographed copy.

But by far the most civilian assistance throughout the effort came from Mr. Ronnie Foreman of Belfast, Northern Ireland, a longtime friend. He believed strongly that my tale needed to be told, not just for my children but for a broader audience. He provided not only encouragement but much solid counsel and was the first person to read the draft manuscript in its totality. Thanks to his clever mind the need for a glossary was obviated by my elimination of almost all acronyms! But Ronnie and his wife Norma's greatest contribution was the offering of their condo on St. Pete Beach, Florida, whenever they were not using it. This allowed me the solitude of the condo in which to research and write and was of immeasurable value. I am deeply indebted for their support and encouragement.

And last but surely not least I must thank some individuals who labored through the entire manuscript with an eye toward clarity, understanding and readability. Those folks are David Wynsen, Nick McDonald, Jesse Myers, Claire Donovan and Bill Cain. Their efforts ensured that I fielded a readable and meaningful document. I hope you agree.

This is far from an exhaustive list and I regret not being able to list everyone who contributed to this epistle in various ways. Like soldiering, the whole effort was fun.

The correctness or any error of fact relating to what is in these pages rests solely with me.

Larry Redmond

APPENDIX 1 - "REDMOND'S RULES"

1. *Lead, Follow or Get the Hell Out of the Way*
2. *Things get worse under pressure. Stay cool*
3. *Do the unexpected, it will likely work*
4. *Always do what you believe is right, even if you don't like it*
5. *Take care of the troops and they will take care of you*
6. *No plan survives the first contact with the enemy*
7. *Never back away from a fair fight or one where you have a tactical advantage*
8. *Think it through, don't do dumb things*
9. *People are gullible, Americans more so than most*
10. *Stay on top of your equipment accountability, it is a career breaker*
11. *The worse the weather the more you will be required to be out in it*
12. *Where you sit determines what you see*
13. *Being smart and persevering is good, but nothing beats dumb luck*
14. *The degree of civilization is inversely proportional to the proximity to combat*
15. *Forgive and forget, but first get even*
16. *Shame on you if you don't love killing! Think attack*
17. *Murphy is alive and well out there -- if it can go wrong it will*
18. *No plan is <u>certain</u> once you cross the line of departure; you can be <u>certain</u> it will change*
19. *Never fool around with Mother Nature, she wins every time*
20. *"When in doubt, tell the truth" - Mark Twain*
21. *"They also serve who only stand and wait" John Milton*
22. *Believe it, Communism is a disaster for the common man*
23. *Never argue with a 4 star; it's like wrestling with a pig, you lose and get dirty*
24. *Finding a job is a job!*
25. *There is life after the military, when the time is right go for it*

APPENDIX 2 - US ARMY RANKS

COMMISSIONED OFFICERS

O1   Second Lieutenant (2LT)
O2   First Lieutenant (1LT)
O3   Captain (CPT)
O4   Major (MAJ)
O5   Lieutenant Colonel (LTC)
O6   Colonel (COL)
O7   Brigadier General (BG)
O8   Major General (MG)
O9   Lieutenant General (LTG)
O10 General (GEN)
General of the Army
      (Reserved for Wartime)

WARRANT OFFICERS

W1   Warrant Officer 1 (WO1)
W2   Chief Warrant Officer 2 (CW2)
W3   Chief Warrant Officer 3 (CW3)
W4   Chief Warrant Officer 4 (CW4)
W5   Chief Warrant Officer 5 (CW5)

ENLISTED PERSONNEL

E1 Private (PVT)
E2 Private (PV2)
E3 Private First Class (PFC)
E4 Specialist (SPC)
E4 Corporal (CPL)
E5 Sergeant (SGT)
E6 Staff Sergeant (SSG)
E7 Sergeant First Class (SFC)
E8 Master Sergeant (MSG)
E8 First Sergeant (1SGT)
E9 Sergeant Major (SGM)
E9 Command Sergeant Major (CSM)
E9 Sergeant Major of the Army (SMA)

ABOUT THE AUTHOR

Colonel Larry Redmond, U. S. Army (RET), was commissioned a Lieutenant of Infantry in 1962 upon graduation from Providence College. During the next twenty-four years he served in various command and staff positions with the 101st Airborne Division, 8th Special Forces Group Airborne, XVIII Airborne Corps, the 82d Airborne Division and other special operations units. He commanded airborne soldiers at platoon, company and Special Forces "A" Team and Infantry Battalion levels. He served two combat tours with the 101st Airborne Division. His overseas assignments included Panama, Thailand, England, Israel and two tours in Vietnam.

Mr. Redmond holds a bachelors degree, two masters degrees and is a graduate of the Navy Command & Staff College and the British Royal College of Defence Studies. He holds the Silver Star, two Bronze Stars, the Purple Heart, the Combat Infantryman's Badge, the Expert Infantryman's Badge and numerous other awards. He is a Master Parachutist, a Vietnamese Master Parachutist and a Brit Para, and was Ranger and Special Forces qualified. He is a Distinguished Member of the 327th Regiment, the 505th Regiment and is a member of the Special Forces Regiment.

Following his military service he worked as an Ombudsman for then GTE Government Systems and later General Dynamics Communications Systems representing those corporations with Army, Marine and Special Operation units around the country.

Mr. Redmond is now fully retired and lives in Poinciana, Florida with his wife of fifty-three years, Mary Elizabeth Devlin of Boston. They have three grown children. He remains active in many military organizations.

Made in the USA
Charleston, SC
22 December 2015